"Bow Tie"
page 226

"Roman Stripe" *variation - page 222*
"Stars" *variation - page 212*

"Center Diamond" *page 199*
"Multiple Patch" *page 202*

"Baskets"
page 216

"Sunshine and Shadow"
page 198

"Center Diamond"
page 199

"Bars"
page 200

Tips for Quilters

Plus 63 of Your Favorite Quilt Patterns

By the editors of FC&A

Tips for Quilters

Plus 63 of Your Favorite Quilt Patterns

By the editors of FC&A

Acknowledgments

Tips for Quilters Plus 63 of Your Favorite Quilt Patterns by the editors of FC&A is compiled from previously published *Tips for Quilters* by Rachel T. Pellman, copyright © 1993 by Good Books, Intercourse, PA 17534; *Amish Quilt Patterns* by Rachel T. Pellman, copyright © 1984 by Good Books, Intercourse, PA 17534; and *Small Amish Quilt Patterns* by Rachel T. Pellman, copyright © 1985 by Good Books, Intercourse, PA 17534. We wish to thank Good Books for their assistance with this project.

We especially wish to thank the following for their help and permission to picture their quilts in this book:

Sunshine and Shadow (color insert) by The People's Place.

Bars, Roman Stripe, Stars, Multiple Patch, Baskets (color inserts) and Center Diamond and Bow Tie (cover and color inserts) by Delores Schuster.

Photograph Credits

Sunshine and Shadow (color insert) by Jonathan Charles and Good Books.

Center Diamond, Multiple Patch, Bow Tie, Baskets, Roman Stripe, Stars (color inserts) by Robert Shapiro.

Cover photos by Robert Shapiro.

We have made every effort to ensure the accuracy and completeness of these instructions, photos, and drawings. We cannot, however, be responsible for human error, typographical mistakes, or variations in measurements and individual work.

Seventh printing March 1998

ISBN # 0-915099-75-6

Contents

Contents

Chapter 18 Amish Quits 177

Amish Quilt Patterns — *Large Version* 196

Amish Quilt Patterns — *Small Version*   260

Contents

She seeketh wool, and flax, and worketh willingly with her hands.

She layeth her hands to the spindle, and her hands hold the distaff.

She is not afraid of the snow for her household: for all her household are clothed with scarlet.

She maketh herself coverings of tapestry; her clothing is silk and purple.

She maketh fine linen, and selleth it; and delivereth girdles unto the merchant.

She looketh well to the ways of her household, and eateth not the bread of idleness.

Favour is deceitful, and beauty is vain: but a woman that feareth the Lord, she shall be praised.

Give her of the fruit of her hands; and let her own works praise her in the gates.

Proverbs 31: 13,19, 21-22, 24, 27, 30,31

Congratulations! You hold in your hands the quintessential quilting book.

Packed with over 1,000 tidbits of quilting advice and more than 60 patterns, *Tips for Quilters Plus 63 of Your Favorite Quilt Patterns* will provide you with years of pure quilting pleasure.

For your convenience, we've divided the book into two parts. The first section is crammed full of quilting advice from more than 400 quilters all across North America, from Pickering, Ontario to Tyler, Texas.

We've broken this section down into chapters, such as Selecting Fabrics, Making Templates, Appliqué, Binding, etc., making it easy to find answers to those common, and not-so-common, quilting questions you're likely to have.

In the second half of the book, we've collected together the most beloved designs of the traditional Amish patterns plus many unique variations. This section contains its own separate introduction, which provides complete instructions for assembling each quilt. Directions for both full-size and crib quilts are included.

We hope you enjoy this book as much as we've enjoyed putting it together for you. May it inspire you to new levels of creativity and send your quilting pleasures soaring to new heights!

— **Your Quilting Friends at FC&A**

1

Selecting fabric

Coordinating fabrics

❖ I look for balance, keeping whites, yellows and extra bright colors interspersed evenly through the whole quilt. I make sure I use enough of an accent color so as not to look like an accident and to make the quilt sparkle.

— Darla Sathre, Baxter, MN

❖ Sometimes the pattern itself seems to call for certain fabrics; a Grandmother's Fan, for example, would seem appropriate in soft, Victorian-looking colors. Patterns like the Ohio Star or Eight-Pointed Star need bright or dark main colors for the star points which I want to emphasize.

— Marilyn Umble, Atglen, PA

❖ Usually I choose a print first, then pick colors from the print to match the solids or the smaller design prints I want to include.

— Betty Boyton, Gordonville, PA

❖ When I'm planning to appliqué, I squint my eyes to see if the colors I've chosen blend.

— Sharron van Meter, St. Charles, MO

❖ First, I usually pick a large floral or a pattern with colors I like. I then pick a variety of prints to match the colors in the main fabric.

— Geneva Herod, Ashland, VA

❖ I try to have contrast in the colors I choose. The quilt pattern also determines my color choices. I often use a little black to get a more dramatic effect.

— Loraine Arnold, Rhinebeck, NY

❖   I put fabrics together and take them to the window or outdoors. I think artificial light masks true color coordination. I learned this through trial and error.

— Lee Cook, Falmouth, MA

❖   I usually start out with a favorite piece of fabric and work from that to choose the remainder. However, I find that in doing so, I sometimes end up not using the "favorite piece," because the others blend so well that I need to make another choice for the primary fabric!

I think I am most successful when I purposely try and clash the fabrics in a project. I try to use a great variety of hues, tints, textures and pattern sizes. This gives the finished project more interest and movement.

— Terry Festa, Clinton, CT

❖   If I'm matching things for a certain room, I take swatches of wallpaper, carpet or whatever else is available with me when I shop for fabrics. I choose fabrics with a variety of sizes and textures of prints.

— Anna Buchanan, Belleville, PA

❖   I always start with one fabric I love and build on that. However, in the end, I seldom use that fabric because it stretches my imagination into other areas of color.

— Suellen Fletcher, Noblesville, IN

❖   Whenever I find a good light color, I buy a yard because it's always harder to find lights. I try to mix large prints, small prints, color values, etc.

— Nancy Wagner Graves, Manhattan, KS

❖   I am always on the lookout for interesting, unusual prints. When I find them, I always buy at least one yard.

— Vanya G. Neer, Bradenton, FL

❖   Before I go for fabric, I usually have a good idea of what I want. Then I find a quiet corner of the store and start piling up fabric until I get the colors I want. I'm usually worn out from getting and putting away bolts of fabric!

— Hazel Lightcap Propst, Oxford, PA

❖   I try not to use a dead white background. Instead, I find neutral fabric with a slightly textured look for the background.

— Shirley Liby, Muncie, IN

❖   I always try to have at least one dark and one light fabric in each quilt. I stay away from stripes, but I do like to work with small checks.

— Barbara Nolan, Pleasant Valley, NY

❖   I love to prepare or buy a border and then blend fabrics with the border color.

— Lou Ann Philpot, Murry, KY

❖ If I am working with a photo of a finished block or quilt, I try to match *values* (lightness and darkness), rather than trying to match fabrics or colors exactly. I achieve the same feeling as the quilt in the photograph, but I've made my own choices!

— Sue Seeley, New Bern, NC

❖ When planning a color-coordinated quilt, I start by choosing a fabric with more than one color. I choose the remaining fabrics highlighting colors from that piece of fabric. I often add an accent in a different color.

— Peggy Smith, Hamlin, NY

❖ When buying fabric for a large area, I roll out a yard or two and then stand back with my eyes several inches above the table height. From that vantage point I can determine if there is a stripe in the design that I couldn't see up close. I like to mix geometrics with prints of softer designs. I love stripes and checks.

— Carol Trice, Wayne, PA

❖ I use a variety of fabric patterns and solids. A good mix of prints makes a quilt sparkle and moves the eye over the surface of the quilt.

— Marilyn Bloom Wallace, Alfred, ME

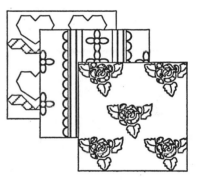

❖ I always pick one fabric that has spark, that is more outstanding, and that adds pizazz. I avoid choosing colors that blend so well that nothing predominates.

— Barbara F. Hummel, Punxsutawney, PA

❖ I never use solid-colored fabrics. For background fabrics I choose very subtle printed fabrics, like white printed on white or natural color printed on muslin. I buy a variety of lights, mediums and darks.

— Gail L. Kozicki, Glen Mills, PA

❖ I prefer small prints for small pieces in quilts. I buy large prints only for wide borders.

— Jane S. Lippincott, Wynnewood, PA

❖ When choosing the main fabric for a quilt, I never look at the fabric bolt by itself. I stack the bolts I think go well together with the main color on top. I drape the top fabric down over the stack so I can see how it looks with each of the other selections and whether it is a coordinated stack.

— Mary Wheatley, Mashpee, MA

❖ I look for fabrics with color combinations which are either opposite — or neighbors — on the color wheel. I vary the hues and values within these color choices.

— Elaine F. Asper, Stroudsburg, PA

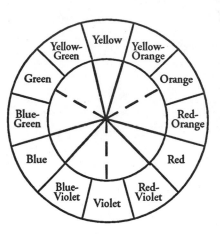

**Color
Wheel**

❖ I like different textures of prints. Sometimes I choose five or six different prints in a particular color for a large project, rather than more yardage of just one or two prints, because I think the finished project looks better. I especially do this if I am working on a monochromatic project — just blue and white fabrics, for example.

— **Linda Hampton Schiffer, Columbia, MD**

❖ I like to choose colors I don't wear when I select quilt fabrics. It gives me an opportunity to play with different colors.

— **Candy Horton, Greenfield, OH**

❖ I like to select all my fabrics at one time when possible. I feel like I get a better blend of colors.

— **Mary E. Martin, Hagerstown, MD**

❖ I always rely on my first instincts in picking out fabrics. It is usually love at first sight, and I don't try to second-guess myself. I never spend too much time in the material shop so I am not tempted to change my mind.

— **Barbara McGinnis, Ocean City, NJ**

❖ I open solid fabrics to a single layer. The shade usually looks quite different than when you look at all the layers in a bolt.

— **Dorothy Humphrey, Webster, NY**

❖ Some of my most interesting quilt blocks are those in which the colors are not overly coordinated. I also try to buy a variety of print sizes and types, including stripes and plaids.

— **Darla Sathre, Baxter, MN**

❖ I rarely choose print fabrics with much, if any, white background. I find white sticks out like a sore thumb and is not a good blender. Of course, if all my prints have some white, it can work.

— **Doris Amiss Rebey, Hyattsville, MD**

❖ I check the backs of fabrics. There are often interesting, more sub-dued patterns on the fabric back that can be used as the "right" side of the fabric.

— **Alison Schwabe, Englewood, CO**

❖ I always try to lay the materials out together in the approximate order and amount that they would be in the finished quilt. I then look at them from many angles.

— **LuAnne S. Taylor, Canton, PA**

❖ I use the Grafex color-match system (by Ohio Graphics Arts Systems, Inc. of Cleveland, Ohio 44128 and available at many art stores). With over 200 colors, I find it most helpful, and I can easily carry it in my purse. I make notations of those colors I want to match or coordinate on the back of the color or my fabric sample cards.

I glue-stick a small sample of each of the fabrics in my "stash" on an index card, noting the yardage I have on hand and the place where I purchased it. I store these cards in a zip-lock bag for easy reference while I'm shopping. A business-card folder also works well for organizing and carrying 3 1/2-inch x 2-inch samples.

If you can't find a color-match set, you can use a selection of flat-paint chips from your local paint store, organized on a scrapbook post.

— **Ann Reimer, Beatrice, NE**

❖ I start with fabrics I like, but I also try to use pieces that I don't care for. I think this is the way I grow from making a nice quilt to creating a great quilt. Sometimes just a small amount of that ugly color is the perfect complement to my quilt!

— **Linda Sterling, Belchertown, MA**

❖ When choosing a print, I squint my eyes to see the dominant color and then choose other fabrics to go with that color.

— **Teresa Reily, White Plains, NY**

❖ I step back a distance to view fabrics I am considering. Fabric can look quite different from this vantage point, and that is usually how a quilt is viewed.

— **Sally Price, Reston, VA**

❖ I play with the fabrics. Because I'm nearsighted, taking off my glasses gives me the same view I would get from a distance.

— **Sara Harter Fredette, Williamsburg, MA**

❖ I go into a quilt shop with an open mind. I have found that if I go looking for a specific fabric or color, I spend twice as much time choosing fabric.

— **Leslie Lott, Englewood, CO**

❖ I try to stay with colors either on the cool or warm side. I don't use both in the same quilt.

— **Maryann England, Thogamond, CA**

Quality checks

❖ I scrunch the fabric up in my hand to see how easily it wrinkles. I buy only known brands of fabric in as much quantity as I can afford.

— **Mary Puskar, Forest Hill, MD**

❖ I open fabric to check the entire 45-inch width to see if it is printed on the straight of grain. This is important if I am going to use it as a large strip for a border or sashing.

I ask to have fabric cut in the store, *not* torn. Tearing breaks thread violently and "runs" into fabric weakening and pulling threads. This is especially visible on dark fabrics.

I never buy through a catalog. I like to see and feel the fabric.

— **Dorothy Reise, Severna Park, MD**

❖ If I put my hand under fabric and can see skin color through it, the fabric is too thin.

— **Jennifer L. Rhodes, Lancaster, PA**

❖ I always check fabric carefully for flaws before buying it.

— **Dorothy Alice Shank, Sterling, IL**

❖ I sniff fabrics I am considering for a fishy scent — some dye smells never disappear. I also rub fabrics to check their sizing content. Sizing is a substance applied to the surface of fabric during manufacture to give it more body and stability. Too much sizing makes a very stiff fabric.

— **Kelly Wagoner, Albuquerque, NM**

❖ If I am going to appliqué, I want fabric that holds a crease well. If I will use it for patchwork, I prefer something that will crease less.

I prefer fabrics that have a smooth and fine "hand" or feel. I check how densely the fabric is woven. The loosely woven, cheaper cottons do not wear well, in my experience. I also find that fabrics woven with larger, coarser threads do not wear well.

— **Linda Hampton Schiffer, Columbia, MD**

❖ I choose fabric that has a crisp feel before I wash it. The tighter the weave in the broadcloth, the more durable the fabric will be.

— **Mary Kay Mitchell, Battle Creek, MI**

A case for 100-percent cotton

❖ I prefer tightly woven 100-percent cotton fabric. This provides the most consistent "feel" in my quilts. Polyester is sometimes too crisp or stretches when it is stitched.

— **Laura Barrus Bishop, Boerne, TX**

❖ I use blends sparingly if they are the only choice for a particular color. I prefer 100-percent cotton.

— **Carol Findling, Beatrice, NE**

❖ I do a lot of appliqué using only 100-percent cotton fabric. I find blended fabrics hard to work with because they fray along the edges.

— **Margaret Jarrett, Anderson, IN**

❖ I always select *good quality,* 100-percent cotton fabric. Trying to save money by buying low-quality fabric that won't stand up to wear and washing is really false economy.

— **Marjorie Mills, Bethesda, MD**

❖ One hundred percent cotton doesn't creep when it is cut, and it creases nicely for appliqué. Because cotton in bright and/or dark colors may bleed, I choose cotton/polyester blends for these colors.

— Ginny Barr, Jackson, OH

❖ I *try* to stick with 100-percent cotton, but there are some fabulous blends out there and I do occasionally buy them! I *always* buy high-quality materials.

— Sherri Driver, Englewood, CO

A case for other fabrics!

❖ I do not worry about fiber content, texture or whether it is "suitable," if it meets the design needs of my project. I do, therefore, have more problems to solve during the construction process, but the end result is worth it.

— Polly Gilmore, St. Joseph, MI

❖ I know cotton is the "in thing," but I avoid it whenever possible. It wrinkles and fades much more than cotton/polyester blends. Blends outwear cotton.

— Mrs. Vernon Kennel, Atglen, PA

❖ I am more interested in color and shades than fabric content. I mix raw silk, blends, cottons, etc.

— Sharron van Meter, St. Charles, MO

❖ I like cotton/polyester blended fabrics because they don't wrinkle as much.

— Elmira S. Snader, New Holland, PA

❖ I always buy cotton/poly for children or baby quilts because they wash and wear better, and their colors are more durable.

— Carol Farley, Grasonville, MD

Helpful "tools"

❖ For the quilt back, I am certain to use fabric of equal quality to the quilt top. If the backing is of a looser weave, it is impossible to attain the finest quality quilting stitches, for even the most experienced quilter.

I prefer to have enough fabric to allow for two seams on the back when it is not possible to have just one piece, with the panels being of equal size. That allows me to avoid having seams where folds are often made (the center), or where the quilt hits the edge of the bed, both of which hasten wear.

— Ann Reimer, Beatrice, NE

❖ I like to use a Valu-Seeker (a piece of red acrylic) which neutralizes all colors to shades of white, gray and black. This allows me to see the color values of the fabrics I have selected, and I can be sure I will not lose a color in my design.

— Jean Turner, Williams Lake, BC

❖ "Peepholes," used in solid doors to allow the person inside a view of who is outside, are a great tool for viewing fabrics. The "peephole" gives the impression of seeing fabrics from a distance and makes it easier to judge dark, medium and light values of fabrics.

— Laura J. Jones, Greenville, SC

Fabric bargains

❖ I buy a lot of fabric pieces at garage sales and at a resale store. I always look at home first, though, and try to use what I have on hand!

— Pat Probst, Columbus, OH

❖ I buy many of my fabrics from garage or estate sales.

— Jane Cunningham, Murray, KY

❖ I always check out discounted fabrics. The $1.00-a-yard fabric may not be something I really love, but it can make a neat and inexpensive backing for quilts and wall hangings.

— Laurie A. Enos, Rochester, NY

❖ Sometimes I shop flea markets, yard sales or Goodwill shops for new or "used once and didn't like" garments that I wash and cut up for quilt fabric.

— Mildred Pelkey, Glen Burnie, MD

Cautions!

❖ I buy remnants of fabric only if I remember having seen them on a bolt in the past.

— Helen Kusnitz, W. Hempstead, NY

❖ I am very careful about selecting directional fabric and include only a few in my fabric collection.

— Mildred Fauquet, Lincoln, NE

❖ I try not to shop if I am in a bad mood or not feeling well. It affects what I choose. I like to shop early in the morning when the sunlight is best. I can get a better idea of fabrics' true colors.

— Susan Ketcherside, St. Charles, MO

❖ I choose fabrics without large open spaces in the prints. Too much open space can appear as a solid when the fabric is cut into small pieces.

— Faye Meyers, San Jose, CA

❖ I always buy extra fabric. It may be a while before I complete the project, and fabrics are discontinued rather quickly. There is no such thing as too much fabric, especially if you love scrap quilts as much as I do!

— Bonnie Zabzdyr, Wright City, MO

❖ I am certain to mark backing panels so that all the fabric on the quilt back runs in the same direction. If the fabric is turned end for end, its nap will cause it to appear as different shades.

The floral prints of calico fabrics are sometimes, in effect, stripes. I drape the fabric over something, and then view it from across the room to determine the width of the pattern repeat and prominence of the stripes. I check to see if the floral "stripes" run with the grain line.

If they don't, I lay the templates with the design of the fabric, rather than the grain line, to avoid the illusion of inaccuracy. This is especially important to take into consideration when the fabric is to be used in larger areas, such as in a border.

— Ann Reimer, Beatrice, NE

❖ I always try to select the same weight of fabrics. Some deep colors use a coarser broadcloth to absorb the darker dyes, so I attempt to use the same type of greige goods ("raw" fabric before it is dyed or printed) throughout. I never mix poly/cotton blends with 100-percent cotton in the same quilt.

— Johnette Zwolinski Shoberg, Globe, AZ

❖ I always buy one-half yard more of each fabric than I actually need, to cover for error.

— Carol Farley, Grasonville, MD

Additional tips

❖ A quilt design or a special fabric dictates to me what colors should be in the quilt. I do not make quilts to match rooms. The colors in a quilt, like art, do not have to match a room to be effective. I make a quilt just to create, not specifically for the purpose of decorating my home.

— Terry Festa, Clinton, CT

❖ Using several different muslins in a quilt top makes it look old, as if it is unevenly faded. I want my quilts to have that old, loved look.

— Barbara Riley, Elk Grove, CA

❖ I try to buy fabrics of similar weight. I like quilt patterns with lots of pieces, so trying to keep that in mind, while also coordinating colors and prints, can sometimes be hard for me.

— Barbara Ashton, Sharon Hill, PA

❖ I seldom purchase enough fabric initially, so I carry very small swatches of all my fabrics and buy more as needed.

— Rose Hankins, Stevensville, MD

How to shop!

❖ I like to shop with a friend who shares my fabric preferences. We combine the amounts we each need, then buy a longer length and split it lengthwise, so we each have enough length for lattices or borders. This works especially well with stripes.

— Phyllis A. Kroggel, Tucson, AZ

❖ If I am uncertain of fabric content, I do a burn test. To do that, burn a scrap, and if the ash is soft and gray, the fabric is cotton. If the result is a hard beaded residue, the fabric is a blend.

— Patti Welsh, Yorktown Heights, NY

❖ I never accept a fabric on the basis of a good price, unless I have first accepted it for some other criteria. Nor do I reject a fabric as being too expensive before I carefully consider its contribution to a quilt. Particularly in small projects, a piece of expensive fabric may be exactly what I need to give the finished piece that extra touch. The additional expense is minimal.

— Linda Hampton Schiffer, Columbia, MD

❖ I take a needle along and "fake quilt" through the fabric to see how easily it will actually quilt. If the needle doesn't glide easily through the fabric, I avoid buying it. Sometimes I will purchase it anyway if I can't find a pattern I like better, but I do not like fabric that is too tightly woven and quilts hard.

— Marilyn Umble, Atglen, PA

❖ I like to go shopping with someone who has different tastes than mine and ask them for their opinion, or let them make one selection for me!

— Joyce Trueblood, Cromwell, CT

❖ When fabric shopping, I keep the day free to do nothing but select my fabric. I don't take little children or anyone else who will distract me.

— Hazel Lightcap Propst, Oxford, PA

❖ I do *not* look at price until I have decided on fabric and color.

— Charlie Weckerle, Roseburg, OR

❖ Before prewashing, I cut a small triangular piece from each selvage edge corner to prevent raveling. The small triangular pieces I save for color-matching. I keep a small notebook in my purse with my swatches taped in place with notes regarding yardage requirements. If I happen to be out and pass a quilt shop, I can pop in and match up colors without having to guess or remember what shade of blue, green, etc., I need.

— Irene J. Dewar, Pickering, ON

2

Prewashing fabrics

Methods for prewashing

❖ I prewash fabrics in Orvus soap and warm water in the washer. I dry them in the dryer on the permanent press cycle, just as I do quilts.
— Ellen Victoria Crockett, Springfield, VA

❖ To prewash, I run a little warm water in the washer, swish the fabric around a bit, and then dry it on medium heat.
— Maryalice DeLong, Elwood, IN

❖ If I think the colors will run or bleed, I boil them until the water is clear. I change the water a few times and add a little vinegar. Other prints I wash in the washer with hot water. I dry everything in the dryer on "Hot" in small lots.
— Jacqueline E. Deininger, Bethlehem, PA

❖ I prewash fabrics by soaking them in a solution of 1/2 teaspoon Epsom salts to one gallon cold water. I rinse them well and then line dry them. The salt solution helps to prevent fading and bleeding of colors if the quilt is to be washed.
— Audrey H. Eby, Lancaster, PA

❖ I prewash fabrics the same way I plan to wash the quilt. If the quilt is for a child, I prewash the fabric using a spray or stick prewash (Stain Stick or Spray & Wash).
— Cheryl Ferriter, West Springfield, MA

❖ I dunk fabric in lukewarm water to check for colorfastness. I keep dunking until the sizing is out; then I dry it until it is slightly damp and iron it.

— Carol Findling, Beatrice, NE

❖ I run hot water over fabric in a small basin. This immediately allows me to know if dark fabric will run.

— Lois Mae E. Kuh, Penfield, NY

❖ I prewash in hot water and Orvus soap through at least two washes for colors that are likely to bleed. Other fabrics get only one wash. I rinse in salt water.

— Suellen Fletcher, Noblesville, IN

❖ If I feel a dark fabric or any fabric may run, I test a smaller piece in a pint jar with warm water and Orvus quilt soap. No fabric enters my sewing room until it's been prewashed in Orvus soap. I use this because it has no additives. If I ever want to dye or over-dye a fabric, I will be able to. Fabrics that might have a residue of fabric softener on them will not dye as well.

— Sue Seeley, New Bern, NC

❖ I wash dark or bright fabrics in the sink so I can see if they will bleed. Once, for a group quilt, I washed 22 fabrics that way. I found one piece that bled for over an hour with repeated washing. When I returned to the store to see how much this fabric had faded, I was amazed to discover it was exactly the same color as the fabric on the bolt! It must have been full of excess dye. It was a very useful lesson on why prewashing is so important.
— Doris Morelock, Alexandria, VA

❖ I prewash using Orvus Paste and repeat the final rinse twice. I then put the wet fabric between two pieces of white paper towels and let the fabric dry. If any color runs onto the paper towels, I re-wash the fabric and dry it between the paper towels again.

— Debra Botelho Zeida, Waquoit, MA

❖ I keep a jar of small white cotton squares from an old sheet that I put in the washer when I prewash fabrics. That allows me to see if the color runs, because the white square absorbs bleeding color.

— Florence Donavan, Lodi, CA

❖ I repeat the rinse cycle to make sure all the soap is removed from the fabric. I dip out a bit of the last rinse water with a white Styrofoam coffee cup to make sure the color is not bleeding.

I sometimes put a few drops of very hot water in the one corner of a piece of fabric, then blot it to determine if it is colorfast.

— Ann Reimer, Beatrice, NE

❖ If I think a fabric may not be colorfast, I put it in a container with boiling water until the water is cool. I repeat that until the water remains clear, then I dry and iron the fabric.

— Irma Harder, Mountain Lake, MN

❖ My prewash formula is as follows: less than one-half yard fabric, I do it in hot water in the sink; more than 2 yards, I wash it in hot water in the washing machine. Anything in between, I take into the shower with me. I use detergent only if fabrics come from a store that allows smoking, or if the fabric seems dirty.

— Ann Foss, Brooklyn, NY

❖ If I make a full-size quilt, I wash all the material first before sewing it together and quilting it. If I make something smaller, like a baby quilt or wall hanging, I put the top together, then wash the top and back before I quilt it. I always prewash reds alone in case the color runs.

— Jean Shaner, York, PA

❖ I use warm water and just a little liquid soap to soften the water for prewashing fabrics. I think it is better to line dry, because I feel the dryer tends to "distort" the cotton, especially small pieces.

— Lee Cook, Falmouth, MA

❖ I prewash fabric in my washing machine with Wisk laundry detergent in warm water. I always rinse fabrics twice to remove any detergent residue.

— Gail L. Kozicki, Glen Mills, PA

❖ I put my fabrics in the washer and dryer. That way I know there is not a chance of shrinkage. This also makes quilting much easier.

— Helen L. Anderson, Titusville, NJ

❖ I sort color shades, then wash fabrics in hot water with a dash of white vinegar.

— Charmaine Caesar, Lancaster, PA

❖ I snip off all four corners of the fabric to prevent raveling. I sort it by color and put it in the washer with the family laundry. I hang it up to dry. Since I snip the four corners I can always tell what's been washed.

— Sherri Driver, Englewood, CO

❖ I prewash materials by hand in a dishpan full of very hot water. I then put the fabric in the washing machine on the spin cycle to take out the excess water, and finally into the dryer.

— Terri Good, Marietta, PA

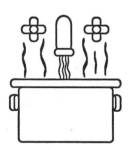

❖ I separate fabrics into light, medium and dark loads by color, so that it is already separated in piles for me to use or to put in my collection for future use. I use 1/4 cup of Orvus soap for one machine load and add 1/2 cup of vinegar and 1/2 tablespoon of salt to set the color.

— Pearl Mok, Los Angeles, CA

❖ I handwash it, roll it in a towel, then line dry it.

— Anona Teel, Bangor, PA

❖ I prewash in warm water on the gentle cycle and do *not* use deter-

gents. A detergent removes fabric preservatives that I want to retain because I may store the fabric for a period of time.

If the preservatives are allowed to remain, my quilt may last longer. After I've ironed the fabric, I place a one- to two-inch strip of masking tape on the fabric as a reminder that "this fabric has been washed and is ready to cut."

— Mary M. Weimer, Clinton, MD

❖ If I have more than three yards, I soak the fabric in medium to hot water in the bathtub overnight. If I have less, I put it with a load of laundry in the washing machine.

— Doris Miotto, Thorold, ON

❖ I fill the tub of my washer with very hot water. I wash one color at a time, starting with the lightest. I swish each piece in the washer. If the piece does not give up any color, I toss it into the dryer to dry.

— Margaret M. Metique, Scarsdale, NY

❖ I prepare an index card with a sample of each fabric, the color number, the textile manufacturer's name, when and where I purchased it, and the price per yard. Next, I hand-rinse my smaller pieces of fabric with warm water in a white sink. I count and note on my card the number of rinses it takes until the water remains clear.

With larger pieces of fabric, such as the backing, I cut off a 1/4 yard piece and rinse it, as described. I then place the larger piece in my washer on a warm wash/rinse setting, and run it through *half* the number of times it took for the 1/4 yard portion. I include a sheet of white fabric or toweling in the last cycle to double-check that the colors no longer run.

— Ann Reimer, Beatrice, NE

❖ I leave my fabrics folded to prewash them. I draw the hottest tap water I can get from the faucet, then lay the folded fabric in the sink and leave it until it's thoroughly saturated. I then drain the water, press out as much excess water as possible, and hang the fabric on the line to dry. If the fabric bleeds, I rinse it until the hot water is clear, or I discard the fabric.

— Carolyn Shank, Dayton, VA

❖ I wash dark and bright colors separately in hot water with one tablespoon Synthrapol detergent and 1/4 cup soda ash (sodium carbonate) per wash load. All purchased fabrics go directly to the washroom before ever seeing my sewing room!

— Katy J. Widger, Los Lunas, NM

❖ I presoak all fabrics separately in two parts vinegar, one part warm water, and two tablespoons salt. Then I wash it in the washing machine with laundry soap and cold water.

— Judy M. Sharer, Port Matilda, PA

Ways to save a bleeding fabric

❖ To set dye in fabric, I soak it in a sink of hot water with 1/4 cup vinegar and an eyedropper's worth of iodine. I let the fabric soak one hour. Then I rinse it.

— **Kathy Evenson, Fergus Falls, MN**

❖ I throw a muslin scrap into the wash water with each fabric. The muslin scrap absorbs any bleeding color, so I know if a fabric is not colorfast.

— **Donna Barnitz, Rio Rancho, NM**

❖ When I bring my material home, I take it right to the laundry room. I hand-wash it, rinse it and dry it in the dryer. Any material that bleeds, I wash several times, then I let it sit in water (one gallon plus one cup white vinegar) for half an hour before rinsing it twice. Vinegar seems to work better than salt. When it is dry, I cut off the selvage and put the fabric in my sewing room. The cut selvage lets me know the fabric was washed.

— **Mary E. Isle, Deerwood, MN**

❖ To salvage a bleeding fabric, try a vinegar rinse — or wash with Ensure and iron *hot*.

— **Barbara Monay, Annapolis, MD**

❖ To prevent bleeding, I wash fabric with Synthrapol detergent (available through mail order from Dharma Trading Co., San Rafael, CA). Synthrapol is made especially to rid fabric of excess dyes without changing or damaging the original colors.

— **Cheri Ruzich, Live Oak, CA**

How to prevent raveled edges

❖ I cut a triangle off each corner to prevent raveling and fraying. This also reminds me that the fabric was prewashed. Small scraps can be prewashed in a mesh lingerie bag on the delicate cycle.

— **Judi Manos, West Islip, NY**

❖ I open my fabric before placing it in the machine, so that the fold line from being wrapped on the bolt has a chance to fade. Clipping loose threads and untangling fabric before placing it in the dryer makes fabric come out of the dryer needing very little care.

— **Janice Muller, Derwood, MD**

❖ Sometimes there are grease marks on a piece of fabric which I have sometimes been able to remove with shampoo for oily hair. I line dry fabric because the dryer tends to fray fabric ends and to soften it.

— **Connee Sager, Tucson, AZ**

❖ I serge (overlock stitch on a serger sewing machine) the ends before prewashing so the fabric doesn't fray. Before I had a serger, I used my pinking shears. Most of the time I put the fabric in the washer without detergent and just let it go through the entire cycle.

— Dottie Doughty, Oklahoma City, OK

❖ I usually serge the ends to prevent raveling, then throw it in the washer. The stitching lets me know the fabric has been washed and which is the right side, if I am using a solid color. I made a 60" board that fits over my ironing board, so it is easy to iron wide fabrics.

— Thelma A. Stein, Tavares, FL

❖ If fabrics are 1/2 yard or smaller, I fold them, then put them in a "wash bag" to wash them. I also clip their corners no matter what size the piece of fabric. Both of these practices reduce the raveling.

— Laura S. Hemenway, Fort Washington, MD

Pressing after prewashing

❖ I remove fabrics from the dryer immediately and steam-press them. If they are too wrinkled, I dampen them and iron them dry.

— Jacqueline E. Deininger, Bethlehem, PA

❖ If I have a lot of fabric to wash, I cut it into small sections of one or two yards each. It is easier to iron the pieces that way.

— Tommie Bandy Freeman, Carrollton, GA

❖ I put fabrics through the rinse and spin cycle of my washer, then remove and iron them with a dry iron. The fabric steams a lot, and it requires a lot of ironing, but by ironing the fabric when damp, it regains that new crisp feeling again before I cut it.

— Marilyn Umble, Atglen, PA

❖ I prewash with hot water, machine-dry the fabric to a damp stage, and then hot-iron it until it is completely dry. I press fabric (no sideways strokes) to avoid distorting its grain. Hot water for prewashing shows me if the fabric will run, and heat from a hot iron sets the dye.

— Barbara Monay, Annapolis, MD

❖ I hardly ever prewash, but I do steam-iron fabrics.

— Alma Mullet, Walnut Creek, OH

❖ I never press fabric till I'm ready to use it, and then only the amount I expect to use. Too much ironing and too hot an iron causes fabric to lose its crisp color and finish.

— Jane E. Crowe, Boyertown, PA

❖ When ironing fabrics, I find it helpful either to drape each piece over an old-fashioned drying rack, or hang it from clamp-type pant hangers, or from wire hangers with a horizontal cardboard crease-saver.

— Ann Reimer, Beatrice, NE

❖ After prewashing fabric, I iron it while it is still damp. Sometimes I use a little sizing spray on its reverse side to make the fabric firmer for cutting out small quilting pieces.

— Marabee J. Seifert, Easley, SC

❖ When prewashing a very large piece of fabric, I mark the selvages at 24" intervals. When the fabric comes out of the washer, I fold it in half lengthwise, matching the marks, and then line dry it. I can then press the fabric folded in half and be sure it is properly aligned.

— Joyce R. Swinniz, Mooresville, IN

❖ When I've finished prewashing, I iron the fabric and fold it twice lengthwise, and then I fold it accordion-style. This makes for easy strip-cutting.

— Jeanne Curtis, Yuba City, CA

Additional tips

❖ I have some finished pieces that I made with fabric that I carefully prewashed. But when I washed the finished product, the color bled through on the quilting stitches. The fabrics were washed in city water at our old house — the quilt was washed in our new home with well water. I do find this makes a difference.

— Marilyn Bloom Wallace, Alfred, ME

❖ I use one gallon of water to four tea bags to make a tea dye. I boil the tea for 15 minutes. I then test four fabric swatches for my favorite shade by soaking one for 15 minutes, another for 20, another for 25, and still another for 30 minutes in the tea dye. Then I iron each swatch dry and compare them. I determine the length of the tea bath for a particular fabric from my test swatches. I then submerge the fabric and add l/2 cup vinegar and l/2 tablespoon salt to the tea bath to set the color and prevent bleeding. I tea-dye to make the quilt look old.

— Pearl Mok, Los Angeles, CA

❖ After prewashing, I keep fabrics covered with bags, sheets, etc., to keep them dust free and clean.

— Jane S. Lippincott, Wynnewood, PA

❖ I do not prewash because I like working with fabric that still has the sizing in it. I feel the fabric has more stability, which allows for greater accuracy in piecing.

— Susan Saladini, Freehold, NJ; Dale Renee Ball, Silverdale, WA

❖ A good reason to rinse fabrics is to remove its sizing, making it much easier to "needle."

— Ann Reimer, Beatrice, NE

❖ I pull wet fabric hard in all directions to straighten its grain.

— Joan Lemmler, Albuquerque, NM

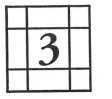

Making templates

Materials and methods for making templates

❖ I like to use washed sheets of plastic that come in packs of bacon. They are just the right size to keep in the sewing box to make templates. One side is smooth; one side pebbly.
— Jean Harris Robinson, Cinnaminson, NJ

❖ When I can get it, I make my templates from Lexan, put out by Parma for Radio Control Cars. It is clear and flexible and cuts easily with a scissors, but it is also thick enough to use with a rotary cutter. (I work in a hobby shop, which deals with R.C. Cars!)
— Rosalie W. Keegan, Enfield, CT

❖ I often use graph paper to draw templates; then I glue-stick them to recycled plastic place mats. I allow the glue to dry before cutting them out with my paper scissors.
— Laura Reif Lipski, Lindenhurst, NY

❖ We use lots of gallon bottles of water. I cut out the flat areas and use them for templates; I swipe the pens my husband uses for marking photo negatives. They mark permanently on slick surfaces.
— Connee Sager, Tucson, AZ

❖ My daughter is an X-ray technician, so I use old X-ray film for templates. (I try to avoid obvious bones!)
— Sharron Van Meter, St. Charles, MO

❖ To make templates for pieced patterns, I draw a full-size design on graph paper — using graph paper appropriate for the block (4, 5, 6, 7, 8 or 10 lines to the inch). I redraft each template piece on separate pieces of graph paper and cut them out, leaving a l/4- to l/2-inch margin around their outer edges. I then glue the graph paper to template plastic with rubber cement (coating both the plastic and the graph paper) and cut along the drawn lines.

— Marilyn Bloom Wallace, Alfred, ME

❖ I like to use template plastic that is marked like graph paper. The lines help to maintain accuracy.

— Ada L. Bishop, Beatrice, NE

❖ If the pattern is printed on a sheet of paper, I put rubber cement on the paper and lay a sheet of template plastic over the glue. I let it set five to 10 minutes and then cut the pieces out. I can read all grain lines, pattern piece numbers and cutting instructions through the plastic.

— Kathy Evenson, Fergus Falls, MN

❖ For appliqué, I like a new heat resistant plastic called Templar. I draw around the Templar template on the wrong side of the material, leaving a 1/4-inch seam allowance. I dampen the seam allowance slightly with spraystarch, using my finger or a small brush (do not spray directly on the fabric).

With a dry iron, using the side of the iron, I push the seam allowance over the Templar — it will not melt. I then remove the Templar, and my piece is ready to be appliquéd with its seam allowances already turned under.

— Judi Manos, West Islip, NY

❖ I make templates from heavy plastic lids of ice cream pails, etc

— Edna Schrock, Haven, KS

❖ For appliqué templates, I use outdated laminated tax charts. They're good for dozens of appliqué pressings.

— Vicky Jo Bogart, Fargo, ND

❖ My personal favorite to use is frosted .075 mm. acetate, available at art supply stores. I can write on it with either pencil or pen. An acetate template allows me to view its most effective placement on the fabric's pattern.

— Donna Humlan, Richmond, VA

❖ I use acetate (plastic) sheet protectors from discarded reports and papers to make templates. The clear plastic is easy to see through to trace pieces, and I can mark on it with a permanent black pilot marking pen.

— Nina Lord, Annapolis, MD

❖ I use the plastic sheets used as desk protectors. They are very reasonable in price and readily available in stationery shops. When I cut out the plastic template pieces, I am very careful to cut on my drawn line. I make note on each template which quilt pattern it is part of and its size. I mark which side should lie on the grain line, and I also make note whether the template includes the seam allowance or not.

— Irene J. Dewar, Pickering, ON

❖ I went to the local car dealer in town and asked if I could have their plastic signs when they were through with them. The plastic is heavy enough to make nice templates. Part of the plastic is clear, and some of it has color. I can separate templates for various projects by color.

— Lois C. Ruiz, Murray, KY

❖ I iron freezer paper together and make a template using a double layer of that. If a template is copied onto paper, I iron that piece to freezer paper. It's not as durable as plastic, but if I am using it infrequently, it is satisfactory.

— Jennifer Asbury, Delta, PA

❖ For appliqué designs, I use tracing paper to copy the design and then use "Tack a Note" adhesive stick to attach it to the paper side of plastic-coated freezer paper. I carefully cut out the design. I lift the tracing paper from the freezer paper and discard it because the glue reacts badly to a hot iron. With the waxed side of the freezer paper down, I iron it to the right side of the fabric. I then use either scissors or a rotary cutter to cut out the design. The freezer paper pattern can be used repeatedly.

I sometimes use a copy machine to copy the design and then trim it to size. I then apply "Tack a Note" adhesive stick to the back of the template and place the template on the fabric. It won't slip when I use a rotary cutter. The pattern can be lifted from the fabric and re-applied repeatedly without harming the fabric. "Tack a Note" adhesive stick is designed to make any paper self-sticking and is removable.

— Janice Muller, Derwood, MD

❖ For templates that will get repeated use, I use plastic. If the quilt blocks are all going to be different, I make templates from freezer paper. I iron the paper to the fabric, and then when piecing, I use the edge of the freezer paper as the sew line and peel off the paper when the block is complete.

— Barbara F. Hummel, Punxsutawney, PA

❖ I trace template pieces onto freezer paper (I can easily see through it) and iron the paper onto manila folders or poster board. For *very* permanent templates I use WARP's rug runner plastic. It's smooth on top, striated on the bottom, can be easily marked with a black fine point "Sharpie" marker, and easily cut with scissors. It is available in hardware and paint stores in rolls 30 inches by five feet, or by the foot.

— Mary Seielstad, Schenectady, NY

❖ When making freezer paper templates for appliqué, I fold a strip of paper many times (like for paper dolls) and cut one. This accurately cuts six to eight templates at a time.

— Melissa Stiles Hess, LaConner, WA

❖ For appliqué templates, I cut freezer paper without the l/4-inch seam allowance. I iron the template onto the right side of the fabric and cut around the template, leaving a 1/4-inch seam allowance of fabric around the template. I then peel the template off the fabric and lay the fabric right side down on the ironing board. I replace the template, this time with the sticky side up, on top of the fabric and center it on the shape. It should fit exactly, exposing a l/4-inch seam allowance around the edges. Seam allowances can be folded over the top of the template (clip corners as necessary) and ironed onto the sticky template.

To keep the template from shifting while I iron the seam allowance down, I iron a small section on one side, then the other side, then on the top and then the bottom, continuing to flip all the remaining seam allowance onto the freezer paper. I now have an entire appliqué piece, ready to hand- or machine-appliqué onto my quilt.

With the freezer paper left in, the unit is secured from stretching while I stitch, and it can be ironed into place on the quilt. Once appliquéd onto the quilt, I remove the paper by cutting a hole from the back side of the quilt. I can pull the paper right out because after I've sewn it on, it has a perforated edge. For real tight spots, I use tweezers to grab hold and pull.

— Cheri Ruzich, Live Oak, CA

❖ I use a stiff poster board for templates, but I am always careful when I am marking not to rub too closely along the edge of the template which would wear it down, eventually making the pieces too small. Just a fraction of an inch can make everything out of true measure.

— Sharon Heidi, Mt. Lake, MN

❖ I make my templates from sandpaper (it doesn't slide on fabric) or sometimes old manila folders.

— Helen Kusnitz, W. Hempstead, NY

❖ For appliqué, I trace or draw the design on tissue paper and then transfer it with carbon paper to a manila file folder, cut it out, and label it carefully.

— Phyllis A. Kroggel, Tucson, AZ

❖ If a template is printed and can be cut out, I put contact paper on both sides of it and then use that as a pattern.

— Mary Puterbaugh, Elwood, IN

❖ I use cereal boxes. My husband can always tell when I need to cut more templates — that's when I purchase the largest size boxes of cereal our grocery store carries! After cutting the cardboard, I use a glue stick to glue fine sandpaper on the backs to prevent the templates from slipping.

— Sherri Lipman McCauley, Pleasant Valley, NY

❖ I use stiff plastic bonnet board. I trace my pattern on the bonnet board, then cut it out carefully with an Exacto knife.

— Grace S. Miller, Mt. Joy, PA

❖ I paste the paper template pattern (with seam allowances included) onto the very stiffest mat board I can find. I keep scissors expressly for cutting out these templates. This board is stiff enough to cut with a rotary cutter or scissors.

— Marilyn Umble, Atglen, PA

❖ I like using a thin, good quality cardboard for templates. The type that comes in underwear packages is ideal.

— Leesa Seaman Lesenski, Whatgly, MA

❖ I've used stiff paper plates for making templates.

— Judy M. Sharer, Port Matilda, PA

❖ The cardboard backs from legal pads make excellent template material. I ask my friends who work in offices to save them for me. I mark each one with the pattern name and block size.

— Ruth Day, Sturgis, SD

❖ If the pieces are for a large project or for long-term use, I have my husband cut them out of masonite board. I use a heavy template plastic for shorter projects.

— Donna Humlan, Richmond, VA

❖ I draw and draft my patterns directly onto accurate graph paper, then glue the graph paper (with rubber cement) onto artist's mat board, a very dense, thin, and sturdy cardboard. I then carefully cut out the templates using a single-blade craft knife. These templates are accurate for marking with a sharp pencil.

For more permanent templates, I also use graph paper for drafting the pattern pieces, but then I glue the graph paper to the sticky adhesive paper covering a sheet of 1/8-inch Plexiglas and have my husband cut out the patterns on his band saw. I peel off the adhesive paper and have a permanent template suitable for use with my rotary cutter. The Plexiglas can be marked according to grain line and size with a black permanent marking pen.

— Katy J. Widger, Los Lunas, NM

❖ When I plan to use a pattern several times, I like to use Plexiglas. This works especially well for triangles which need to be cut on different angles. On each side of the template I place a chart (covered with clear contact paper), showing how to cut the triangles.

— Judith Eve Nisly, Partridge, KS

❖ If I want a template to last and plan to use it for several quilts, I go to the local glass company and have it made from Plexiglas.

— Mary McCormick, Maguson, IL

❖ I prefer hard plastic templates. My husband cuts them out for me from a sheet of acrylic he purchases at the hardware store, and then he gently sands the edges.

— Bonnie Zabzdyr, Wright City, MO

❖ My husband used his band saw to cut templates for me out of an old plastic file cabinet that I was going to throw away.

— Loraine Arnold, Rhinebeck, NY

❖ The curved edge of a 45 RPM record is just right and makes a great template for some of my Drunkard's Path quilts.

— Myrna L. Rambis, Anderson, IN

❖ I use Electric Quilt software for templates if possible.

— Patti Welsh, Yorktown Heights, NY

❖ For appliqué, I use tear-away interfacing for templates, transferring the markings with pencil.

— Teresa Ernest Steinstraw, Denton, TX

❖ For appliqué templates, I iron freezer paper to the right side of the fabric, cut outside the paper for my seam allowance, and roll the seam allowance under to the edge of the freezer paper with my needle as I go.

— Ib Bartlet, Schenectady, NY

Quilting templates

❖ I sometimes trace a quilting design on bridal veil fabric and lay this on top of dark fabric. The pattern can be traced with chalk, white pencil, or a thin piece of worn-down hand soap. When I trace patterns onto bridal veil fabric, I use large paper clips to secure the pattern to the veil.

— Katie Esh, Ronks, PA

❖ To make stencils, I trace the design on template plastic, place a nail in a block of wood so the point of the nail extends through the block, heat the nail point over a candle flame (holding onto my wood block "handle"), and press the nail into the plastic to make holes for a pencil to enter for marking. I use a Berol pencil (an architect's tool) to connect the dots after tracing them onto the fabric.

— Lela Ann Schneider, Boise, ID

❖ I pierce holes in corners of templates using a hot ice pick. I make dots through the holes and connect the dots with a pencil to mark sewing lines.

— L. Jean Moore, Anderson, IN

❖ I trace quilting patterns onto plastic, cardboard or vinyl floor covering. I cut them out using a buttonhole scissors or a bent toenail scissors. The curve in the scissors' blade makes cutting curves less difficult.

— Katie Esh, Ronks, PA

Adjusting template sizes

❖ As I learned to do once upon a time in grade school art class, I draw a grid over the design and reduce or enlarge the template by drawing it into a smaller or larger grid

— Ada L. Bishop, Beatrice, NE

❖ I first use a proportional wheel (available in an art store) to determine the percent by which I should enlarge or reduce the pattern to fit my needs, then use a photocopying machine to do that. Those wheels are great! I can be very accurate.

— Donna Barnitz, Rio Rancho, NM

❖ I buy large sheets of graph paper so I can draft the whole block and add seam allowances in another color. I then use tracing paper and trace individual templates showing their seam allowances.

—Laura Reif Lipski, Lindenhurst, NY

❖ When I need to adapt a pattern, I go to the school library and use the opaque projector to enlarge patterns.

—Jennifer L. Rhodes, Lancaster, PA

❖ I adjust by resizing templates on an opaque projector and then cut them out of thin sheets of acetate purchased at a plastic store.

—Pearl Mok, Los Angeles, CA

❖ I often draft small patterns (less than one page in finished size) on my computer and use my drawing software to size the finished template.

—Linda Hampton Schiffer, Columbia, MD

❖ I swear by graph paper, but lately I have been using "The Electric Quilt," a computer program.

—Judith Lavine Smith, Washington, DC

❖ I use graph paper to figure out the ratios if I am enlarging. Generally, though, I use freezer paper and cut a block the exact size I want it with no seam allowances, and then either fold or use a ruler to draw the template shapes. For example, if I need a 10-inch block and am making a nine-patch design, I cut out a 10-inch piece of paper and fold it into thirds in both directions. The crease lines on the paper would be the template lines.

—Joy Rubenstein-Moir, Holtsville, NY

❖ Most blocks can easily be redrafted with graph paper or by folding paper. I have a pantograph I use for appliqué. It works well to enlarge a small design.

—Dorothy Reise, Severna Park, MD

❖ Some things I just reduce or enlarge on a copy machine. Other times I draw the pattern to the scale I want using the "Auto Cad" program on my computer.

—Barbara Aston, Sharon Hill, PA

❖ I keep plastic bags of templates — triangles, squares, diamonds and hexagons. I go through them, and often I can find the right sizes for the pattern I want to make.

—Muriel D. Austin, Hingham, MA

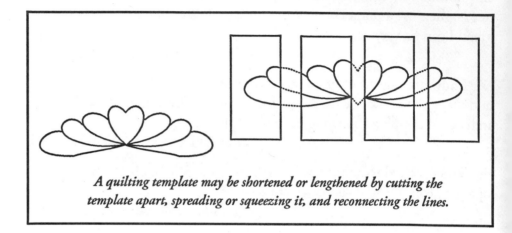

A quilting template may be shortened or lengthened by cutting the template apart, spreading or squeezing it, and reconnecting the lines.

❖ To adjust the size of a quilting template, I transfer the design to a piece of paper and lay it on the fabric border to see how sections of the design fit into one-fourth of the length of the border. I can then add to or subtract from the paper design to make it fill the appropriate space. With this knowledge, I can use the plastic template, but adjust it accordingly to fit my particular border.

When I work with light fabrics, I sometimes put the design, adapted to the proper size on plain paper with a dark marker, underneath the fabric, so I can use it as a reference point to see where and how to place the plastic template for marking. For appliqué, I use the copier to enlarge or make the templates smaller.

— Edna Nisly, Partridge, KS

❖ I find that commercial stencils can always have a loop added or deleted to fit a square border on a quilt. I also play with designs on paper, rearranging the design elements of one or several templates. For borders, I match corners first — everyone checks to see if the corners are rounded beautifully. If the rest of the design doesn't fit, I can fudge somewhere in the middle or, better yet, with each repeat of the design or template.

— Sherri Driver, Englewood, CO

❖ To enlarge or reduce a pattern, I first draw the design in one color. I then draw a grid of squares over the design using a different color. On another sheet of paper I make the same number of squares in the size block I want the finished pattern to be, then draw my design to correspond with the first set of squares.

— Joyce A. Walker, Ft. Smith, AR

❖ Marry an engineer. I did — so this is not a problem here. It involves him in my quilting and he's a whiz at math. Life is wonderful!

— Judy Mocho, Albuquerque, NM

❖ I use template plastic with a grid to aid in accuracy, but I always check my re-drawn patterns by making a paper paste-up before I cut the fabric. This saves lots of time and prevents errors.

— Shirley Liby, Muncie, IN

❖ I draw my quilting designs onto sew-in interfacing. To adjust the size, I cut portions of the pattern apart and stretch or scrunch them as needed to fit the sides and ends of a quilt.

— Alix Nancy Botsford, Seminole, OK

❖ To adjust quilting templates, I work details at the very ends and at the very center first, then adjust spacing between the details. Part of it is by calculation and the rest by eye.

— Susan Loweth-Melton, Olney, MD

❖ When adjusting quilting templates, I make a paper template the actual size of the border and fold it into fourths. I then adjust the template so that each quarter comes out the same and so that the ends are all the same.

— Virginia L. Fry, Fulton, MD

Organizing templates

❖ I store templates in plastic bags stapled to patterns in an alphabetized loose-leaf notebook.

— Shirley J. Odell, Manteca, CA

❖ On all templates, I mark with permanent marker: the pattern name, block size, grain line direction arrow, and a letter which corresponds to a letter on the drawn diagram. I do not mark the number to cut or the color, since I may want to use it over again with some other project.

— Terry Festa, Clinton, CT

❖ I use heavy plastic for making templates. After I've finished using them, I place them in a file in alphabetical order. I clip all pieces of the template together and attach a graph of the finished design on paper.

— Margaret Jarrett, Anderson, IN

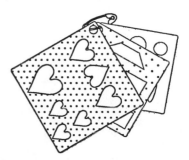

❖ To keep templates together, I use a paper punch to put a hole in each piece. I then put them on a safety pin.

— Jo Anne Parisi, West Springfield, MA

Additional tips

❖ When making templates, I use a large needle and pierce the plastic at each corner of the piece being made. I then use a ruler and a fine point permanent marker to draw the lines connecting these points. I cut the piece out, using scissors set aside for paper and plastic, and cut inside the drawn line. I use a rotary cutter to cut plastic templates. Nicked blades or blades too dull to cut fabric will still work well on template plastic.

— Sue Seeley, New Bern, NC

❖ At the hardware store, I buy sandpaper with pressure sensitive adhesive on the back and place a small square on the backside of each template to prevent slipping while I trace.

— Freda Gail Stern, Dallas, TX

❖ I use sheet plastic for templates. This has a hard enough edge to mark against with a pencil. However, when I use a rotary cutter around the template without the marking lines, I need something hard over the template to cut against so that I don't slice the template. Clear Plexiglas or a hard clear plastic dressmaker ruler works pretty well.

— Elaine W. Good, Lititz, PA

❖ I cut the flatter parts out of vinegar jugs, Clorox bottles, and milk jugs, then slip them under a rug and forget them until I need them. They become fully flattened in no time!

— Dorothy Dyer, Lee's Summit, MO

❖ I put both sewing lines and cutting lines on my templates so I can lay templates over the pieced block to check for accuracy.

— Sherri Driver, Englewood, CO

❖ After I've cut the templates out of plastic, I place them over the original patterns to be certain they match exactly.

— Kathy Mason Vetter, Colorado Springs, CO

❖ I trace templates onto plastic and cut them with a rotary cutter. I always make sure light is coming from the right (I'm right-handed) when I'm cutting templates so I don't get a shadow on the line I'm cutting.

— Harriet S. Meade, Clinton, CT

❖ I use a laundry marker to write on templates to identify each piece. I also put "S.A.A." (seam allowance added) so I know I don't have to add it again!

— Thelma A. Stein, Tavares, FL

❖ I iron the freezer paper template onto the fabric, layer other fabrics underneath, and cut multiple layers. I can use the rotary cutter and ruler without the template moving.

— Jo Ann Pelletier, Longmeadow, MA

❖ If I use triangular templates for machine-piecing, I clip off the corners 1/4 inch from the seam line. This results in accurate and uniformly sized pieces, and prevents having "dog-ears" shadowing through the light fabrics.

After I have prepared my templates, I lay them out on a newspaper with the frosted side up and give them a light coating of spray adhesive (Scotch 3M "Spray Mount" Artist's Adhesive or a similar product works well). It is best to do this in a well-ventilated area. After the adhesive has dried for a few minutes, the templates will be ready to use or store in a file folder. This coating prevents templates from slipping on the fabric or in my file folder. Sometimes I find it necessary to re-treat the templates with an additional spraying of the adhesive.

— Ann Reimer, Beatrice, NE

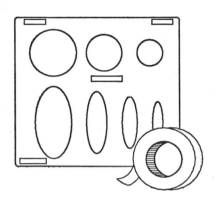

❖ I cut templates out of template plastic with old scissors. I then place colored electrical tape around each template to help create a ridge. This helps to prevent slippage and allows me to place a clear ruler on top of it and align the edges, so I can cut with a rotary cutter and not trim away my template underneath.

— Lela Ann Schneider, Boise, ID

❖ I put a small piece of masking tape on the back of plastic templates to keep them from slipping.

— Abbie J. Christie, Berkeley Heights, NJ

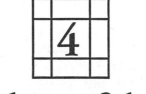

Marking fabrics

Marking tools

❖ My favorite marking tool for fabrics is a silver pencil. It shows up on both dark and light colors, and it washes out easily. Also, I can get a finer point than with chalk pencils.

— Cindy Cooksey, Irvine, CA

❖ I mark lightly using a special fabric lead which is only graphite (no oil/petroleum). Silver architect's pencils (Berol Verithin) are good. Soap slivers are great on medium to dark fabrics

— Carol Findling, Beatrice, NE

❖ A #2 hard Pentel pencil gives me a consistent line on all my fabrics.

— Suellen Fletcher, Noblesville, IN

❖ I keep red, yellow, turquoise and white colored pencils on hand for marking multicolor prints.

— Ann Foss, Brooklyn, NY

❖ If the fabric is part light and part dark, yellow is a good color for marking because it shows up well on both.

— Nancy Wagner Graves, Manhattan, KS

❖ Mechanical pencils with .5 or .7 lead are excellent for marking because they leave narrow marks and the pencil never needs to be sharpened.

— Judi Manos, West Islip, NY

❖ I generally mark with a blue/purple water-soluble pencil and wash the quilt after completion to remove markings.

— Franie Shaffer, Coatesville, PA

❖ I mark on the wrong side of the fabric using a pencil or an *old* permanent marker pen — one that the ink comes out of very lightly.

— Muriel D. Austin, Hingham, MA

❖ I love using white tailor's chalk on darker fabrics because it comes off without leaving any marks.

— Barbara Forrester Landis, Lititz, PA

❖ For most marking, I use a #1 or #2 lead pencil, break off the eraser end, and sharpen both ends to eliminate trips to the pencil sharpener. On dark fabrics, I use a Berol prismacolor canary yellow pencil. These are available in artists' supply stores. Again, I sharpen both ends.

— Mary Seielstad, Schenectady, NY

❖ I save soap slivers to use for marking dark fabrics.

— Elaine F. Asper, Stroudsburg, PA

❖ This sounds like a no-no, but it's okay. I trace around plastic templates with a ball-point pen. The ball-point rolls easily and doesn't stretch the fabric, and I cut just *inside* the marks, which removes them.

— Sherri Driver, Englewood, CO

❖ For dark fabrics, I use a Berol white or silver pencil. For light fabrics, I use an Aquarelle black watercolor pencil. These wash off.

— Linda Hampton Schiffer, Columbia, MD

❖ When marking the sewing line on fabric, I like to use a silver, white or yellow marking pencil. When marking a cutting line, I like to use a fine point, permanent marker which shows up well and will be cut away. I normally use black. In the case of dark fabrics, I use the silver, white or yellow pencil since the black does not show up.

— Terry Festa, Clinton, CT

❖ I like a permanent, fine, felt-tip pen for marking the cutting line of pieces. The pen marks without pressure which might pull the fabric out of line, and it makes a fine line so it is easy to cut accurately. Because it is permanent, it does not bleed into the piece when I wash it. Obviously, I cannot mark stitching lines in this way, only the cutting lines.

— Barbara Monay, Annapolis, MD

❖ I prefer using chalk over pencil and find that if I make a dotted line, rather than a solid line, the fabric isn't as likely to move. It also means there is less marking to remove later.

— Alison Schwabe, Englewood, CO

❖ I've had good luck with the blue water-soluble pen. I make dots instead of marking complete lines, and I mark lightly, just enough ink to see. Then it's easy to soak it out completely in clear, cold water.

— Nina Lord, Annapolis, MD

❖ BIC pens are good for marking the wrong sides of fabrics for piecing because they do not bleed or run.

— Marabee J. Seifert, Easley, SC

❖ I've learned never to use an ink pen! Even when I cut exactly on the line, the ink may bleed past the seam allowance, and it never washes out completely!

— Lynne Fritz, Bel Air, MD

❖ I like to mark with double pencils, so that I'm drawing both the sewing line and the cutting line at the same time.

— Peggy Hamilton, Hillsboro, OH

❖ I do not use purple disappearing markers if I need to press the marked areas, because heat makes the marks permanent.

— Janice Muller, Derwood, MD

❖ When marking, I don't hold my pencil straight up, because it will drag on the fabric and the line will not be accurate. I lay the pencil up against the pattern on an angle and mark in one long swoop. If the pencil mark is thick, I cut inside the mark for piecing.

— Dorothy Reise, Severna Park, MD

❖ I use a US General white chalk pencil for marking dark fabric — not using too much pressure — and a 2 1/2 black Ticonderoga pencil for light fabrics. Both remove easily.

— Irma H. Schoen, Windsor, CT

❖ For me the easiest way of marking is with thread, either by using tailor tacks or basting. Tailor tacks are stitches made in the fabric at strategic points, using a contrasting thread so they are easily seen. They are removed when no longer needed for placement guidance. Basting stitches are long stitches that outline an area to be quilted and are removed when quilting is completed.

— Lois C. Ruiz, Murray, KY

Appliqué marking

❖ For appliqué, I work over a light box, tracing my appliqué design onto the background fabric with a pencil. I then place my appliqué pieces over the penciled pattern.

— Dale Renee Ball, Silverdale, WA

❖ I mark appliqué designs on the right side of the fabric, since appliqué is sewn on the right side and piecework on the wrong side. Being able to see my seam lines helps me to maintain accuracy in both hand and machine work.

— Mildred Fauquet, Lincoln, NE

❖   For appliqué, I generally do not mark the design. Instead, I put a copy of the entire design on freezer paper over the background fabric. I slide the piece to be appliquéd between these until it is in the right place and put a pin through all the layers. I then turn the fabric over and pin from the back side, catching just the background fabric and the appliqué piece. I remove the pin attaching the freezer paper and am ready to appliqué.

— Joy Rubenstein-Moir, Holtsville, NY

❖   For appliqué, rather than marking directly on the background fabric, I mark the pattern on tracing paper and lay this over the background piece to position the appliqué pieces.

—Vicki Jones, Rushville, IN

❖   I mark as little as possible. I use a light box and a placement pattern to place the appliqué pieces.

I use 1/4-inch masking tape to mark quilting lines whenever I can. It can be easily peeled off when I've quilted alongside it, and I have no marks to remove.

—Violette Denney, Carrollton, GA

❖   For appliqué, I mark placement lines on the background fabric slightly smaller than the actual templates, so the markings won't show when the appliqué is completed.

— Maryann England, Thogarnond, CA

❖   When I do hand-appliqué, I draw the lines lightly on the right side because I do needle-roll style appliqué.

— Judy Mullen, Manieca, CA

Maintaining accuracy

❖   I usually use a very fine mechanical pencil and a sandpaper board to mark fabrics. I start at one corner of the template and draw halfway toward the middle of the pattern, then I go to the opposite end and again draw toward the middle. This helps to keep the fabric from stretching.

— Debra Botelho Zeida, Waquoit, MA

❖   I use sandpaper self-adhesive dots to keep templates from slipping. I also recently was taught how to notch templates and fabric for matching. For example, templates can be made with notches, showing where they connect to each other. When marking fabrics, transfer the notches to the fabric. Corresponding pieces can then be perfectly aligned by matching notches.

— Pearl Dorn, Fresh Meadows, NY

❖   I keep my pencil sharpened so each piece is marked the same. The

fatter the pencil lead, the further it marks from the template.
— Barbara Ashton, Sharon Hill, PA

❖ I use fine sandpaper under my fabric and also glue sandpaper to the underside of my templates. This keeps the fabric and the templates from slipping. Small pieces of fine sandpaper glued to the underside of rulers will help keep them from slipping.
— Cheryl Ferriter, West Springfield, MA

❖ I like to use Basic Board by Craftistic Products underneath fabric to keep it from shifting when I am marking it. When marking, I extend my lines 1/4 inch beyond each intersection. This forms a very clear point for the corner.
— Doris L. Orthman, Wantage, NJ

❖ My husband made me a marking surface with a piece of fine sandpaper (a whole sheet) glued to an 8-inch x 12-inch piece of hemosate from a hardware store. It helps to keep the fabric from shifting.
— Mary Puskar, Forest Hill, MD

❖ I make dots at the corners of the template before I start to draw, so that they can be reference points in case the fabric moves.
— Marion Lumpkins Reece, Richmond, VA

❖ I like to use double-sided tape to hold the pattern to the fabric when I mark.
— Marlene Parrish, Stevensville, MD

❖ I use a sandpaper board for marking. It is a sheet of Plexiglas with sandpaper glued on with rubber cement. You can make a portable board by using a file folder with two sheets of sandpaper glued to it.
— Fran Lange, Orange Beach, AL

❖ I use dash marks instead of a continuous line when marking cutting lines. I've found fabric does not move if I use this method.
— Alyce C. Kauffman, Gridley, CA

❖ I always use a sandpaper board underneath my fabrics when tracing templates. The sandpaper stabilizes the fabric. I find it an invaluable aid when marking fabrics on the bias — the fabric does not shift and my lines are completely accurate.
— Elaine Untracht Pawelko, Jamesburg, NJ

❖ I keep a box of 20 to 30 sharpened pencils next to me when I'm marking fabric, and I change whenever a point begins to dull. I use a layer of sandpaper underneath the fabric to secure it and rubber cement, dried, on the backs of templates to keep them from shifting.
— Linda M. Pool, Vienna, VA

❖ I always cut on the same side of my marked lines for accuracy and consistency.
— Carol McDowell, Cavan, ON

Making a light table

❖   I use my washing machine with a storm door window over it as a light table.

— Joy Rubenstein-Moir, Holtsville, NY

❖   I have a large piece of Plexiglas which I purchased for $40.00 that I can place on top of my quilt frame. I use it as a shadow box by putting a light underneath it when I don't have a quilt set up.

— Dale Renee Ball, Silverdale, WA

❖   I have an extension table with extra boards. I take the boards out, place a clear glass in their place, and put a light under the table. This creates a light table. The light underneath makes it easy to see through the fabric for tracing markings.

— Ada Miller, Millersburg, OH

Additional tips

❖   In piecework, I figure out how many pieces I need of each fabric and mark everything at once on that fabric. I then move on to the next fabric and cut it all out later while I'm watching TV.

— Carol MacDowell, Cavan, ON

❖   I never mark on a damp day. The marks fade faster.

— Carlene Horne, Bedford, NH

❖   I find it is usually easier to mark on the wrong side of the fabric, but I need to make sure the pattern is flipped if there's a wrong and right side to the pattern design.

— Grace S. Miller, Mt. Joy, PA

❖   I put curves on the bias. There is less problem with raveling on fabric edges.

— Ellie Sienkiewizcz

❖   I always have the straight of the grain on the outside edge of each block because that helps to prevent the fabric's stretching and distorting.

— Mary E. Isle, Deerwood, MN

❖   The more accurately the pieces are cut on the grain, the less the patch will ripple as it is sewn together.

— Jane E. Crowe, Boyertown, PA

❖   When marking fabrics, I keep the point of my pencil as close as possible to the template, gradually rolling it in my hand to keep the point sharp.

As I cut quilt pieces, I sometimes arrange them on sheets of graph or plain paper which I have sprayed with a light coating of spray adhesive that has then dried. This keeps the block pieces arranged neatly. Sometimes I pin them to a square of Pellon interfacing or string each group together on a thread.

— **Ann Reimer, Beatrice, NE**

❖   I mark fabrics in the same light that I will primarily use for stitching. Daylight marks don't always work at night and vice versa.

— **Polly Gilmore, St. Joseph, MI**

❖   Yellow markings on dark fabrics are especially easy to see at night.

— **Susan Campbell, Flint, TX**

❖   I try not to buy "busy backs," especially of dark fabrics. This affects my selection when I can't choose between two fabrics. I will choose the one with the lighter back because I can see markings on it more easily.

— **Marion Lumpkins Reece, Richmond, VA**

❖   If I am marking a directional print, I like a clear, see-through template for accuracy.

— **Judy Steiner Buller, Beatrice, NE**

❖   I place directional arrows in the seam allowance of cut pieces to indicate the straight of grain.

— **Thelma Anderson Swody, Stonington, CT**

5

Cutting fabrics

Using bias and straight of grain

❖ A quick way to check lengthwise grain of fabric is to stretch it. It stretches more across the grain than with the grain.

— Edna Nisly, Partridge, KS

❖ I am very careful when working with fabric cut on the bias. When piecing, I make sure bias edges are not on the outside edge of a block, so they do not stretch the block out of place.

— Betty Boyton, Gordonville, PA

❖ I cut all pieces with the grain of fabric going the same way. If the straight of grain and a bias are mixed, the quilt pieces will not fit together as well.

— Elizabeth Chupp, Arthur, IL

❖ When cutting borders, I try to use lengthwise grain as much as possible, so there is less chance of a ripple or wave on the border edge.

— Sue Seeley, New Bern, NC

❖ I make my blocks for the background of appliqué work with the straight of grain running in the same direction. Even though fabric appears to be one color, it may, in fact, have a nap. Also, a quilt is stronger if the fabric straight of grain runs lengthwise through it.

— Carol Trice, Wayne, PA

❖ If you sew bias pieces onto straight of grain pieces, the stitching will be less apt to stretch and rip.

— Mary Wheatley, Mashpee, MA

❖ When I sew a bias edge to a straight edge, I always make sure the straight edge is on top as I feed the fabrics through the machine.

— Cheri Ruzich, Live Oak, CA

❖ When cutting points (as in leaves or flower buds), I cut the point across the grain. The fabric lies flatter and is easier to sew.

— Vicki Jones, Rushville, IN

❖ I place the longest portion of each piece on the straight edge (grain) of the fabric. For example, you should never have the long side of a triangle on the bias!

— Alice H. Traynor, Mercersburg, PA

❖ When piecing triangles within a given block design, I find it really helps to keep the straight of grain perpendicular to the finished sides of the block. If the overall effect depends on a specific design or direction other than straight of grain, I stitch the biased edges so as to minimize stretching by beginning at the center and stitching out.

— Susan Loweth Melton, Olney, MD

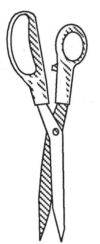

❖ I think the grain of the fabric is less important than the pattern of the fabric I plan to cut.

— Laura S. Hemenway, Fort Washington, MD

❖ One of the most challenging things for me in cutting fabrics is to be alert for one way designs or patterns in the fabric. Keeping designs all going the same direction enhances the finished project considerably.

Sometimes, on first glance, one does not notice a directional design, but by looking more closely, one can sometimes see a pattern.

— Judy Steiner Buller, Beatrice, NE

❖ The sharper my scissors, the better. I prefer to cut my curved appliqué pieces on the bias, as much as possible, to take advantage of the "give" that is present on the bias.

— Carol Kelley, Carrollton, GA

Tips for accuracy in cutting

❖ When cutting with a rotary cutter, I try to cut all pieces of the same size at the same time of day. I find shadows can affect the size of the finished strip.

I also use the same type of ruler throughout the project. That way the width of the lines should always be the same.

— Sue Seeley, New Bern, NC

❖ If I start a project using one ruler, I use it all the way through. I learned (the hard way) that not all rulers measure the same.

— Laurie A. Enos, Rochester, NY

❖ I use spray on glue on the pattern pieces. That holds them in place, but I can still reposition them if necessary.

— Shirley Taylor, Yuba City, CA

❖ I make sure the entire piece of fabric is on the table when I cut out my pieces. If some of it hangs over the edge of the work surface, it pulls the fabric and distorts the cut.

— Rhondalee Schmidt, Scranton, PA

❖ I mark on one layer, then fold or stack the fabrics to cut through three or four (never more than four) layers. I always place a pin through the center of the layers to prevent their shifting.

— Sherri Driver, Englewood, CO

❖ When I want to cut several layers of fabric at the same time, I hold them together with binder clips, used for holding papers together. They are not as long as clothespins, so they interfere less.

— Lois Mae E. Kuh, Penfield, NY

❖ When cutting more than one layer at a time, I like to iron the layers together first. That helps keep them together more securely.

— Shan D. Lean, Middleton, MA

How to use fabric efficiently

❖ I cut the biggest pieces first, using the rotary cutter whenever possible. The leftover scraps from the bigger pieces (borders and sashing) can be used for the smaller pieces.

— Pearl Mok, Los Angeles, CA

❖ I mark and cut from one half of the fabric (22 inches in length) first. Then I mark and cut, beginning at the top of the remaining 22-inch length piece. This tends to leave me with a more usable piece of fabric as a leftover.

— Mary Seielstad, Schenectady, NY

Additional tips

❖ For single triangles, whenever possible, I first cut them out in strips, then in squares, then as either two or four triangles, rather than cutting completely around each template one by one.

— Julie McKenzie, Punxsutawney, PA

❖ I set aside a whole day to cut out my quilt, do the marking, and then package and label all the pieces. That way I don't have to get out the fabric and clean off my dining room table more than once. It takes a lot of time, but it is well worth it in the long run.

— Thelma A. Stein, Tavares, FL

❖ I stack my fabrics right sides together whenever possible for cutting, which means I have to handle the pieces less when I'm ready to stitch them.

— Lorraine Moore Lear, Del City, OK

❖ When cutting fabrics for triangles, I stack several fabrics right sides together and in alternating colors, so that two triangles are cut in position to be sewn together. When I'm ready to sew them, I use a darning needle to pick up the triangles, allowing the two colors to stay together. They adhere to each other and are perfectly lined up for sewing.

— Katie Esh, Ronks, PA

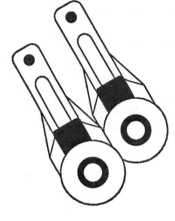

❖ For hand and machine piecing, I use a 1/4-inch seam allowance. For appliqué, I use only a 1/8-inch seam allowance.

— Eleanor Larson, Glen Lyon, PA

❖ I cut 1/4-inch seam allowances for appliqué and trim them to l/8 inch as I stitch.

— Jean A. Schoettmer, Greensburg, IN

❖ Especially for appliqué, I find a 1/4-inch seam allowance is too wide and makes unnecessary bulk. I prefer to use about a 1/8-inch seam allowance, and then space my stitches a little closer together.

— Laurie L. Rott, Fargo, ND

❖ I always make stems for flowers with bias binding.

— Franie Shafer, Coatesville, PA

❖ I keep two rotary cutters on hand — one for fabrics and the other for template plastic, paper and even cardboard.

— Judi Manos, West Islip, NY

❖ I find it is important to have sharp scissors and to make long, sure cuts using the entire scissors blades, rather than short "bites" with just the inner portion of the scissors blades.

— Johnette Zwolinski Shoberg, Globe, AZ

❖ I never use good scissors to cut batting because it dulls the blades, and I hide my good scissors from the rest of my family! I keep the rotary cutter away from children and stock lots of Band Aids!

— Lela Ann Schneider, Boise, ID

❖ I think appliqué scissors (with a wide bill on one side) are very helpful to avoid a wrong cut.

— Nina Lord, Annapolis, MD

❖ If you suffer from arthritis, try a pair of Gingher's Lightweight scissors. Although these scissors cannot be resharpened and must be replaced periodically, they make cutting easy and pleasurable.

— Elaine Untracht Pawelko, Jamesburg, NJ

❖ I think rotary cutting of straight of grain and bias strips is the way to go. Not being good in math, I have found it helpful to remember four numbers needed to cut out triangles with a rotary cutter. I pasted them on the wall in my work area so I can refer to them as I need to. They are 1.414 and .707 to figure the long or short side of triangles — and 7/8 inch or 1 1/4 inch, needed to calculate the amount of seam allowance needed. I would be lost in figuring measurements for quilts and rotary cutting their pieces without these formulas.

— **Rosie Mutter, Bechtelsville, PA**

❖ A kitchen base cabinet with a Formica top makes a great cutting table and gives me storage capability.

— **Mary Puskar, Forest Hill, MD**

❖ If fabric is not very tightly woven, I spray it with starch and iron it dry before cutting or marking it.

— **Loyce Wood Sage, Gallup, NM**

Figuring Measurements for Rotary Cut Triangles from Squares

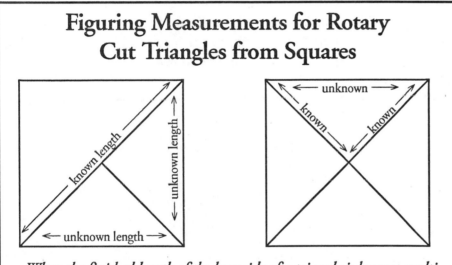

When the finished length of the long side of a triangle is known, multiply that number by .707 to give the measurement of the short sides of the triangle.

Add 7/8-inch seam allowance on two sides of the square to get the proper size triangle when the square is cut in half diagonally.

When the finished length of the short side of the triangle is known, multiply that number by 1.414 to give the measurement of the long sides of the triangle.

Add 1 1/4-inch seam allowance on two sides of the square to get the proper size triangle when the square is cut in quarters diagonally.

❖ If a fabric for piecing or appliqué is too soft to handle, I spray it lightly with sizing (spray starch) on its reverse side and iron it. That

makes it much easier to cut accurately. The stiffness works out as I quilt. I like Clover shears with a serrated blade for cutting appliqué pieces.
— **Pat Brousil, Columbia, MD**

❖   Cutting several wall hangings at a time saves lots of time. I make up a chart for each one, stating how much of which fabrics I need. As I cut each color, I mark it off on the chart. Each "kit" goes into a small box, along with the chart, so I don't forget how I've planned to make it!
— **Judith Eve Nisly, Partridge, KS**

❖   I snip any grades, curves or corners to within a thread or two of my pencil line.
— **Leesa Seaman Lesenski, Whately, MA**

❖   Before cutting all the fabric up into little pieces, I cut only enough for one block to make sure the templates are accurate.
— **Linda Sterling, Belchertown, MA**

❖   I organize fabric by color, separating prints from solids. I save all strips and separate them into labeled boxes (1 inch, 1 1/2 inches, 2 inches, 2 1/2 inches, 3 inches, 3 1/2 inches). When I need a strip of any of these sizes, I just pull down the appropriate box and go from there. I can also use these strips to cut whatever size squares I need.
— **Susan Campbell, Flint, TX**

6

Tips for doing piecework

Efficiency at the sewing machine

❖ I do continuous-line sewing between pieces. For example, if I have a lot of equal squares to be pieced, I don't cut each apart as I sew, but let the machine sew on air between patches, then cut them apart afterwards.

— Betty Boyton, Gordonville, PA

❖ If I'm in a car or a place where I can't sew, I pin the pieces that go together along the seam lines, and when I'm in a position to sew, I do it then — it's much faster!

— Maryalice DeLong

❖ I chain-sew small units of a block together, and then chain-sew the larger units of the block from left to right. I then butt horizontal seams together.

— Lois Mae E. Kuh, Penfield, NY

❖ I employ a "thread bunny" to keep my machine from eating the pieces! A "thread bunny" is a small scrap of fabric which you put under the presser foot as you begin to sew. When you start a set of patches on the "thread bunny," you can feed them under the presser foot with less chance of their being chewed by the needle or having the machine stall. Using a "thread bunny" to begin and end sewing also eliminates long threads on the sections being pieced. Because the sections are chain-pieced closely together, the tails of long thread stay on the "thread bunny" at the beginning and the end of each section.

— Lynne Fritz, Bel Air, MD

❖ In making Log Cabin patches, I cut long strips the width of the logs. I trim strips to the appropriate length as I finish sewing each section.

— Mary Jane Musser, Manheim, PA

❖ I sew like pieces together, one after another, as long as I can stand it! Repetition makes the task go faster. When I get tired, I change to a series of other like pieces, eventually going back to those I left.

— Lauren Eberhard, Seneca, IL

❖ I feed pieces through one after another for speed piecing. If I am going to sew two identical shapes together (for example, two triangles), I place the two fabrics right side together when I cut them out. Then, when I'm ready to piece, I pick up the pairs and they are perfectly aligned.

— Gail L. Kozicki, Glen Mills, PA

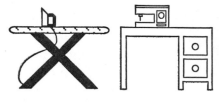

❖ I use my thumbnail to finger-press seams when I'm sewing and wait to run to the ironing board until I've completed the patch.

— Marilyn Umble, Atglen, PA

❖ I press a lot, so I lower the ironing board to the same height as my sewing machine and move it as close as possible.

— Harriet S. Meade, Clinton, CT

❖ I prepare extra bobbins in advance for quick changing as I need them.

— Sandy Buckman, Webster, NY

Efficiency in hand-sewing

❖ Thread snips, tiny spring-action snippers, save time over scissors when I hand-piece.

— Fran Lange, Orange Beach, AL

❖ I pin all pieces of a block to wax paper and keep it flat in a zip-lock baggie. This is great for traveling — all pieces are ready to sew. When I pin pieces together, I use a threaded needle in place of a pin where I should begin sewing. I use silk pins on the rest of the piece.

— Carolyn K. Inglis, Hudson, NH

❖ I pin pieces to a pillow on my lap for hand-piecing.

— Doris McCloskey, Annapolis, MD

❖ When hand-piecing, I keep several needles threaded with a neutral shade of thread — it saves time!

— Rosemarie Fitzgerald, Delaware, OH

❖ I machine-piece only large pieces. I mark each one and pin it carefully. I hand-piece small parts for greater accuracy.

— Laurie L. Rott, Fargo, ND

Precision in piecework

❖ I use a "Little Foot" on my sewing machine. It makes a perfect 1/4-inch seam.

— Betty Hutchinson, St. Charles, MO

❖ When I sew bias and straight of grain pieces together on the sewing machine, I try always to put the piece with the straight of grain on the bottom, so that it stabilizes the bias piece.

— Carol MacDowell, Cavan, ON

❖ When I sew two pieces of fabric together and one is cut on the bias, I always put the bias (stretchy) piece down against the machine so that the feed dog will help to ease in the fullness.

— Marilyn Umble, Atglen, PA

❖ If my blocks turn out to be a little larger than I need, I trim equal amounts from each side to square it up. This keeps the design more precise. If the full amount is trimmed from one side, the design is cock-eyed.

— Jennifer Strand, Sacramento, CA

❖ When I make templates, I drill a hole where the sewing lines intersect. Then I mark this dot on the wrong side of my cut pieces. When I match my fabric pieces together, I put a pin right through the dot on both pieces. Then when I sew the pieces together, I make sure to sew through that dot. With this method, all the corners match up perfectly.

— Jennifer Strand, Sacramento, CA

❖ I make templates with seam allowances from frosted mylar. I take a 1/8-inch hole punch and mark the corners of each square and the tips of each triangle. When I trace the template onto fabric, I mark dots at each hole punch. When I join the blocks, I match the dots to assure accuracy.

— Susan Ketcherside, St. Charles, MO

❖ I draw templates onto plastic, marking the stitching line and adding a 1/4-inch seam allowance. I cut the template on the seam allowance line. At the corner of each stitching line, I punch a hole using a 1/8-inch paper punch. When tracing the template onto fabric, I mark a dot at each hole. I can then connect dots using a ruler, and I have my sewing line.

— Alice H. Traynor, Mercersburg, PA

❖ I find that working in daylight is better than night light.

I pin all adjoining seam points on both sides of the seam intersections before sewing them together.

— Jacqueline E. Deininger, Bethlehem, PA

❖ When I piece, I do not press open seam allowances; instead, when I sew two pieces together with seam allowances, I turn the seam allowance of one piece to the right and the seam allowance of the other piece to the

50 ·

Tips for doing piecework

left. The center point matches more easily.

— Audrey H. Eby, Lancaster, PA

❖ I turn seam allowances in opposite directions. I always have the seam allowance on top turned toward me as I sew. It is less inclined to slip because it is supported in place by the opposite seam allowance.

— Katie Esh, Ronks, PA

❖ I've found that in machine-piecing, it is safe to press the seams open, rather than to the side. This improves accuracy in piecing.

— Lynn Parker, Taylors, SC

❖ I press seams in opposite directions to match up seams exactly. When matching seams, I sew 1/2 inch across the matched area, check to make sure I am being exact, then sew the entire seam. This saves a lot of ripping out.

— Susan M. Miller, Centreville, MD

❖ I iron a seam as it was sewn before pressing it to one side. This relaxes the seam and helps it to press flatter.

— Hilda G. Pruett, Macon, GA

❖ Silk pins help keep seams exactly where I want them.

— Suellen Fletcher, Noblesville, IN

❖ When pinning piecework, I insert pins at both ends of a seam first, then in the center, and finally add them wherever else they are needed.

— Ann Foss, Brooklyn, NY

❖ When piecing stars or fans, I stitch inside my stitching line a tad to make the points meet. Once the star is pieced, I take a thread and go from dot to dot at the center of the star, the whole way around. (I mark these dots at the intersections of seam lines when I mark the fabric for cutting.) I pull the thread tight and tie it off. I have a perfect center every time.

— Faye Meyers, San Jose, CA

❖ I do all machine-piecing on the same machine so the seam allowances will be consistent.

— Marjorie Mills, Bethesda, MD

❖ When I draw stitching lines, I always draw my corners first. If they are exact, it really helps.

— Joy Rubenstein-Moir, Holtsville, NY

❖ "Butting" at the intersections of vertical and horizontal seams helps immeasurably. I sew the horizontal seams first and press one seam up, the other one down. Before sewing the vertical seam, I slide the two pieces together until they lock into place. Corners match better than with pinning.

— Ada L. Bishop, Beatrice, NE

❖ When I am matching seams while sewing, I pin down the allowance that is folded toward the needle to prevent the presser foot from pleating the allowance in the wrong direction.

— Linda Hampton Schiffer, Columbia, MD

❖ I have a Pfaff machine with a built-in walking foot that makes things easier without trying.

— Monika Jones, Grants Pass, OR

❖ I like templates with "snubbed off" corners so I can match pieces precisely.

— Judith Lavine Smith, Washington, D.C.

❖ I sew using a scant 1/4-inch seam allowance to allow for the fold when I press the seams to one side.

— Terry Festa, Clinton, CT

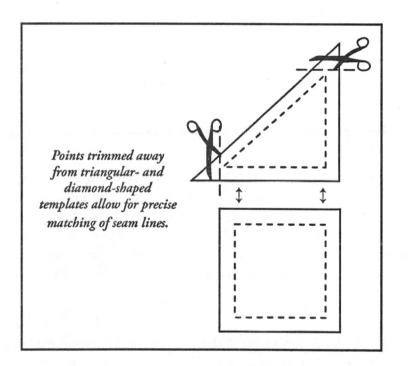

Points trimmed away from triangular- and diamond-shaped templates allow for precise matching of seam lines.

❖ I use the same ruler to measure, draw and cut, from the start of the project to the end! An inch on one brand of ruler is not necessarily the same as an inch on another brand.

— Terry Festa, Clinton, CT

❖ I pin with silk pins, taking small bites with the pins. I regularly check my alignment by pushing a pin through a seam marking at a 90-degree angle to see that it comes out at the corresponding mark on the piece on the other side.

— Barbara Monay, Annapolis, MD

❖ I like the PBS slogan for woodworking — "measure twice, cut once." I use good equipment, in good condition, and work carefully.

— Joyce Trueblood, Cromwell, CT

❖ I make a sample block for a pieced project and then measure each finished block against the sample for an exact match.

— Kelly Wagoner, Albuquerque, NM

❖ I check the sections with my mini-square ruler as I piece a block and square them as I go along to make sure the block will be accurate when it is finished.

— Phyllis A. Kroggel, Tucson, AZ

❖ When I get ready to machine-piece, I take a piece of 1/4-inch graph plastic and check that the needle of my machine is set to an exact 1/4-inch measurement. If it isn't, I move it.

— Ann Stutts, Grants Pass, OR

❖ I like Simplicity's "pleating pins" (size 12, 3/4 inch 275 count) for pinning sections of a quilt together. They are also quite helpful for attaining smoothly rounded curved patch sections.

I pin curved patch pieces over an old darning egg or light bulb when I pin the convex and concave edges together. After pinning the edges and center, I further subdivide the seam with pins, as needed, for the size of the patch. This works well for both hand and machine construction.

— Ann Reimer, Beatrice, NE

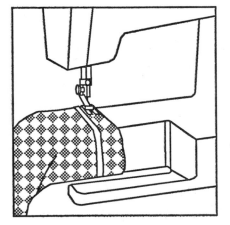

❖ I make sure my seams are 1/4 inch by first marking a line on a 3 inch x 5 inch card, 1/4 inch from one edge. I lay the card under the presser foot with the card edge horizontal to the edge of the presser foot and then lower the needle until it touches the line. I place a piece of masking tape along the edge of the card on the machine. When sewing, I run the fabric along the edge of the masking tape for a perfect 1/4 inch seam allowance.

— Marabee J. Seifert, Easley, SC

❖ I place a rubber band around the free arm of my sewing machine. When I place it 1/4 inch from the needle, it makes a ridge that holds the fabric away from the needle, thus allowing for an accurate 1/4-inch seam allowance.

— Roberta P. Nelson, La Conner, WA

❖ In a class with Blanche Young, I learned of her "Dr. Scholl Shoe Pad Sewing Guides." I take a 3 inch x 7 inch shoe pad and cut it into 1/4 inch x 1 inch pieces. Placing a ruler with a 1/4-inch line under the needle, I place one of the 1/4 inch x 1 inch pieces along the straight edge of the ruler. I now have a 1/4-inch seam guide to sew perfect 1/4-inch seam allowances.

— Kathy Evenson, Fergus Falls, MN

❖ I let my index fingernail grow out and "finger pin" the seams at the sewing machine. I press seam allowances only with a dry iron towards the darkest fabric.

— Diana M. Garrison, Silver Spring, MD

❖ When drawing my pattern on fabric, I extend my lines at intersections to help the piecing be precise.

— Cathy Krautkremer, East Stroudsburg, PA

❖ Maintaining an overall lengthwise grain line on the quilt top results in the pieces fitting better, puts less strain on the fabric, and allows the quilt to hang more evenly.

— Ann Reimer, Beatrice, NE

❖ I'm a hand-piecer, so my templates are cut without seam allowances. I trace around plastic templates on the wrong side of the fabric. This mark becomes my seam line. Then, setting aside the template, I use a Quilter's Rule (6 inches), which has a 1/4-inch lengthwise seam guider, and cut with a miniature cutting wheel.

— Carol Trice, Wayne, PA

❖ For a fan — or other pattern with very critical angles — I carefully trace the pieces without seam allowances onto freezer paper. I cut the paper pieces out and iron them to the wrong side of the fabric, then cut out the fabric, leaving 1/4 inch around all the sides for seam allowances. The paper edges thus serve as a sewing line to keep the angles true and to prevent bias edges from stretching. When I've finished stitching, I peel the freezer paper off and press the blocks.

— Barbara Monay, Annapolis, MD

❖ I've found a method that works for piecework squares that use only straight lines. Iron block-size pieces of freezer paper together on a low iron setting without steam. You will need as many block-sized pieces of freezer paper as there are blocks in the quilt. (I've used up to six layers at one time.) Experiment with the iron first, since, if you are not careful, the paper will stick together and not come apart.

Always put the plastic side down and slide the iron quickly along the paper. Only the barest touch evenly across the surface is necessary, but iron all the way to the edges so the paper will lie reasonably flat. Using a cutting board, plastic ruler and sharp pencil mark out the quilt block on the top sheet only. Label all pieces of freezer paper alphabetically, according to the order in which they will be sewn together. Also, mark each piece of paper with its corresponding color, fabric selection, and design.

Cut the square precisely, using a rotary blade and being sure to cut through all layers without shifting the ruler or paper. After the pieces are all cut, separate each individual stack of templates and mark each pile so that all templates in each group can be placed onto the appropriate piece of fabric.

At the ironing board, iron the fabric free of wrinkles, then reset the iron to a medium setting without steam. Make sure when you iron the templates onto the fabric that the grain of fabric is lying correctly. Iron templates at least 1/2 inch apart to be sure each piece will have a 1/4-inch seam allowance. To cut pieces apart, use a clear plastic ruler and cut 1/4 inch outside the edge of the freezer paper

To sew, leave the freezer paper on the fabric, using it as a guideline. Check alignment by sticking a pin straight through the two pieces of fabric. The pin should enter one side and exit the other precisely on the seam line and at the corners of seams. You can also hold the patch up to light and visually align the pieces. Remove freezer paper after the square is completed. Press and check the block again for accuracy.

I find that with this technique the fabric does not stretch on the bias as much. I still need to iron and measure at each step of the construction process, but I find my accuracy is much improved with less ripping and resewing.

— **Sharon L. Leali, Jackson, OH**

Organization tips

❖   I always carry a zip-lock plastic bag with needles, thread, scissors and quilt pieces pinned onto paper towels — one square per towel. I stack them in the bag.

— **Sharon Honegger, Hawthorne, NY**

❖   I keep a tin or small box with everything I need in it — thread, needles, scissors, thimble and pieces cut and ready to sew. I can readily pick it up as I go out the door, so I can piece in the car, at auctions, while waiting for my daughter, etc.

— **Judi Robb, Manhattan, KS**

❖   I sometimes work in "shifts," first cutting all my templates, then cutting the fabric pieces, and finally putting each block in a marked baggie. This makes it easy to take projects with me.

— **Debra Botelho Zeido, Waquoit, MA**

❖   I use knitters' stitch-holder pins to carry thread that has been wound onto bobbins to save space when traveling.

— **Laura Reif Lipski, Lindenhurst, NY**

❖   I pin my cut pieces to paper in the pattern design so I don't sew wrong seams together.

— **Carol A. Medsker, Englewood, CO**

❖   I like to lay out all the pieces in their proper order on a flannel fabric and remove them as needed. I start with a puzzle laid together and work to a finished piece. The visualization helps me.

— **Carol Kelley, Carrollton, GA**

❖   I work on two or three quilts at one time. I cut and sew during the daytime. I put partially completed blocks into dishpans (one for each quilt) and lay them aside. After supper I pin everything together while I watch TV. The next day I'm ready to sew the next step.

— Mary Lou Mahar, Williamsfield, IL

❖ I use cookie sheets or 8-inch x 11-inch cardboard (backs from paper pads) with a piece of felt attached to place individual blocks in their proper arrangement for piecing. I also put a clip-board across my drawer to the left of the sewing machine and on it place the pieces I want to pick up to sew in sequence. On my right, I put a basket into which I place the finished pieces.

— Laura Reif Lipski, Lindenhurst, NY

❖ I chain-sew whenever possible. I stack and number piles with self-sticking labels. I also use this method to identify various pieces (A, B, C, etc.).

— Rosie Mutter, Bechtelsville, PA

❖ I place individual blocks on my design board and stitch them in sections, replacing each one as it's finished. This is an easy way to avoid assembly mistakes. I machine-piece and use the assembly-line method when the blocks are all alike.

— Phyllis A. Kroggel, Tucson, AZ

❖ On small pieces, I mark in the seam allowances the letter or number of the corresponding piece so I can easily tell which piece is sewn to which piece. On "nearly" equal sides of triangles I mark the seam allowances for the outer edge. Coding in the seam allowances can make piecing easier.

— Mary Seielstad, Schenectady, NY

❖ I arrange all pieces in the order in which I will sew them before I begin to piece.

— Helen L. Anderson, Titusville, NJ

❖ I like a sewing room arranged so that the iron is one step away — or better yet, so I can stay in my chair while pressing pieces.

— Sherri Driver, Englewood, CO

❖ I glue sandpaper to a heavy cardboard piece that fits in my lap. I lay pieces of my quilt block out on the sandpaper, and they stay put until I get them all sewn together.

— Joyce A. Walker, Ft. Smith, AR

❖ When I'm working with a repetitive pattern like Trip Around the World, I number the fabrics, make a diagram on graph paper, and sew them together by my diagram.

— Grace S. Miller, Mt. Joy, PA

Additional tips

❖ If I have trouble doing a project, I put it away for a while, then get it out and restart. I am not as mad at it when I do it this way!

— Roberta S. Bennsky, Annapolis, MD

❖ I keep thread in the freezer (in plastic bags). It will last for years without developing dry rot.

— Betty Boyton, Gordonville, PA

❖ I file a few fabric pieces for repair for each quilt I make. If I give a quilt as a gift, I save little pieces of fabric that can be used for repair if necessary, and give them along with the quilt.

— Arline M. Rubin, New York, NY

❖ I use ponytail rubber bands around spools of thread and bobbins to prevent the thread from unwinding.

— Laura Reif Lipski, Lindenhurst, NY

❖ I sew pieces together of the exact widths I want and strip-cut them.

— Jacqueline E. Deininger, Bethlehem, PA

❖ I find that good pressing is the best shortcut to accurate piecework.

— Dorothy Reise, Severna Park, MD

❖ When I don't feel like working on a major project, I take my small scraps and fit triangle and square templates on them, cut them out and put various sizes in plastic bags. When a pattern comes along that I want to start, I adapt it to fit my triangles and squares, and I'm ready to roll.

— Muriel D. Austin, Hingham, MA

❖ If a large piece is made out of smaller ones, I strip-piece the components of the piece first, iron the seams, and then lay the larger template on the top of my "new" fabric. I draw markings on the large template to show the placement of the component fabrics so that each large piece is exactly like all the others.

I save scraps from strip piecing, cut them into various shapes, and keep them for scrap quilts.

— Doris Miotto, Thorold, ON

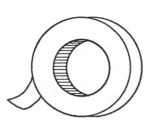

❖ When I put a border on larger quilts, I begin pinning and sewing from the middle of the quilt and move down to the end, then return to the middle and pin and sew in the opposite direction. That prevents the ripples that can come from sewing the border from one end to the other.

— Roberta S. Bennsky, Annapolis, MD

❖ I use quilting thread to hand-piece my blocks. It's stronger, so I think it holds my blocks together better.

— Theresa Lepert, Schellsburg, PA

❖ I always keep a roll of 1/4-inch masking tape on my extra sewing machine spindle and tear a short strip whenever I want to start or stop exactly 1/4 inch from the end. It helps a lot when the edge adjoining is not square. And a piece can be re-used several times.

— Carol Findling, Beatrice, NE

❖ I turn my ironing board "backwards," so the iron rests on the narrow pointed end, and use the wide end to press blocks.

— Jean H. Robinson, Cinnaminson, NJ

❖ I don't over-iron; I feel it ruins the fabrics.

— Carlene Horne, Bedford, NH

❖ I press seams toward the darker fabric whenever possible. If this is impossible, I "grade" the darker side of the seam by trimming it narrower than the light fabric to prevent shadowing through a lighter fabric.

— Ann Reimer, Beatrice, NE

❖ Even though my work may be very precise, sometimes when I have many colors in a quilt and I can only match one of them with the thread color, a stitch here and there shows through on the right side. I sometimes use a permanent, fine point magic marker that matches the fabric color and dab the thread gently. It disappears magically!

— Terry Festa, Clinton, CT

❖ When joining light and dark fabrics, I use thread to match the darker piece being joined. The thread is almost invisible, the desired result. This applies to both hand and machine methods.

I like to have a pressing board within easy reach so that I can press each seam as I sew. Though there are many pressing boards available, you can make one with supplies you likely have on hand. Start with a 15- to 16-inch square of wood, 1/2 to 3/4 inch thick. Cover it with an old Teflon coated ironing board cover and pad. If you don't have a pad, a piece of Thermolam (needle punched fleece which has been specially formulated to tolerate heat) works well. Cover the board with the padding, clipping the corners to eliminate bulk, and tack the edges to the back of the board.

Carefully stretch a section of the old ironing board cover over the padding until it is taut, mitering the corners as one does in making a bed, and tacking the edges to the back. Cover the tacks with tape or self-adhesive felt, or glue on a leftover piece of Thermolam to protect the top of the sewing machine cabinet from scratches.

Next, use a fine-line laundry marking pen to mark expanding squares on the pressing board. After determining the center of the square, mark the squares in 1/2-inch graduations, 2 1/2 inches through 14 1/2 inches. Use a triangle and a quilting ruler with 1/2-inch markings to assure complete accuracy. Note the size of each square at the center of each bottom, horizontal line. These markings will indicate at a glance if quilt pieces are accurate in size, as they are pressed on their respective sized square!

A small travel iron with a sharply pointed tip is handy to use with the pressing board. Both items are quite portable and can easily be slipped into a quilter's bag for travel.

— Ann Reimer, Beatrice, NE

Tips for doing appliqué

Preparing

I baste seam allowances under on appliqué pieces. It makes the whole process easier, and I can sew faster.

— Helen L. Anderson, Titusville, NJ

When I do appliqué, I make a freezer paper pattern, then iron that to the back of the fabric. I cut the design, adding 1/4-inch seam allowances. I then use a fabric glue stick and glue the 1/4-inch allowance onto the freezer paper and allow it to dry. The template is then ready to be appliquéd.

— Barb Grauer, Owings Mills, MD

I do not mark the appliqué pattern onto the background fabric (I dislike having to deal with the problem of removing any marks that show when I'm done), but lay the square over the pattern to see where to place the next piece or put the pattern on by eye. I find that eyeballing placement is accurate enough.

— Linda Schiffer Hampton, Columbia, MD

In appliqué I always spray all pieces with spray-starch and then press them to stabilize the fabric. I baste under seam allowances and press, so all curves are smooth.

— Carol MacDowell, Cavan, ON

I cut fabric with a 1/4-inch seam allowance. I then cut a cardboard template the size of the finished appliqué. Next I cut a piece of aluminum foil a bit larger than the fabric. I place these three layers — foil first, then

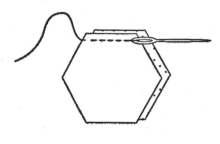

fabric (right side down), then the cardboard template—on the ironing board. I fold the foil and the fabric firmly around the edges of the cardboard and press with a hot iron on both sides. I allow the foil to cool completely before removing it and the cardboard. And I have fabric with its edges pressed under, all ready for appliqué.

I find file folder cardboard works better than heavier cardboard and that I can press several layers of fabric at once.

— Edna Nisly, Partridge, KS

I cut doubles of each appliqué piece, sew them together (right sides together), slit open the back, turn right side out, and press. Then I topstitch it by machine, right next to the edge. The piece is now ready to be appliquéd.

— Kay Hineman, Rushville, IN

I cut Templar heat resistant plastic to the actual size of the template and fabric piece, then press seam allowances around the edges of the Templar before sewing. This gives me a more accurate idea about how to place each piece, since the seam allowances are already turned under.

— Judi Manos, West Islip, NY

I prefer sketching-in where I want pieces to be, rather than drawing their absolute placement. As long as I get the leaves under vines, for example, the piece has a more personal touch than if I place it precisely like the pattern.

— Jorita J. Groves, Bushland, TX

I like to use Wonder-Under with appliqué designs. The double adhesive on Wonder-Under allows me to machine-appliqué without pinning.

— Janice Muller, Derwood, MD

I finger press seam allowances under, and then trim them to a scant 1/8 inch. That makes them much easier to sew.

— Elaine C. Langley, Greenville, SC

When I work with blocks of appliqué, I finger press the background block into fourths to help me place the appliqué pieces accurately and uniformly.

I always cut out all of my freezer paper pieces at one time and then iron them onto the selected fabric. As I cut out the pieces, I place them on the background fabric to see if the colors look good together. If I don't like it, I change the fabric until it suits me. This way I can see what the finished square will look like before I start to appliqué.

— Virginia L. Fry, Fulton, MD

I use Do-Sew. It is like Stitch Witchery without the adhesive. Lay the Do-Sew over the fabric (which is right side up). Trace the outline of the design onto the Do-Sew. Sew on the traced line. Trim and clip around the edges of the sewn line. Cut a slit in the Do-Sew. Turn the shape inside out. The edges are finished and ready to be appliquéd.

— Jennifer Strand, Sacramento, CA

To prepare pieces for appliqué, I place the cut-out piece of fabric right side down onto an old dryer sheet, old fabric or Fusible Web. I sew around the edge of the appliqué piece. I cut a slit in the backing so I can turn the appliqué piece right side out. Then I smooth and press it. Next, I place it wrong side down on the background material, pin it in place, and sew it on invisibly, catching the edge of the appliqué. Fusible Web eliminates pinning and works well for scallops and curves.

— Lela Ann Schneider, Boise, ID

I like to use freezer paper to make the templates, and then press the paper onto the back of the fabric. That allows me to cut 1/8- to 1/4-inch seam allowance, then press it over the paper, thus creating a good sharp edge to sew along.

— Lois C. Ruiz, Murray, KY

I put a gathering stitch in the seam allowances of simple appliqué pieces. Leaving the cardboard template in, I gather in the seam allowance and press. Then I remove the cardboard and appliqué.

— Leesa Seaman Lesenski, Whately, MA

Work in process

I always use a machine embroidery weight thread when doing machine-appliqué. Polyester thread causes puckering.

— Vicki Jones, Rushville, IN

For doing inverted parts, like on a heart, I sew down to within about 1/4 inch of the inverted area, stop and fold back the other side. I then continue to the inverted point. When that is sewn, I pull the folded part back out and continue on.

— Susan Campbell, Flint, TX

When pinning, I use Sequin Pins. They are only 1/2 inch long and give me more accuracy. I use them mostly for appliqué, but find them helpful also for doing miniatures.

— Irma H. Schoen, Windsor, CT

I don't baste, but use the small l/2-inch craft straight pins to hold appliqués in place.

— Virginia C. White, Gallup, NM

After cutting out the appliqué pieces, I prepare them by sewing two identical shapes together (right sides together), slitting open the back, and turning them right side out. I baste the edge of the piece, with the underneath layer pushed back just a hair. Then I baste the piece to the background and appliqué with the ladder stitch.

— Sara Harter Fredette, Williamsburg, MA

After my appliqué is finished, I cut away the background fabric and any additional layers from behind it. This makes quilting a lot easier since there are not so many layers to quilt through.

— Beulah Little, Hamden, OH

A very small seam allowance — a scant 1/8 inch for appliqué — means a minimum of clipping so the corners and points are nice and smooth.

— Ruth Cottrell, Irving, TX

I use my needle to turn under the seam allowance just ahead of where I am stitching, so pressing or basting is not necessary.

— Nina Lord, Annapolis, MD

I use thread to match the color of the piece being applied. It is important to pull the thread taut, though not too tight to create distortion.

— Connie Downey, Muncie, IN

I use a fabric glue stick instead of pinning and basting to hold design pieces to the foundation fabric in stained glass appliqué.

This also works well for black bias strips. I can get a nice smooth curve, it stays put while I appliqué, and it doesn't gum up the needle either.

— Connie Downey, Muncie, IN

I use a toothpick for turning seam allowances under as I sew.

— Vanya G. Neer, Bradenton, FL

I staple pieces to the background fabric to make the work easier to carry around with me. This way I don't have to worry about pins falling out or catching my thread.

— Gail L. Kozicki, Glen Mills, PA

I use "cutwork appliqué" wherever possible. I mark the template on a square or chunk of fabric and attach it on the background fabric with short pins. Then I cut around the shape, leaving a 3/16-inch seam allowance, and needle-turn it under, just a couple of inches at a time as I stitch it to the background.

— Mary Wheatley, Mashpee, MA

Appliqué is so much easier when I use Sequin Pins to turn the fabric under a little ahead of my sewing. They are shorter and my thread doesn't get caught while I stitch.

— Suellen Fletcher, Noblesville, IN

I use a blind stitch and invisible nylon thread to appliqué on the machine.

— Myrna L. Rambis, Anderson, IN

I've found that a very short blind stitch with invisible thread can be used to appliqué by machine. This gives the appearance of having been done by hand after it is quilted.

— Edna Nisly, Partridge, KS

I don't mark the background fabric. Instead, I keep my colored pattern lying on the light box, where I can refer to it constantly, and pin several pieces onto the background at a time. This eliminates the need to remove markings from the background when I'm finished.

— Teresa Ernest Steinstraw, Denton, TX

I cut templates from freezer paper and iron them to the right side of my fabric. I cut outside the paper, using the edge of the paper as a seam line. This eliminates the need to mark my fabric. I have a light table my father made for me, so I don't mark the background fabric either. I pin the pieces in place on the light table using small safety pins.

— Joyce Trueblood, Cromwell, CT

I have sometimes used iron-on fusible material to make the appliqué adhere to the background block. Then I machine-appliqué it. This is a quick shortcut for children's quilts.

— Judy Williams, Stevensville, MD

I like to pin appliqué from the back. Then I have no tangles in the thread!

— Shan D. Lear, Middleton, MA

Organization

When doing hand-appliqué, I package the necessary pieces in zip-lock bags for each block so I can take them with me and work when I wait.

— Eleanor Larson, Glen Lyon, PA

I cut all appliqué pieces out at the same time and place them in position on a paper pattern. I have no hunting, then, for which piece goes where. If several pieces are nearly alike in shape, I number the pattern where the pieces belong and number the corresponding fabric pieces in their 1/4-inch seam allowances.

— Marabee J. Seifert, Easley, SC

If I'm doing a layer appliqué, such as a flower or Sunbonnet Sue, I stack the pieces in reverse order (last piece first), then run a knotted thread through all the pieces. It is easy to pick up and take with me, and I don't have to look everywhere for a leaf or hand that has dropped.

— Sissy Anderson, Lithonia, GA

Additional tips

I find that using a magnified light helps me in creating precise appliqué.

— Kay Hineman, Rushville, IN

I make bias strips for appliqué stems, i.e., I cut 5/8- to 3/4-inch strips, fold them into thirds, and baste down the center

— Suzanne Dwyer Chambers, Silver Spring, MD

When using bias tape for stems, open the bias tape on one edge and stitch one side of the stem to the background fabric by machine. Refold the bias tape over the machine stitching and hand-appliqué the remaining edge.

— The Old Country Store, Intercourse, PA

I use a lap board for appliqué. A piece of ceiling tile cut to about 11 inches x 14 inches covered with flannel works well

— Jean A. Schoettmer, Greensburg, IN

I use a quilling needle to remove the paper from between the backing and the piece being appliquéd. To do this, insert the needle into the space left open. Then catch the paper with the forked end of the needle. By turning the needle either clockwise or counterclockwise you can roll the paper into a small cylinder and remove it through the opening.

You can make a quilling needle by taking a large, long-eye darning needle and sawing or cutting the very tip of the eye end with a wire cutter. Be *very careful* when doing this, because the small piece of metal has a tendency to fly into space. I hold both the needle and the cutters inside a paper bag and away from my face.

— Lois C. Ruiz, Murray, KY

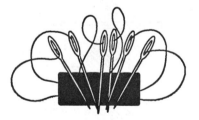

I keep a magnet with lots of size 10 needles threaded with all the colors I'll be using on a project. I never unthread one color for another. I study the pattern and number the sewing sequence of each piece.

— Ann Govinlock, Alexander, NY

I've discovered 100 percent silk thread for appliqué. It is smooth and takes dye well, so its colors are clear and vivid.

— Charlotte L. Fry, St. Charles, MO

8

Tools of the trade

Tools for marking

❖ I use a tiny washer I got in a store with a tiny hole in the center to trace outside a marked line. Larger washers can be used in the same way to mark wider spaces. I place my pencil in the center hole and "roll" the edge of the washer against the previous line. It makes another line outside the marked line, the exact distance as the width of the washer.

— Katie Esh, Ronks, PA

❖ If I need a circle, sometimes I get the right size from the lid of a can of cocoa. It is metal and will never bend. I keep it with my templates.

— Dorothy Geiger Hoffman, Conneaut, OH

❖ I sometimes use Scotch tape that is sticky on both sides to prevent the fabric layers from shifting.

— Diana M. Garrison, Silver Spring, MD

❖ I use a mini hand drill from my husband's toolbox (it looks like a big pencil) to make holes in templates. I place the template plastic on top of a magazine for drilling.

— Jennifer Strand, Sacramento, CA

❖ I've used a metal shish kebab skewer, heated in the flame of my gas stove, to melt a small hole in the corner of plastic templates so I can mark corners for accuracy.

— Julie McKenzie, Punxsutawney, PA

❖ I use a toothbrush to get rid of eraser dirt after erasing pencil marks

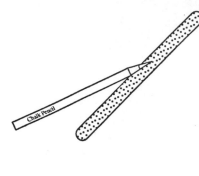

Chalk Pencil

when I've finished quilting.

— Joan Vanover, Easton, PA

❖ I sharpen chalk pencils and other soft pencils with an emery board.
— L. Jean Moore, Anderson, IN

❖ I use a piece of rug gripper web to hold my ruler in place and keep it from slipping.

— Nancy L. Scott, Baltimore, MD

Tools for cutting

❖ I have an old metal 12-inch ruler that is 2 inches wide. It has become my favorite! The sides can't be slivered by the rotary cutter, and it always provides a straight edge.

— Lynne Fritz, Bel Air, MD

❖ I use an Exacto knife to score my plastic pattern pieces. I run the knife along a metal ruler, and then I can snap the pieces apart. I get a straighter edge on pattern pieces than I get by cutting them out with scissors.

— Barbara Ashton, Sharon Hill, PA

❖ I like to use a carpenter square.

— Sharon Heide, Mt. Lake, MN

❖ I was making a miniature log cabin diamond Christmas tree skirt. I was doing it with strip piecing and a rotary cutter. I didn't have a ruler with a 60° marking on it, so I used my husband's engineering triangle (20°, 60°, 90°).

— Audrey Romonosky, Poughkeepsie, NY

Tools for piecing

❖ I always hold my 4-inch embroidery scissors in my hand while sewing. It comes in handy, not only for cutting, but as a stiletto for pushing little edges under the presser foot, etc.
— Donna Fite McConnell, Searcy, AR

❖ After all my squares are completed for a quilt, I lay a clear Plexiglas square, the size of the desired finished square, on top of each one. I mark an "x" in the center of this Plexiglas and center it on each quilt block, then trim away or add on borders accordingly to make all the blocks the same size. If Plexiglas is not available, I use a large piece of heavy cardboard and cut a center 3-inch square out of it so I can center it over the block.

— Barbara Nolan, Pleasant Valley, NY

❖ I use a bodkin or fine crochet hook to move small pieces under the presser foot when I machine-piece.

— Sherry Carroll, Delta, PA

❖ Fourteen years ago my first quilting teacher used an old hat pin to guide patches under the pressure foot and keep the points together. I still do this today.

— Mary Puskar, Forest Hill, MD

❖ I wax the metal sewing table of my sewing machine with car wax (not furniture wax) so that pieces will glide over it. This is especially helpful when I am machine-quilting.

— Terry Festa, Clinton, CT

❖ I have a piece of walnut wood, about 1/2 inch square, 6 inches long, and tapered to a fine point at each end (a different angle at each end) which I use to finger press fabric seams. It works better and gives a sharper crease than a fingernail.

— Doris Amiss Rebey, Hyattsville, MD

❖ I use the Little Foot presser foot to make precise 1/4-inch seams when I am machine-piecing.

— Carolyn Shank, Dayton, VA

❖ I use plastic coffee stir sticks (the round hollow kind) to guide fabric through the sewing machine. They are just ridged enough to guide the fabric, and, if I hit them with the needle, they don't break the needle or cause any damage to my machine.

— Lois C. Ruiz, Murray, KY

❖ A seam ripper helps to feed seam allowances under the presser foot. Seam allowances often tend not to want to go in the direction I want them to move.

— Irene J. Dewar, Pickering, ON

❖ I use a computer table with a dropped area built for a computer keyboard. My sewing machine sits in the dropped area. My table is adjusted so the plate of my sewing machine is level with the table surface.

— Janet Jo Smith, Littleton, CO

❖ I use very thin Swiss pins, about 1 1/8 inches long, in piecing. I can pin pieces together, matching seams perfectly, and sew over the pins.

— Annabelle Unternahrer, Shipshewana, IN

Tools for appliqué

❖ I use tweezers to take freezer paper out of appliqué work.

— Lisa Tizzoni, Olyphant, PA

❖ I use hemostats (a medical clamping tool) to pull out my freezer paper from appliqué work and for turning squares for cathedral windows.

—Maryann England, Thogamond, CA

❖ I use an orangewood manicure stick for turning appliqué pieces right side out.

— Sara Harter Fredette, Williamsburg, MA

❖ An orange stick or metal nail file works well for turning seam allowances over to glue. It allows me to keep my hands cleaner.

— Doris Amiss Rebey, Hyattsville, MD

❖ When doing appliqué, I sometimes roll the 1/8-inch seam allowance under with a damp round toothpick which I've been holding in my mouth.

— Johnette Zwolinski Shoberg, Globe, AZ

❖ When appliquéing by the needle-turn method, I sometimes use a wooden toothpick to help me turn under the raw edges. The wood grabs the tender threads and allows me to put them under the appliqué.

— Peggy Smith, Hamlin, KY

❖ A very small crochet hook helps me push a seam under to appliqué or helps me pull out a curve.

— Donna Conto, Saylorsburg, PA

Tools for quilting

❖ I use a single-edge razor blade to cut ends of threads when quilting. Tug slightly on the thread, then slice it off as close to the quilt as possible. No tails!

— Bethel Triplett Moore and Karen Moore, Fairfax, VA

❖ When I am quilting in the ditch or through seams, I lay a bar of bath soap on my quilt and every now and then stick my needle in the soap. This makes the quilting easier.

— Bealah Little, Hamden, OH

❖ Hardware stores have a wide selection of masking tape widths. I am not limited to the standard 3/4-inch tape for marking large quilted areas.

— Bethel Triplett Moore and Karen Moore, Fairfax, VA

❖ I use the fingertip of the index finger from latex gloves to help push and pull my needle.

— Shirley Taylor, Yuba City, CA

❖ I keep a small pair of needle-nose pliers on my frame. I use them to pull the needle through the material. It works very well.

— Helen L. Anderson, Titusville, NJ

❖ I wind a rubber band around my thimble, creating a no-slide surface to help pull my needle.

— Joyce Buschhaus, New Bern, NC

❖ If the needle is difficult to pull through fabric and batting, I pinch the needle with a piece of rubber from a tourniquet that I saved after I had blood drawn for a blood test. I use a piece about 1-inch square.

— Judith Ann Govotsos, Monrovia, MD

❖ A fabric-covered board (3 inches x 24 inches) is great to lay on the quilt frame to hold tools, thimbles, scissors, small lamps, etc.

— Jennifer L. Rhodes, Lancaster, PA

❖ I use a carpenter's square to make sure the quilt corners are square before I mark the quilting pattern and begin to quilt. I use cups, saucers, plates, spools and a potato masher (interesting curves!) for quilting templates.

— Kelly Wagoner, Albuquerque, NM

❖ I love to use cookie cutters for marking quilt designs and sometimes even for appliqué designs.

— Rhondalee Schmidt, Scranton, PA

❖ I use a #13 crochet hook to pull those knots that have popped out back into the batting.

— Virginia C. White, Gallup, NM

❖ I wear a rubber finger grip on my index finger. I buy them at the office supply store and cut the tips off. It slides down to the second knuckle and acts as a needle gripper when I pull the needle through the quilt.

— Bonnie Zabzdyr, Wright City, MO

❖ I buy tubular party balloons and cut a section about 1 inch long from the closed end. I wear this on my right index finger. It allows me to hold the needle securely without gripping it when I'm quilting. I wear it when I appliqué, too. It's thin and comfortable.

— Phyllis A. Kroggel, Tucson, AZ

❖ When I find that it is hard to pull the needle through quilting, I use the 1/2-inch rubber band that comes around fresh broccoli in the grocery store. I insert my thumb and forefinger into the "donut hole" of the rubber band, then widen the distance between my thumb and forefinger until I have picked up the rubber band.

I place the needle along the outside edge of the rubber band, pushing the needle and the rubber band between my thumb and forefinger. I pinch the needle between my thumb and forefinger, with the rubber band on each side of it so it cannot slip.

I tie a ribbon or yarn onto the rubber band, then safety-pin the ribbon onto the section of the quilt where I am working. Then I don't lose the small rubber band all the time.

— Pearl Mok, Los Angeles, CA

❖ I use a rubber jar lid remover to pull my quilting needle through a tough fabric. (This is a circle of rough textured rubber used to remove stubborn lids.) My grandmother used an old piece of leather.

— Joyce A. Walker, Ft. Smith, AR

❖ I use a finger cot which watchmakers use to keep body oils off watch parts. It's better than a separate needle grabber because it stays on my finger all the time. Finger cots can be found in drugstores near gauze and bandages.

— Lee Ann Hazlett, Freeport, IL

❖ I use rubber fingers, available in office supply stores, instead of a thimble. I wear one on my right thumb for traction.

— Mary Seielstad, Schenectady, NY

❖ I use black electrical tape to protect the fingers on my left hand from pricks while I quilt.

— Marjorie Mills, Bethesda, MD

❖ I use a baby feeding spoon (with hook handle) with my left little finger through the hook and my thumb resting in the bowl of the spoon as a striker plate for my quilting needle. Sure saves my left thumb!

— Mary-Leigh Schensnol, Fallbrook, CA

❖ I sometimes use the kind of tape normally used to wrap baseball bat handles on my finger instead of a thimble for appliqué.

— Connie Downey, Muncie, IN

❖ When stitching white on white, I like to use a fine tatting floss that is waxed. It gives the quilting a greater dimension, plus the stitching is stronger.

— Lynn Parker, Taylors, SC

❖ When I free-form machine quilt and want to use metallic threads, I use a spring needle, and not the spring that attaches to the needle screw arm. You can use a size 80/12 topstitch needle. Also, loosen the top tension a notch or two.

One tool that I find useful is a stiletto. A stiletto does everything that some persons do with their seam rippers, but it does it with much greater ease. For fabric pieces that try to slide apart while sewing, I stab the two pieces and then run them under the presser foot with the stiletto until they are held tightly by the foot. A stiletto is also great for fetching the bobbin thread loop from under the raised presser foot. The stiletto, when rubbed across the top of the fabric toward the foot and needle while sewing, will gracefully ease extra fabric bulk into the seams without puckers.

— Cheri Ruzich, Live Oak, CA

Tools for travel

❖ I take along a light bulb with high wattage to put in lamps in motel rooms so I can see better for sewing.

— Laura Reif Lipski, Lindenhurst, NY

❖ I use knitting needle protector tips on my small scissors when I carry them in my bag.

— Ann Stutts, Grants Pass, OR

❖ I carry a magnet when traveling with sewing projects in the event that I need a quick pick up of spilled pins!

— Laura Reif Lipski, Lindenhurst, NY

❖ A battery-operated portable neck lamp is great for train- or bus-travel sewing.

— Laura Reif Lipski, Lindenhurst, NY

❖ When traveling, I use a small bar of soap for a pincushion. It lubricates needles and prevents pins from rusting. I also use empty paper towel rolls around which I wind binding, fusibles, etc. It prevents creasing. It is also how I carry blocks when I travel. The blocks can be stored around the tube to prevent folds.

— Susan Ketcherside, St. Charles, MO

❖ I find a tote bag is a necessity when I attend quilt shows. I prefer one with a strap that crisscrosses over my back and allows my hands to be free. If I use a fanny/waist pack, I don't need a purse and my hands are also free.

— Laura Reif Lipski, Lindenhurst, NY

❖ I have a pocket-size sewing kit for traveling — a Sucrets box into which I put several needles, a pill container with 10 to 12 pins, a safety pin, needle threader, thimble and sharp folding scissors. It also holds two quarters for telephone calls and two of my business cards. I put a spool of thread into the same pocket as the Sucrets box. Then I add a bag holding my fabric "project" to my tote/handbag. This arrangement is great for the car, planes, dentist's office, etc.

— Polly Gilmore, St. Joseph, MI

❖ Take a few extra programs home from quilt shows. They can be cut up and used to glue proper identification onto the back of pictures. Write in the back of a program the number and name of each picture taken.

— Laura Reif Lipski, Lindenhurst, NY

❖ When traveling, I place straight pins and threaded needles in an empty 35 mm film container. I line the inside of the top with magnetic self-stick tape (1/2 inch wide).

This helps prevent a great mess if the pins spill on planes or in hotel rooms. The lid snaps on and I leave a little piece of thread hanging outside, so I can easily find the needles I need.

— Helene Kusnitz, W. Hempstead, NY

❖ I use a large manuscript clamp to attach sewing bags or plastic bags containing my sewing supplies to either a shoulder seat belt or my skirt, pants or jacket when I travel.

— Laura Reif Lipski, Lindenhurst, NY

❖ Label all your tools and supplies when you travel with other quilters!

— Laura Reif Lipski, Lindenhurst, NY

Organizational tools

❖ I like to keep my needles in the package they came in, so I know what size they are. I found that by putting a strip of adhesive-backed magnetic tape on the needle package, I have a place to put my needle. I don't lose so many, and when I am done, it goes back in the correct package. This has also been a real help when I baste. I would always lay the needle on the quilt top, and then could not find it easily on some of the fabrics.

— Barbara Ashton, Sharon Hill, PA

Eyeglass Case

❖ I use old eyeglass cases (envelope style) to store rotary cutters. I store many of my smaller and larger items in a small plastic fishing tackle box.

— Carol Findling, Beatrice, NE

❖ I keep needles, ripper, thimbles, marker, etc. in a clear plastic makeup pouch. It stays right by my chair, and I can see at a glance what's in it. I also have a pincushion on the right arm of my chair with 20 pockets.

— Tommie Bandy Freeman, Carrollton, GA

❖ I'm a lover of the plastic bag. I make mini-quilts, and I can carry a whole quilt to piece in a little plastic bag in my purse. It also makes me feel virtuous for recycling my plastic bags (the clear ones, of course).

— Vicki Krausz, Denver, CO

❖ Our group has discovered that carrying supplies for projects (thread, scissors, etc.) in clear plastic, zippered cosmetic cases is a very convenient and inexpensive way — even having one case for each project.

— Quilting Friends, Richmond, IN

❖ I have a clear plastic hair dryer holder on the wall beside my cutting/ work table. I keep rotary cutters, marking pencils, small rulers, scissors, etc. in the three compartments close at hand. My table is from Ikea and has legs of adjustable heights, so I can have it waist high and save my back! A three-basket rolling cart sits beside my machine for more convenient storage of equipment and necessities.

— Nancy Jo Marsden, Glen Mills, PA

❖ I sometimes use clothespins to keep strips in place. I number the clothespins, attach them to strips, and hang them in numerical order.

That way there is no mix-up when I sew.
— Elaine C. Langley, Greenville, SC

❖ I use a small felt-lined tray for beads and sequins for embellishments.
— Polly Gilmore, St. Joseph, MI

❖ A golf tee, with a small magnet glued to the top, slips in the holes on a spool of thread and holds a needle or thimble.
— Susan Harris Smith, IN and Leesa Seaman Lesenski, Whately, MA

Tools for basting

❖ I use safety pins in place of basting.
— Mary-Louise Miller, Rochester, NY

❖ When using safety pins to baste a quilt to be quilted, I use a grapefruit spoon to close the pins. It sure saves lots of sore fingers! Put the serrated edge of the spoon under the point of the pin and snap it closed! It takes a little practice.
— Lauren Eberhard, Seneca, IL

❖ I use a butter knife for closing safety pins. Place the pin in the quilt, press the knife to the pin's point, turn the knife at a slant and fasten the pin. It's painless.
— Lela Ann Schneider, Boise, ID

❖ I use a soup spoon with a round bowl when basting quilts. As the needle comes up from the wrong to the right side, I move the bowl of the spoon under the tip of the needle. This allows me to grab and pull the needle up easily — with no pricks.
— Mary Wheatley, Mashpee, MA

❖ I baste prior to quilting my quilts on the tile kitchen floor. I use basketball knee pads and elbow pads. I have also used gardeners' kneeling pads. All work well.
— Jorita J. Groves, Bushland, TX

❖ For pin-basting on a tabletop or the floor, I use heavy brass bar weights and old "lead ducks" (drafting weights) to hold the backing fabric taut around the edges. I then place the batting and the quilt top over the backing and carefully reposition each weight, one at a time, before I start pinning.
— Nina Lord, Annapolis, MD

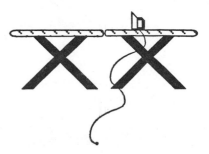

Tips for pressing

❖ When ironing a large quilt top or back, I put the iron on an extension cord and place two ironing boards end to end. I can work down the whole quilt at once.
— Barbie Mockenhaupt, Palmdale, CA

❖ For a quick press by my machine at home or when attending a class, I use a Radio Controlled Airplane Monokote Iron and a small ironing pad. The Monokote iron "High" setting is almost the same as a "Cotton" setting on a home iron. The Monokote iron has a wooden handle, an iron head 1 1/2 inches wide and 5 inches long, is pointed, and is Teflon-coated.

— **Corinne Airola Manley, The Colony, TX**

❖ I use an old non-aerosol hair spray bottle filled with water when I need just a touch of dampness for pressing. It puts the water in just a small spot, so I can use the iron point to press. It helps avoid too much pressing.

— **Carol Findling, Beatrice, NE**

❖ For filling my steam iron, I use a liquid soap container that has been rinsed well to remove all traces of soap. Its top opens to squirt water into the iron. It prevents spills, and it's not an open container that collects dust and lint.

— **Alyce C. Kauffman, Gridey, CA**

❖ I have several hat pins or corsage pins at the end of my ironing board. Sometimes I use them to hold fabric straight while ironing to make sure it doesn't stretch.

— **Mildred Pelkey, Glen Burnie, MD**

❖ My husband made a large rectangular table top that locks to my ironing board so that I can open fabric for pressing. It also makes a big surface for planning.

— **Dorothy Humphrey, Webster, NY**

Additional tips

❖ When hand-piecing in really hot weather and wearing shorts, I lay an old sleeve holder on my leg above the knee so I can pin to the holder, as if it were my third hand. You can use pants or a skirt also!

— **Helen M. Erickson, Grants Pass, OR**

❖ I use a crochet hook to push corners out, and a bobby pin to run the ribbon through pockets on quilted ornaments.

— **Susan Alexander, Baltimore, MD**

❖ Instead of a fabric glue stick, I sometimes use school paste, thinned with water, and apply it with a small brush.

— **Trudy Kutter, Corfu, NY**

❖ I find the tip of my letter opener (pointed but not sharp) perfect for pushing out and smoothing the seam allowances inside mitered binding corners before I stitch them into place on the back of the quilt.

— **Nina Lord, Annapolis, MD**

❖ A curling iron helps bend bias curves and ribbons. A broken bone knitting needle is good for trapunto.

— Polly Gilmore, St. Joseph, MI

❖ I stand two small pocket mirrors upright, with their two edges together, next to a patch I'm designing. Then I fan open the outer edges to varying angles so that I can visualize how the fabric might best be cut out to create a new design, for example, in a star pattern.

I use the end of a large knitting needle to push out a corner without putting a hole in the fabric.

— Becky Humphries, Vancouver, WA

❖ I use a chopstick when stuffing small doll arms, etc.

— Lisa Tizzoni, Olyphant, PA

❖ I use a wooden letter opener to poke out corners.

— Freda Gail Stern, Dallas, TX

❖ I use a dentist pick for stuffing small shapes.

— Kaye Schnell, Falmouth, MA

❖ I use a children's mini-kaleidoscope to get an idea from one quilt block how a whole quilt would look. I look through a sheet of red transparent plastic to neutralize color, so I can tell the difference between dark and light fabrics in relation to each other.

— Dianne Wernick, Baltimore, MD

❖ There are three things I could not do without — now that I have them! They are: a real sewing machine table — the machine sits lower than the rest of the table; an office-type chair — upholstered, with adjustable height, and on rollers; and a floor lamp that can be turned in any direction, including up and down.

— Harriet S. Meade, Clinton, CT

❖ To keep safety pins from rusting, I place a moisture-absorbing packet (from vitamins) in a bag or jar of pins.

— Joyce Buschhaus, New Bern, NC

❖ When entering a quilt show, I start to my left. Most people automatically go right.

— Laura Reif Lipski, Lindenhurst, NY

❖ I keep a long magnet on a handle to "sweep" the floor for pins.

— Elizabeth Hanson Sammons, El Segundo, CA

❖ I have a ping-pong table in my workroom, so I don't have to crawl on the floor when laying out a quilt. It has fold-down sides which I put up when I work with extra large quilts.

— Ona G. Jones, Hull, MA

❖ I have an unused buffet in my back room. It is just the right height on which to do my cutting. I used it basically for storage, until one day I needed to cut just one small piece and did it on the top of the buffet. Now I use it all the time.

— Barbara McGinnis, Ocean City, NJ

❖ Surgical scissors are great for ripping out small stitches.

— Nancy Ann Callaway, Elwood, IN

❖ When doing a lot of handwork (piecing, appliqué and quilting), I like to prop up my feet (at least one foot) on a small foot stool, six to eight inches high. Sometimes I use the rung of a chair or a low drawer of the sewing machine cabinet. It helps to prevent a backache and gives me more of a lap to work out of.

— Laura Reif Lipski, Lindenhurst, NY

❖ To remove dust and lint from my sewing machine, I place a plastic cap over the end of my vacuum hose. I poke a hole in the center of the cap and place a plastic straw in the hole. Then I turn the vacuum on and, using the straw, I am able to get into the small crevices of the machine and get lint that a brush leaves behind.

— Judi Manos, West Islip, NY

❖ I start a blank sheet of paper with each quilt, and on it I put the name of the quilt, the date I began, the pattern and fabrics I used, etc. As I progress with the quilt, I take notes — problems, solutions, changes, etc. I put this paper, the drafted design on the graph paper, templates and small swatches of fabric I'm using into a clear plastic protector. When the quilt is finished, I add the date it was completed, maybe a sketch of the quilt design (or pattern I made), the amount of thread I used, and a picture of the finished quilt. The plastic protector is a pocket with three rings punched in the margin so it can be used in a binder. Presto — instant records of my quilts!

— Dorothy Reise, Severna Park, MD

❖ For stained glass work or celtic, I use old corset steels to form my own bias binding. I fold the fabric in half (wrong sides together), press it, and stitch along the raw edges. I trim the seam allowance, insert the corset steel, put seam allowances to the back and press.

— Pauline J. Morrison, St. Marys, ON

❖ I use a small, soft brush to pick up any stray threads and lint from the top or back of the quilt.

— Edna Nisly, Partridge, KS

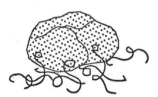

Use a soft eraser
to remove threads.

❖ A soft eraser removes threads after ripping out seams.

— Doris Amiss Rebey, Hyattsville, MD

❖ I use a pair of six-inch "Mayo" surgical scissors, available at medical supply houses. These have a blunt, curved lower blade so I do not accidently cut the fabric layers underneath when I trim seams.

— Bethel Triplett Moore and Karen Moore, Fairfax, VA

Preparation for quilting

Choosing quilting designs

❖ I find that crosshatching and other lines quilted close together enhance larger quilting designs in the foreground.

— Lou Ann Philpot, Murray, KY

❖ I place wax paper over the area of the quilt top for which I am selecting a quilting design. I use a regular pencil to scratch the wax paper surface with the proposed quilting lines. The quilt top units show through the paper, allowing me to study each block and its quilting design, and decide if it is appropriate.

— Rosie Mutter, Bechtelsville, PA

❖ On a piece of cling-wrap (about 24 inches x 24 inches) I draw the quilting design with a colored pencil and lay it on top of the finished top. If I like this, I draw it on the top itself. If I don't, I start again with another design.

— Doris Miotto, Thorold, ON

❖ I lay out several choices drawn on typing paper on the quilt block to see what each will look like.

— Molly Wilson, Gonzales, TX

❖ I choose quilting designs that make the backs of my quilts as pretty or prettier than the fronts. I like to use a plain backing that shows off the quilting.

— Dorothy Reise, Severna Park, MD

❖ I let the pattern design suggest the quilting design. For instance, if I appliqué flowers, I look for a flower or leaf quilting design.

— Connee Sager, Tucson, AZ

❖ I select a design to flow with the design of the pieced blocks. Where plain blocks are adjacent to pieced blocks, I place the template under clear mylar and trace the design of the pieced block onto it, and then use those designs for quilting on the plain block.

— Dorothy Logan, Harrisonburg, VA

❖ I like to choose something that complements, or draws the eye to the pieced or appliquéd design, and does not compete with it.

— Audrey H. Eby, Lancaster, PA

❖ I look to the quilt to see what is needed. If the quilt has a lot of angles, quilting curves can soften the sharpness.

— Laurie A. Enos, Rochester, NY

❖ I use simple lines if there is a strong fabric pattern which hides the stitching and fancier designs if the fabric is rather plain and will allow the quilting to show.

— Carol Findling, Beatrice, NE

❖ Sometimes the name of the quilt just lends itself to a design. When I made a quilt called *"Mormor"* (which is Swedish for "Grandmother") and used Christmas red and green fabrics, I felt it had to be quilted with hearts. Both "Grandmother" and "Christmas" mean love to me.

— Sue Seeley, New Bern, NC

❖ I think it's nice to repeat my piecework in my quilting, such as quilting fans on a Fan quilt or hearts on a Heart quilt.

— Ilene Bontrager, Arlington, KS

❖ If it is an old-fashioned-looking quilt, either by fabric or pattern, I choose simple designs, such as crosshatching or straight lines in the border, which do not detract from the pattern. If the pattern has a lot of curves, circles or open spaces, as appliqué patterns often do, I choose a fancier design (hearts, flowers, etc.). In other words, I match my quilting designs to what the quilt itself says.

— Marilyn Umble, Atglen, PA

❖ I choose my quilting designs to match the rest of the quilt; for example, baskets with basket-weave quilting.

— Elsie Schlabach, Millersburg, OH

❖ On bird quilts I use feathers.

— Mahlon Miller, Hutchinson, KS

❖ I try to choose designs that require a minimal amount of starting and stopping, and I place them so that there will be a minimum number of knots and few chances of quilting coming loose.

— Joyce A. Walker, Ft. Smith, AR

❖ I try to match the flow or theme of the appliqués or patterns or major fabrics. On appliqué work I frequently echo-quilt what has been appliquéd.

— Brenda Shaw-Nielsen, Washington, DC

❖ I try to match the quilting design to the style of the quilt. If the quilt has an antique appearance, I use an antique quilting design. Likewise, at the other extreme, I use new designs on a contemporary quilt.

— Terry Festa, Clinton, CT

❖ I look at quilting stencils and select particular elements from the design to use in different areas of the quilt. I like to use the complete stencil in a border and parts of it in a block.

I love to quilt but get bored easily, so I like changes — lots of curves, sharp turns, flowers — all in the same work, if possible. The design must mean something to me in relation to the piecework or appliqué pattern.

— Ginny Barr, Jackson, OH

❖ I find that the smaller the finished quilt (miniature size), the more the piece lends itself to simple, less-cluttered geometric designs, especially if the border is a tiny print. I use small prints and find that intricate quilting patterns not only get lost, but seem to "muddy" the look of the finished piece.

— Jane E. Crowe, Boyertown, PA

❖ I determine the overall quilting design by the proportion of the piecing on the top. If the pieces are small, then I quilt the design closer together.

— Johnette Zwolinski Shoberg, Globe, AZ

❖ I look at the designs in the fabric to see if there are shapes to repeat.

— Teresa Reily, White Plains, NY

❖ I pin several quilting patterns on my quilt and hang it up or drape it over a table so I can look at it once in a while. It just hits me one day which one to use.

— Thea Campbell, Simpsonville, SC

❖ With appliqué I try to add details with quilting that complete the design — veins in leaves, petals on roses, tendrils with clumps of grapes.

— Betsy Hughes, Midlothian, VA

❖ I like to accentuate the pattern with the quilting stitches. I often use outline stitches around the main pattern and then fill in the background with lines or crosshatch.

—Violette Denney, Carrollton, GA

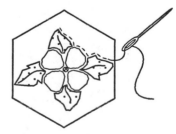

❖ I hang my stencils on a pegboard according to their size. I check the size of my borders or blocks and try all of that size templates to see which one coordinates with the pattern of my quilt.

— Mary Lou Mahar, Williamsfield, IL

❖ I make quilting templates for the spaces that need to be enhanced. I usually limit the number of motifs on one quilt. I prefer to use only one or two motifs on the surface, plus glorious gridding!

— Ellen Swanson, Hamilton, VA

Marking quilting lines

❖ I mark quilting designs lightly with a lead pencil. To trace the design onto fabric, I pull apart an extension table and place a piece of glass over the open space. I set a lighted lamp on the floor underneath the table. Then I place the pattern and fabric on the glass, and I can see the pattern through the fabric.

— Audrey H. Eby, Lancaster, PA

❖ I use a silver or white pencil. If I am marking a design that is not a cutout template, I tape the design to a piece of Plexiglas, prop the ends of the Plexiglas on two bar stools, and set a lamp on the floor underneath to make a light box.

— Julie McKenzie, Punxsutawney, PA

❖ I use a light table, which I use for viewing slides, or my Lucygraf to enlarge the design, and draw directly onto the fabric what they project. Sometimes I place a sheet of graphite transfer from a #2B pencil between the fabric and my final tissue drawing. I use a "metal pencil" purchased in Japan and poke a hole along the lines of my drawing. An old ball-point pen without ink or a straightened out paper clip also works well.

— Pearl Mok, Los Angeles, CA

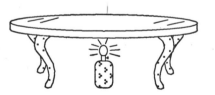

❖ I use a light box and mark plain blocks before piecing the complete top.

— Marie A. Beltz, McConnellsburg, PA

❖ I sometimes use my glass-top coffee table as a light box by just putting a lamp underneath it. I tape the design on top of the glass and position the quilt on top of that. I then trace the design.

— Terry Festa, Clinton, CT

❖ If I am quilting 1/4 inch from the ditch, I use 1/4-inch masking tape as my guide. It doesn't leave any chemical residue that can harm the fabric in the future.

— Laurie A. Enos, Rochester, NY

❖ I mark with a lead pencil. It won't bleed, fade or disappear. There's always a pencil around, so I don't have to make a special purchase. Pencil marks erase or wash out easily. For dark fabrics on which pencil is hard to see, I use white chalk.

— Lynne Fritz, Bel Air, MD

❖ I sharpen school chalk and mark as I go. It's easy to use, although it brushes off easily. Sometimes that's an advantage.

— Pat Probst, Columbus, OH

❖ I use pencil and chalk pencils. I do straight lines with different widths of masking tape. I constantly check angles with rulers and triangles.

— Rosalie W. Keegan, Enfield, CT

❖ A used, thin, sliver of soap is especially good for marking dark fabrics.

— Mrs. Vernon Kennel, Atglen, PA

❖ My mother's method is to use straight pins to mark lines of small areas or simple curves. You then follow the pin heads and remove the pins as you complete the stitching.

— Rosie Mutter, Bechtelsville, PA

❖ I use a mechanical pencil lightly on light fabrics. On dark fabrics, I transfer the design to tulle (netting often used for bridal veils), and trace it onto the top of the quilt with silver or white pencil. I usually mark with dotted lines so that so much of the pencil does not rub off onto the thread.

— Joy Rubenstein-Moir, Holtsville, NY

❖ On light fabrics I use a technical pencil with a very fine lead. Then, I dot my design; I don't draw solid lines. I don't want to see any lines of any kind. Yes, it takes time to dot, but the end results are absolutely worth it.

— Ann Leatz, Victorville, CA

❖ When I use the blue water-soluble pen to mark a design, I use only enough dots to indicate the gist of the design (cross-over points, etc.). I don't draw heavy lines.

— Nina Lord, Annapolis, MD

❖ Pencil is my Number One choice. I also use water-soluble Dixon pencil or Aquarille lead pencil, but never a blue or purple felt-tip pen. I use only markings that I know will come out. The Hera marker works well, especially on plain colors.

— Marilyn Bloom Wallace, Alfred, ME

❖ On dark fabrics I mark with slivers of soap. The marks don't disappear as fast as the powders.

— Muriel D. Austin, Hingham, MA

❖ On dark fabrics I like to use old slivers of bar soap or small travel soaps to mark quilting designs. They show up well on dark fabrics and are simply removed in one washing. Do not use perfumed soaps!

— Susan Ketcherside, St. Charles, MO

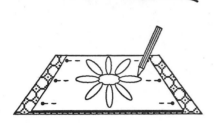

❖ On dark fabrics, I trace the pattern I plan to use onto Do-Sew or lightweight Pellon with a yellow or light blue pencil. I then pin the copy in place on the fabric and slip a piece of light-colored dressmaker's tracing or dressmaker's carbon paper between the fabric and the design. I pin it to hold, and then go over the design with a "dead" ball-point pen to transfer it to the fabric.

— Mary Seielstad, Schenectady, NY

❖ A silver, hard, wooden pencil is my favorite for dark colors. It sort of sparkles in the light.

— Judy Mocho, Albuquerque, NM

❖ If I have to mark, I use a silver pencil *very lightly*, which usually flakes off as it is being quilted. I use medium to heavy "Sew-in" stiffening to make quilting stencils. I pin them on with safety pins and quilt around them. They can then be unpinned, relocated, and used again.

— Alix Nancy Botsford, Seminole, OK

❖ I use chalk pencils and light pencil marks. If the markings will show on the fabric, I mark the lining and quilt from the back side.

— Hilda G. Pruett, Macon, GA

❖ I use a very thin pencil or 1/4-inch masking tape. Pencil markings must be very light. If you use masking tape, apply it, then remove it as soon as you're finished. Otherwise the adhesive will cause problems.

— Sue Dieringer-Boyer, Walkersville, MD

❖ I usually use a chalk pencil. It's thick and must be sharpened often, but its markings are completely removable with water.

— Sherri Driver, Englewood, CO

❖ I have a large piece of Styrofoam (made to paint signs on), over which I stretch my quilt and pin the edges so the top does not shift while I'm marking. A large sheet of cardboard also works.

— Edna Nisly, Partridge, KS

❖ I use surgical tape, pencil or colored pencils for marking.

— Pat Segal, Mechanicsburg, PA

❖ I use colored pencils for marking, trying to match or go with the colors of the quilt.

— Mrs. Ora C. Nisly, Hutchinson, KS

❖ I use a tailor's chalk pencil. It is easy to remove when quilting is complete.

— Kathy Mason Vetter, Marmora, NJ

❖ I only use chalk if the designs need to come off and won't be covered by appliqué. Chalk lasts longer and takes a bigger thrashing than we give it credit for.

— Cheri Ruzich, Live Oak, CA

❖ I don't usually mark on my quilts. I quilt along the lines of the blocks of the piece in some way that looks good to me. For motifs in blank blocks, I trace the design onto unprinted newsprint and pin or thread-baste that onto the block. I then quilt along the lines marked on the paper. The paper tears away afterwards, leaving no marks to clean off the cloth.

— Linda Hampton Schiffer, Columbia, MD

❖ When doing small projects like a pillow top, I mark straight lines with masking tape. For curved designs, I trace the design onto tissue paper, baste the tissue paper to the pillow top, and quilt over the marked lines. I pull off the tissue paper when I've finished.

— Audrey Romonosky, Poughkeepsie, NY

❖ Quilting designs can be made from lightly-sticking contact paper. Stick the paper to the quilt top. Quilt around the design, remove the paper, and move ahead to the next location for quilting.

— Sally Price, Reston, VA

❖ I think masking tape is great for straight lines. However, I do not leave it on the quilt overnight as some residue may stay on the fabric. Sharp-edged soap works nicely and smells good while I work.

— Brenda J. Marshall, St. Marys, ON

❖ I do not mark quilting designs. Instead, I use masking tape whenever possible. I make larger patterns out of wide masking tape, shaped with an Exacto knife, and then carefully place the tape.

— Carol A. Blake, North Kingsville, OH

❖ I use a big, blunt-edged needle and a flannel-covered board. I place the quilt top over the board and pull the needle down across the design. That leaves a shadow that stays — even in a frame.

— Vicki Jones, Rushville, IN

❖ I use the back of a crochet hook to make a hard mark on the fabric. The mark will stay until the fabric is washed and is easily seen.

— Kathy Powell, Vancouver, WA

❖ I do a lot of measuring, making sure to mark designs by starting in the middle and working out to the sides. I trace quilting designs with a lead pencil.

— Terri Good, Marietta, PA

❖ I use a Papermate Sharpwriter pencil that uses a very fine lead. I prefer dots to lines.

— LaVerne A. Olsen, Willow Street, PA

❖ A good lamp over my shoulder is an absolute necessity because my lines are so fine.

— Doris Morelock, Alexandria, VA

❖ I either use a water-soluble marker, or I cut out the design on contact paper. Contact paper templates can be reused several times, and they do *not* leave any sticky residue

— Darla Sathre, Baxter, MN

❖ I don't mark unless it's absolutely necessary. I use masking tape for straight lines; I also make freezer paper stencils. I don't press them on; I just pin them to the quilt top, quilt around them, then move them to the next area. When they're too worn to use, I replace them with new ones. When I do mark, I use my faithful Berol 2H pencil and a light hand.

— Ginny Barr, Jackson, OH

❖ One time I put the template down and did a close running stitch in thread and quilted close to that. I did not want the silk wallhanging to have any marks.

— Doris Miotto, Thorold, ON

❖ I mark *after* the top batting and backing are basted together because the softness makes my lines lighter. By the time I finish quilting, the lines are almost gone.

— Pat Brousil, Columbia, MD

❖ I have found that, for me, the best way to mark my quilt is not to mark on it at all, but to simply quilt it "freestyle" with no lines to follow except my own ideas. This is not practical for every quilt, so sometimes I use a wash-out blue pen and either draw directly on the quilt top, without using a template, or use a light table and trace the design onto the quilt top. I also use white contact paper cutouts that I quilt around with great success.

Another method I use frequently is to trace the quilt design, again using my light table, onto lightweight "deli paper," and then carefully pin the deli paper pattern directly onto the quilt top. I then sew over the top of the deli paper, using either a clear appliqué foot or a rolling foot, carefully following the pencil lines I have drawn on the paper. When I finish quilting, I simply tear the paper away, and no marks remain on the quilt. This method works best for "quilt as you go" blocks and small quilts, although I have used it successfully for doing borders on larger quilts.

— Katy J. Widger, Los Lunas, NM

❖ When using masking tape for straight lines, I find that if I quilt *only* along the right side of the tape, I can see better and don't quilt too close to the tape, which helps me avoid getting a sticky needle.

— Carol A. Medsker, Englewood, CO

❖ Sometimes I'm not absolutely certain of my design choices until I stitch! I use tape for straight lines, paper shapes to quilt around for simple motifs, and cornstarch dots on dark fabrics.

— Ellen Swanson, Hamilton, VA

❖ I go to the auto parts store and buy 1/4- and 1/2-inch wide masking tape. It comes in larger rolls and is much cheaper.

— Kay Jackson, Harrison, AR

Removing marked lines

❖ I use a water-soluble pencil. When I'm done quilting, I spray the quilt with a mist bottle of cool water. The lines disappear.

— Mary Kay Mitchell, Battle Creek, MI

❖ I use a very soft white rubber eraser.

— Jacqueline E. Deininger, Bethlehem, PA

❖ I use Orvus quilt soap and warm water.

— Suellen Fletcher, Noblesville, IN

❖ Usually I wipe my quilt with a wet terry cloth to remove markings. Sometimes I just wash the whole thing in the machine.

— Rosalie W. Keegan, Enfield, CT

❖ If I don't get the markings out through normal washing, I've had luck with Fels-Naptha soap. Orvus Soap works well, too.

— Donna M. W. Lantgen, Rapid City, SD

❖ Chalk wears off quickly. Pencil marks can be erased with the right eraser.

— Doris McCloskey, Annapolis, MD

❖ I wash it in the washer or rub it lightly with a towel saturated with Formula 409.

— Lou Ann Philpot, Murray, KY

❖ I use a soft toothbrush to remove chalk pencil. For blue pen, I wet a paper towel, use it to blot the marks, then lay the quilt on my dining room table overnight. I treat blue marks until they are gone on the surface, then I soak the quilt in cold water in the washing machine (if it is a queen or king, I use the bathtub), gently squeezing the water in and out. I spin the quilt damp-dry after washing it with a small amount of detergent or Ivory flakes in warm water on the gentle cycle.

— Dorothy Reise, Severna Park, MD

❖ Since I use chalk, it is easy to remove. If some chalk marks remain, I dampen a clean white washcloth, wring it almost dry, and rub it over the chalk marks. Sometimes I will do a single block, roll it in a towel, then flatten and smooth the damp piece on my clean kitchen counter to dry.

— Connee Sager, Tucson, AZ

❖ I don't usually remove markings because they are covered by stitches, but I do use an art gum eraser if necessary.

— Freda Gail Stern, Dallas, TX

❖ I use a white eraser (the kind in a plastic casing shaped like a pencil), water and a damp *white* washcloth.

— Marilyn Bloom Wallace, Alfred, ME

❖ I use baby shampoo in cold water.

— Susan Saladini, Freehold, NJ

❖ I use Spray 'n Wash and a toothbrush. It's best to wash the entire piece when finished, but ... I don't always!

— Mary Seielstad, Schenectady, NY

❖ I use a wet sponge over the pencil lines to remove them.

— Sherri Lipman McCauley, Pleasant Valley, NY

❖ A soft brush will remove most of the silver Berol Verithin markings.

— Edna Nisly, Partridge, KS

❖ If I have used water-soluble pens, I make sure I use plain water to rinse the markings out, because soap will set the ink, leaving permanent marks on the quilt. If I used pencils, I wash the quilt with a good quilt soap.

— Judy Williams, Stevensville, MD

❖ I use a mixture of three ounces of water, one ounce of rubbing alcohol, and three drops of Ivory dish detergent. I mix it together, apply it with an old toothbrush, and then rinse it with water.

— Anona Teel, Bangor, PA

❖ If all the pencil marks don't "quilt away" during the quilting process, I use three ounces of rubbing alcohol mixed with one ounce (two tablespoons) of water, and two to three drops of dishwashing liquid soap. (Be sure to test a small area for colorfastness first.) I hold an absorbent paper towel underneath the quilt, then gently brush the pencil lines with a very soft toothbrush and this mixture. This recipe was shared with me by a group of fellow certified judges while attending a national quilt show many years ago.

— Ann Reimer, Beatrice, NE

❖ Pencil marks should be as slight as possible. Should there be heavy pencil marks on the quilt, I use a German eraser known as Mars-Plastic to erase them. That eraser is about the best I have seen.

— U. Khin, Rocky Ridge, MD

❖ To remove chalk, I wash the quilt in the machine. To remove blue marker, I soak the quilt in cold water for four hours, drain it and wash it in cold water with cold water laundry soap. I rinse it three times.

— Meg T. Zechiel, Ontario, CA

❖ I rub markings off by holding the project in both hands and rubbing the material against itself.

— Jane S. Lippincott, Wynnewood, PA

❖ I remove pencil marks by using Baby's Wet Ones.

— Esther S. Martin, Ephrata, PA

❖ For wash-out markers, I use a spray bottle of tepid water and mist the entire area. After it has dried, I do it again to remove any remaining color. I find that markings made by other methods generally disappear as I'm quilting. If not, a soft damp cloth removes them.

— Alice Turner Werner, St. Charles, MO

❖ When I am through quilting, I lay my quilt on the living room floor at bedtime and mist it with a plant mister bottle to remove the blue marks. White powder usually brushes off before I want it to.

— Mary Lou Mahar, Williamsfield, IL

❖ I saturate a cloth with rubbing alcohol and rub it gently over marks to remove them. Sometimes I wad up scraps of batting and use them like an eraser to remove marks.

— Mary Wheatley, Mashpee, MA

❖ I remove fat chalk pencil marks with plain cold water. I use a *new* clean sponge and just dab at the marks. In 12 hours, the lines are gone.

— Barbara Nelson, Pleasant Valley, NY

❖ I feel very confident that when I mark my quilts with a *green* (no other colors) *Ultra-fine Flair* pen, the green disappears — removed without any worry — when I proceed to carefully rinse or wash it.

— Dorothy VanDeest, Memphis, TN

❖ For hard to get at areas, I have used a Q-tip dipped in water with or without a mild soap.

— Mary M. Weimer, Clinton, MD

❖ If you have used a blue marking pen, it is extremely important to remove all the ink. I like to use a spray bottle of water and generously spray each area as it is completed, allowing it to dry flat overnight.

When I have completed and bound the entire project, I put the quilt in the washing machine and fill it with cold water — without soap. I allow the quilt to soak in the water for about 10 minutes.

I am careful not to agitate the quilt so I don't add stress to the stitches. I then spin the water out and dry the quilt in the dryer or outside, spread on a sheet. If the blue markings are not removed in this way, the chemical sits in the quilt's batting and in the fibers of the fabric. If the sun or soap comes in contact with the chemicals, it is possible to have permanent yellow or brown stains left on the quilt. I have also heard reports of fabric that has disintegrated because of markings that were not fully and properly removed.

— Terry Sesta, Clinton, CT

❖ I use a clean art gum eraser-cleaner, available at office supply stores. This also works to remove pencil marks left from appliqué work on either the background or around the appliqué patches.

— Ginny Barr, Jackson, OH

❖ Spray 'n Wash removes pencil marks. I use that, then soak the project in the washer, gently agitate it and rinse. All pencil marks come off and it looks great!

— Jo Ann Pelletier, Longmeadow, MA

❖ I use hair spray to remove ink and Easy-Wash for most other stains. I remove markings with a fabric eraser or a Pentil Clic eraser. The Clic eraser is more precise because it is smaller.

— Jennifer Strand, Sacramento, CA

❖ Sometimes I use a T-shirt scrap to rub away extra marks. I use a blue water-soluble pen sparingly, and to remove its marking, I soak the project and allow it to dry, repeating until no spots reappear. I always use clear water for soaking — no detergent until all the blue stains are gone.

— Nina Lord, Annapolis, MD

❖ A Magic Rub Faber Castell is a great eraser for smudges.

— Jean Harris Robinson, Cinnaminson, NJ

❖ I don't mind washing a quilt if necessary to remove markings. I like the way a quilt puckers up with washing — it looks used and loved.

— Barbara Riley, Elk Grove, CA

Sources of inspiration

❖ When I can't figure something out, I try to imagine and practice what pioneer women would have done, like folding paper bags for patterns or using dishes for quilting designs to make good circles.

— Muriel D. Austin, Hingham, MA

❖ I look mostly at the patterns and designs all around me. Patterns on wallpaper, bathroom tile, even on the bottoms of my sneakers, have inspired my quilting designs. Living in the Southwest, I am also constantly inspired by the designs and patterns used on pottery and in woven tapestries by other natives of this area. I also like to modify and redesign old, classic quilting patterns.

— Katy J. Widger, Los Lunas, NM

❖ Currently I am quilting a design I made by folding and cutting a 12-inch square of paper, snowflake-fashion. My first "snowflake" turned out to be just what I needed.

— Irene J. Dewar, Pickering, ON

❖ I like to do either freehand designs or use household or kids' items for stencils. One of my favorites was my toddler's wooden puzzle pieces, interlocked. They made an interesting design!

— Lynne Fritz, Bel Air, MD

❖ Great children's ideas are found in many coloring books. Bed linens have nice floral and geometric designs.

— Helen Kusnitz, W. Hempstead, NY

❖ One of my quilting designs came from a grave marker in a graveyard that I photographed.

— Dale Renee Ball, Silverdale, WA

❖ Sometimes I get ideas from wallpaper or a greeting card. I have also made my own designs.

— Helen L. Anderson, Titusville, NJ

❖ Choosing a quilting design is my excuse to go to the quilt store for a stencil. Usually they cost under $3.00, and I get lots of enjoyment looking at the fabrics and books for very little money.

— Vicki Krausz, Denver, CO

❖ When I read quilt magazines, I keep a Fine-Line Sharpie marker in my hand. If I run across something I like or want to try, I make a marker note with the page number on the magazine cover.

— Pat Probst, Columbus, OH

❖ I get ideas from all sorts of books and drawings — even coloring books and paper towels.

— Corinne Airola Manley, The Colony, TX

❖ I look at all sources — architecture, art, flooring, wallpaper, doodles, baskets. I just got a book on Sashiko, which will likely inspire my next patterns. When I quilt by machine, sometimes I just do it freely — no markings. I make it up as I go along. It can be quite fun!

— Joyce Trueblood, Cromwell, CT

❖ Sometimes carved work on old buildings inspires my quilting patterns.

— Sissy Anderson, Lithonia, GA

❖ I use magazines for inspiration and subscribe to four or five. I catalog the magazines using a 3 x 5 card for each. I indicate on the card categories of projects. For example, "**" indicates quilts I want to make. Or when I need to choose a border, I pore over my magazines.

— Nolen Provenzano, North Potomac, MD

❖ I save napkins, greetings cards and pictures to use as inspiration for quilting designs. Then, I (or my husband) cut the plastic template when the template is needed. I also use quilt design books.

— Marion Lumpkins Reece, Richmond, VA

Batting choices

❖ I prefer polyester batting. I like light batting for small quilts, regular

batting for larger quilts, and fat batting for tied comforters.

— Karen M. Campbell, Germantown, MD

❖ I like the look that Mountain Mist quilt batting gives a finished quilt. If I want a very old-fashioned flat look in a quilt, I like Mountain Mist's 100-percent cotton batting, although it is harder to quilt because it is more densely woven. One hundred percent cotton also works nicely in a wallhanging since it doesn't puff out nor stick out from the wall as much.

— Marilyn Umble, Atglen, PA

❖ If the quilt will likely be washed, then I choose a durable, washable, puffy batting. If the quilt is for display only or for hanging on a wall, I prefer a thinner batting.

— Audrey H. Eby, Lancaster, PA

❖ I like quilts to look and feel older. Thin batting gives that appearance. You can make smaller quilt stitches with thin batting. Thermore is a good thin batting and also eliminates fiber migration.

— Jean Shaner, York, PA

❖ Buying the 96-inch wide batting in large rolls is less expensive. The wide batting is also much smoother than individual batts.

— Elizabeth Chupp, Arthur, IL

❖ If I want a fluffy look, I use polyester. For a flat antique look, I use at least part cotton, Mountain Mist or Hobbs.

— Melissa Stiles Hess, La Conner, WA

❖ I use thinner batting when I plan to hand-quilt, and thicker batting when I machine-quilt or tie.

— Melissa Myers, Indian Head, MD

❖ I choose my batting according to the amount of quilting I will do — lightweight for profuse quilting; heavyweight for scant quilting.

— Jacqueline E. Deininger, Bethlehem, PA

❖ Hobbs dark batting is great for dark quilts because any fibers that might pull through the fabric are not as visible.

— Doris McCloskey, Annapolis, MD

❖ Since I only hand-quilt, I use only lowloft or Fairfield Traditional. I find that Mountain Mist batting pulls apart too easily.

— Faye Meyers, San Jose, CA

❖ For bed-size quilts I use Mountain Mist Regular or Fairfield Lite. These keep the quilt light and soft. For wall-size quilts I use Fairfield Traditional for body and stability.

— Rosie Mutter, Bechtelsville, PA

❖ If I make a wall hanging that will be folded to mail, I always use polyester, because cotton batting leaves a crease after it has been folded.

— Judi Robb, Manhattan, KS

❖ I avoid cotton batting because it tends to ball up if the quilting is not close enough to hold it in place.

— Judy Williams, Stevensville, MD

❖ For things that will be washed often, I use polyester. I prefer lowloft (antique-looking) quilts. For anything I make that will be for "good" use (that is, for my bed and not my children's), I use cotton. I use almost exclusively Mountain Mist Blue Ribbon cotton batting, because I like its "drape" and feel and the way it works.

— Linda Hampton Schiffer, Columbia, MD

❖ I prefer thick, fluffy batting so that the quilting designs are more puffy and more visible.

— Elaine Nolt, Versailles, MO

❖ I use extra loft for my grandchildren because I want their quilts to be cozy.

— Sharron Van Meter, St. Charles, MO

❖ I can do smaller stitches with thinner batting.

— Ann Foss, Brooklyn, NY

❖ For my Amish-style quilts, I like cotton. My stitches are not as small, but I like the flat look.

— Joy Rubenstein-Moir, Holtsville, NY

❖ I like Mountain Mist. I think it has fewer thin spots or thick spots!

— Virginia A. Arthur, Wellston, OH

❖ I've used Mountain Mist for years, but have now gone to Hobbs. It migrates and beards less through the fabric of the completed quilt top or bottom.

— Dorothy Humphrey, Webster, NY

❖ I match batting to fabric: cotton for all cotton, etc.

— Joyce A. Walker, Ft. Smith, AR

❖ I frequently use Osnanburg cloth in place of batting for wall hanging quilts.

— Brenda Shaw-Nielsen, Washington, D. C.

❖ For hand-quilting, I like polyester lowloft batting. I like the way it looks and drapes. I do not like to hand-quilt through a cotton or cotton-blend batt since the needle drags and makes my hand ache. I will, however, split cotton batting for mini-quilts and hand-quilt through that with no problem.

For machine-quilting, I still prefer polyester lowloft batting. Although I have no problem quilting through cotton batts, and I like the way that they scrunch up slightly after being washed, they tend to leave more of a crease after being folded. I find that a Thermore batting holds this crease as well.

I like all my quilts to be washable, so I tend to stay away from wool batting.

— Terry Festa, Clinton, CT

❖ Sometimes a thin cotton blanket or bath towel works well for wall hangings. I also use good parts of old mattress pads.

— Mildred Pelkey, Glen Burnie, MD

❖ If I machine-quilt, I use 100-percent cotton batting. The cotton tops and backs seem to cling together.

— Kathleen Bishop, Washington D.C.

❖ To keep the scale correct, I use only lightweight batting for miniatures.

— Jane E. Crowe, Boyertown, PA

❖ I like to open prepackaged batting, spread it flat, and allow the batting to "relax" for at least 24 hours. If I don't want to wait the 24-hour period, I place the batt in a warm dryer and fluff it for about five minutes to remove its creases.

— Ann Reimer, Beatrice, NE

❖ I fluff batting in the dryer for a few minutes to increase its loft, even up its holes, and prepare it to produce a more uniform quilt.

— Lela Ann Schneider, Boise, ID

❖ To give quilts an old-fashioned look, I put a cotton flannel sheet between the layers without prewashing the flannel. After the quilt is quilted, I wash and dry it. The shrinking of the flannel sheet puckers the top, creating an old look.

— Kathy Evenson, Fergus Falls, MN

❖ I enjoy 80/20 cotton/polyester batting because I like a flat look, and it doesn't beard as easily.

— Leslie Lott, Englewood, CO

❖ I use natural fibers *only* (cotton, wool or silk) to avoid the toxic fumes always emitted by polyester.

— Alix Nancy Botsford, Seminole, OK

❖ I like cotton because it is easy to quilt and feels good to the touch. I like its appearance quilted. I also like cotton because it is a proven fiber. I am concerned that polyester batts will lose their stability. I am also concerned that polyester batts may be an environmental toxin to my family and the earth.

— Diana M. Garrison, Silver Spring, MD

❖ I avoid polyester batting because it would be devastating in a fire.

Even if the quilt top were not burned, the heat could melt the polyester.

— Linda Franklin, Camas, WA

Additional tips

❖ I can be more precise with quilting lines if I do marking for quilting on the quilt top before it is sandwiched with the batting and backing.

— Dorothy VanDeest, Memphis, TN

❖ I baste most of my seams down the way I want them to lay, so when I quilt I have no moving seam allowances. I remove the basting as I quilt.

— Joan Vanover, Easton, PA

❖ If I am machine-quilting, I use fingertip moistener like bank tellers and secretaries use. It makes my fingers lightly tacky, so I have a better grip for machine-quilting.

— Susan Ketcherside, St. Charles, MO

❖ Quilters are obsessed with getting tiny, beautiful, perfect stitches — and they are important! The thing that really impresses me in a finished quilt, however, is the overall design of the quilting — the amount, the balance, the way it emphasizes the pieced or appliquéd design. I love heavy quilting grids in background areas. Carefully *designed* quilting makes masterpiece quilts!

— Ellen Swanson, Hamilton, VA

❖ Storing sharpened marking pencils in a toothbrush travel container protects their points.

— Ann Reimer, Beatrice, NE

❖ I try to have consistent amounts of quilting in the body of the quilt, as well as in its borders, so that the quilt hangs or falls properly.

— Terry Festa, Clinton, CT

❖ I never like to copy a traditional design exactly, so I always make small changes.

— Marabee J. Seifert, Easley, SC

❖ Often, if it is possible to stitch in the ditch, I do that. Then I go back and add in some hand-quilting. Quilting in the ditch holds the area together so that then I can quilt much easier by hand without having all kinds of basting pins or threads in the way.

— Leslie Lott, Englewood, CO

Quilting

Frame options

❖ I use a round 18- to 20-inch frame for large quilts. I like to be able to turn the frame as I work and to be more mobile than a floor frame allows (for which I do not have the space, anyway).

I have also found a rectangular frame to be useful — especially for doing borders. It's easy to attach and detach the frame's plastic "pipes."

— Marjorie Mills, Bethesda, MD

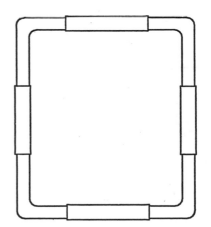

❖ First, I put my wall quilt in a small stretcher frame (four rails) and quilt the border and area around the main blocks. I then remove the quilt and complete the more intricate designs in a Q-Snap Frame.

I can place my small stretcher frame on a table and extend it over the edge in order to quilt. No stands are necessary.

For large quilts, I use five stretcher rails — three long (114 inches) and two short (84 inches). I pin the quilt length (all three layers) to the first long rail and half the quilt width (three layers) to the two short rails. I pin the quilt bottom and top to the remaining long rails, then roll it up halfway to store it on the extra length of short rails. The batting I let loose.

After I've quilted the first half of the top, I unpin it. I then move the first rail, on which the quilt has been rolled, forward on the short rail. I stretch and pin the rest of the top, back and bottom to the two short rails.

This is essentially the same method as that of a roller frame, but this requires only half the space of a full four-rail stretch. I use C-clamps to keep the rails in place.

— Rosie Mutter, Bechtelsville, PA

❖   I use a hoop with three legs that attach to a base. This leaves both my hands free for quilting. It even works well in a car.

— Sue Seely, New Bern, NC

❖   I use a 14-inch round hoop on a stand that fits in my lap. It is the most comfortable, portable frame I have found. My arms are short and I have a bad back. With a lap frame, I can move the quilts in any direction I choose. A plain hoop without the lap stand needs to be balanced on one's left forearm. I get very sore shoulders from that.

— Marilyn Bloom Wallace, Alfred, ME

❖   I prefer an 18-inch wooden hoop. It is portable and allows me to quilt a large area at a time. The Q-Snap squared frames are good, too, and indispensable for miniatures, because they prevent the end result from being distorted.

— Cindy Cooksey, Irvine, CA

❖   I like a hoop on a stand from Sullivan Woodworks. It allows me to sit on the sofa to quilt. I can pull it in over me and swivel it, so I can turn my work. That way I can sit with the rest of my family to watch TV and still quilt.

— Judi Robb, Manhattan, KS

❖   I use a small wooden eight-inch hoop, even for a large quilt, because I can reach under the hoop so easily.

— Debra Botelho Zeida, Waquoit, MA

❖   I use a 16-inch wooden hoop for quilting. It is larger than the usual 12-inch block so I can see the whole block as I quilt. Also, it is a portable size.

— Laurie A. Enos, Rochester, NY

❖   The type frame I use for quilting depends on the quilt pattern. If it is mostly curved, I lap-quilt on a hoop. If it is mostly straight, I use an old floor frame I ordered from a Sears Catalog 25 years ago!

— Alice Turner Werner, St. Charles, MO

❖   I use 14-inch hoops for my most fancy quilting, but first I stabilize the quilt by doing all the straight stitching on a large frame.

— Scarlett von Bernuth, Canon City, CO

❖   I purchased long boards at our local lumber store — 1-inch x 2-inches in various lengths — suitable for crib- or queen-size quilts. The corners are held together with C-clamps. I position the four sides on top of our pool table. This position is higher than normal, but easier on my back, because I must sit straight.

— Brenda J. Marshall, St. Marys, ON

❖   My carpenter husband made 3 1/2-feet-long rails, 5/8 inch x 1 1/2 inches. They are held together at the corners with C-clamps. I tacked strips of fabric on the rails, and the whole thing makes an excellent frame for my wall hangings.

— Ilene Bontrager, Arlington, KY

❖ I like a big frame in which I can stretch my entire quilt back and top, so it quilts very nicely.

— G.B., Smicksburg, PA

❖ I use a floor model Q-Snap frame. It holds the quilt firmly in shape, and I can adjust the tension for ease in quilting. The size fits into my living room; a full-length frame would be too big.

— Ada L. Bishop, Beatrice, NE

❖ A stretch frame that exposes the entire quilt is wonderful for a whole group of people quilting together. I use that kind for a "sister's day" quilting party. My roller frame, made by my husband, is the best for quilts that I work on alone. It doesn't take up much space in my room and is easy to operate alone.

— Grace S. Miller, Mount Joy, PA

❖ I have a large frame that accommodates eight people for any really large quilts for fund-raisers. This large frame is great because I can just leave all the thread, thimbles and needles right on top of the quilt when the phone rings or I have to prepare dinner.

— Barbara Nolan, Pleasant Valley, NY

❖ I like to set my frame inside my picture window and quilt with the help of natural light.

— Anna Buchanan, Belleville, PA

❖ Living in a small house, I find that a frame that can be put away quickly is best. My husband made me a frame consisting of two boards as long as a quilt is wide and two boards as long as my arm. They are connected by C-clamps and rest on sawhorses. I roll the quilt as I go.

— Rhondalee Schmidt, Scranton, PA

❖ For miniature quilts, I like a square lap-size frame, so I can turn it and always quilt towards myself. For large quilts, I want a big enough frame so that I can stretch out the quilt completely. I do sometimes pin every 12 inches and roll one side in. It takes less space.

— Edna Nisly, Partridge, KS

❖ For lap-quilting, I use a Q-Snap frame because it's lighter in weight, and my hand doesn't get tired holding it.

— Lee Ann Hazlett, Freeport, IL

❖ I use a king-size Zook quilting frame. There's no need to baste the three layers together before quilting, and it's fairly easy to put the biggest quilt in by myself. With the frame's three-pole construction, I can adjust the tension on the top or the backing individually. I have an eight-foot florescent light on the ceiling above the frame. I also use a secretary chair. It glides easily from one end of the quilt to the other.

— Ginny Barr, Jackson, OH

❖ My favorite is a 15-inch lap frame that I prop on the edge of a TV-tray. I've done king-size quilts this way, and when I was finished, I could still sit without a backache. I can tip the frame on the tray to catch the best light and readjust my chair easily.

— Judy Mocho, Albuquerque, NM

❖ My husband made a frame consisting of four boards — 1 1/2 inches x 24 inches. At each end of each board is a slit 4 inches long and l/4 inch wide. (The slits allow me to use the frame for a variety of sized quilts.) I stapled fabric onto one side of the boards. I use wing nuts to hold the boards together. I like the frame because most of my quilting is on small items. The frame doesn't take a lot of room to store, and it is easy to use.

— Judith Eve Nisly, Partridge, KS

❖ I use a small lap frame. I can turn it so that I can quilt in any direction possible. For borders, I use two pieces of elastic pinned to the quilt and pulled tight around my frame.

— Hilda G. Pruett, Macon, GA

❖ I use a large hoop. I usually quilt at our game table in the family room and let the table support the weight of my quilt.

— Diane DeBolt, Anderson, IN

❖ A floor frame encourages correct posture. I find a director's chair to be the right height and to give the best support. If I don't rest my arm on the quilt frame, I have better control, and I don't put extra pressure on the tendons in my arm and hand.

— Bea Kasebier, Bangor, PA

❖ I baste a towel to the edges of a quilt, so I can quilt into a corner when I am using a hoop.

If the PVC pipe frame begins to lose its grip, wrap it tightly with rubber bands, and submerge it in very hot water for a while. Remove it and let it cool.

I use the Hinterbury frames on a stand. I have a square, 22 inches, 29 inches and the edge bar. Since these turn a complete circle and move to any angle, they are most convenient to use.

— Irma H. Schoen, Windsor, CT

❖ For pillow tops, small wall hangings and quilts, I use a 14-inch hoop that my dad attached to a 14-inch round board with three dowel rods. It's about six inches high. This allows the hoop to stand alone on a stool or my lap, and I have both hands free to quilt.

— Carolyn Shank, Dayton, VA

❖ I use a Q-Snap frame and just quilt on my lap. I like to quilt on my

bed so I can bend my knees up and prop my work on my knees.
— Stephanie Braskey, Pottstown, PA

Putting quilts in frames

I use a heavy woven plaid or striped fabric on the edges of my quilt rails, being sure that the fabric is straight when I attach it. The plaids and lines in the fabric then serve as my accuracy check when I attach the quilt backing to the rails. I mark the center of each rail and the center point along each side of the quilt. When they are lined up, I can be sure the quilt is straight in the frame. I use a square or 90-degree triangle to make sure the quilt is square at each corner before I do any quilting.
— Carol A. Findling, Beatrice, NE

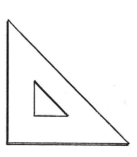

❖ I put my backing on the roller bar of the quilt frame first. If this is straight, I have no problem with the batting and quilt top. I pin the batting and quilt top only along the top edge of the frame and let the extra batting and quilt top hang over the other side of the frame to the floor. As quilting progresses, I roll the quilt and pull up the extra batting and top. I try to keep the backing as taut as possible when I stretch it in the frame.
— Janet L. Haver, Punxsutawney, PA

❖ My kitchen floor has blocks, so I can lay my quilt on the floor, using the floor markings as a guide to be sure it is straight in the frame. I use staples to attach the edges to the frame. It doesn't slip at all when it is stapled.
— Peggy Hamilton, Hillsboro, OH

❖ Sometimes opposite sides of the quilt are not equal, because the cross-grain of the backing fabric was stretched unevenly when the quilt was basted. I measure the backing after it has been stretched to be sure both ends are the same length. I also mark my quilting frame. This is an important part of the whole process to make the quilt hang evenly.
— Dorothy VanDeest, Memphis, TN

❖ I have had the best success with my large frame when I have basted the quilt backing to both sides of the quilt frame, then rolled the backing back and forth until it looks exactly straight. I then lay the batting on carefully and, finally, the quilt top. I pin the top along the edge and let the excess batting and top hang over the end. This allows quilting from only one side, but produces a very straight accurate look.
— Ethel Martin, Maugansville, MD

❖ I find that if fabric is stretched too hard in the frame, it is harder to quilt. It stitches more easily if it is stretched just lightly enough to make sure everything is straight, but not so it is quite taut.

When I use round, wooden hoops, I wrap them with the self-sticking tape athletes use to wrap sprained joints. This prevents the quilt from slipping in the hoop and prevents snags.

— Ann Reimer, Beatrice, NE

Quilting without a frame

❖ I prefer not to use a frame. By basting in a grid about 4 inches apart, I can keep my quilt from shifting. I can cuddle up with the quilt and quilt!

— Alix Nancy Botsford, Seminole, OK

❖ I can't use a frame. I must have my left thumb on top of my work, so I fold my quilt, wall hanging or pillow to the size of my work area, then tuck the ends under my legs.

— Carol Sucevic, Hopwood, PA

❖ I never quilt on a frame or even a hoop. I prefer the flexibility of not using a frame. I place a quilt on top of a hoop on a stand, just to keep it off the floor, and quilt the area that hangs over onto my lap.

— Darla Sathre, Baxter, MN

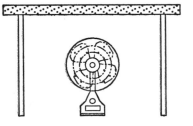

❖ I pin-baste with lots of pins and quilt in my lap. In hot weather, I support the quilt on a card table and put a fan under the table. It looks funny, but it works for me. I use no frame, even for large quilts, and feel more comfortable being able to move my quilt around easily.

— Betty F. McGuire, Clinton, CT

❖ Bending over a frame hurts my back. I stretch my quilt on an old wood frame, pin it all over with brass pins, and take it off to quilt.

— Florence Donovan, Lodi, CA

❖ I do not use any frame. I stretch out the back of my quilt across two or three tables and, using masking tape, I tape all edges down tightly. I lay the batting over the back, and then the top over that. I then baste the three layers together, starting in the middle, either by needle and thread or by using tiny brass pins, sewing or pinning every four inches. I have no puckers on the back when I quilt in my lap.

— Kathy Evenson, Fergus Falls, MN

❖ I have found that a quilting frame slows me down. I quilt without a frame, starting in the middle of the quilt and working out from all directions to keep the quilt nice and flat. I use safety pins to secure the three layers.

—Virginia L. Fry, Fulton, MD

❖ I do my quilting without a frame. I pin-baste about a fist apart all over the quilt. My projects are not limited to wall quilts. I have done many queen-size quilts this way. I find a quilting frame's tension to be too tight for my quilting technique.

— Barbara Tone Lister, Highlands Ranch, CO

❖ I don't use a frame. My idea of lap-quilting is to drape the whole quilt over my lap and get to it.

— Ann Foss, Brooklyn, NY

❖ I quilt on my lap with no frame. I pin-baste my quilts every three to four inches, and the layers just don't shift, so I don't bother to use that awkward frame.

— Sherri Driver, Englewood, CO

❖ I make miniature quilts. When a top is pieced and marked, I place it on a cutting board with its batting and backing in place. I use a rotary cutter to trim it to its finished size. Before lifting it, I pin its edges in preparation for binding. Then I use quilt pins to anchor the piece through and through so it doesn't shift as I quilt. When all the pinning is finished, I lift the piece from the cutting board. I bind and hem the piece before going on to do any quilting. I do not use a frame of any sort to quilt.

— Jane E. Crowe, Boyertown, PA

Techniques for starting and stopping

❖ I knot my thread and bury the knot in the batting. I begin the quilting line with one backstitch to anchor the thread. I also end with a backstitch, then knot and bury the thread. I try to keep the "knot burying" in the quilting line to avoid its being seen through the fabric.

— Lynne Fritz, Bel Air, MD

❖ Because I am right-handed, I start on the right side and work left.

— Peggy Hamilton, Hillsboro, OH

❖ I start in the middle of the quilt, go left to the side, go back to the middle, and go right. When I finish that row, I move down to the next row in the middle and do the same thing.

— Margaret Jarrett, Anderson, IN

❖ To begin, I pull my thread up one stitch-length away from my starting point and tug to bury the knot. I start with a tiny backstitch and continue. To end, I tie two small knots, insert my needle at my last stitch, coming out about one inch away, and tug to bury the knots. Then I clip the thread.

— Faye Meyers, San Jose, CA

❖ I begin with a knot pulled through into the batting and end with tunneling back through the stitches.

— Rosie Mutter, Bechtelsville, PA

❖ I start with a small quilter's knot and insert my needle into the fabric about a half inch away from my starting point, having the point of the needle emerge on the quilting line. I pop the knot into the batting and begin quilting. I end by knotting and pulling the knot down into the last stitch, then come out a half inch away, leaving a long tail. Finally, I clip the thread.

— Vanya G. Neer, Bradenton, FL

❖ I use the no-knot method. I put the needle in, facing where I want to start, and sew back over the thread. To end, I make a knot close to the surface, put the needle in the fabric heading back to the stitches that I've made, but only through the batting. I come up through a stitch an inch or so away, I go back down and through the batting to the last stitch, then bring it up and out.

— Joy Rubenstein-Moir, Holtsville, NY

❖ I begin quilting by tying a knot in my thread, then slipping the needle into the batting and popping the knot through the top layer. I end by taking a stitch, bringing my needle up in a seam, then putting my needle back in the seam line, bringing it back up an inch away. I end by cutting the thread.

— Connee Sager, Tucson, AZ

❖ To begin, I knot the thread and sink the knot into the batting with the tail just under the section I'm about to quilt. My first few stitches anchor the tail. To end, I wrap the thread around the needle and work the knot to about a half inch from the quilt top. I then sink the knot into the batting.

— Marilyn Bloom Wallace, Alfred, ME

❖ I knot my thread and pull the knot through (between the top and back of the quilt), about an inch from where I intend to start quilting. When ending, I take about three stitches backward, exactly on top of the last ones I quilted.

— Mary Jane Musser, Manheim, PA

❖ I begin with a small knot and pop it into the batting. To end, I take one backstitch, having the point of the needle emerge to the side, one or two inches away from the previous quilting. I make a small knot close to the fabric and run my needle under a quilting stitch, emerging on the other side of the quilting. I repeat that two more times.

— Sherri Driver, Englewood, CO

❖ I begin by pulling a knot through the top side and taking a backstitch. To end, I make three tiny knots (by wrapping the thread once around the needle) and pull the knots back into the quilt. These knots run back along the lines of the quilted stitches.

— Sherry Carroll, Delta, PA

❖ I knot at the beginning and the end. If I scratch the fabric as I pull the knot, it goes through more easily.

— Mary F. Martin, Hagerstown, MD

❖   I start quilting in the center of the quilt, but do not tie off the thread when I reach the edge of my hoop. The tail of thread can be left and I can re-thread it for continued quilting when I've moved the hoop.

— Sharron Van Meter, St. Charles, MO

❖   When doing machine-quilting, I begin and end by reducing the stitch length to zero and then taking a couple of stitches.

— Sue Dieringer-Boyer, Walkersville, MD

❖   I start about 10 to 12 needles, depending on my design, then I quilt as far as I can reach and leave the needle there, picking it up again when I roll the quilt in the frame.

— Elaine W. Good, Lititz, PA

❖   To end, I make a small knot and pull it through the fabric to bury it in the batting. I reinsert the needle exactly where it came out after tugging the knot. I push it through the batting about an inch. The point emerges, but before the eye comes out, I turn the needle in the batting and push it again (against the point), having the eye emerge. I pull the needle out (eye first) and clip the thread. This leaves a longer tail in the batting.

— Mary M. Weimer, Clinton, MD

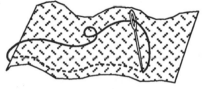

❖   If I have a long, continuous design, I take a very long thread, pull it halfway through the fabric, and quilt in one direction.

Then I thread the other end and stitch the other way. I backstitch at both ends.

— Lee Ann Hazlett, Freeport, IL

❖   I start a line of quilting by popping the knot through the top layer and hiding it in the batting. I end a section by weaving the thread through the batting under a few lines of quilting stitches and clipping the tail close to the quilt's surface.

— Terry Festa, Clinton, CT

❖   I begin by coming up from the back, pulling my knot through so that it stays in the middle; then I backstitch and begin quilting. To end, I wrap my thread around the needle twice, go down through the top, and come out as far away as the needle will push through, leaving the tail buried in the batting.

— Susan Campbell, Flint, TX

❖   I end a line of quilting differently, depending on my location. If I'm close to a seam line, I make a tiny stitch through the top and batt only and run my needle away from the quilting line to come out in the seam line.

I put the needle in the same hole it came out, go about an inch ahead in the batt, and resurface into the seam line. I do this once more, then cut the thread close to the quilt top. The thread pulls back into the batt. (All these stitches are through the top and batt only.)

If I end "out in the open spaces," I insert the needle close beside the last stitch taken and push it into the batt about an inch or so away. I then bring the needle (tip only) out of the quilt top, turn the needle in another direction in the batt (eye first), and bring the needle completely out of the top. I cut the thread close to the quilt top, and the thread buries itself in the batt.

— Ginny Barr, Jackson, OH

❖ I begin with a fine knot that I can pull through to the batting and anchor it by splitting the thread with my needle on the initial stitch. I end by weaving the needle back through the completed stitching.

— Susan W. Caccamise, Edgewater, MD

❖ I knot the end of my thread and pull the knot from the bottom into the batting to begin. I tug a little to bury the knot. When I'm ready to end, I draw the needle all the way through the top. Then I wrap the thread two or three times around the point, return the needle as close to the last stitch as possible, and pull it through to bury the knot.

— Lynn Parker, Taylors, SC

❖ Because my ending knots sometimes pop back to the surface, I now end by putting the needle in alongside several just-completed stitches. I bring most of the needle out, but I leave the eye in and, turning the needle, push the eye underneath stitches to the opposite side of the quilting line. This time the eye comes out but not the point. I push the point under another stitch and back to the other side. The thread is now wrapped around my stitches, and the end is long enough that, even with lots of wear, it won't work out. This also works well when I need to move from one quilting area to another and the distance is more than a needle's length.

— Sissy Anderson, Lithonia, GA

❖ I begin with a knot and end with a knot and pull both inside. If I still have a long thread, I knot it for the next section before I cut it off. Then I cut between the two knots (one buried and one on top). That practice saves time and frustration.

I quilt until I have only a little thread in the needle. I backtrack under two or three stitches. Then I loop the thread around a stitch and pull the thread into the batting and cut off what's left.

— Roberta S. Bennsky, Annapolis, MD

❖ I knot the thread and leave a 3/8-inch tail. I bury the needle in the fabric from left to right and come up with the tail buried, then quilt over it from right to left. To end, I knot the thread at the last stitch and pull the knot and thread under the batting, leaving a length of thread as long as the needle will allow.

— Nolen Provenzano, North Potomac, MD

❖ After hiding the knot between the layers, I am careful not to pull my first few stitches snug, to keep the knot from showing its ugly head on the backside.

— Johnette Zwolinski Shoberg, Globe, AZ

❖ I do not like to knot the thread, because I think it makes a hole when it is pulled through the fabric. I start by inserting the needle about one inch from where I am going to start quilting and pull the needle carefully up, leaving a tail. I backstitch two times and then start quilting. I use this same method at the end by backstitching a couple of times, then pulling the needle out about one inch further along, and finally snipping the beginning and end threads off. I have done all of my quilts this way, and the quilting does not come out when the quilts are washed.

— Virginia L. Fry, Fulton, MD

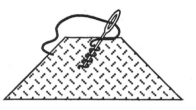

❖ I wrap my needle about four times (like for a French knot) and slip the thread down over my needle to make the knot. Then I pop this from the back side of the quilt into the batting. To end, I wrap my needle about four times again, go back in the hole of my last stitch and pop this knot into the batting.

— Rosalee Crawford, Alba, TX

❖ I pull a knot through to the middle layer to start quilting. To end, I take one backstitch, and then take another small stitch, having the point of the needle emerge at the end of the last stitch.

With the eye of the needle still in the fabric, I wrap the thread just used in the fabric around to the right side of the needle and under the point. I bring thread from the eye of the needle to the left of the needle and under the point. The threads cross under the needle. Then I pull the needle carefully through. This makes a small knot at the end of the stitch. I bury the end of the thread by taking a stitch into the batting layer. I let the needle emerge and clip the thread.

— Shirlee Hugger, Martha's Vineyard Island, MA

❖ When machine-quilting, I begin by pulling the bobbin thread up to the top and then take both the top and bobbin threads to the back of the presser foot. I take three tiny stitches with my machine on the "satin stitch" setting, then dial my machine up to the desired stitch length and begin quilting. I finish off the same way. If I am doing "free motion" quilting, I also start out by pulling the bobbin thread up to the top and take three tiny stitches before beginning to quilt. When I am finished, I bury the top threads and the bobbin threads in the batting.

— Katy J. Widger, Los Lunas, NM

Recording yards of quilting thread

❖ I record the amount of quilting thread in a quilt by first using one spool with 250 yards, then measuring the rest in lengths of 10 or 20 yards at a time.

— Elizabeth Chupp, Arthur, IL

❖ First, I use one spool of 250 yards. For the rest, I wrap thread around a yardstick, 40 or 50 yards at a time, then put it back on the spool.

— Judy Miller, Hutchinson, KS

❖ I cut all quilting thread in one-foot lengths. Each time I cut a length, I make a mark on a 3 inch x 5 inch index card. When the quilt is finished, I count the marks and divide by three to determine the yards I used.

— Barbara J. Swartz, Mercer, PA

❖ I measure thread by the yard and then pin the cut threads on the quilt. I just pull a new thread when I need one.

— Mrs. Vernon Kennel, Atglen, PA

❖ I measure a 50-yard length with a yardstick and roll it back onto an empty spool.

— Rosie Mutter, Bechtelsville, PA

❖ I wrap thread around the length of a yardstick and record the number of rounds on a piece of masking tape on the yardstick (one round equals two yards).

— Mary Jane Musser, Manheim, PA

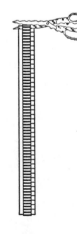

❖ Several years ago when my mother-in-law and we girls made a quilt to sell, we needed to keep track of the number of yards of quilting thread we used. We each threaded a number of needles with four feet of thread in each one. We each recorded the number of needles we threaded, and we used only our own needles. When the quilt was finished, we had a record of how much quilting thread we had used.

— Ilene Bontrager, Arlington, KS

❖ I measure 50 or 100 yards by wrapping the thread around a yardstick (the long way) and then cutting both ends so I have one-yard pieces.

— Grace S. Miller, Mount Joy, PA

❖ I fasten two C-clamps to my quilt frame, exactly 36 inches apart. I tie the end of the thread to one of the clamps and make loops around both clamps, counting two yards for each loop. I cut all the threads at each of the clamps and place them into an open magazine, with the ends of the thread coming out of the top and bottom of the magazine. Then I close the magazine. I record the number of yards and the date. I place the magazine within easy reach so I can pull out one thread as I need it.

— Edna Nisly, Partridge, KS

❖ When I thread my needle, I use about 14 to 16 inches at a time. That lasts approximately five to seven minutes, depending, of course, upon the intricacy of the quilting designs. Considering that I waste from two to four inches of thread at the end of each piece of thread, I use about 12 inches of thread for sewing every six minutes. By calculating the time I spend quilting each quilt, I get a fairly accurate estimate of the amount of thread I use on each quilt.

— U. Khin, Rocky Ridge, MD

❖ To keep a record of how many yards of thread I use, I thread 20 needles, each with 18 inches of thread. When I've emptied all the needles, I know I've used 10 yards of thread.

— Theresa Lepert, Schellsburg, PA

❖ I always use more than one full spool, so I only measure on the second spool, measuring off two yards at a time. A long thread saves both time and thread.

— Rosa Nisly, Hutchinson, KS

❖ I put a safety pin in the corner of the quilt for each new spool of thread I use.

— Coleen Swettman, Vancouver, WA

❖ I have a 2-inch x 2-inch x 40-inch board with two small nails on the top side, a yard apart. I wrap my thread around those nails, which allows me to keep track of the yards of thread I use.

— Ida Hilty, Berne, IN

❖ My grandmother taught me to keep a pad of paper and pencil on top of my quilt in progress and make a tally mark each time I thread a needle. This allows me to calculate how much thread I used and how much time I spent on the project.

— Barbara Riley, Elk Grove, CA

❖ Being a beginner at quilting, I keep records on everything I do in making a quilt! I save the spools until I have the project finished. Then I add the information to the sheet in my notebook about that particular project. Since I usually have more than one thing going at the same time, I use colored dot stickers to mark the spools for different projects.

— Lois C. Ruiz, Murray, KY

Making knots

❖ I thread my needle while the thread is still on the spool, and do not cut the thread until I make my knot. To form the knot, I slide my finger down the length of thread I want to use. I wrap the thread around the end of my finger two or three times. I then run the needle under the loops from the base of my fingernail to my fingertip, pulling the entire length of the thread through the loops. This forms a small knot, and I clip the thread just below the knot.

— Kay Jackson, Harrison, AR

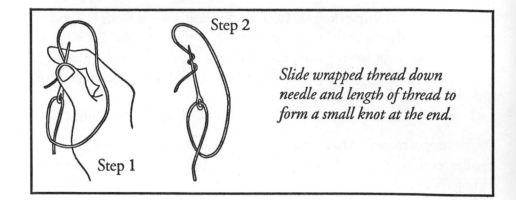

Step 2

Slide wrapped thread down needle and length of thread to form a small knot at the end.

Step 1

❖ To make a small knot for quilting, I thread my needle, then bring the long end of the thread up to the needle, laying it parallel to the needle with the end beside the needle's eye I pinch the end of the thread against the needle with my right hand. With my left hand, I wrap the thread two or three times around the pointed end of the needle. I grasp the wrapped needle with my left hand and pull the pointed end of the needle with my right hand, sliding the wrapped thread down over the length of thread to form a small knot at the end. The number of wraps around the needle determines the size of the knot.

— Rosie Mutter, Bechtelsville, PA

Additional tips

❖ If I must eat chocolate while quilting, I eat M & M's!

— Joy Rubenstein-Moir, Holtsville, NY

❖ I start quilting in the middle of the quilt and work towards one long end, then towards the other end. Next I work from the middle of one side, ending up in each corner, and then I do the same on the other side.

— Helen R. Altherr, Jackson, OH

❖ I keep a small paper bag with my quilting supply box to gather the small pieces of thread.

— Mary Ruth Williams, Dahinda, IL

❖ A quilt that never gets done is no fun; therefore, I find scheduling helps me. I usually quilt the border on all four sides before I start rolling in. I also roll the ends instead of the sides, making it a shorter distance to quilt. I can usually attain my goal — to roll after four hours of quilting — the amount of time I usually quilt per day.

— Judy Miller, Hutchinson, KS

❖ My husband built a simple lamp stand using a 2 x 2 set on two crossboards for feet. My long-arm drafting light has a bolt which extends about two inches. He modified this bolt and holder and inserted the cup portion into the top of the 2 x 2 stand (36 inches high). The bolt fits into

the cup and I have a portable light that can be placed exactly where I need it.

— Carol Findling, Beatrice, NE

❖ On one bed-size quilt for our mountain cabin, I used polyester batting and crosshatched every 10 inches, then finished the edges. The quilt is able to be used, but I'm now adding crosshatching every inch. I always have that project to work on at the cabin!

— Barbie Mockenhaupt, Palmdale, CA

❖ I baste my projects well, using an "ugly" color of thread. I am more inclined to work on the project knowing I am removing the "ugly" thread as I go. The more basting in the quilt, the better the quilt will be (less shifting), and the more "strings" there are to remove (creating tiny "goals" to achieve).

— Lela Ann Schneider, Boise, ID

❖ I hate basting, but here is a great shortcut. Pin the top, batting and backing together as usual. I baste in a grid with the rows of stitching four inches apart, using a milliner's needle. I start by placing the thread spool in the center of the quilt. I'm right-handed so I baste on the left first, but this can be reversed if you prefer. Keeping the spool lying down in the center of the quilt, thread the needle. Baste from the center to the left (or right) edge. Take two backstitches and remove the needle. Take the spool and unroll it so the thread is six inches past the other edge of the quilt. Cut the thread at that point. Thread the needle. Baste this side as above. Baste the entire quilt in this method. I alternate horizontal and vertical rows.

I like to use yellow for basting thread, because it can be seen against white as well as darks.

— Joy Rubenstein-Moir, Holtsville, NY

❖ I use a baby's nail scissors to clip threads when I quilt. The blunt end will not puncture the quilt.

— Connee Sager, Tucson, AZ

❖ I find quilting at a large quilting frame is less tiring when I use an office chair with adjustable height, swivels and casters that allow me to move along the side of the quilt. I roll the sides of the quilt in often so I need not reach in so far. I end up with neater work and I'm less tired.

— Edna Nisly, Partridge, KS

❖ My chair is important for quilting. I use an adjustable secretary's chair which is on rollers.

— Violette Denney, Carrollton, GA

❖ I've learned never to quilt when I'm under stress. If I do, I have to take that section out the next day because the stitches are too tight. Quilting should be a pleasure.

— Kaye Schnell, Falmouth, MA

❖ Quiltmaking amplifies my frustration or my contentment. If I am unsettled in my life, it is usually a good idea for me not to start a new project. If I return to an old one, I can lose myself in it, rather than facing a million decisions I am not able to make at the time.

— Linda Franklin, Camas, WA

❖ I like to quilt the longest section of quilting possible without cutting my thread. Having my hands clean keeps the needle from sticking and pushing hard. I always use glazed quilting thread. It sure reduces knots and tangles and seldom tears.

— Mabel Rissler, Barnett, MO

❖ My mother always said, "You're not a good quilter until you can quilt a circle without stopping!" Now if you think about that, that's good advice, because in order to quilt a circle, you must move your needle at every angle possible.

— Grace S. Miller, Mount Joy, PA

❖ By using longer thread, I can make more time. I don't need to knot, cut thread and start again. I also put in a dozen stitches or more before I pull the thread through.

— Elaine Nolt, Versailles, MO

❖ I try not to use too long a thread so that my stitches will be more uniform.

— Lois C. Ruiz, Murray, KY

❖ To make my quilting as continuous as possible, I often back my needle through to reach another line. When I reach the end of a line, I insert the needle and emerge a distance away in the direction I want to go. I do not pull the needle completely out, but point the eye end toward the goal. I repeat as often as necessary, emerging at the line I want to do next. A tiny backstitch anchors the thread and prevents my pulling the thread too tightly. I think a quilt is strongest if the threads are as long as possible.

— Elaine W. Good, Lititz, PA

❖ To go from one section of quilting to another, I "walk the needle." To do this, I push the needle in as if I were going to make a stitch, but I don't go through the quilt back. Instead, I push the needle in three-quarters of the way, then flip it, so that I am then pushing the pointed end. I keep flipping the needle along inside the quilt until I reach the spot I want to get to.

— Joanne Kennedy, Plattsburgh, NY

❖ When piecing or quilting a variety of colors together, I choose light gray-colored thread. The gray takes on the hue of whatever color it is against. For dark colors, I choose dark gray thread.

— Karel Fisher, New Holland, PA

❖ I find that making miniature quilts is a good way to make many quilts in a year that are affordable — both in time and money. I've learned that quilts which are the most complicated to make may not be the prettiest, and that blocks which are very simple to make can look complicated, depending upon the way they are set or the blocks that sit next to them. Creative ways of setting blocks can make a few blocks go a long way.

— Susan Campbell, Flint, TX

I like to quilt one stitch at a time (but not stab stitch). I think the stitches are prettier and go deeper into the fabric layers, instead of just lying there, kind of flat-looking!

— Susan Campbell, Flint, TX

❖ I prefer solid colors in my hand-quilted work to enhance the sculpturing effect of the quilted pattern.

— Johnette Zwolinski Shoberg, Globe, AZ

❖ When I wanted to improve my stitches and have more stitches to the inch, I found it helpful to use a needle a size smaller than I was using previously.

— Judy Miller, Hutchinson, KS

❖ The smaller the needle, #10 or #9, the smaller the stitches.

— Marilyn Stephens, St. Marys, ON

❖ I use a rolling lint-remover to get rid of loose threads. I go over the back of the quilt carefully and remove all threads before I sandwich the layers for quilting. Removing threads at this point is far less time-consuming than trying to pick them out (if they shadow through) after the quilting is completed.

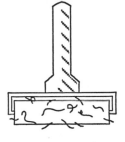

— Ann Reimer, Beatrice, NE

❖ If I cannot find quilting thread to match the fabric, I've found it works to dip a spool of regular matching thread in melted paraffin, then let it cool and dry before I use it. I like this better than running the thread over bee's wax because the paraffin does not leave a wax residue.

— Irma Harder, Mountain Lake, MN

❖ The more quilting put into a quilt, the lighter the quilt feels.

If I quilt every day, even if only for half an hour, I quilt better and faster than when I do it only occasionally.

— Rachel Tamm, Allentown, PA

❖ I aim for even stitches. They get smaller as I practice. When I haven't quilted for a while, it takes a little time for me to regain the technique. During those times, I quilt on something "non-critical," until I'm comfortably back into the swing of things. Background music and/or pretty views and good company make quilting especially pleasant.

— Nina Lord, Annapolis, MD

❖ I begin at an inconspicuous place (in the ditch, etc.) until I have re-established my needling rhythm. That way my first awkward (and maybe uneven) stitches don't show as much.

— Barbara N. Neff, Cypress, CA

❖ When quilting in a frame, or otherwise as well, I always quilt straight lines first.

— E. Ann Warkentin, Enid, OK

❖ Quilting is much easier and smaller stitches are more possible with thin batting.

— Lisa Tizzoni, Olyphant, PA

❖ I tie my scissors and needle puller to a ribbon and attach the ribbon onto my frame.

— Donna Barnitz, Rio Rancho, NM

❖ A nail hammered into the frame holds my spool of thread.

— Barbie Mockenhaupt, Palmdale, CA

❖ I safety-pin a scrap of bright fabric to the place where I've stopped quilting. That eliminates wasting time searching for where I ended.

— Harriet S. Meade, Clinton, CT

❖ I enter each quilt's progress in a journal, recording my daily work. I may have four or five projects going at a time. I record design problems, progress, my feelings about a piece, changes, batting type and the amount of time I spent each day I worked. I do this for my own curiosity and as a historical record. Also, when my children were little, I often felt I hadn't accomplished anything at the end of the week. A review of my journal revealed I had accomplished more than I realized!

— Barbara Tone Lister, Highlands Ranch, CO

❖ One of the most important things for me is to keep a diary of all my projects. It helps me to be able to check back on machine settings or techniques that I used successfully in past projects. I always add a recommendation to my notes, so that if I don't like a particular aspect of a project, I might avoid it in the future.

— Janice Muller, Derwood, MD

❖ I keep a small notebook in which I note when I work on a quilt — the date and time and what was going on in the news. It makes interesting reading, and I know how much time I actually spent on a quilt.

— Donna Barnitz, Rio Rancho, NM

❖ Quilting in public is a wonderful way to get conversations started with strangers. I find it therapeutic and it gives me a sense of carrying on our traditions and history. Quilting an old top makes me feel as if I'm joining hands with a sister from the past.

— Lynn Crowe, Anderson, IN

Sore fingers

Prevention

❖ I try to prevent my hands from becoming too dry. When they're dry, they become injured more quickly and heal more slowly.

— Joyce Trueblood, Cromwell, CT

❖ I use a thimble to push the needle and rubber finger cots to pull it.

— Jacqueline E. Deininger, Bethlehem, PA

❖ I cut a length of adhesive tape and in the center build a three or four-layer square of the same tape. I place that thick section on my finger where the needle hits underneath the quilt. It protects my finger, yet I can feel the point of the needle when it comes through the layers of the quilt so that I can do eight to 10 stitches per inch.

I keep a Gingher snippers on a ribbon around my neck and attach the tape "protector" to it when I'm not quilting. Also on my ribbon (or chain) is my needle case, a spool of quilting thread and my thimble cage. All my necessary tools are always handy.

— Carol Findling, Beatrice, NE

❖ I try to quilt some every week. It keeps my finger tough and forms a callus on the tip.

— Nancy Wagner Graves, Manhattan, KS

❖ I find my fingers get less sore if I quilt only an hour or so at a time.

— Sharon Heidi, Mt. Lake, MN

❖ I use a thimble on the third finger of both hands.

— Margaret Jarrett, Anderson, IN

❖ I alternate the fingers that I prick underneath the quilt. I apply a dab of Mycitracin on the sore ones at bedtime. By the next day, they are all better.

— Rosalie W. Keegan, Enfield, CT

❖ I never wash dishes without rubber gloves. If I do, my callus softens up, and that's not good.

— Shan D. Lear, Middleton, MA

❖ I don't do dishes (or water sports) before quilting. Water softens the skin.

— Mary Seielstad, Schenectady, NY

❖ The warm water bath from washing dishes is the best thing I've found to prevent sore fingers, although in today's world of electric machines, I always draw groans over that statement!

— Doris Morelock, Alexandria, VA

❖ I never quilt with wet hands. If I plan to quilt after washing dishes, I wear rubber gloves.

— Barbara Riley, Elk Grove, CA

❖ I use small pieces of black electrical tape on the fingers that are underneath the quilt. The tape is sturdy but not bulky like leather.

— Marjorie Mills, Bethesda, MD

❖ I soak my fingers in peroxide and buff them with an emery board when I finish quilting. I cannot quilt a beautiful stitch without the needle touching my fingers underneath the quilt.

— Lou Ann Philpot, Murray, KS

❖ I soak my sore fingers in Listerine mouthwash solution for a couple of minutes twice a day.

If there are rough spots on my fingers due to needle pricks, I smooth them out with a nail file. I find the action quite healing and comfortable, and then I'm ready for quilting again.

— U Khin, Rocky Ridge, MD

❖ I paint my fingers with New Skin, an over-the-counter liquid "Band-Aid" that can be purchased at a drugstore.

— Freda Gail Stern, Dallas, TX

❖ I buy paper tape at the drugstore. It looks like a small Band-Aid but isn't slick like one. It acts like an extra layer of skin.

— Bonnie Zabzdyr, Wright City, MO

❖ I limit the amount of time I spend at each quilting session. If my hands begin to feel uncomfortable, I do something else for a few hours. I try to schedule my time, so I don't have to do a lot at the last minute when there is a deadline.

— Phyllis A. Kroggel, Tucson, AZ

❖ I wrap masking tape around my finger.

— Margaret Morris, Middle Village, NY

❖ I collect old leather gloves and cut the tips off the fingers. The tips fit well and save my fingers.

— Helen L. Anderson, Titusville, NJ

❖ I wear a leather thimble that covers as far as the second joint on my finger, since I always seem to slip and stab myself there.

— Vicki Krausz, Denver, CO

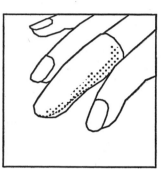

❖ My thumbnail breaks along the side from gripping the needle to pull it through. If I use a finger cot on my thumb, I don't have to press as hard, and it saves my thumb. I also cut a piece of leather from an old work glove and put a couple of tiny darts in it so it fits the surface of my thumb (on the side opposite the nail). Then I slip it inside the finger cot for "pushing."

— Julie McKenzie, Punxsutawney, PA

❖ I buy a thimble which is a little larger than my finger and tape my finger with a Band-Aid. I remove the Band-Aid very carefully so that it holds the mold of my finger, then insert it into the thimble. (I trim off any excess Band-Aid that extends outside the thimble.) It gives me padding, so that my finger is not constantly rubbing against the metal part of my thimble, and protects my long fingernail.

— Pearl Mok, Los Angeles, CA

❖ DMC and Piecemaker needles make my fingers less sore than some brands of needles.

— Edna Nisly, Partridge, KS

❖ I use surgical tape on the fingers that I have under the quilt and take turns between the two fingers. When one gets sore, I tape it, and it stays out of the way so I can use the other one. DMC needles also help.

— Mrs. Ora C. Nisly, Hutchinson, KS

❖ I dip my fingers in rubbing alcohol, both before I start to quilt and when I stop.

— Fannie Troyer, Mt. Hope, OH

❖ I paint my fingertips with clear nail polish before I start to quilt.

— Esther S. Martin, Ephrata, PA

❖ On my underside hand, I allow the needle to touch my fingernail instead of my finger.

— Ruth Cottrell, Irvin, TX

❖ I place a Band-Aid around my ring finger where the rim from the thimble presses.

— Mary Jane Musser, Manheim, PA

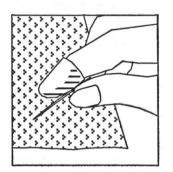

❖ I use a thimble on my index finger and a leather thimble with a large metal guard for my thumb. It takes a while to adjust to all this paraphernalia, but my fingers thank me.

— Kay Hineman, Rushville, IN

❖ I sometimes use rubber fingers like office people and bank tellers use. They are light enough that I can still feel the needle coming through, but thick enough to provide a barrier against needle pricks.

— Susan Ketcherside, St. Charles, MO

❖ My mom taught me to let the needle go between my index and middle fingers under the quilt. I soon learned to feel when the needle pierced the lining, so that I could immediately let the thumb with the needle on the top hand bring it back up. I've had no blood on my quilts. Thanks, Mom!

— Betty Hutchinson, St. Charles, MO

❖ I use two thimbles. On my underneath hand, I use an "Ivory"-type thimble — the kind used for scrimshaw. It has a perfectly smooth flat top and no markings.

— Debra Botelho Zeida, Waguoit, MA

❖ I use two leather fingers — the tip of an old one inside a new one, and sometimes even a Band-Aid under that.

— Harriet S. Meade, Clinton, CT

❖ I soak my fingertips in chlorine bleach. It makes them tough.

— Loyce Wood Sage, Gallup, NM

❖ I wrap my underneath finger with surgical paper adhesive. Sometimes I use Coban — 3M surgical tape that adheres to itself. It protects sore fingers, yet allows me to feel the needle.

— Doris Amiss Rebey, Hyattsville, MD

❖ I put Aloe Vera salve on my fingers when I stop quilting for the day, and again at night upon retiring to keep my fingers soft. I find DMC needles to be more blunt and that is very helpful.

— Judy Miller, Hutchinson, KS

❖ A plastic, curved guitar pick that slides along my underside finger helps keep it from getting sore. A pick costs between 50 cents and a dollar at most music stores, versus two to three dollars for a finger guard at the local quilt store.

— Lynn Parker, Taylors, SC

❖ I use Dermiclear tape, a Johnson & Johnson product. Band-Aids make my needle sticky.

— Alma Mullet, Walnut Creek, OH

❖ I use moleskin on spots on my fingers that I know will get sore.

— Betty Richards, Rapid City, SD

❖ I use Micropore tape on my thumbs.

— Sharon L. Leali, Jackson, OH

❖ Pressing fingertips in alum (available from any drugstore) helps to toughen fingertip calluses.

— Ann Reimer, Beatrice, NE

❖ I use wide adhesive tape to wrap my left middle finger and left thumb. I use a thimble on my right middle finger.

— Donna Jean Boyce, Long Beach, CA

❖ I place plastic shields inside a leather thimble for my thumb when I quilt away from myself. I use a metal thimble with a ridge on my middle finger and white bandage tape on my underneath forefinger. The tape grips the needle and allows me to feel, but it doesn't permit the needle to pierce my skin.

— Lela Ann Schneider, Boise, ID

❖ When I finish quilting, I wash my hands in warm water and rub them with turpentine. Then they are ready for the next time.

— Zelda Lynch, San Augustine, TX

❖ I massage the underside finger vigorously before a quilting session.

— Quilting Friends, Richmond, IN

❖ I work slowly, and, believe it or not, this helps a great deal.

— Ann Leatz, Victorville, CA

❖ I quilt one stitch at a time, pushing the needle down and then pulling the needle up, while holding the needle without a thimble and with the quilt in a frame. No sore fingers!

— Violette Denney, Carrollton, GA

❖ When I have had a break between quilting times, I build up quilting time slowly and wait for my calluses to develop. It usually takes no longer than three days.

— Carol Kelley, Carrollton, GA

❖ I allow a callus to develop on the finger I use underneath the quilt. And I put only enough pressure on the needle to push it through to the other edge of the quilt sandwich until I touch the underneath finger.

— Elaine Untracht Pawelko, Jamesburg, NJ

❖ For me, the size of the needle makes a difference. The points of the #9 and #10 are sharper.

— Erma Landis, Sterling, IL

❖ I use a thimble and a rubber secretary finger on my index finger. This really helps me pull the needle through.

— Judy Mullen, Manieca, CA

❖ I use a leather thimble on my "pusher" finger and a metal "Aunt Becky's" on my underneath finger. This is a bent piece of metal that goes over the finger. The needle comes straight down through the quilt, glances off the "Aunt Becky's" and goes back up through the quilt.

— Irene J. Dewar, Pickering, ON

❖ I purchase white plumber's tape at the hardware store for my fingers. It is pliable, thick, can be cut into small pieces, and can be reused. It is also inexpensive compared to some tapes on the market for quilters, and a roll lasts a long time.

— Lois C. Ruiz, Murray, KY

Cures

❖ I put vitamin A and D ointment on my fingers at bedtime and BenGay or Muscle Rub at the base of my thumb near the wrist.

— Jacqueline E. Deininger, Bethlehem, PA

❖ If I do get sore fingers, I use Chap Stick on them overnight. It helps!

— Margaret Jarrett, Anderson, IN

❖ I use a Band-Aid with Vick's salve left on overnight to take away the throbbing.

— Eleanor Larson, Glen Lyon, PA

❖ Sometimes I just have to resort to another hobby for a short time!

— Doris McCloskey, Annapolis, MD

❖ Soaking my fingers for a few minutes in a mixture of water and hydrogen peroxide takes the sting out of them.

— Faye Meyers, San Jose, CA

❖ An antibiotic ointment such as Neosporin or Bacitracin really takes out the soreness. Doing dishes in hot soapy water also helps.

— Mary Puskar, Forest Hill, MD

❖ I put White's A and D Ointment on the sore area and then lightly bandage it. If it's a fingertip, I like to use a shaped bandage. Sore spots usually heal in 24 hours.

— Connee Sager, Tucson, AZ

❖ I buy Bag Balm from our farm supply store. A big container doesn't cost any more than a tiny container in a quilting store. Some of my friends bought some from me.

— Tommie Bandy Freeman, Carrollton, GA

❖ When I find my hands very dry from working with fabric all day, I put Bag Balm all over my hands and then wear cotton gloves to sleep. By the next day or two, my hands look great.

— Sue Seeley, New Bern, NC

❖ For hard surfaces on my skin, I use Bag Balm. It softens my skin in a couple of days.

More often I have a split in the skin, and for that I use Sayman Salve First Aid cream. It has camphor in it which takes out soreness overnight. It's been a family remedy for years.

— Bonnie Zabzdyr, Wright City, MO

❖ I massage Neutrogena or Bag Balm into my fingertips. Both help, but Neutrogena smells better.

— Barbara Waymire, Wichita, KS

❖ After I'm finished quilting, I dunk my fingers in alcohol. It really helps heal and toughen fingers.

— Charlotte L. Fry, St. Charles, MO

❖ I use Aloe Vera lotion. It's also got vitamin E in it, and the combination seems to heal very quickly.

— Mary Seielstad, Schenectady, NY

❖ I use Silvedene cream for finger pricks.

— Charmaine Caesar, Lancaster, PA

❖ I use Campho-Phenique liquid. I rub it on my sore fingers in the evening when I go to bed. It helps!

— Ida Schrock, Haven, KS

❖ I use Eucerin cream to keep my skin soft.

— Linda Hampton Schiffer, Columbia, MD

❖ I soak my fingers in magnesium salts and warm water.

— Laura Barrus Bishop, Boerne, TX

❖ I use vitamin E liquid or prick a vitamin E capsule with a pin, squeeze and apply it on my sore finger. It helps heal and also smooths the rough skin.

— Judi Manos, West Islip, NY

❖ Avon Rich Moisture Hand and Nail Cream is the best I've ever used.

— Mrs. Vernon Kennel, Atglen, PA

❖ I use lots of hand cream, Nivea or Curel.

— Pearl Dorn, Fresh Meadows, NY

❖ If my fingers are really sore, I put some fingernail polish remover on them. It sounds bad, but it works!

— Vicki Jones, Rushville, IN

❖ Sheep and Undertakers! Apply Lanolin (sheep fat available from a druggist) at bedtime and wear white cotton "undertaker" gloves over your hands to bed. The soreness usually heals overnight.

— Kelly Wagoner, Albuquerque, NM

❖ I like Revlon's Professional Cuticle Massage Night Cream.

— Brenda Shaw-Nielsen, Washington, DC

❖ I wash dishes three times daily.

— Mary Ann Mazur, Dublin, OH

Sore fingers

❖ I soak my fingers in hot water for a few minutes.

— Inez Chen, Ft. Washington, MD

❖ I coat my sore fingers well with after-shave lotion.

— L. Jean Moore, Anderson, IN

❖ I apply aloe vera juice many times a day. At night I put a piece of aloe vera plant directly on the sore and cover it with tape.

— J. Newman, St. Marys, ON

❖ Neosporin helps heal very quickly. For especially callused and pricked fingers that catch and snag on everything, a pumice stone rubbed softly but firmly across the rough spots works wonders.

— Cheri Ruzich, Live Oak, CA

❖ I sometimes use Cortizone cream.

— Fran Lange, Orange Beach, AL

❖ Neutrogena Norwegian Formula Fragrance-Free Hand Cream has been like magic for me; it returns chapped and bleeding hands to normal in two days!

— Abby Breslaw Shipper, Hartsdale, NY

❖ Rub Vaseline into your hands and cover them (socks work well) overnight.

— Lela Ann Schneider, Boise, ID

❖ I use Sulfa Urea cream which I get at veterinary supply stores. It is used for cows' udders but works well for fingers, rough heels or fingers that split in cold weather.

— Jean Turner, Williams Lake, BC

❖ I wash my hands frequently with soap and warm water and try to soak in warm water for 15 minutes several times a day. I apply Neosporin or another antibiotic to any breaks in my skin.

— Nina Lord, Annapolis, MD

❖ I wash my hands well, rinse them with peroxide, and use a liberal amount of Neutrogena Unscented Hand Cream at bedtime.

— Jeannine Dougherty, Tyler, TX

❖ I soak in powdered alum water.

— Mildred Duley, Yates City, IL

❖ I use one 13-ounce container of plain petroleum jelly, five to six teaspoons of medicinal turpentine (the label reads "oil turpentine"), and a scant teaspoon of oil of wintergreen. I warm the petroleum jelly in a pan of warm water over low heat and stir in the other two ingredients. I save tiny jars (baby food, pimento and jelly samples) and fill them with the balm.

— Jennifer Asbury

❖ I use Vicks Vapo-Rub when I go to bed at night, and my fingers are restored by morning! This is an excellent remedy for chapped hands, too!

— Ellen Swanson, Hamilton, VA

❖ I use Bag Balm or our quilter's hand cream which is: equal parts Bacitracin, A&D Ointment and Revlon Hand and Body Lotion. I mix it well and keep it handy to use after washing my hands and at night.

— Carolee Kidd, Albuquerque, NM

❖ I use brown vinegar applied with a cotton ball to sore fingers.

— Patty Miller, Charles City, IA

❖ I use Vaseline every night.

— Marlys Klein, Scarsdale, NY

❖ I use Bag Balm or Watkins Salve.

— Thelma A. Stein, Tavares, FL

❖ I exercise my hands by making a fist, then extending my fingers. I repeat this several times, then gently shake my hands.

— Jean Livell, Dallas, TX

❖ To prevent tendonitis or repetitive motion syndrome, I take breaks and play piano (otherwise known as cross-training)!

— Elaine W. Good, Lititz, PA

❖ Take a day off and read the latest quilt book or go buy more fabric!

— Ann Govinlock, Alexander, NY

Needles and thimbles

Choosing a thimble

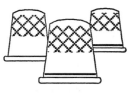

❖ I have different size thimbles to compensate for swelling in my fingers. I look in junk shops, because I like the feel of silver and can often find a bargain.

— Debra Botelho Zeida, Waquoit, MA

❖ I like to have more than one size thimble, so on days when my fingers feel extra thick (especially after hours of quilting), I can switch to a larger, more comfortable size.

— Darla Sathre, Baxter, MN

❖ I like a plastic adjustable thimble with space for a long fingernail. It's very inexpensive and can be dunked in hot water and reshaped when necessary.

— Freda Gail Stern, Dallas, TX

❖ I like to buy old, used thimbles because I like the idea of carrying on a tradition with both the craft and the tools. When I use an old thimble, I feel a kinship with a quilter from some other time.

— F. Elaine Asper, Stroudsburg, PA

❖ I don't use a thimble. I wrap my middle finger with masking tape. This "thimble" lasts for about a week of stitching. At night it can be removed, but it doesn't fall off while I work. I shift the tape to a new place when holes occur.

— Ann Foss, Brooklyn, NY

❖ I don't use a thimble. I put heavy tape on the middle fingers of both my hands, covering the tips of my fingernails. On heavier projects, I use an Indian leather thimble on my first finger.

— Carol Farley, Grasonville, MD

❖ I use leather thimbles which I make myself. I stitch around a piece of leather with my sewing machine and use a glue stick to dab my finger before putting the thimble on. It stays on well.

— Florence Donavan, Lodi, CA

❖ I use a leather thimble with elastic, and often put a new one over my old one for added life.

— Susan Thomson, Houston, TX

❖ I have been using the same brass thimble for 14 years. Brass heats up to body temperature. It's like having an extension on my finger.

— Carlene Horne, Bedford, NH

❖ I have about 10 thimbles of different sizes and brands. I just keep trying different ones on until I find one that fits that day. Temperature, nail length or the condition of my hands dictates the size I need at any particular time. I do like the ones with ridged tops. I always use a metal thimble.

— Alice Turner Werner, St. Charles, MO

❖ I wet my middle finger and blow in the thimble before inserting my finger. That helps to keep the thimble on my finger.

— Scarlett von Bernuth, Canon City, CO

❖ If a thimble is too large, I run a piece of 1/4-inch masking tape around the bottom edge of the inside, and then the thimble fits quite snugly.

— Mary M. Weimer, Clinton, MD

❖ I seem to cut the thread when using a normal silver thimble, but if I use antique bone and ivory thimbles, I don't have any problem with them. I always look for spares at antique shows.

— Muriel D. Austin, Hingham, MA

❖ I look for deep indentations that will hold a needle eye and a size that is just a bit snug. Then I flatten the sides of the thimble slightly with a hammer so the cross-section is oval, rather than perfectly round. That helps the thimble fit better since my fingers are not perfectly round. If I buy a thimble in winter, I will probably need one a size larger for warm summer days when my hands get puffy.

— Barbara Monay, Annapolis, MD

❖ I use an ordinary thimble, set it on a solid surface, place a penny on it and hammer the end flat. I then use the base of a small ball hammer and make an indentation in the end of the thimble. I find this much easier to work with than the high ridge thimbles. Most quilting thimbles are too small for me. My fingers have broad tips.

— Rachel Tamm, Allentown, PA

❖ I have long fingernails and very tiny fingers. I found that the leather thimbles with openings on top for fingernails did not give me adequate protection against needle jabs. I now use a small, metal tailor's thimble. I had my husband hammer one side of the thimble flat to fit the contours of my finger. It feels like a leather thimble.

— Elaine Untracht Pawelko, Jamesburg, NJ

❖ If I am hand-quilting, I use a flat spoon-like thimble with dimples because I can rock the needle up and down without excessive wrist motion. If I try to quilt using a sewing thimble with a ridge, I can't rock the needle properly. My hand begins to hurt.

— Corinne Airola Manley, The Colony, TX

❖ Following surgery on my hands, I discovered it hurts to push with a thimble on the end of my finger. So I push from the side. A tailor's thimble works well this way.

— Bea Kasebier, Bangor, PA

❖ I have small fingers and have trouble finding a thimble small enough. I lick my finger so my thimble stays on better!

— Jan Kerr, Punxsutawney, PA

❖ The thimble on my upper hand must have good dimples to hold the needle. The best are old sterling silver ones which I can often find at flea markets or antique shops. On my underneath hand, I use a thimble that is as dimple-less as possible. I tap the top flat so it doesn't catch the needle.

— Carolyn K. Inglis, Hudson, NH

❖ I use a leather thimble with a metal tip in the end. My fingers sweat, and this type of thimble allows my fingers to breathe.

— Ann Leatz, Victorville, CA

❖ I like a thimble with a lip around the top. I think it makes it easier to push the needle from many different angles. When I work at a frame, I use a soft leather thimble on my thumb so that I can quilt away from myself, pushing with my thumb where necessary.

Sometimes I'll wear both my middle finger quilter's thimble and my leather thumb thimble, so I can quickly change direction without adjusting my body position.

— Nina Lord, Annapolis, MD

❖ I have tried all kinds of thimbles but none works as well as "nature's thimble" — the callous on my finger!

— Lisa Tizzoni, Olyphant, PA

Choosing a needle

❖ I prefer a #10 needle. The smaller the needle, the smaller the stitches and the greater my speed.

— Audrey H. Eby, Lancaster, PA

❖ I use a Colonial #12. It seems to be strong enough not to bend, and I can thread it easily.

— Shan D. Lear, Middleton, MA

❖ I use #10 Hemming's large-eye needles. I think they are the best. I can use a #12 only if there are no seams and I can thread them in daylight.

I like Richard Hemming and Son #10s. I think platinum needles are great, but they don't last long enough for their cost.

— Florence Donavan, Lodi, CA

❖ I like small needles. DMC's #9 are easier on my fingers; they don't prick as much.

— Mrs. Ora C. Nisly, Hutchinson, KS

❖ I find Richard Hemming and Son needles from England are the best. They have large eyes and do not bend as easily as other brands.

— Jean Karen Witteveen, Thorold, ON

❖ I think John James needles are the greatest because they are very sharp and very strong. I've had a pack of 25 for a year. My other brands get used up in a single quilt by either bending or breaking.

— Laura J. Jones, Greenville, SC

❖ The DMC needle is the best that I have found to save my fingers. They are more dull, but still easy to use.

— Judy Miller, Hutchinson, KS

❖ I like a Richard Hemming large-eye needle. It is easy to thread and does not break easily.

— Nancy Lee McCabe, Flint, TX

❖ I prefer #12 Piecemaker needles for hand-quilting. They don't seem to bend or break as easily as other needles.

— Donna Fite McConnell, Searcy, AR

❖ I use John James #9 or #10 needles. They don't bend like the others and stay a bit sharper. I change needles often when I quilt. I do the same with sewing machine needles, changing after each project.

— Roberta S. Bennsky, Annapolis, MD

❖ Colonial #10s are one inch long, excellent for quilting, and their eyes are reasonably easy to thread. I use my needle as a gauge, laying it down beside my quilting stitches to check if I am attaining a uniform number of stitches per inch.

— Ann Reimer, Beatrice, NE

❖ I mostly use a #12 Piecemaker. They do not bend, have very sharp points, and thread more easily than other #12 needles I have used.

— Virginia L. Fry, Fulton, MD

❖ I use #12 Clover needles. They are short enough to produce a small stitch, but sturdy enough not to break.

— Betsy Hughes, Midlothian, VA

❖ I use DMC brand needles. I don't think my fingers get sore as quickly.

— Ida Hilty, Berne, IN

❖ I use Susan Bates #10 quilting needles. I can see to thread them. Other brands that small are hard for me to thread.

— Mary Lou Mahar, Williamsfield, IL

❖ I choose a needle that helps me make small stitches and that glides smoothly through the fabric. I use a Piecemakers #12 for quilting and John James sharps #11 for appliqué.

— Barb Grauer, Owings Mills, MD

❖ If the fabric is tightly woven, I use a #8 needle. If the fabric is easy to quilt, I use a bigger needle — #7.

— Elaine Nolt, Versailles, MO

❖ I like to use smaller needles on thin quilts and a size larger on quilts with heavy batting.

— Mrs. Mahlon Miller, Hutchinson, KS

❖ I choose the size needle according to the thickness of what I have to quilt. I use a smaller needle to achieve smaller stitches when I quilt over several layers of appliqué, since it's harder to go through the many layers.

— Donna M. W. Lantgen, Rapid City, SD

❖ I prefer quilting with sharps since I have large hands and need a longer needle.

— Mrs. Vernon Kennel, Atglen, PA

❖ I use the smallest appliqué needle that I can thread.

— Doris L. Orthmann, Wantage, NJ

❖ I do make it a point to test-stitch my fabric with the needle I plan to use before I begin sewing. So many times charts tell me one thing and my machine tells me another. Needle size should be in relation to thread size and fabric weight.

— Dorothy VanDeest, Memphis, TN

❖ I do a small amount of work with different sizes of needles, and then choose the one I like best for the particular project.

— Jeannine Dougherty, Tyler, TX

❖ I don't like a fat shaft on a needle and needles vary. I choose them by feel.

— Vicki Krausz, Denver, CO

❖ I like a very fine #12 between needle. Usually needles made in England are much thinner than others. They are also a tiny bit shorter. If they are hard to thread, they are the right ones!

— Denise S. Rominger, Cranbury, NJ

❖ I always use a #10 embroidery needle. It is thin, sharp and has a longer eye, and I can run five to six stitches onto it before pulling it through.

— Kaye Schnell, Falmouth, MA

❖ With thin batting, I use a small, thin needle. With thicker batting, I use a longer needle. Most of the time I use a #9.

— Rhondalee Schmidt, Scranton, PA

❖ I prefer a #7 needle because it is longer and stronger.

— Loraine Arnold, Rhinebeck, NY

❖ I use a #10 between quilting needle at home because I use a very snug tension on my frame. When I quilt where the frame tension is looser, I use a #9 between quilting needle. For appliqué, I use a #9 between quilting needle.

— Ginny Barr, Jackson, OH

❖ I often choose a thicker needle because they do not bend. Bent needles cause uneven stitches. I look for needles with sharp points (burrs on needles can be felt with fingertips) and a good smooth finish. I also check the eye by sawing thread through it — to see if the eye cuts the thread.

A magnifying glass helps me to see if the eye was cut cleanly. If my quilting starts off badly, I try another size or brand needle. My touch changes from day to day.

— Barbara Monay, Annapolis, MD

❖ I use #9 new needles for quilting, then save them for handwork other than quilting stitches. I keep changing needles as they get dull. Needles do wear out and lose their point. I use the old needles for putting on buttons, etc.

— Shirley Liby, Muncie, IN

❖ Number 10, nickel-plated needles work best for me. Any #10 works, but the nickel-plated tend to break and bend less.

— Sharon L. Leali, Jackson, OH

❖ My old faithfuls are #10 betweens. I no longer hesitate to change them because I've come to appreciate a sharp, smooth needle and use my thriftiness for other things!

— Alana Clark Robbins, Los Lunas, NM

❖ I discovered that a milliner's needle works well for appliqué. I sometimes use it also for hand-piecing. Generally, I use a #12 because it creates fine stitches.

> — Faith Hart Banas, Ludlow, MA

❖ For machine-sewing, I try to use a thin #11 sharp (not ball-point) needle to make the smallest hole in the fabric. For hand-sewing, I still feel most comfortable with long needles, which are hard to find in thin sizes. Long sharps are my favorites.

Even with encouragement from other quilters, I cannot manage betweens. Beading needles are great on silk and make invisible hems.

> — Abby Breslaw Shipper, Hartsdale, NY

❖ I like to use an appliqué needle for quilting. It is sharper and thinner, and its longer length does not impede me.

> — Quilting Friends, Richmond, IN

❖ I use only a #8 platinum needle. Each one lasts at least four years.

> — Jean Turner, Williams Lake, BC

❖ I choose a #10 between because it has a larger eye. A larger eye needle permits less friction on the thread, thus keeping it from fraying. I can use a longer length of thread.

> — Jean A. Schoettmer, Greensburg, IN

Threading needles

❖ I always thread the end I cut from the spool. I wet the needle instead of the thread.

> — Mrs. Vernon Kennel, Atglen, PA

❖ I cut the end of the thread on the diagonal, so that it will slip easily into the tiny eye of my needle.

> —Ada L. Bishop, Beatrice, NE

❖ I cut the thread at a slight angle to make the edge a point instead of blunt. I do not wet it because that causes the thread to fray.

> — Bonnie Zabzdyr, Wright City, MO

❖ I never wet the end of the thread because it could cause the fibers to swell, making it impossible to thread.

> — Mary Pat Sloan, Panama City, FL

❖ I cut thread on an angle and turn the thread facing me. With my other hand, I place the needle on the thread. I am needling the thread instead of threading the needle.

> — Peggy Smith, Hamlin, KY

❖ If I have difficulty in threading a needle, I put the eye of the needle in my mouth and leave a little saliva on the end. The thread goes right through with ease.

> — Dorothy VanDeest, Memphis, TN

❖ I thread several needles at once onto the spool. I knot the end of the thread so as to keep them from slipping off. When needed, I cut off a length of thread with a needle and reknot the thread on the spool.

— Melissa Myers, Indian Head, MD

❖ I like threading a whole package of needles onto a spool of thread. I keep the spool in a wooden holder with a magnet for the needles. This keeps them easily accessible and from becoming unthreaded.

— Laura Reif Lipski, Lindenhurst, NY

❖ My girlfriend used to thread several needles for her mom and leave them on the curtains!

— Lynne Fritz, Bel Air, MD

❖ I cut the thread with a sharp scissors, wet the end, and pull it firmly between the fingernails of my thumb and index finger to flatten it, then slide the thread through the needle.

— Helene Kusnitz, W. Hempstead, NY

❖ I find that thread has what I call a "wrong" side and a "right" side. I hold a piece of thread between my forefinger and thumb and pull it through. The right side has the smoother feel. I thread from the top end of the smoother feel. Usually this is the beginning end as you pull it off the spool.

— Rosalee Crawford, Alba, TX

❖ I cut the thread at an angle, hold it between my thumb and pointer finger with 1/8 inch sticking out, and bring the needle eye to it.

— Shan D. Lear, Middleton, MA

❖ I thread the needle, then knot the cut end. This keeps the thread from becoming tangled, since by doing this, I am sewing with the weave of the thread and not against it.

— Betty Boyton, Gordonville, PA

❖ At our quiltings, we sometimes have an elderly lady who can't quilt anymore use a needle threader and thread needles for everyone.

— Mrs. Mahlon Miller, Hutchinson, KS

❖ Put a piece of white fabric or paper directly behind the eye of the needle to make it more visible. I do not try to thread a ragged end into the needle.

— Marilyn Bloom Wallace, Alfred, ME

❖ For hand-piecing or lap-quilting, I use a lapboard on which I've stuck a 1 1/2 inch x 3 inch white press-ply sticker. I use this as my background for the needle eye. It is much easier to thread the needle when I hold it against something white.

— Mary Seielstad, Schenectady, NY

❖ I hold my thread above the needle eye and point down through the eye.

— Loyce Wood Sage, Gallup, NM

❖ I beeswax the thread to slide it into the eye.

— Donna Conto, Saylorsburg, PA

❖ I use Chap Stick year-round. Before I wet the thread, I oil my lips. The small amount of Chap Stick left on the thread that ran between my lips gives enough stiffness to thread the eye easily.

— Polly Gilmore, St. Joseph, MI

❖ I thread 20 needles at a time so as not to slow down once I start. On a good day I can do this three times!

— Helena A. Bagdonas, Brockton, MA

❖ Use younger eyes! I have my children or friends with good eyes help me. They thread many at a time, and I set them out of the way, but close to where I stitch.

— Dale Renee Ball, Silverdale, WA

❖ I thread several needles onto the spool early in the morning when I see most clearly, and then pull them off as I need them.

— Barbara Forrester Landis, Lititz, PA

❖ I hold the needle against a dark solid material. It helps me see the hole.

—Vicki Krausz, Denver, CO

❖ I stick my needle in a dark fabric on my quilt to thread my needle. The needle is steady, and I can see the eye easily.

— Judy M. Sharer, Port Matilda, PA

❖ I like to thread and knot many needles all at once and put them in a pincushion.

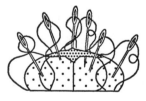

— Rhondalee Schmidt, Scranton, PA

❖ I use a needle threader. I put eight or 10 needles on the threader, pull the thread through them, leave the threader attached to the spool, put the needles in a pincushion, and take off one at a time as I need it. I also sometimes have several needles in a quilt at the same time.

— Alice Turner Werner, St. Charles, MO

❖ I thread as many needles as I have, knot them and hang them on the edge of my quilt so they're ready to go.

— Thelma A. Stein, Tavares, FL

❖ I recently learned that the eye of a needle has a "right" and a "wrong" side. If my thread doesn't go through on the first try, I turn the needle and try from the other side. It's amazing how often this works!

— Mary Puskar, Forest Hill, MD

❖ When I am teaching kids to quilt, they often pull their needles off the ends of the thread. So, I've devised this practice: I thread a needle with a single thread and knot the end. I pull the needle up close to the free end and pierce the thread with the point of the needle. I pull the needle through the thread, thus locking it on the thread. The children can then sew and finish off normally, but the needle needs to be cut free with scissors.

— Barbara Monay, Annapolis, MD

❖ I cut the thread and thread it right away, so I don't give the thread a chance to get dull at the end.

—Vi Angle, Rosebury, OR

❖ I thread the needle from the spool before cutting the thread. I think it frays less. I always cut thread at an angle.

— Theresa Lepert, Schellsburg, PA

❖ I thread a whole package of needles onto the spool, then pull off one needle and one length for quilting at a time. Each time, I anchor the tail of thread onto the top of the spool. I do this when I'm fresh and when I can use natural light to keep from having eyestrain.

— Shirley Liby, Muncie, IN

❖ I fold the end of the thread over the eye end of the needle to crease it, then push the crease through the eye and pull until the short end comes through.

— Jane K. Boyarski, Downingtown, PA

❖ I take a small piece of paper and fold it, then lay the thread into the fold and insert it into the eye of the needle.

— Dorothy Geiger Hoffman, Conneaut, OH

❖ I apply hair spray to the tip of the thread.

— Leesa Seaman Lesenski, Whatgly, MA

❖ I pinch the thread between my fingers, just letting a centimeter or so protrude. This makes the thread very stiff and easy to thread.

— Debbie Chisholm, Fallston, MD

❖ I cut thread on an angle and thread a dozen needles at a time. When all are empty, I count them and thread them again. If I don't have 12, I look for the missing!

— Caryl L. Burgan, Valhalla, NY

❖ A pair of magnifying clip-on glasses is extremely helpful for me.

— Joan Lemmler, Albuquerque, NM

Additional tips

❖ I've timed myself to find out how long it takes to quilt an 18-inch length of thread. I hang a strawberry or other small pincushion from my lamp or over the work area of the quilt. Into the strawberry I place needles threaded with 18 inches of thread (not longer, because the thread will receive too much wear). I pre-thread the amount of needles I will need to fill the amount of time I estimate I'll have to quilt This serves as a good discipline and yardstick towards a goal.

I use a separate pincushion just for quilting to keep those needles separate.

— Jeannine Dougherty, Tyler, TX

❖ I occasionally glance at the red strawberry or some other bright object in the room to refocus my eyes and help eliminate eyestrain

— Ann Reimer, Beatrice, NE

❖ I use only two needles at a time on a quilt so that I don't lose track of them or drop them on the floor for feet to find My mother threads and knots eight to 10 needles at a time in order to discipline her time. When she has emptied the allotted number, her day of quilting is over.

— Barbara Waymire, Wichita, KS

❖ I like to prepare needles in the following way for travel: I put my thread in an old pill bottle and bring the thread out through a hole in the lid. I then thread an entire package of needles without cutting the thread and put them into the bottle. As I need it, I pull a needle and a length of thread from the bottle. I leave the remaining needles in the bottle, with the end of the thread secured under the edge of the bottle cover to prevent it from slipping inside.

— Debra Botelho Zeida, Waquoit, MA

❖ If I find a thread that knots or ravels too much, I run it through beeswax, even if I'm simply piecing. If I don't want to change to different thread because color is important, but I am still having a problem, I iron the thread after running it through beeswax to melt the wax into the thread.

— Sue Seeley, New Bern, NC

❖ Years ago, Marie Johnson of Lincoln, Nebraska, showed me how to wax my quilting thread. She slowly and carefully heated wax normally used to seal jelly glasses. When it was hot (a steamy appearance rose faintly from the pan), she carefully lowered the spool of quilting thread into the wax with metal tongs and gently rolled the spool until tiny bubbles stopped rising from the thread. She removed the thread with the tongs and placed it on a rack until it was cool enough to touch. That procedure not only makes threading very easy, it also eliminates the need to secure the thread to the spool each time a thread is pulled off. You can't do this with Styrofoam spools, however.

— Mary Pat Sloan, Panama City, FL

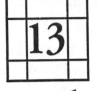

Planning color layout

Preplanning with fabric

I like to use the color wheel to find dramatic complementary schemes (i.e. blue/orange, red/green, purple/yellow). I used to use paper and colored pencils. Now I don't bother; I just fold my fabric into little piles and lay them out like fans to see what looks good.
— **Kathleen Bishop, Washington, DC**

I make several prototypes after I have sketched the design on paper. Using the actual fabric is much better than relying on the sketch alone, because color and subtle patterns can affect the final look.
— **Suzanne S. Nobrega, Duxbury, MA**

I drape possible fabrics over a stuffed armchair and let them sit there for about a week, adding or subtracting as I want to. I try to arrange them in proportion to the amounts I will use and in relation to each other as they will be in the quilt.
— **Melissa Stiles Hess, La Conner, WA**

If I'm making a scrap quilt, I hang the pieces on my design wall and play with them till I like the arrangement. I leave it up for a couple of days to see if I still like it and then sew it together.
— **Nancy Wagner Graves, Manhattan, KS**

Many times I lay fabric on the floor in a room for a day or two, then walk by and see how it catches my eye. I usually end up rearranging the pieces.
— **Helene Kusnitz, W. Hempstead, NY**

I have a design wall covered with felt for planning a 6 feet x 6 feet size piece. It really helps me to be able to lay out large tops.

— Ellen Victoria Crockett, Springfield, VA

I have a queen-size flannel sheet nailed to the wall. I try different colors by moving them around and standing back to look. Fabric pieces will stick to flannel just by smoothing them on.

— Judi Robb, Manhattan, KS

I buy what I think will work, then make a sample, and either go with it or change a color or two. When I think I have it, I use a 25x magnifier flat sheet. That really gives me a "finished" look.

— Lauren Eberhard, Seneca, IL

I want contrast, so I put pieces on a piece of batting taped to the wall and stand back and look at it.

— Dale Renee Ball, Silverdale, WA

I used to do everything on paper first, even pasting tiny pieces of fabric on a design so I knew what it would look like finished. Now I'm into scrap quilts, and I create on a flannel board hung from the ceiling. If I like it on the board, I take it down and sew it.

— Dorothy Reise, Severna Park, MD

I use Pellon Fleece on my wall for planning my quilts. The fleece hangs on the wall of my bedroom so that I can stare at it while I lie in bed.

— Joy Rubenstein-Moir, Holtsville, NY

After cutting out the pieces in the colors I think I want, I place them in the proper design on my coffee table for a day or so. I look as I go past, and also from a distance as I come down the stairs. I make changes until I'm happy with what I see.

— Barbara Aston, Sharon Hill, PA

I sometimes find it helpful to photocopy a large sheet of each fabric that I plan to use in my quilt. I use the setting (usually the lightest setting) that gives the best copy of my darkest piece of fabric, and then use that same setting for each piece to keep uniformity in color values. I use these photocopies to make a trial paste-up block. Planning the quilt out in black and white helps assure me of an effective balance of color values.

I spray the back of a sheet of graph paper with spray adhesive, press it to the back of a piece of fabric, and weight it with a large book until it has dried. I repeat the process for each fabric I will use in the quilt. Using paper-cutting scissors, I turn the graph paper side up and cut out all the squares, rectangles and triangles I need for my block and border designs, glue-sticking (Dennisons' 1 oz. Glue stick works well) the pieces to a sheet of graph paper to produce a paste-up miniature of my quilt. I make several different paste-ups to find the most effective use and balance of the lights, mediums and darks. This is not only a helpful planning exercise, it also gives me a frameable block for the wall or a greeting card for a fellow quilter.

— Ann Reimer, Beatrice, NE

If in doubt, I cut selvages 1/2-inch wide, glue the strips to marked squares on 1/4-inch graph paper, then cut the paper into appropriate pieces and glue them to another sheet of graph paper as a mockup. When complete, I take a picture with a Polaroid camera, and instantly my eye sees it as a full-size quilt. I can then make adjustments where I see problems, insert needed accents, or change a piece here and there.

— Carol Findling, Beatrice, NE

I like to use mirrors at right angles when trying something new. I make one block and then put it in front of mirrors to see what four will look like. Sometimes I just cut exact size pieces and lay those in front of the mirrors.

— Sue Seeley, New Bern, NC

I place two mirrors at a 90-degree angle on two sides of a sample quilt block to see how they would look set together.

— Audrey Romonosky, Poughkeepsie, NY

I lay all fabrics on top of an unmade bed, leave them there a day or two, and then rearrange them or use them as I originally planned.

— Rose Hankins, Stevensville, MD

I lay itsy-bitsy pieces of material on paper to create a miniature block. I rearrange the design until I like it, then I transfer it to clear contact paper. This way I have a color arrangement to follow and a color chart for future reference, all in one.

— Judith Eve Nisly, Partridge, KS

My local fabric store sells 1/8-yard cuts of any bolt, so I buy eight or 10 1/8-yard pieces and lay my palette of colors on the dining room table. Over a period of a few days, I look at them each time I walk by the table. I gradually remove the less desirable prints till I get down to the three or four I want. I then go back to the store and purchase the full amounts I need for the quilt.

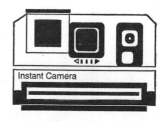

Instant Camera

— Jacqueline E. Deininger, Bethlehem, PA

I sit with my fabrics around me in morning light and choose. Morning light is least forgiving when matching colors. If the arrangement looks good then, it will look good in any light. I take a snippet of each color and lay them together someplace where I can back away and look at them, off and on, before I make a final decision.

— Jane E. Crowe, Boyertown, PA

I lay out fabrics that I have on hand to make my color choices until I get close to what I want. Then I cut small samples to take shopping for my final selection.

— Barbara N. Neff, Cypress, CA

I use a red sheet of clear plastic and place it over fabrics to tone out color, to determine each fabric's intensity (dark, medium or light) in relation to other fabrics, and to discover the emphasis each fabric will bring to a pattern.

— Lela Ann Schneider, Boise, ID

I preplan my whole quilt on a flannel planning wall. I use a reducing glass (or wrong end of binoculars) to view my overall piece in progress from "a distance." This makes it easy for me to pick out the wrong choices.

— Shirlee Hugger, Martha's Vineyard, MA

I use a wallboard to arrange colors. I then view them with a hand mirror, looking into the mirror over my shoulder or looking through the wrong end of binoculars to get better color perspective.

— Nell Jackson, Taylors, SC

I work by a sunny window or outside at a picnic table. I cut 1/2-inch strips of fabric and then cut them into 1/2-inch squares. Then I sort fabric by color in a 12-cup muffin tin. I attach the fabrics to graph paper using clear glue so I can peel off the pieces and rearrange them until the design pleases me.

— Diana M. Garrison, Silver Spring, MD

I was making a Log Cabin quilt and wanted a way to organize my squares without having piles to gather up every time. So I pinned each square to an old sheet of the same size. That way I could rearrange them as I wanted, and they kept still. When I settled on the final arrangement, I just folded up the sheet till I was ready to sew the blocks together. This method would work for any block quilt.

— Jane Lippincott, Wynnewood, PA

If I am going to make a pieced block quilt, I always make four blocks first. If I don't like the finished blocks, they become the center of a quilt or a wall hanging or tablecloth. I have an idea of the outcome before I begin, but I am always open to change, even if I've used graph paper and set out the pattern in colored pencil.

— Doris Miotto, Thorold, ON

Preplanning without fabric

I use graph paper and colored artist's pencils to plan some of my quilts. A color wheel is also helpful.

— Cheryl Ferriter, West Springfield, MA

I like to have color schemes that go together. I work with Electric

Quilt Software to design and plan whenever I can.

— Patti Welsh, Yorktown Heights, NY

I think the easiest way to see "what and where" is to do a drawing of my design — a nine-block (nine-patch) rendition. I color in with pencils or crayons to get a close idea of what the overall quilt will look like. If I'm not sure how I want the color design to be, I make a few photocopies of the drawing or sketch of the nine blocks, and then I have several to color in different arrangements. I always make a sample block!

— Mary Seielstad, Schenectady, NY

If I'm doing an original design, I graph out a sample quilt and make several photocopies of it. Then with crayons or colored pencils, I try many combinations. Often I find secondary patterns I was not aware of in the original pattern.

— Peggy Smith, Hamlin, KY

I color blocks on graph paper, then work with paint chips, and finally paste up a block to size.

— Ib Bartlet, Schenectady, NY

I sketch my design on graph paper, then I borrow my son's crayons and play until I find a combination I like. My son promised to give me my own box of crayons for Christmas!

— Rhondalee Schmidt, Scranton, PA

I draw my design on graph paper and color it with colored pencils. If it's really complicated or "daring," I make mock-ups of the quilt by spraying index cards with adhesive and gluing swatches of the fabric to the cards. Then I cut out the pieces and glue them (rubber cement is good, so I can change my mind) to my graph paper design, mounted on poster board. I make the whole quilt design this way. I like to hang the poster board and look at it in that position before I cut the entire quilt.

— Julie McKenzie, Punxsutawney, PA

My designs are determined by the value (lightness or darkness) of the colors. When I design on graph paper, I fill in the shapes with dark, medium and light pencil strokes. I also have a flannel design wall where I can "stick up" pieces and see their effect from a distance. I find this to be very important.

— Sherri Driver, Englewood, CO

If I design on paper, I like to use watercolor paint in a tube to create the color.

— Janet Jo Smith, Littleton, CO

After I have the idea, I draw it on graph paper and then color it with colored pencils. It is extremely important that I draw this to scale so I am able to tell if one color is out of proportion.

— Coleen Swettman, Vancouver, WA

Binding quilts

Preparation for binding

❖ I always machine-baste the edges of the quilt top, the batting and the backing together before I cut off the excess batting and backing, because it's difficult to get all three layers together once they've been cut. I like to hand-sew the binding with quilting thread because it's stronger.
— Marian Umble, Atglen, PA

❖ I trim all excess fabric from the edges of the quilt and pin the binding on before sewing it on.
— Sharon Heide, Mt. Lake, MN

❖ For binding, I use 2 1/2-inch bias strips. I sew the long strips together, press 1/2 inch in on each side, then fold the strip in half and press it like a double-fold bias tape. This takes longer, but I have more control over it that way.
— Verna Mae Sessions, Yakima, WA

❖ I always use pins to make sure all the layers are together and even, and then pull them out before they go under the sewing machine foot so they don't get caught.
— Jane S. Lippincott, Wynnewood, PA

❖ I make a small running stitch all around the edge of the quilt to keep all the layers together before I apply the binding.
— Patricia Fielding, Stone Mountain, GA

❖ I mark the centers of both the quilt and binding. Then I match the centers and ends to make the binding fit correctly. I also use a walking foot on my machine. It helps to feed all the layers of the quilt evenly through the machine.

— Gail L. Kozicki, Glen Mills, PA

❖ While the quilt is still in its frame, I hand-baste through all its thicknesses about 1/4 inch from the outside edge of the quilt top, along all four sides. This holds all the thicknesses neatly together when I sew on the binding.

— Mary Jane Musser, Manheim, PA

❖ I first pin the binding on, distributing the fabric evenly so it doesn't pucker, then I sew.

— Arline M. Rubin, New York, NY

❖ After I cut and join the pieces for the binding, I spend extra time ironing it, so that there are no ripples and pleats. This gives me a head start on getting the binding on straight all the way around.

— Barbara McGinnis, Ocean City, NJ

❖ I pin the binding to the quilt on a flat surface before taking it to my sewing machine.

— Teresa Reily, White Plains, NY

❖ When I put the quilt in the frame, I baste the top to the batting and lining, so that when I'm ready to bind, it is much easier to put the binding on. I like to use a bias binding.

— Erma Landis, Sterling, IL

❖ I use a long ruler and a rotary cutter to straighten all the quilt edges before I apply the binding.

— Linda M. Pool, Vienna, VA

Measuring for binding

❖ Using a piece of dental floss or macramé string (they are not stretchy), I measure the quilt through the middle from top to bottom and from side to side. I cut the binding the same lengths as these pieces of string. When I start stitching the binding to one side, I sew an inch or so, then stop to measure my binding for that side, easing in the side of the quilt so that it fits, and so that each side is the correct length when I've finished.

— Carol Trice, Wayne, PA

❖ Measure, measure, measure. I measure the top and bottom of the quilt, and measure my binding to this same measurement. If my binding measures the same for top and bottom (allow for miters if necessary) and for both sides, my quilt will be a perfect rectangle (or square).

— Mary Wheatley, Mashpee, MA

❖ I break each side of the quilt and binding into four equal measurements as I stitch each side. I pin the binding to the quilt on the first side, matching marks I've made at each interval. I sew one side to the pivot point making mitered corners. I make the pivot, and then measure the next side and pin the binding in place. I measure and pin after each pivot. My pieces are very flat and don't wobble.

— Barbara Tone Lister, Highlands Ranch, CO

Applying binding

❖ I'm careful not to pull the quilt as I sew the binding to the right side, because that will make the quilt wavy on its edges. Bias binding is lovely to put on, but fabric cut from straight of grain works also. I use thread to match the background fabric so the stitches won't show. The last thing I cut when cutting pieces for a quilt is the binding. After cutting strips 2 1/2 inches wide, I sew them together, press them in half, and loop them together in a bundle with a rubber band around them. They stay with the rest of the quilt as I sew it. It makes my work go faster, and I never worry about what on earth I will use to bind this quilt!

— Dorothy Reise, Severna Park, MD

❖ I apply my binding to the top immediately after the top is finished. After the quilt is quilted, I blindstitch the already applied binding to the back.

— Joy Rubenstein-Moir, Holtsville, NY

❖ I apply the binding by hand because I like the finished product better.

— Lee Cook, Falmouth, MA

❖ To eliminate extra bulk in the corners, I start sewing the binding on a side of the quilt rather than at a corner.

— Terri Good, Marietta, PA

❖ To machine-stitch the binding to my quilts, I use a fusible thread in my bobbin. When I turn the binding to the other side for the second stitching, I quickly press it with the iron and it holds in place without the use of pins.

— Judy Williams, Stevenville, MD

❖ If I do small projects, such as Christmas ornaments, potholders, minis, etc., I use fusible thread in the bobbin when I apply the binding. I can then simply fuse the binding to the back of the quilted item. It's quick and easy!

— Susan Ketcherside, St. Charles, MO

❖ I always double the fabric on the binding so it will be more durable. I pull the fabric firmly while I apply it and use a lot of pins.

— Betty Boyton, Gordonville, PA

❖ I use straight strips of binding for straight edges. I sew by machine on the back side of the quilt and turn the binding to the front. I figure since

I'm hand-quilting, I want the hand-sewn part of the binding on top to match the hand-quilting.

— Florence Donavan, Lodi, CA

❖ The quilting pulls the quilt together a bit, so the outer edge is a bit larger than across the center of the quilt. For this reason I ease in the quilt by stretching the binding just a bit, so the edge doesn't wobble when it's finished.

— Edna Nisly, Partridge, KS

❖ As I handstitch the backside down, I pin ahead of the stitching a few inches.

— Mary Puskar, Forest Hill, MD

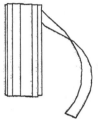

❖ When I turn the binding to the back side for final hemming, I am careful to keep the bias parallel, front to back. Stretching or folding it unevenly will cause the binding to wrinkle.

— Ginny Barr, Jackson, OH

❖ When I apply the binding, I start in the middle of a section and work out to the corners, using a walking foot to sew the binding on.

— Irene Daniels, Webster, NY

❖ To prevent buckling, I sew bias binding to the quilt top only. I then hand-sew the binding to the back of the quilt and quilt along the bound edge border.

— Charlie Weckerle, Roseburg, OR

❖ When starting the binding, I create a tail of about 2 inches, folded at a right angle to the quilt. As I complete the binding, I sew about an inch past the stitching starting point and cut the binding off. When I blindstitch the binding, the beginning point is covered by the "bias" of the right angle, and the binding is at an angle, rather than a straight line across. The slanted line is more pleasing to the eye.

— Marion Lumpkins Reece, Richmond, VA

❖ I always put bindings on by hand. Going around twice controls the fullness.

— Winifred W. Rexrode, Shiremanstown, PA

❖ I like to use a millinery stitch to handstitch one side of the binding. I take a small stitch through the quilt backing and binding, slide the needle through the fold of the binding, and take another small stitch.

— Jean Harris Robinson, Cinnaminson, NJ

❖ I take extra care not to stretch the binding. Stretching can cause the edge of the quilt to ripple.

— Harriet Velting Kennon, Franklin, IN

❖ I pin a great deal at right angles to the seam. Sometimes I do a double row of basting and then sew in between the basting lines.

— Arline M. Rubin, New York, NY

❖ Sometimes I run a basting stitch on the edge of the binding and gather it up if there is fullness. It seems to work for me. The basting stitch can be pulled out after the binding is on.

— Lee Cook, Falmouth, MA

❖ I lay the binding next to the feed of my sewing machine and place the quilt on top. I can control both edges more accurately.

— Nell Jackson, Taylors, SC

❖ When sewing binding onto the quilt by machine, I shorten the stitch length. It seems to help take up some of the fullness of the fabric

— Lois C. Ruiz, Murray, KY

Straight bindings

❖ To begin, I make enough binding to go around the quilt easily. (Add up the length of all four sides, add 12 inches, then add another 20 inches or so for good measure). I use straight grain binding most of the time.

I sew strips together so the seams are at 45-degree angles. Then I fold the binding in half at the ironing board and press the entire length.

The beginning of the binding needs to be angled. To do that, I fold the straight end of the binding strip to form a 45-degree angle. I press and trim the folded seam allowance to 1/4 inch. I place the opened binding on the front of the quilt, right sides together. Then I pin a 4-inch section in place and stitch the binding to the quilt with a 1/4-inch seam, going through a single layer of binding for about 3 to 4 inches. I stop and break the thread. This first stitching creates a pocket to receive the tail of the binding at the end.

I fold the binding in half again and begin new stitching through both layers at the spot where I stopped the first stitching, continuing to stitch around all edges of the quilt. I stop my stitching, needle down into the quilt, about 5 inches from the end.

I judge approximately where the end of the binding is by laying it over the beginning of the binding. I then cut it straight across, forming the "tail." I insert the tail into the pocket and mark the angle of the beginning of the binding. I pull out the tail and cut it 1/4 inch below the marked line.

Then I insert the tail back into the pocket and pin the remaining binding back to the sewing machine needle. I continue stitching through all layers until I reach the stitching that shows on the double layer of the binding.

When the binding is hand-stitched to the quilt back, all the seams are angled so that there is minimal bulk at the starting/stopping spot. (See the following diagram.)

— Marilyn Bloom Wallace, Alfred, ME

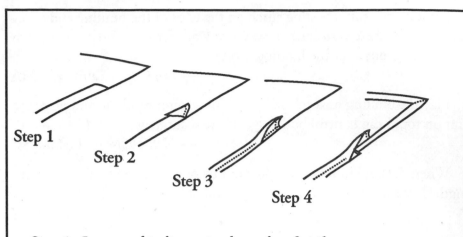

Step 1: *Lay open binding strip along edge of quilt.*

Step 2: *Fold fabric at a 45-degree angle. Trim seam to 1/4 inch.*

Step 3: *Stitch binding to quilt through a single layer of binding for 3 to 4 inches. Refold binding and begin stitching through all layers where previous stitching stopped. Continue around quilt edges returning to starting point.*

Step 4: *Trim end of tail that meets beginning of binding at 45-degree angle. Insert ending tail into pocket. Fold binding and continue stitching through all layers to meet beginning stitches.*

❖ On small hangings, I use a continuous binding cut on the straight of the fabric and usually doubled. On full-size quilts, I cut the doubled binding strips and attach the top and bottom, and then the sides, usually mitering the corners.

— Marjorie Mills, Bethesda, MD

❖ I think it is wasteful to do bias binding on straight edges. Also, length grain binding helps prevent rippled outside edges on my quilts. I use bias bindings only when I finish curves.

— Linda Hampton Schiffer, Columbia, MD

❖ I like to use straight binding because it makes quilts, and especially wall hangings, hang squarely and helps to keep them from stretching out of shape. I only use bias binding on curved edges.

— Gloria West, Grier, SC

Bias bindings

❖ I stitch bias binding to the top side of my quilt before trimming away excess batting and backing. After the binding is stitched, I trim all edges even with the edge of the binding, fold the binding over the raw edges, and whipstitch the binding in place. I prefer a very narrow binding.

— Betty Hutchinson, St. Charles, MO

❖ I cut a bias strip 2 inches wide and press it in half. I sew the raw edges of the strip to the raw edges of the quilt. Then I fold the binding over to the backside and whipstitch the fold to the back. The fold makes the final edge. It works very well.

— Ruth Ann Penner, Hillsboro, KS

❖ I find bias binding that I make myself is the most forgiving — and mistakes are more easily hidden if I use the same fabric for the border and binding.

— Brenda Shaw-Nielsen, Washington, DC

❖ To make a corded look to my binding, I add a short strip of batting, about 1-inch wide, as I fold the bias strip to the back. It really looks neat.

— Thelma A. Stein, Tavares, FL

❖ I starch bias binding and am careful not to stretch the binding when I sew it. I cut my binding 3 1/2-inches wide and fold it in half because the double thickness works better. I stuff my binding with batting as I whip it down to give it a nice rounded effect.

— Scarlett von Bernuth, Canon City, CO

❖ I always finish bias binding on an angle. The finish is unnoticed and smooth.

— Shirley Liby, Muncie, IN

❖ Bias binding will last longer on a quilt than fabric cut on the straight of grain, because there will be more threads on the edge with bias.

— Dana Braden, Dallas, TX

❖ When scalloping the edge of a quilt, I always cut the binding on the bias so I have some stretch to work with in the points.

— Marian Umble, Atglen, PA

❖ I always use double bias binding. It stretches easily to allow easy binding of corners and curves.

— Ellen Victoria Crockett, Springfield, VA

❖ If the quilt has curves, it must have bias binding. Using a stiletto, I hold the binding in place while stitching slowly and carefully. I pivot at the inside angles and curves, and I miter the outside angles.

— Marilyn Bloom Wallace, Alfred, ME

❖ I pin a lot! I use continuous bias bindings on any quilts with curves.

— Joy Rubenstein-Moir, Holtsville, NY

❖ Bias binding is much easier than straight grain for all my projects, because it is flexible and forgiving of my small errors in calculation.

— Katherine Lombard, Deerfield, NH

❖ I cut binding on the crosswise grain. I make my strips seven to eight times wider than the finished binding is to be (1 3/4- to 2-inch strips for 1/4-inch final binding). Then I sew the strips together, end to end, and press the seams open. I fold them in half right side out, press them and baste them, if I want to. I then line up the raw edges of the binding with the raw edge of the quilt, baste them together, and stitch. I fold the binding over to the backside and stitch the folded edge to the back side of the quilt.

— Elaine W. Good, Lititz, PA

❖ I cut bias binding 2 1/2-inches wide and fold it in half to make a double binding. I sew through both layers of binding and all the quilt layers with a 1/4-inch seam, then trim the raw edges, turn the binding to the back, and sew it down. To begin and end, I leave about a 6-inch tail unsewn at the beginning and stop sewing about 12 inches before I reach the starting point. I remove the quilt from the machine, lay out the binding ends to meet each other, then cut off the ends, allowing a 1/2-inch overlap. I stitch the ends of the binding together with a 1/4-inch seam and finish sewing the binding to the quilt.

— Julie McKenzie, Punxsutawney, PA

❖ If I make my own bias tape, I have more elasticity than with commercial bias tape. Even curves and turns create no problem.

— Jean Harris Robinson, Cinnaminson, NJ

Negotiating curves

❖ I mark curves and sew the binding on before I trim close to the curves.

— Cheryl Ferriter, West Springfield, MA

❖ I miter corners and stitch curves by hand to ease the binding evenly. Then I machine-stitch.

— Mildred Fauquet, Lincoln, NE

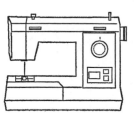

❖ If I have curves to bind, I run a stitch under the turn and pull it lightly to gather it to turn the corner.

— Sharon Heide, Mt. Lake, MN

❖ I go slowly and shorten the stitch length in the tight areas. This makes it easier to make perfect curves.

— Sue Dieringer-Boyer, Walkersville, MD

❖ I often use a steam iron and hand-mold the binding on curves.

— Barbara Forrester Landis, Lititz, PA

❖ To negotiate curves, I leave the needle in the fabric at the inside corner of the scallop, lift the presser foot, and pivot the fabric before going on to the next scallop. I feed the fabric in to the presser foot, smoothing into the curves.

— Gail L. Kozicki, Glen Mills, PA

❖ I find that narrow binding works best on turns and curves.

— Mrs. Ora C. Nisly, Hutchinson, KS

❖ I baste first, easing the binding into the curve, then sew. This takes more time but saves my temper!

— Kaye Schnell, Falmouth, MA

❖ I make a small pleat at the "v" of curves and corners.

— Betty F. McGuire, Clinton, CT

❖ I try to sew with the concave side on the top, and I mark the center of the turn or curve with a pin.

— Loyce Wood Sage, Gallup, NM

❖ I ease the bias binding around the curves, using more stitches closer together on the inside of the curve and fewer on the outside of the curve.

— Sandra Fulton Day, Oxford, PA

Square corners

❖ I prefer to sew binding on one end of the quilt, cut it off, lay the binding out, and sew the next piece on, and so on, rather than sewing it on as a continuous piece.

— Marilyn Yoder, Mt. Hope, OH

❖ To finish square corners, I bind the top and bottom, trim them, then finish the sides, allowing the side bindings to extend about one inch beyond the edge. To finish the binding, I fold the ends in so that all raw edges are covered, then handstitch the binding in place.

— Fannie Troyer, Mt. Hope, OH

❖ When making square corners, I flip the horizontal over the vertical on one side and the vertical over the horizontal on the other. I find the corners look more square this way!

— Joyce Trueblood, Cromwell, CT

❖ I like to round the two corners at the foot end of the quilt and just bring the binding around the curve. This helps to keep the corners off the floor, especially when the bed is low. I leave the head end corners square, because they are usually tucked under the pillow.

— Mrs. David L. Miller, Partridge, KS

❖ I sew binding on each side of the quilt, then on the top and bottom. I sew the top and bottom bindings out over the side bindings.

— Katie Esh, Ronks, PA

Mitered corners

❖ I use a 1/4-inch seam allowance and stop stitching 1/4 inch from the corner. I fold the binding up at a 45-degree angle from the corner, then fold it back down on itself, and align it with the next side to be bound. I begin stitching again at the point where the previous stitching stopped. This forms a nice mitered corner. When I hand-sew the binding down, I also sew the mitered corners down, front and back.

— Nancy Wagner Graves, Manhattan, KS

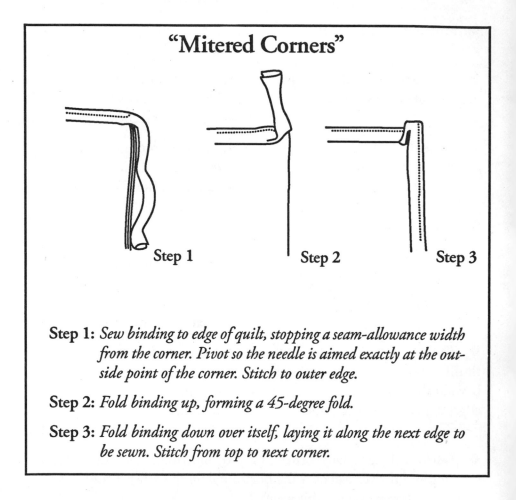

"Mitered Corners"

Step 1   Step 2   Step 3

Step 1: *Sew binding to edge of quilt, stopping a seam-allowance width from the corner. Pivot so the needle is aimed exactly at the outside point of the corner. Stitch to outer edge.*

Step 2: *Fold binding up, forming a 45-degree fold.*

Step 3: *Fold binding down over itself, laying it along the next edge to be sewn. Stitch from top to next corner.*

❖ I miter the corners when I do the binding. I sew up to the seam allowance's width from the edge of the corner (for example, I generally do 1/2-inch seam allowances on binding, so I sew up to exactly 1/2 inch from the edge). I stop sewing with the machine needle down. I pivot the corner so that the needle is now aimed exactly at the outside point of the corner. I sew along this line all the way out to the corner and off the edge. I raise the presser foot and cut the thread. I fold the binding up, so that the unsewn edge of binding that will be sewn next is parallel to and above the edge of the quilt and the fold in the binding is at a 45-degree angle (along the line just sewn to the point of the curve). I hold the binding at the just-finished edge and fold it down over itself, so that it lies along the next side to be sewn. I leave a little (1/8 inch or so) extra fold at the point. Then I begin sewing again at the top edge and go on to the next corner. When I am done and fold the binding to the back to sew it down, I have a perfectly mitered corner. I stitch the binding to the back of the quilt by hand.

— Linda Hampton Schiffer, Columbia, MD

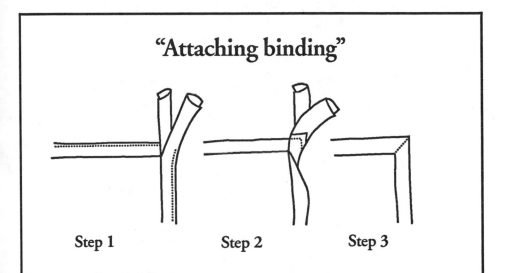

"Attaching binding"

Step 1   **Step 2**   **Step 3**

Step 1: *Using 1/4-inch seam allowances, stitch binding to quilt edges, stopping 1/4 inch away from each corner.*

Step 2: *Fold quilt corner until top is aligned vertically with side of quilt. Mark center point of binding. Mark a 45-degree angle on each side of center point to form a "v." Stitch on marked line 1/4 inch above stitched line.*

Step 3: *Turn binding right side out.*

❖ I use the following method for binding: 1) Cut binding strips to equal the width and length of the quilt, plus 2 1/2 inches extra on each end. 2) Using the 1/4-inch seam allowances, stitch the binding to the quilt edges, stopping stitching at the 1/4-inch seam allowance on each corner. 3) Mark the center of the binding. 4) Fold the quilt corner until the top edge is aligned vertically with the left side of the quilt. Mark a 45-degree angle to each side of the center line, forming a "v" on the binding, and stitch on this line. Trim the binding to 1/4 inch from the stitching. Repeat with the remaining corners. 5) Turn the binding. Both sides will be mitered. Blindstitch the binding to the back of the quilt over the seam line.

— Jean H. Robinson, Cinnaminson, NJ

❖ I have a trick I use. I put binding on two sides of the quilt and stitch it down to the backside. On the remaining two sides, I fold the fabric at the ends of the binding to make it look like it's mitered. The ends of the binding are folded at 45-degree angles to the center of the binding, creating a "v" at the end. The angles are handstitched in place. The finished product looks pretty good.

— Jorita J. Groves, Bushland, TX

When hand-sewing binding on the back side, I continue stitches all the way through from the back to the quilt top at the mitered corners. I close the fold of the mitered corner on the back with small stitches, running from the base of the corner to the outer point. At the outer corner, I stab through to the front of the quilt and close the miter fold, going from the outer corner to the inner corner. I stab through again to the back of the quilt and continue stitching to the next corner.

— Dorothy Reise, Severna Park, MD

❖ Be sure the bias is exactly on grain, and the miters will just fall in place.

— Dorothy Humphrey, Webster, NY

❖ When using mitered corners, I stitch the folds closed, not only for a more finished appearance, but to prevent snagging and to assure longer wear.

— Ann Reimer, Beatrice, NE

❖ I usually miter corners and trim out as much excess seam allowance as possible, so the corners will not be bulky.

— Connie Downey, Muncie, IN

❖ I like mitered corners and generally use continuous binding, stitching directly onto the quilt. Using a folded binding, I stitch the binding to one side of the quilt, stopping 1/4 inch from the edge. I backstitch about a 1/2 inch, cut the thread, and lift the presser foot. I measure a fold of binding twice the finished binding width, mark that with a pin, and leave it unattached. I hand-press the stitched binding out over the raw edge of the quilt.

I then lay the pin marking the end of the free loop along the seam just stitched and insert the needle at the pin where the previous stitching stopped. I backtrack several stitches and then proceed to stitch the next side, continuing until all four sides have the binding attached.

To finish the corners, I fold the quilt diagonally until its vertical and horizontal bindings are lined up against each other. I mark the center point of the binding, then draw a line at a 45-degree angle from the corner of the stitching to the center, and from the outer fold to the center. I stitch along these lines, forming a point, then trim close to the stitching, and turn it right side out. Both sides are then mitered.

— Nina Lord, Annapolis, MD and Jean Harris Robinson, Cinnaminson, NJ

Additional tips

❖ For place mats, I like to use extra-wide, double-folded bias tape for binding. I straight stitch one side in the first fold line. Then I turn the binding to the other side and sew it down with a medium zigzag.
— Karen M. Campbell, Germantown, MD

❖ I just got a 1/4-inch foot for my Bernina that works extremely well for applying binding and piecing accurately.
— Debra Botelho Zeida, Waquoit, MA

❖ I always fold binding in half, doubling it, because the binding is the first thing to wear out.
— Faye Meyers, San Jose, CA

❖ I use an Evenfeed Foot on my sewing machine when I apply binding to avoid puckering.
— Rosie Mutter, Bechtelsville, PA

❖ I use a 2-inch strip to make a 1/4-inch binding; the extra thickness of doubling the fabric adds extra body to the binding.
— Pearl Mok, Los Angeles, CA

❖ I use a walking foot to sew binding on so it won't bunch and fold sideways.
— Virginia C. White, Gallup, NM

❖ I am very careful not to stretch binding. I prewash my bindings so they will not shrink. I pour boiling water over purchased binding still on the card and let it dry to avoid ironing and stretching.
— Loyce Wood Sage, Gallup, NM

❖ If I'm short on binding, I cut the corners off the quilt and round them. That requires much less fabric.
— Vi Angle, Rosebury, OR

❖ I like trimming the back and batting 1/4 inch longer than the top so the binding feels full when folded and tacked down.
— Alana Clark Robbins, Los Lunas, NM

❖ I use 1/2-inch seams for binding so it never comes off.
— Vi Angle, Rosebury, OR

❖ I find fabrics with glitter gold and silver do not work well for borders and binding. Maybe it's me, but I have had troubles! They are heavy and stiffer.
— Helen M. Erickson, Grants Pass, OR

❖ Before sewing on the binding, I like to trim the batting at a 45-degree angle on the corner where the binding pivot point will occur. This prevents a lot of bulk in the corner.
— Carolee Kidd, Albuquerque, NM

❖   Sometimes I don't bind a wall hanging; instead, I stitch the perimeter with the batting on the bottom and the right sides of the fabrics together, then turn it right side out, press it, and quilt 1/4 inch inside the edge after stitching the opening shut (any quilting would need to be done after this procedure).

— Sara Harter Fredette, Williamsburg, MA

❖   When putting a sleeve on the back of a quilt, I take a strip of fabric that matches the backing, finish the raw edge at the two ends, and fold it in half lengthwise. Then before sewing on the binding, I pin the sleeve to the raw edge and sew it on with the binding. I can then sew down the bottom fold of the sleeve by hand.

— Sharleen White, Arnold, MD

❖   To make gathers for a quilted project such as a pillow or baby quilt, I set the sewing machine to the largest zigzag stitch and sew carpet thread or dental floss on top of the fabric. Then I pull up the heavy thread or dental floss to gather the fabric.

— Kathy Evenson, Fergus Falls, MN

❖   Since I'm usually working on more than one quilt at a time, I make the outside border 2 inches to 2 1/2 inches wider than its final size. That way I always have enough fabric for binding it in the same fabric, even though it might be two years before that quilt gets finished. When I'm ready, I simply cut off the 2 inches to 2 1/2 inches around the quilt and have enough for its binding.

— Jean Harris Robinson, Cinnaminson, NJ

Signing and dating quilts

Documentation with pens

❖ I use Pigma pens on a muslin square. I turn the edges under and appliqué it to the back of the quilt.

— Karen M. Campbell, Germantown, MD

❖ I sign and date all my quilts with a Pigma pen 01. I also sketch a special design around my name and date! I feel this adds a personal touch.

— Betty Hutchinson, St. Charles, MO

❖ I spray-starch the muslin square that I will be using and then iron freezer paper to the back of it for stability. I also use a ruler to line the paper side of the freezer paper so that my writing is straight on the fabric. The lines show through clearly enough to make it easy to write on them. Sometimes I use a rubber stamp (to reflect my mood) in the top left corner. I may include a few lines of poetry that I select that conveys the message of the piece, followed by my name, date, city and state. I then set the inks with a hot iron. Then I appliqué the muslin square to the back of the quilt.

— Janice Muller, Derwood, MD

❖ I like to make a smaller version of the blocks in the quilt, line it, and appliqué it to the back of the quilt as a pocket, using a Velcro dot as a fastener at the open end. I write my signature and date in indelible ink on the quilt under the pocket, and write other information on paper or cloth and place it inside the pocket.

— Ada L. Bishop, Beatrice, NE

❖ I use a pen that will not wash out to write on the back side of the quilt. If the backing is white, I embroider instead so there isn't any chance of the ink going through to other layers.

— Faye Meyers, San Jose, CA

❖ Sometimes I cross-stitch a label. Most of the time I find a design I like, trace the design over a light box with a Pigma pen, and then print or write my name, the quilt's title and date. Sometimes I add paint to designs.

— Judi Robb, Manhattan, KS

❖ I use an indelible marker and sign my initials and the date on the back of the quilt. For a Freedom quilt for my 21-year-old son, I wrote a small story about his quilt on a piece of fabric and sewed it to the back of the quilt.

— Barbara Nolan, Pleasant Valley, NY

❖ I sign my quilts with a very fine permanent marker pen in the lower right front corner. On the back, somewhere towards the middle, not on a removable label, I print the information plus the name of the quilt.

— Alison Schwabe, Englewood, CO

❖ I use a Pigma Micron #5 pen for my name and a #1 for drawing flowers. I spray-starch the fabric first. Taping the fabric down provides more stability for writing.

— Ann Judge, Queenstown, MD

❖ I draw faint guidelines on a large piece of muslin, which I then put in a hoop intended for liquid embroidery. The lower hoop is solid and provides a firm surface for writing. I write slowly, carefully and legibly and allow the inscription to set for 24 hours, then iron it to further set the ink. I hem the two inner edges and attach the outer edges to the quilt by catching them in the seam when I attach the binding. I appliqué the inside edges to the quilt.

— Bethel Triplett Moore and Karen Moore, Fairfax, VA

Documenting with embroidery

❖ I embroider using only a single strand of floss and very tiny stitches.
— Ruth Ann Penner, Hillsboro, KS

❖ On large quilts, I embroider my name, either with outline stitch or cross-stitch, and the date. Then I make a muslin label using the typewriter with the pattern name, my name, address and the date the quilt was finished and attach that to the quilt over my embroidered name.

— Elizabeth Haderer, East Quoque, NY

❖ I use an embroidery stitch to label quilts. I sign my name in pencil and then embroider over it so it is in my own handwriting.

— Pat Segal, Mechanicsburg, PA

Documenting with cross-stitch

❖ Ever since my wife, Yvonne M. Khin, and I started making quilts, we have always attached a label to each — homemade by Yvonne Khin in cross-stitch — giving the name of the quilt, who quilted it and when. When more than one person is involved in making the quilt/quilts, we stitch their names in addition.

— U. Khin, Rocky Ridge, MD

❖ I make a cross-stitch label with my name, town, date and the quilt's name, bind it with a matching fabric from the front of the quilt, and sew it on the back. If the quilt is made for someone special, I also include their name and the occasion.

— Judi Manos, West Islip, NY

❖ I cross-stitch on 14-count Aida and appliqué it to the back side of the quilt. For children's quilts, I frequently use checked gingham for the back and have a ready-made stitch-grid.

— Joan Lemmler, Albuquerque, NM

Documenting with quilting

❖ When marking quilting designs on a quilt, I mark my initials and the date on a corner of the quilt, and then quilt that information along with the quilting pattern.

— Audrey H. Eby, Lancaster, PA

❖ On one of the borders of only the quilt top, I mark and quilt with quilting thread my name and the date when I made the quilt. I don't try to go through to the back. If I have worked on only one quilt from start to finish, I have sometimes quilted in the date I began it, the date I completed it, and "made for _____ by _____ (my name)."

— Mary Wheatley, Mashpee, MA

❖ I quilt information into my quilts, incorporating it into the design — along the curve of stems or along the lines of hatching, so it becomes integral to the quilt. I sign it in permanent ink on the back, along with basic information — made for whom, the occasion, my name and town, the year and size. I also attach muslin with information and care instructions.

— Carol Findling, Beatrice, NE

Other methods

❖ I include all information on a typed muslin piece — the batting I used, my method of construction, the pattern, maker and the date made — and appliqué it to the quilt. I also embroider my name and the completion date somewhere on the back.

— Mildred Fauquet, Lincoln, NE

❖ When I finish the binding, I always appliqué a heart on the back and write for whom the quilt was made, the date it was finished, my name and address, the pattern and what book it came from.

— Shan D. Lear, Middleton, MA

❖ Lately I've been typing all the information on muslin and then cutting it into a heart-shaped label. I use my maiden name, as well as my first and last names, so that I can be traced.

— Sara Harter Fredette, Williamsburg, MA

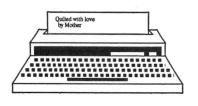

❖ I make labels on the computer by ironing muslin to freezer paper and printing directly on the muslin. I go over the printing with Pigma pen and iron it to fix the ink.

— Ellen Victoria Crockett, Springfield, VA

❖ I have a fabulous machine that does alphabets, so I stitch my own labels and hand-appliqué them to the back. I have begun to piece quilt backs, either with ugly leftovers (for a scrap quilt) or by repeating a design element. I always sew in a light solid patch, and that becomes my built-in label. I like the idea of the label that is part of the back because it cannot be removed. I also like to tell the story of the quilt, if there is one.

— Sherri Driver, Englewood, CO

❖ My backs are pieced in a way that suits the front. When I piece, I insert a light panel that I have machine-embroidered or written on with a permanent ink Pentel product. My label includes the title of the piece, my name and/or others if it was a group project, my city and state, the date I completed it, and the size. If the item is for sale or a show, I also list the fiber content and batting.

— Barbara Tone Lister, Highlands Ranch, CO

❖ I am part of a close circle of quilting friends who decided to do a sort of friendship quilt. Each member made a block for each of the other members. The label on my finished quilt is a circle with pieshaped wedges. It represents the six of us. Each pie-shaped piece is the background of the block that person chose. With each name is a simple floral appliqué that shows the fabrics each person is using for her quilts. This is more ambitious identification than I usually do, but then it represents many people.

— Dorothy Humphrey, Webster, NY

❖ I tape muslin to typewriter paper. I type twice onto the muslin, as much information as I want to say. I put a vinegar/water (equal parts) cloth on top and then iron it to help set the type. This allows the quilt to be washed over and over again.

        — Jo Ann Pelletier, Longmeadow, MA

❖ I am working at a way to create a pretty and interesting label directly on the back of the quilt itself to eliminate the possibility of an appliquéd label falling off. I am still experimenting with copper plate calligraphy to get a Victorian look (although my quilts are not Victorian). I now make sure I include the name of the recipient and the occasion, in addition to my personal information with the date.

        — Abby Breslaw Shipper, Hartsdale, NY

❖ I make a label on my sewing machine, attach it to the back of the quilt, and quilt through it.

        — Jean Turner, Williams Lake, BC

❖ I have used fabric picture transfer medium to include photos on the backs of family quilts.

        — Betty Kegerreis-Fulmer, Quakertown, PA

Additional tips

❖ I keep a notebook of sayings or quotes I particularly like and sometimes use one of those on my quilt labels.

        — Bonnie Zabzdyr, Wright City, MO

❖ When signing fabric with a pen, I iron a piece of freezer paper to the back to help stabilize the fabric. This is especially useful for signing friendship blocks.

        — Susan Ketcherside, St. Charles, MO

❖ My friends make fun of me and say that I end up writing a book about my projects! I always include my name, age, address, the name of the quilt, for whom it was made and why, that person's address, and the type of fabric and batting I used. If it is a project that I made in a class, I include the instructor's name and the location of the class. I have several antique quilts that are not signed and am saddened that no one knows who put all that work and love into those quilts.

        — Linda Nixon, Cardiff, MD

16

Storing quilts and wall hangings

Storing while in process

❖ I fold and store my quilts in plastic shopping bags while they are in process, but I make sure they are not sealed tightly. This lets them breathe but keeps them clean.

— Carol Trice, Wayne, PA

❖ I use shopping bags to separate fabric for a project in progress from my large fabric stash.

— Sally Price, Reston, VA

❖ I made a big cloth bag in which I can carry the quilt in progress.

— Donna M. W. Lantgen, Rapid City, SD

❖ When traveling, I put quilts in process in a black plastic bag between my legs in the car and pull up as much quilt as I need to work in the hoop.

— Dorothy Reise, Severna Park, MD

❖ When working on quilts, I keep them covered with a sheet in my sewing area.

— Mildred Fauquet, Lincoln, NE

❖ I keep the quilt I'm working on in a clothes basket.

— Cindy Krestynick, Glen Lyon, PA

❖ For a project in progress, I store its pieces — cut, ready to sew and finished blocks — in plastic fish containers. I used to get them free from the grocery or fish market, but now they cost a dollar each. They are a good size (15 inches x 11 inches x 5 1/2 inches), have tight fitting lids, and can be stacked.

— Mary Seielstad, Schenectady, NY

❖ When working on a quilt, I always try to hang it over a banister so I can see it come to life and change with the changes in the light in the room. This always warms my heart. I equate it to watching a child grow!

— Doris Morelock, Alexandria, VA

❖ When I have a quilt in the frame, I cover it with a flat sheet and fold it back as I quilt. This keeps it clean and dust-free. I store a finished quilt in a large paper bag.

— Charlotte Shaffer, Ephrata, PA

❖ While my quilt is in process, I roll it on a padded carpet roll.

— Kaye Schnell, Falmouth, MA

❖ I put one project at a time in a large see-through plastic box by Rubbermaid. I never mix projects, thereby eliminating the chance of losing pieces or patterns or, worse yet, directions.

— Barbara McGinnis, Ocean City, NJ

❖ I keep a quilt in process in a small suitcase.

— Dorothy Dyer, Lee's Summit, MO

❖ When working on a quilt, I toss it over a portable towel rack. A friend uses her laundry cart.

— Connee Sager, Tucson, AZ

❖ I have many quilts "in process." I keep them in individual boxes with all their supplies together — instructions, color layout diagram, thread, if special color is being used, quilting ideas, or anything else I want to include in that quilt, plus the date I started it.

— Lee Ann Hazlett, Freeport, IL

❖ I put quilts in process in shallow cardboard boxes (the kind that cases of pop are stacked in) with the ends labeled. I stack these in my sewing room closet, where it's easy to pull out whatever project I feel like working on. I always have lots of quilts started in various stages of completion.

— Darla Sathre, Baxter, MN

❖ When a quilt is in the frame, I cover it with a plastic paint dropcloth. I store the finished quilt in a big quilt box.

— Loyce Wood Sage, Gallup, NM

❖ I get large, clean pizza boxes from the pizza shop and store blocks of a quilt in progress in them. This allows me to keep even large blocks in good shape with no fold marks.

— Barbara Monay, Annapolis, MD

❖ I keep the quilt I'm working on on a cotton flannel blanket, hung over a spring tension rod, positioned in a closet door frame.
— L. Jean Moore, Anderson, IN

❖ I have a quilt basket designed by Helen Mitchum of Mt. Pleasant, North Carolina. The basket is 18 inches high, based on an apple basket pattern. It grows out from a round base, then tapers in at the top to about 18 inches. A king-size quilt and its batt fit in the basket. A section of the quilt in the hoop forms the cover.
— Betsy Hughes, Midlothian, VA

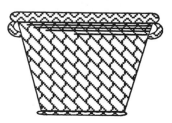

❖ I fold quilts in process over a clothes drying rack. This is also great to hold tops waiting to be sandwiched.
— Alyce C. Kauffman, Gridley, CA

❖ I pin quilts that I'm piecing to foam board. I keep appliqué work rolled and tied in a fabric book with flannel and cotton pages. I put small wall hangings in my daughter's old cotton crib sheets, similar to large pillow cases. Ideally, I'd like to have ultraviolet windows so the sun wouldn't fade any fabrics.
— Diana M. Garrison, Silver Spring, MD

❖ For ongoing projects I use a movable wire cart with drawers (a Scandinavian product). The cart has six drawers, so I can see each project. I keep overflow projects in cardboard soda pop flats.
— Barbara Tone Lister, Highlands Ranch, CO

Storing completed quilts rolled

❖ I keep my completed quilts rolled onto mailing tubes with the front side on the inside of the roll so the stitches aren't stretched.
— Janice Muller, Derwood, MD

❖ When finished, I roll my quilt so I have fewer folds. I place it in a brown grocery bag, then slip another grocery bag down over the top so it is all covered.
— Jean Shaner, York, PA

❖ I get long cardboard tubes from a fabric store and roll my quilts onto them.
— Helen Plauschinn, Pickering, ON

❖ When I've finished, I roll quilts with old sheets, blankets or towels in them to prevent creases from folds and lay them on a long shelf in a large closet lined with more towels.
— Mildred Fauquet, Lincoln, NE

❖ I store quilts folded in half lengthwise and then rolled up. I wrap them in an old, no longer used, 100-percent cotton mattress pad.
— Susan L. Schwartz, N. Bethesda, MD

❖ I roll my quilts like cigars and wrap them with white cotton sheets.

— Kelly Wagoner, Albuquerque, NM

❖ I roll my quilts on cardboard rolls and put them into cloth bags. For those with embellishments, I have used tissue on top of the quilt to protect its surface.

— Janet Jo Smith, Littleton, CO

❖ I store quilts, especially heirloom quilts, in fabric bags where they can breathe. I fold them up lengthwise, roll them, and slip them into a cloth bag or pillow case. I store them upended instead of pressed flat, so they don't crease.

— Mrs. David L. Miller, Partridge, KS

❖ I roll quilts on a long, fabric-covered tube. I prefer to store quilts rolled over a piece of PVC plastic pipe. I place an old sheet under or on top of the quilt before I roll it to give it extra protection from fading or soiling. If I need to fold it before putting it away, I always fold it differently to avoid its wearing on a crease line.

I avoid exposing quilts to untreated wood, such as a cedar chest or closet shelves, by placing them inside a large, washed pillow case.

— Molly Wilson, Gonzales, TX

❖ For storing finished wall hangings, I sew together a long tube made of fabric with three or four fabric loops spaced along its length. I roll the quilts loosely to fit them in the tube. I put up cup hooks to correspond with the fabric loops, inside closets and above their doors, to hang the quilt bags out of the way.

— Marabee J. Seifert, Easley, SC

Storing completed quilts flat

❖ We have many quilts, and we store them flat on huge tables made for that purpose. Sometimes we store them flat on a raised platform, similar to the way carpets are displayed in carpet shops. In this way the quilts are devoid of creases and always appear in good shape. We do not store more than 25 quilts per flat stack.

— U. Khin, Rocky Ridge, MD

❖ I store finished quilts on a spare bed, up to eight deep!

— Ib Bartlet, Schenectady, NY

❖ When we leave home for a period of time, I lay all my quilts flat on our king-size bed and cover them with a spread.

— Dorothy Reise, Severna Park, MD

❖ If the quilts are small, I store them flat and upside down to prevent their fading. If they are large, I hang them inside out over a clothes rod that we hung on one end of my workroom.

— Vicki Krausz, Denver, CO

Storing completed quilts folded

❖ When finished, I store quilts in the closet, refolding them several times a year.

— Donna M. W. Lantgen, Rapid City, SD

❖ I store my quilts folded in acid-free tissue paper.

— Suellen Fletcher, Noblesville, IN

❖ When finished, I wrap quilts and store them in an acid-free paper-lined dresser drawer.

— Cindy Krestynick, Glen Lyon, PA

❖ I like using king-size pillow cases to store quilts, both before and after I finish them. They are long enough so I can turn under the open end and secure that with pins or clips.

— Judy Williams, Stevensville, MD

❖ I store my quilts in a glass quilt chest.

— Anona Teel, Bangor, PA

❖ I am careful to fold and refold quilts periodically while they are in storage. Airing helps them, but I do not do it in sunshine or heavy wind. I am particularly careful to keep the quilts from touching wood shelves or cupboard sides because they contain an acid which eats the fabric.

I also monitor the amount of humidity in the storage area because dampness can cause rotting and mildew damage. The quilts that I hang on the wall, I rotate often to give them a rest.

— Dorothy VanDeest, Memphis, TN

❖ When I finish a quilt, I fold it with old towels in the folds.

— Kaye Schnell, Falmouth, MA

❖ I place my finished quilts in pillow cases and store them in a no-longer-used deep freezer.

— Dorothy Dyer, Lee's Summit, MO

❖ I store my quilts in beautiful old cotton pillowcases, many of which have handmade lace.

— Connee Sager, Tucson, AZ

❖ I try to keep the shades pulled in the rooms where I have quilts exposed to retard fabric fading. Every so often, I remember to refold quilts in order to eliminate permanent creases.

— Terry Festa, Clinton, CT

❖ I sew old sheets into big bags. I store quilts in them under my bed. I refold them in a different way every few months.

— Rita Gorman, Lockport, NY

❖ I wrap my finished quilts in sheets and store them in cedar-lined trunks. I don't let the quilts touch the sides of the trunks, which have been wallpapered.

— Barbara N. Neff, Cypress, CA

❖ I store quilts in pillow covers that have zippers across their ends. They close easily, are fabric, and are not expensive. I can write my name right on the pillowcase.

— Shirley McFadden, Annapolis, MA

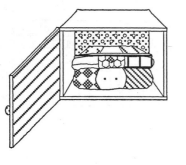

❖ I store finished quilts in a wooden chest that has been sealed with polyurethane paint I refold the quilts every six months. I made a hanger of chain and dowels that I hang from the ceiling for displaying quilts.

— Alyce C. Kauffman, Gridley, CA

❖ I store my finished quilts in an antique pie safe — they're safe from dust, but they can breathe through the holes in the punched tin. Every few months I refold them to avoid creasing.

— Barbara Tone Lister, Highlands Ranch, CO

❖ If you need to fold a quilt to store it, fold it in thirds and roll it, rather than folding it in halves and quarters. This prevents a fold crease running through the center of the quilt.

— The Old Country Store, Intercourse, PA

Additional tips

❖ I drape small pieces over the towel bar on an antique washstand. I find that my being able to look at quilts helps me see things that may inspire my future pieces.

— F. Elaine Asper, Stroudsburg, PA

❖ I store my quilts on large curtain hangers begged from my dry cleaning store.

— Marlys Klein, Scarsdale, NY

❖ I store big quilts by draping them over coat hangers covered with muslin sleeves. I clip them with clothespins and cover them with a large clothing bag.

— Faith Hart Banas, Ludlow, MA

❖ When giving a quilt away, I wrap it in acid-free tissue paper and include a note telling how to store it safely.

— Marion Lumpkins Reece, Richmond, VA

❖ I never store or transport a quilt (finished or unfinished) in a plastic garbage bag. It's too easy to confuse with real trash. I store quilts in a clean, never used, pillowcase. Sometimes I make a matching pillowcase from excess lining material. Acid-free tissue is great for small items.

    — Bethel Triplett Moore and Karen Moore, Fairfax, VA

❖ Every autumn I hang all my quilts on the washline for a day when the wind blows gently.

    — Caryl L. Burgan, Valhalla, NY

❖ When I mail quilts, I never put the word "quilt" on the outside of the package. I just use the letter "Q" in the address name. When I mail to a quilt show, I include a stamped, self-addressed postcard or envelope for them to return so I will know they have received my quilt items.

    — Joyce A. Walker, Ft. Smith, AR

17

Removing spots

Blood

❖ If I find I have blood spots from pricked fingers on the bottom side of the quilt, I use a little hydrogen peroxide on it. The peroxide pulls it right out.
— Sharon Heide, Mt. Lake, MN

❖ Each person's saliva has an enzyme that neutralizes proteins in her/his own blood. Wet a Q-tip with saliva and rub it on the spot to make it disappear.
— Betty Boyton, Gordonville, PA

❖ For bloodstains, chew a ball of white thread, then blot the spot immediately with the wet thread.
— Debra Botelho Zeida, Waquoit, MA

❖ I use a paste made of salt and water to remove blood.
— Helena A. Bagdonas, Brockton, MA

❖ If I'm quilting and bleed on my quilt, I pull a little ball of batting from the edge, soak it in my mouth, and lay it on the blood spot. I allow it to dry and poof — it's all gone.
— Charlotte L. Fry, St. Charles, MO

❖ For blood spots from pricked fingers, soak a cotton ball in cold water. Lay it on the spot on the quilt. When the cotton ball is dry, the blood will be gone!
— Susan Ketcherside, St. Charles, MO

❖ For bloodstains, I use saliva right away. If it is an old bloodstain, I use unseasoned meat tenderizer with a little water and rub it in with a toothbrush. Afterwards, I use a little detergent on a toothbrush to get it out. For greasy stains, I use mild shampoo

— Joy Rubenstein-Moir, Holtsville, NY

❖ I use Spray 'n Wash, lemon juice, peroxide or Baby Wipes to remove blood.

— Carol Farley, Grasonville, MD

❖ On cotton or poly-cotton, I find an ice cube does well at removing bloodstains, even if the stain has set a while.

— Joan Lemmler, Albuquerque, NM

Grease

❖ For grease spots, I take a piece of freezer tape, stick it on the spot, and then pull it off. Most of the grease will lift off. For stains on white fabric, I dip a Q-tip in bleach and apply some to the spots.

— Elaine Nolt, Versailles, MO

❖ I use shampoo for oily hair to remove grease.

— Connee Sager, Tucson, AZ

❖ Baking soda will remove grease products without harming the fabric. Just rub it in gently and vacuum it out.

— Coleen Swettman, Vancouver, WA

Rust

❖ For rust spots, I use Rust Stain Magic which I get at a hardware store.

— Janet Derstine, Telford, PA

❖ If the quilt has iron rust spots, I put a few drops of Willert Home Products, Rust Free, Instant Stain Remover on it and immediately dunk it in water. This is a great product, and I use it on other clothing and carpet, as well as my quilts.

— Betty Hutchinson, St. Charles, MO

❖ If Orvus soap and warm water do not remove a stain, I gently rub a mixture of Zud powder and water on the stain. This has even removed some rust stains from an old quilt.

— Sue Seeley, New Bern, NC

❖ To remove rust spots, I moisten them with lemon juice and then hold the area over steam.

— Dana Braden, Dallas, TX

More ideas for spot removal

❖ For white fabric only, make a paste of dry automatic dishwasher detergent and liquid Prell concentrated shampoo. Apply to the spot with an old toothbrush.

> — Janice Muller, Derwood, MD

❖ Spotto. This is the best stuff in the world! It takes out stains nothing else even fades.

> — Lynne Fritz, Bel Air, MD

❖ I have used Shout, but I have had to wash the whole quilt or a water line would have remained.

> — Margaret Jarrett, Anderson, IN

❖ I try liquid Ivory soap. I rub the spot gently and rinse it thoroughly.

> — Marjorie Mills, Bethesda, MD

❖ I try to avoid spots so I don't have to remove them. I wash my hands before quilting and after lunch breaks and every two hours. Clorox 2 helps a badly soiled quilt.

> — Laura Reif Lipski, Lindenhurst, NY

❖ Most organic stains can be removed with a spritz of liquid Murphy's Oil Soap and then washing it normally.

> — Linda Hampton Schiffer, Columbia, MD

❖ I keep a bar of Fels Naptha (Octagon) soap handy. It works well on clothes stains, too. I make sure the area I am spot cleaning is wet, because the Fels Naptha can stain. Always check for color fastness too!

> — F. Elaine Asper, Stroudsburg, PA

❖ I've found rubbing alcohol to be the best thing for removing spots.

❖ I use a Pentel Clip Eraser to remove pencil marks.

> — Geneva Herod, Ashland, VA

❖ I combine Dreft and Clorox Powder (equal amounts of each) and mix that with water to make a strong mixture. I soak the stain for a long period of time or overnight.

> — Mary F. Martin, Hagerstown, MD

❖ I use Resolve fabric cleaner.

> — Pearl Mok, Los Angeles, CA

❖ I use Magic Wand carefully for some spots. Also, the few times a fabric has bled, I have just washed it again and, luckily, the second time the bleeding has washed out.

> — Patricia Fielding, Stone Mountain, GA

❖ I mix some Woolite and water, rub it into the spot, and put it in the sun. When it's dry, I take clear water, dab the spot, and let it dry.

> — Helen L. Anderson, Titusville, NJ

❖ I've sprayed Shout on a spot.

> — Barbara F. Hummel, Punxsutawney, PA

❖ I use alcohol or hair spray to remove ball-point pen ink.
— Katherine Lombard, Deerfield, NH

❖ A lemon and water rinse and sunshine are a wonderful, old-fashioned and safe way to tenderly bleach a dingy, yellowed or tattletale gray fabric.
— Dorothy VanDeest, Memphis, TN

❖ I quilt heavily in the area of the spot and hope it disappears in the shadow created by the quilting.
— Vicki Krausz, Denver, CO

❖ For any spots, soak them in cold water as soon as possible. This should disperse the soiled spot by removing or loosening up the spot Then wash in Woolite.
Barbara Nolan, Pleasant Valley, NY

❖ I like to use Amway LOC on many spots. Vinegar works for acid-type stains — tomato sauce, grape juice, etc.
— Laura Barrus Bishop, Boerne, TX

❖ For stains such as pencil marks or mud, I use Formula 409 on a towel and first wipe vertically, then horizontally across the stain.
— Lou Ann Philpot, Murray, KY

❖ Stanley Spot Remover takes out most spots. I remove ink by using a few drops of whole milk, then washing it out with warm water.
— Esther S. Martin, Ephrata, PA

❖ I do not use chemicals! I use pure soap or salt and lemon juice and sun, then sponge the spot with distilled water.
— Kaye Schnell, Falmouth, MA

❖ I place a heavy white towel behind the piece and blot with a solution of Ivory liquid and water. The heavy towel underneath keeps the spot from going to another area of the piece.
— Rhondalee Schmidt, Scranton, PA

❖ When old masking tape left a gummy residue that attracted dirt, I had good luck with lighter fluid. I squirted it on, then rubbed it off with a damp washcloth.
— Julie McKenzie, Punxsutawney, PA

❖ Mix l/4 cup household ammonia, 1/2 cup dish detergent, and one cup water in a spray bottle. Spray the soiled area, rub it, and throw it in the washer.
— Dorothy Dyer, Lee's Summit, MO

❖ I have a wonderful formula: three ounces rubbing alcohol, one ounce water, three or four drops liquid detergent. Mix well and use a soft toothbrush to apply. This removes pencil marks well.
— Shirley J. Odell, Manteca, CA

❖ I use toothpaste on ink spots.
— Sara Ann Miller, Fredericksburg, OH

❖ I find that the lye soap I make removes most stains. I've had good luck using baby shampoo on antique quilt blocks with stains.
— Scarlett von Bernuth, Canon City, CO

❖ I use a vet's soap for spot removal or treat spots with Shout.
— Patty Miller, Charles City, IA

❖ I use Fantastic. It may not always remove the spot, but it has never damaged the fabric, and it doesn't leave water spots. I usually "spot" clean.
— Jorita J. Groves, Bushland, TX

❖ If the spot is from human oil, my daughter, who is a beautician, suggests using shampoo.
— Thelma A. Stein, Tavares, FL

❖ I sometimes make a paste of cream of tartar and water, rub it on the spot, let it dry, then rub it off.
— Marjorie L. Benson, Yates City, IL

❖ I try cold water first! Liquid Dial works wonders.
— Nancy Jo Marsden, Glen Mills, PA

❖ I leave a cold-water cloth on the stain for a while. I also use Kiss-Off a lot, and it works well.
— Janet Derstine, Telford, PA

❖ I wet the area of the spot and spray it with Clear Magic (available in automotive sections). I brush it lightly with a soft bristle brush, rinse it thoroughly, then air-dry it out of the sun.
— Teresa Ernest Steinstraw, Denton, TX

❖ Most spots are usually protein-based. I find that if I wet the spot with cold water, then apply a tiny amount of ERA brand liquid detergent, leaving it on a short time, I can lift away the detergent with a wet wash-cloth. The spot comes off with a little rubbing. I must wet the spot first, however, to prevent any color "lifting."
— Jane E. Crowe, Boyertown, PA

❖ To remove spots from old quilts, I use one gallon water, one quart buttermilk and one tablespoon vinegar. I soak the quilt in the solution and then wash it gently.
— Adella Halsey, Wymora, NE

❖ If the spot is in a white section of the quilt, I lay the quilt on a sheet in the sun with a second sheet over the top. I cut a hole in the top sheet to expose the spot, treat it with lemon juice, and allow the sun to bleach it out.
— Carol Sucevic, Hopwood, PA

❖ Vivid will take out spots if the fabric should run after the quilt is put together.

— Roberta S. Bennsky, Annapolis, MD

❖ When I wash my quilts, I use Orvus soap and put them in the bathtub with a sheet laid in the bottom of the tub for lifting them out.

— Cheri Ruzich, Live Oak, CA

❖ I think Lestoil is a magic elixir! Used full strength on almost any color or fabric, it removes just about anything — ball-point ink, pencil, blood (mostly), grease, tomato sauce, lipstick, other makeup, grass, chocolate — it's great — if you can take the smell.

— Abby Breslaw Shipper, Hartsdale, NY

❖ I have never tried this on a quilt, but I've used eyeglass cleaner to take fresh coffee stains out of a blouse.

— Doris F. Kluss, Mason City, IN

❖ A product I use and found safe for most fabrics, especially cotton, is Easy Wash by Van Wyck Products.

— Trudy Kutter, Corfu, NY

❖ I spray wall hangings with Scotchgard. That makes it easier to brush off the dust.

— Marilyn Stephens, St. Marys, ON

❖ I wash small pieces in Cascade dishwashing compound, about a tablespoon to eight quarts of water.

— Jeannine Dougherty, Tyler, TX

❖ I keep a small bottle of distilled water (some waters have staining minerals in them) available while I work on a quilt. Club Soda, 7-Up or any clear, carbonated beverage works well if it is applied immediately. I avoid commercial spot removers because I found them not as effective. Sometimes they create more of a stain when dry than the original spot.

— Joyce R. Swinniz, Mooresville, IN

❖ If I'm in process and have leftover fabric, the same as what is spotted on the quilt, I use the scrap to test the cleaning agent. I also use the scrap to rub against the like fabric on the quilt. It leaves no debris.

— Betsy Jarasz, Youngstown, NY

Additional tips

❖ I never use a colored cloth to remove spots. Some color may be transferred to the quilt.

— Annabelle Unternahrer, Shipshewana, IN

❖ Sometimes a little appliqué can be added without distracting from the design. I have a friend whose dog chewed a small hole in her prized quilt.

She appliquéd a flower over it, and no one will ever know but her and the dog and me!

— Mildred Fauquet, Lincoln, NE

❖ Sometimes if a spot will not go away, a coffee or tea bath will make a quilt look okay. I scorched a top while piecing it. A tea bath made it look fine.

— Leigh Booth, Kintnersville, PA

18

Amish Quilts

Amish Quilt Patterns

The magic of antique Amish quilts has captured admirers everywhere. This section offers patterns, step-by-step instructions, and color suggestions for reproducing many favorite antique Amish quilts.

Why the interest in antique Amish quilts?

Perhaps it is the simplicity and peace visible in the lives of the people who create them that has made their quilts so fascinating. Perhaps it is the combination of energy and restraint in these quilts' simple geometric patterns that gives them such broad appeal.

Perhaps in a modern, fast-moving technological age people grasp for links with the past to find stability. Whatever the reason, there are increasing numbers of people interested in Amish quilts.

Many old quilts from the larger Amish settlements of eastern Pennsylvania and the Midwest have already been purchased from private homes by museums and collectors. The transition happened slowly at first but soon the Amish communities were ravaged by "door knockers" — persons who stopped randomly at Amish homes offering to buy any old quilts. Some homes had old quilts stolen from them while the family was away at church.

That understandably made the Amish community uneasy, so some owners decided to sell their quilts before they were stolen. Some wanted to sell but wished to wait until the market drove prices higher. Others wanted to keep their quilts and got weary of questions. But most did not understand the unusual demand.

Within the Amish community, values and commitments are taught and passed on to the next generations through a way of life. Consequently, for the Amish a tangible symbol of their past is not important or sought after because their basic values are firm and generally not losing ground.

In fact, for them a new quilt seems a more appropriate wedding present than an old one. And so, many old quilts left homes with their sellers happy to have cash instead.

For those outside the Amish community, these old quilts stand as symbols of the past. They speak of a time of long family evenings, winter leisure and handcrafted works of love. Their bold shapes and dark vibrant colors show stability and freedom within specific limitations.

Many persons continue to search for these works of art from the past. But the quilts are increasingly hard to find. These Amish quilt patterns attempt to provide the next best thing — a good reproduction It is not possible with modern dyes and fabrics to duplicate the deep warm colors produced by natural dyes

Some strikingly true reproductions have been made with the use of old fabrics But it is also possible to come close to the old look with careful attention to fabric selection, pattern, scale and quilting designs. These patterns include easy-to-follow instructions so that anyone can make one of these prized quilts.

Amish crib quilts and wall hangings

Antique Amish crib quilts are avidly sought by collectors of Amish crafts. When found, these small treasures bring prices close to, or exceeding, full-sized quilts of the same genre.

The reasons for the high values placed on these small quilts are varied. First, these bedcovers are scarce. Fewer crib quilts were made to supply the needs of a household. A quilt could be made for the crib and remain as the crib cover for a series of different occupants. Obviously, such a quilt went through repeated washings. Often they were used until they were thoroughly worn and then thrown out and replaced. Today, collectors are often willing to pay high prices for a crib quilt even if it shows severe signs of wear.

Secondly, crib quilts are desirable because of their size. They make magnificent wall displays and are more likely than larger quilts to fit on the wall spaces of modern homes.

Then there is the special feeling connected with crib quilts. They stand as a tangible symbol of love and caring. They hold warm memories of childhood, carefree days and restful nights, the secure feelings of loving and being loved.

This section includes patterns that have been reduced in size so that the proportions will be pleasing in a small quilt. Templates for piecing, as well as quilting designs, are given in actual size so that no adaptation is required on the part of the maker. Though they are suitable for crib quilts, these patterns should not be limited to that. They make dynamic wall hangings and can be custom designed to suit both color and space requirements.

When used as wall hangings, these quilts are truly display pieces and can be painstakingly pieced and quilted without fear of the wear and tear of normal use. Or what better gift can be given than a handmade quilt to cuddle and comfort a child through the dark night hours!

Getting started

Good planning is the most basic rule in successful quiltmaking. It will minimize many frustrations! You should know before selecting your fabric which quilt pattern you are going to make, how many colors you will need to complete your choice, and which colors or color families you want to use.

Choosing a pattern

Amish quilts are made in a wide variety of patterns. And many patterns look "Amish" because of the colors used. The three designs that are distinctively Amish are the Bars, Center Diamond and Sunshine and Shadow patterns.

These, by virtue of their simplicity and straight lines, are easy to piece and, therefore, excellent choices for beginners. However, a trademark of these patterns is also their elaborate quilting designs, so to recreate them requires the patience and skill to cover them with tiny, even quilting stitches.

A beginning quilter will be less frustrated by choosing a pattern that can be assembled in straight line units rather than one that requires setting in triangles.

For example, the Nine-patch pattern can be done in a series of straight lines, whereas the Lone Star quilt requires setting a triangle piece into a corner. Study the assembly instructions of a pattern and choose one that provides an adequate challenge without undue difficulty.

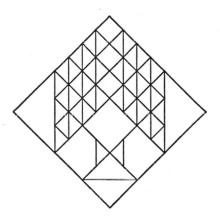

Making a model

Since it is difficult to visualize a grouping of colors and fabrics in a quilt when working with either large bolts or small swatches, it is helpful to sketch a scale model of the quilt onto graph paper and then use crayons or colored pencils to fill in the appropriate colors.

You can get an even more accurate color representation by purchasing small amounts of the fabrics under consideration and cutting them into tiny patches to cover the appropriate areas on the scale model. This is especially helpful when working with those patterns using large geometric shapes. It becomes more tedious when working with patterns involving small patches.

Despite that, it is a very beneficial exercise since it allows the quilter to see in advance whether one fabric is lost or dominant among the others. If, for instance, you are trying to emphasize a particular design within a patch, the surrounding areas will need to provide adequate

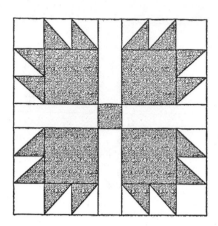

contrast so the design pattern will stand out. This dimension can be achieved with light and dark fabrics or by the use of contrasting colors.

Selecting "Amish" colors

Most Amish quiltmakers did not understand the science of color selection and combinations. They followed their intuitions and used what was at hand. In the past and today, Amish homes are bare by most American standards. Walls are generally painted a plain blue or green. Floors, if carpeted at all, are usually covered with handmade rag rugs. Very little upholstered furniture is used.

In short, these people, because of their commitment to simplicity, have traditionally given very little effort to coordinating room decor and accessories. The same is true of their clothing. The Amish style of dress is prescribed by the church. They are not concerned about the latest styles or fashion colors. These matters have simply never applied to the Amish way of life. Consequently, they are not bound by the surrounding culture's sense of what is proper and what is not.

This freedom from the dictates of society's norms is evident in the color schemes of antique Amish quilts. Frequently, the colors which color theory describes as complementary (opposite each other on the color

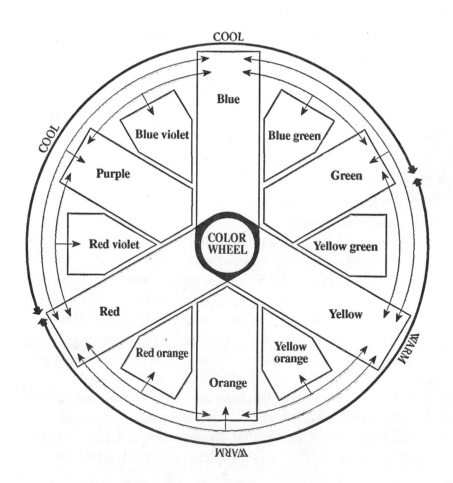

wheel) often appear together in Amish quilts. Probably the makers never knew they had selected complementary colors, but they could see that those colors brought out the best in each other.

Many Amish quilts have accents of black and red, a combination that decorators recognize as a boost for many color schemes. When Amish women emptied their scrap bags they didn't work from a basis of scientific knowledge. They just chose their fabrics in relation to each other. Many times the result was a dramatic color scheme that stands up well today.

It would be unfair to create the impression that all Amish quilts were masterful in color. There are many that are less than pleasingly coordinated. But if you would like to capture the best in antique Amish quilt colors, you will likely be most successful if you try to forget what you know about color and begin with a fresh, new approach.

There are several guidelines you might follow. The fabrics used in antique Amish quilts are almost always solid colors. Printed fabrics seldom appear. The oldest, most traditional Amish quilts come from eastern Pennsylvania, specifically from the Amish of Lancaster County. This earliest settlement tends to be more conservative than some of the groups who later migrated to other areas.

The clothing colors of this group used only part of the spectrum of the color wheel, avoiding those colors known as warm colors — bright reds, red orange, orange, yellow orange, yellows and yellow green. The "cool" colors — burgundies, blues, purples and greens, were the colors permitted for clothing and also used in quilts. Therefore, these more conservative, traditional Amish quilts reflected their community's standards and used a myriad of colors, but only those within the boundaries of that "cooler" spectrum.

Antique Amish quilts from areas outside the eastern Pennsylvania communities were often more daring in their colors. Yellows and oranges appear frequently in Midwestern quilts and those from Pennsylvania counties other than Lancaster. However, these colors were used in conjunction with the traditional darker hues. For example, it is extremely unusual to find an Amish quilt using only a scheme of earth tones.

Play with colors in several arrangements before you make a final decision. See how they stand in reference to each other. Some colors highlight one another and others have a dulling effect.

Try, as much as you can, to approach your color selection in an uninhibited way. The closer you can get to that approach, the more likely it is that you can create a quilt that looks authentically Amish.

Don't forget black

To approximate "Amish" color choices, you will do best by using colors of varying intensities and shades. And don't forget black. Black can be a spark of life in a color scheme. Several shades of black may be more interesting than only one. The varying shades that appear in old quilts happened because they were often scrap quilts, and substitutions were made for fabrics that ran out. You should not be afraid to try substituting one or several similar fabrics instead of using the same one throughout the quilt.

Choosing good fabric

The quality of a quilt is only as good as the quality of each of its components. Therefore, it is essential to choose high-quality fabrics for quiltmaking.

Lightweight 100-percent cotton is ideal for quiltmaking. In addition, 100-percent cottons have a dull finish, making them similar to the old fabrics. (Cottons blended with synthetics tend to have more luster or sheen.) The fabric should be tightly woven so it does not ravel excessively. If you check its cut edges and find it frays easily, the fabric will be difficult to work with, especially in small pieces.

Test it for wrinkling by grasping a handful and squeezing firmly. If sharp creases remain when the fabric is released, it will wrinkle as you work it and will not have a smooth appearance, especially if it is used in large sections on a quilt. It is wise to wash all fabrics before using them to preshrink and test them for color fastness.

Figuring yardage

Aside from the quilt back, one of the areas requiring the largest amount of fabric on pieced quilts (particularly antique Amish patterns) is the border. The border looks best if it does not need to be pieced. Therefore, its fabric should be purchased adequately so as to run the entire length of the quilt. Any fabric remaining along the edges after the borders are cut can be cut into patches for another quilt.

Be sure to calculate seam allowances when figuring yardage. It is a good idea to remove all selvages from fabrics before cutting, so allow for that when calculating the width of fabric you need. Most quilting fabrics are 44 to 45 inches wide.

Since most quilts are wider than that, you will likely need to piece the back of the quilt. When calculating yardage requirements, remember that the back should be five to six inches larger than the quilt top to allow for shrinkage that will occur during the quilting process. You should buy enough fabric so that it can run the full length or width of the quilt without being pieced. Then buy as many lengths or widths as you need to cover the quilt back. Remember to calculate for seams when buying fabric for the quilt backing.

Figure the total yardage you need for patchwork pieces by calculating the amount of fabric you need per block, and then multiply that by the number of blocks of that color in the quilt. Again, remember to allow for 1/4-inch seam allowances on all sides of each patch, and a little extra for cutting mishaps. If there will be fabric left from the borders and back from which patches can be cut, delete that amount from the calculated requirements.

Planning borders

Border treatments vary greatly on quilts. They may be seen as a way to quickly increase a quilt's dimensions to an adequate size, or they may be the frame that highlights the quilt pattern. Sometimes they achieve both at the same time. At any rate, a border should not come as an afterthought. Plan your quilt dimensions with the border in mind. Many Amish quilts have wide, elaborately quilted borders.

The important factor is that the borders be in proportion to the interior pattern of the quilt. This will vary from pattern to pattern.

Pattern templates

The accuracy of a template will make a monumental difference in whether a quilt fits together or not. Templates should be very accurately traced onto a material that will withstand repeated outlining without wearing down at the edges. Cardboard is not appropriate for a template that must be used repeatedly.

More durable materials are plastic lids from throw-away containers or the sides of a plastic milk jug. Sandpaper may be glued to the back of the template to keep it from slipping as you mark the fabrics. Plastic template material is also available today in fabric stores or quilt shops.

Before you cut all the quilt's patches, cut enough for just one block by using the new template. Then assemble the patch to check for accuracy. If changes are required (perhaps the corners don't meet), adjust the template and try again. Always test the template by assembling one block before cutting fabric for an entire quilt top.

Templates may be made with or without a seam allowance, depending on the method of marking, cutting and piecing preferred by the quilter.

Marking patches with seam allowances

This method requires that the template be made with a 1/4-inch seam allowance on all sides. When traced onto the fabric, the marked line is the cutting line. The seam line is 1/4 inch inside the marked line. The advantage of this method is that if you work with very sharp scissors, you can trace the outline on the top layer of fabric, but then cut through several layers of fabric at the same time.

With this method, you may use the template as a guide and cut with a rotary cutter and mat. You will need to punch a small hole in the template at every corner, so that you can mark the "match points" where the patches meet.

Marking patches without seam allowances

This method requires that the template be made the actual size of the finished patch. When traced onto the fabric, the marked line is the stitching line. The cutting line must be imagined 1/4 inch outside this line. The advantage here is that you have a tracing line to stitch along, almost guaranteeing accuracy in piecing. The disadvantage is that each patch must be marked and cut individually. With this method you cannot stack and cut multiple layers of fabrics. Choose the method that works best for you. The important thing is to maintain accuracy by whatever way is most comfortable.

It is extremely important to be precise in marking and cutting. A very minute mistake in either step will be multiplied many times over when you try to assemble the quilt. Ultimately, you want to have a smooth, flat quilt top. To achieve that, the individual pieces must fit together precisely.

Marking and cutting fabrics

There are many ways to mark fabrics. You may use a regular lead pencil to trace the template. However, on some fabrics, especially dark fabrics, the markings are very difficult to see.

There are several pencils designed especially for quilters. Some of these make markings that are soluble in cold water, allowing for easy removal of markings. Some pencils make markings that disappear after a certain period of time. That works well if the pieces marked are used before the time elapses. Whatever you choose, be sure to follow the manufacturer's instructions for its use.

Every quiltmaker should have a good pair of sharp fabric shears. The longer the blade of the scissors, the greater the chances of cutting a continuous straight line. The scissors must be sharp all the way to the point to cut well-defined corners.

Rotary cutting is a fast, accurate cutting method available to quilters today. It requires a rotary cutter, a transparent rotary cutting ruler, a rotary cutting mat, and a sturdy, flat surface on which to place the mat. Pieces are cut with 1/4-inch seam allowances included, and several layers of fabric can be cut at the same time.

Piecing

If the pieces have been cut and marked accurately, piecing the quilt is rewarding and fun. Piecing can be done by hand or machine. Machine piecing is a great deal faster and in many cases makes a stronger seam.

If the pieces have been rotary-cut, they may be lined up so that the 1/4-inch stitching line falls directly under the needle. The raw edge of the fabric may be aligned with the edge of a presser foot, a seam guide, or a piece of masking tape, but it should be exactly 1/4-inch from the stitching line.

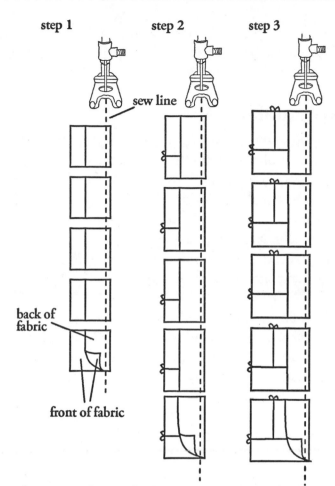

step 1   step 2   step 3

sew line

back of
fabric

front of fabric

In hand piecing, the stitch is a tiny running stitch, sewn along the marked lines, and reinforced occasionally with a backstitch. Care must be taken to keep the seam taut, but not so tight as to cause puckering.

Whether piecing by hand or by machine, follow assembly instructions so that all patches are built in straight seam units whenever possible. When corners must be set in, they can be done either by stitching from the outer edge of the patch to the corner (stopping at the seam allowance), pivoting and sewing out to the other edge, or by starting at the corner, sewing one edge, and then returning to the corner and sewing the other edge. Practice both methods and choose the one most easily completed.

When machine piecing, it is most efficient to stack patches in order and sew all like units at once. This method is called "chain piecing." For example, when making a Log Cabin, sew all the center squares to the first log section, then add all #2 logs, etc. When sewing the patches, do not clip threads between each unit. Rather, feed them through the machine in a continuous row and clip them apart at the end of a group of patches. Repeat the same procedure for adding the next piece to the patches.

It is generally best to press all seam allowances in one direction. Exceptions to this rule are when a dark fabric is next to a light fabric and the seam allowance would show through the light fabric if laid in that direction. A second exception applies when seam allowances would interfere with quilting if pressed in one direction. If these situations exist, it is best to hide or avoid having to quilt through the allowance even if it means they must be pressed opposite from other allowances.

Preparing to quilt

A quilt is a sandwich of three layers: the quilt back, the lining or batting which adds insulation, and the top which is often pieced or appliquéd. The purpose of quilting is to hold together the three layers which constitute the actual quilt — the back, batting and top.

Much of the magic of old Amish quilts is in their hand quilting. They are lavished with quilting designs, leaving few open spaces. This tiny, intricate quilting is essential in reproducing the look of an old quilt. Full-size quilting templates for large quilts and small quilts are included in this book.

Marking those designs on the quilt top can be done in a variety of ways. See "Marking and cutting fabrics" on page 184 for information on quilt-marking pencils. Remember to mark with something that will not rub off easily as quilting requires having hands against the quilt surface. On the other hand, the markings must be completely removable when the quilting is completed so that unsightly lines do not remain.

If you work with fabric that is light enough to see through, the easiest way to mark is by tracing. Outline the quilting designs on paper with a heavy magic marker. Lay the fabric to be marked, wrong side down, on top of the quilting design. Trace, with a fabric marker, or thin-lead pencil over the lines to stitch.

Although this method is easiest, many fabrics used in these quilts are too dark to see lines through the fabric. Therefore, the design must be traced in an alternate way. This can be done by cutting very thin slashes at intervals on the quilting template. This creates a dot-to-dot effect with the slashes. The template is then laid on top of the right side of the fabric and the lines are traced onto the quilt top.

Since templates are used repeatedly, it is wise to make them of a material more durable than paper. Plastic template material is ideal. Straight lines or crosshatching can be marked by laying a ruler on the fabric and tracing along both sides. On large areas, a chalk line can be snapped across the quilt.

When patches are being outlined, no marking around them is necessary. Simply quilt close to the seam to emphasize the patch.

After the quilt top is marked with its quilting lines, it is ready for the actual stitching process.

The type of batting chosen will affect the overall look of the quilt. A polyester batting will give a full, puffy quality to the quilted lines. Cotton batting will be a bit flatter and should be quilted more closely to prevent lumpiness when the quilt is washed. Another option is to use a piece of cotton flannel or an old blanket which will give a flat appearance much like the antique quilts.

Putting the quilt in the frame

Whatever type is chosen, the three layers of the quilt must be stretched and held together throughout the quilting process. This creates a taut surface conducive to quilting.

The most traditional and probably most effective frame is the type that is large enough to stretch the entire quilt out at once. This allows for even tension over the whole quilt. These frames are generally used at quiltings when several persons work on the quilt at the same time. The disadvantages of such a frame are its size and lack of mobility. Since the entire quilt surface is exposed, the frame obviously requires that much floor space. Also, once the quilt is stretched in the frame it should not be removed until quilting is completed. That usually means that the space is occupied for an extended period of time. Many quilters do not have the space required for such a frame.

Another type of frame accommodates the entire quilt at once, but most of it is rolled onto a long rail along one side of the frame. Only about a 3-foot section, along the width of the quilt, is exposed for quilting. As that area is completed, the quilt is rolled onto the opposite rail until the entire quilt is finished.

Even smaller frames are available for quilters with very limited space. These look like giant replicas of embroidery hoops and allow the quilt to be quilted in small sections. A very important procedure before using this type of frame is to baste the entire quilt together through all three layers. Basting should begin at the center and work out toward the edges. Doing this assures that the layers will be evenly stretched while quilting and avoids creating puckers during the quilting process. Do not quilt over the basting stitches because this makes them extremely tedious to remove later.

Making tiny, even stitches

Hand quilting is a simple running stitch. It is done most easily and durably with quilting thread since it is heavier than regular thread and more able to withstand the repeated pulling through the three quilt layers. Quilting needles are called "betweens." These needles are shorter than "sharps," which are considered the normal hand sewing needles. Betweens come in various sizes, which are identified by numbers. Most quilters use a size 7 or 8 to quilt. Some quilters prefer the even smaller size 9 needle. The best way to choose a needle size is to try several and then use the one that seems most comfortable.

A thimble is a must for quilting since the needle must be pushed repeatedly through three fabric layers. The thimble should fit snugly on the second finger of the hand used for pushing the quilting needle.

To begin quilting, cut a piece of quilting thread about 1 yard in length. Thread the needle and make a single knot at the end of the piece. Then insert the needle through only the quilt top about 1 inch from where quilting will begin. Pull the thread through to the knot. Gently tug on the knot until it slips through the fabric and is lodged invisibly underneath the top. This will secure the quilting thread at the beginning. With one hand underneath the quilt and the other on top, push the needle through all three layers until the hand underneath feels a prick. That indicates you've been successful and stitched through all the thicknesses. (Experienced quilters develop calluses from this repeated pricking!)

Then, with the thimble on your upper hand, tilt the needle upward. Use your lower hand to push up slightly from underneath. As soon as the needle point appears on top, reinsert it through the layers again. Continue this process until three to five stitches are stacked on the needle. Finally, pull the needle and thread through the fabric to create the quilting pattern. The stitches should be snug but not so tight as to create puckering. Continue the process of stacking stitches onto the needle until the thread is used. When the length of thread is nearly gone, do a tiny backstitch to secure the thread. Insert the needle again through only the

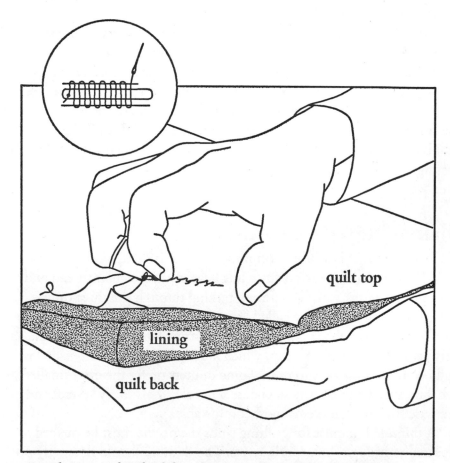

A quilt is a sandwich of three layers — the quilt back, lining or batting, and the quilt top — all held together by the quilting stitches.

To both secure the quilting thread at the beginning and hide the knot, insert the needle through only the quilt top about 1 inch from where the quilting will begin, pull the thread through to the knot, and gently tug on the knot until it slips through the fabric and is lodged invisibly underneath the top.

top layer and make a stitch the length of the needle, away from the quilting design. Pull the needle through the surface and snip the thread with the long stitch left buried underneath the quilt top. Thread the needle and begin again.

The goal to strive for is tiny, even stitches. And they come only with practice! Initially, concentrate on making straight, even stitches, without worrying too much about their size. Try to have the stitch length be the same on both the top and bottom of the quilt. Holding the needle perpendicular to the fabric is crucial for achieving straight stitches. Once you have mastered evenness, try to decrease the size of the stitches.

When quilting curved lines, do not try to stack as many stitches on the needle before pulling it through. No more than two stitches on the needle at a time are best for executing smooth, even curves.

Many quilters today are using their sewing machines to create small, even quilting stitches. Machine quilting is a good alternative, especially for quilters who cannot comfortably hold a small quilting needle due to arthritis or carpal tunnel syndrome. Straight lines of quilting can be sewn easily on the machine. New "even feed" or "walking" attachments are available for sewing machines to make the quilt sandwich go through the machine evenly.

To achieve the small, curved shapes of Amish-style quilting on the machine requires the "free-motion" method of stitching. The feed dogs of the machine are lowered and the quilt is moved around under the needle by hand. This method takes practice, but the results can rival hand quilting.

Either method of machine quilting requires basting the quilt sandwich with safety pins instead of hand basting (which is difficult to remove after machine-stitching). The safety pins can be removed as the quilt is being stitched. Several tools are available to help quilters comfortably insert and remove the safety pins from the quilt.

Binding the quilt

The final step in finishing a quilt is its binding. The binding covers the raw edges along the four sides of a quilt. Bindings, particularly on antique Amish quilts from Pennsylvania, are generally wider than bindings found on many other quilts.

Since the edge of a quilt receives a lot of wear, the binding is often done with a double thickness of fabric. It is not uncommon for bindings on old quilts to have been machine stitched in place, although hand stitching is less obvious.

Bindings can be done in several ways. One of the easier methods is to cut strips of fabric that measure four times the width of the finished binding. These strips can be cut either lengthwise or crosswise on the fabric grain. Lengthwise strips do not need to be pieced, but piecing on a binding is not very obvious and can be done without minimizing the beauty of the quilt.

The binding strips should measure about 1 inch longer than the quilt on two of its parallel sides. On the other two sides, the binding strips should be as long as the quilt's width (or length) plus one inch, plus the double finished binding width from the other two sides.

Fold the binding strips in half, wrong sides together, so that both raw edges meet. Trim any excess lining and backing from the quilt itself. Pin the shorter two binding strips against the two parallel edges of the quilt top's width, with the raw edges of the binding flush with the raw edges of the quilt. Machine stitch in place using a 1/4-inch seam allowance.

Open the seam so that the folded edge of the binding is now the outer edge of the quilt. Sew the remaining binding strips onto the other two sides of the quilt extending out to the folded edge of the attached binding strips. The binding is now folded in half again so that the previously folded edge goes around to the back and covers the seam made by attaching the strips. Hand stitch the binding in place. Fold corners under so that no raw edges are exposed.

Another method of finishing a quilt, less commonly used on old Amish designs, is to simply wrap excess border fabric from the top, bottom and sides of the quilt around to the back where it is stitched in place. Or the extra backing fabric may be wrapped forward over the raw edges to the front where it is stitched in place on the quilt top. However, most old Amish quilts use separate binding. It is frequently in a color which contrasts with the border and is new to the color scheme of the interior of the quilt.

After the binding is completed, you may want to initial and date the quilt so that it can be identified by future generations. If you sign and date with embroidery, that should probably be done on a lower back corner. If you prefer to quilt in the initials and dates, it is usually also done in a corner.

Variations

These patterns are provided for the sizes specified. However, there is great room for variation. If you want a longer quilt, add a row of patches on the top or bottom. If you need a wider quilt, add patches along each side. Border treatments may vary. The borders are meant to frame the quilt and, as long as proper proportions are maintained, they may be pieced in various ways.

The patches are also adaptable for pillows. A grouping of patches may be used together or a single patch can be used and enlarged with the use of borders. Pillows can be finished with piping or ruffles or left plain. Quilt patches can also be used to make potholders, place mats, table runners and tablecloths and other craft projects. The only limit is your own imagination.

To display quilts

Wall quilts can be hung in various ways. One is to simply tack the quilt directly to the wall. However, this will stretch the quilt and may damage the wall. Another option is to hang the quilt like a painting. To do so, make a narrow sleeve from matching fabric and hand sew it to the upper edge of the quilt along the back. Insert a dowel rod through the sleeve and hang the rod by wire or nylon string.

The quilt can also be hung on a frame. This method requires Velcro or fabric to be attached to the frame itself. In the case of Velcro, one side of it is stapled to the frame. The opposite Velcro is hand sewn on the edges of the quilt and attached carefully to the Velcro on the frame. If fabric is attached to the frame, the quilt is then hand stitched to the frame itself. Quilts can also be mounted inside Plexiglas by a professional frame shop. This method, often reserved for antique quilts, can provide an acid-free, dirt-free and, with special Plexiglas, a sunproof environment for your quilt.

A note on our patterns and instructions

The quilts in this book were originally hand-pieced and hand-quilted, in the traditional Amish style. Instructions and templates are provided for hand-piecing, and measurements are given **without** seam allowances.

However, for quilters who prefer to use rotary-cutting and machine-piecing methods, **finished-size** measurements have been noted on each template. To cut squares, rectangles and strips from template shapes, add the 1/4-inch seam allowance all around and cut to that size. For larger squares and strips whose finished dimensions are given, add 1/4-inch to all sides and cut.

To quick-cut right triangles, measure the finished size of the short sides and add 7/8-inch to the length. Cut a square of that measurement and cut the square in half diagonally. When sewn together, the triangles will be the correct finished size.

Total Quilt Assembly Diagram

Diagram 5.

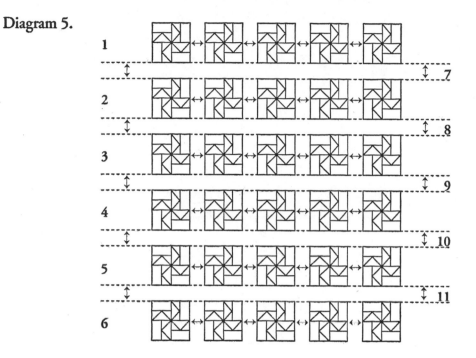

Diagram 6.

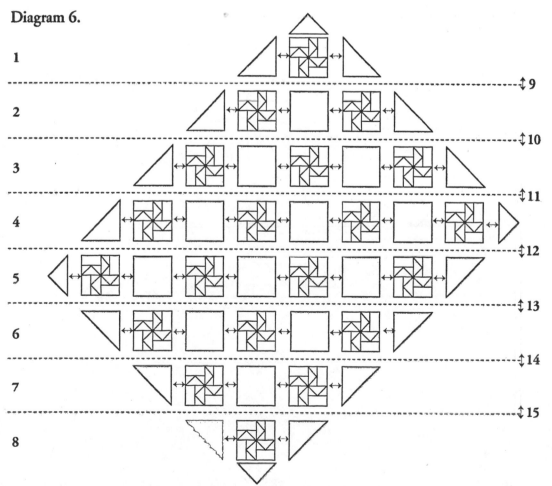

Total Quilt Assembly Diagram
(Small Version)

Diagram 5.

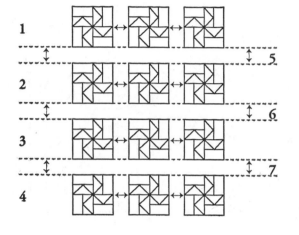

Diagram 6.

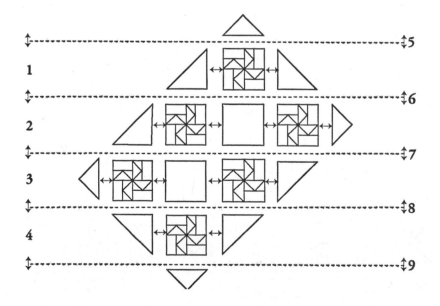

Border Application Diagram

To obtain correct border length, measure length of edge to which border will be applied. Border widths are given with each pattern. When corner blocks are used, sew them to the ends of the last border pieces and then add the border and blocks as a complete section.

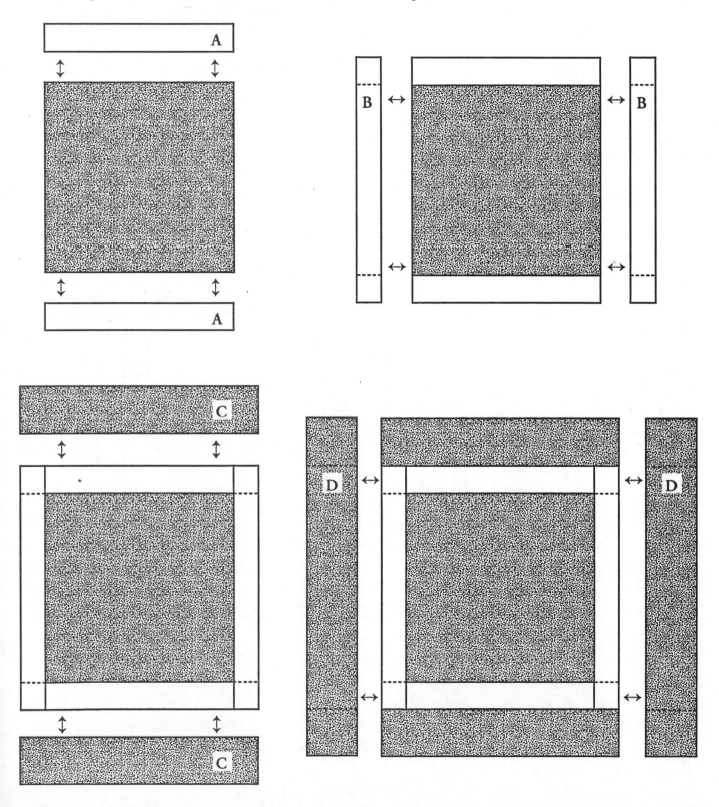

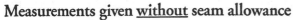

Center Diamond
Approximate size 96 x 96

Variation 1

Measurements given <u>without</u> seam allowance

A — 24 ½ inches square
B — 24 ½ inches x 6 ½ inches
C — 6 ½ inches square
D —

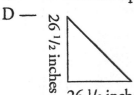

26 ½ inches
26 ½ inches

E — width of inner border 6 ½ inches
F — 6 ½ inches square
G — width of outer border 15 inches
H — 15 inches square

Assembly instructions:

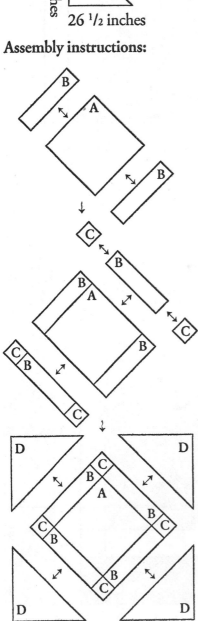

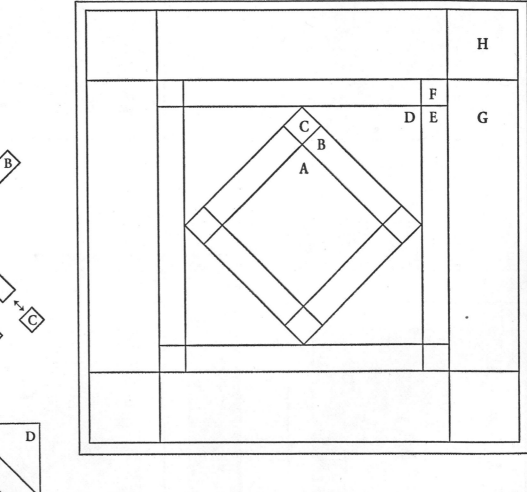

See Border Application Diagram, page 195.

Variation 2

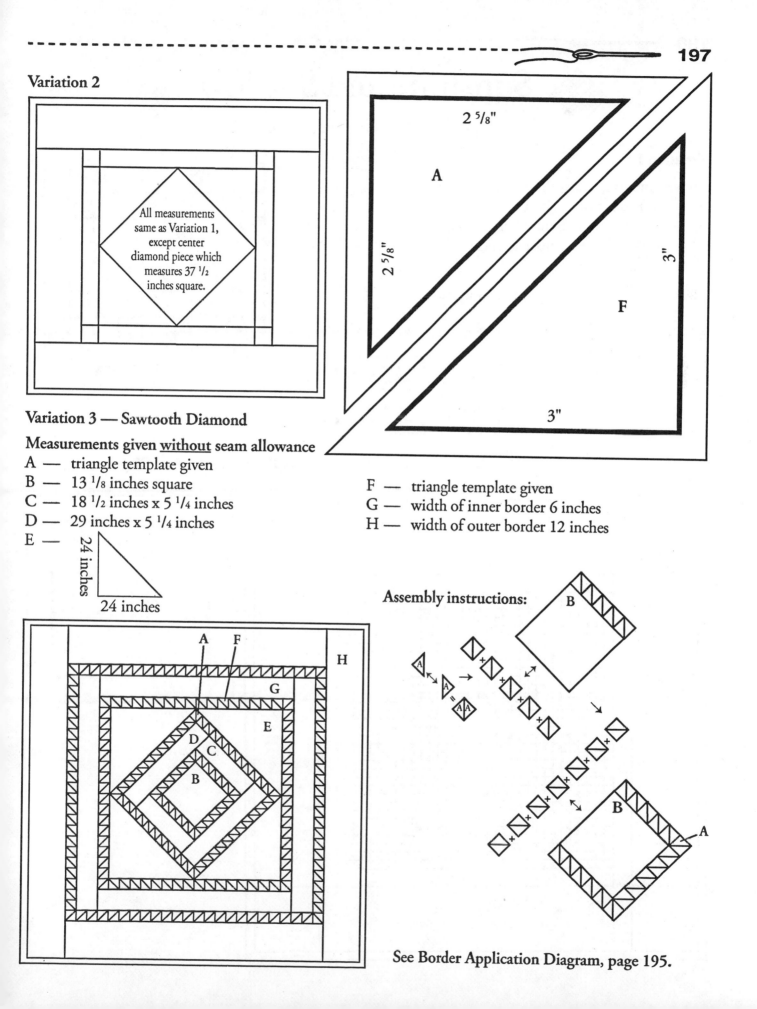

All measurements same as Variation 1, except center diamond piece which measures 37 ½ inches square.

2 ⁵/₈"

A

2 ⁵/₈"

3"

F

3"

Variation 3 — Sawtooth Diamond

Measurements given <u>without</u> seam allowance

A — triangle template given
B — 13 ⅛ inches square
C — 18 ½ inches x 5 ¼ inches
D — 29 inches x 5 ¼ inches
E —

24 inches
24 inches

F — triangle template given
G — width of inner border 6 inches
H — width of outer border 12 inches

A F

H

G

E

D
C

B

Assembly instructions:

B

A

A

A
A A

B

A

See Border Application Diagram, page 195.

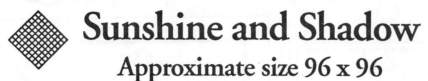

Sunshine and Shadow
Approximate size 96 x 96

Variation 1

Measurements given <u>without</u> seam allowance

A — square template given
B — width of inner border 6 ¹/₄ inches
C — width of outer border 15 inches
D — 15 inches square

Make a center block 33 squares x 33 squares

Assembly instructions:

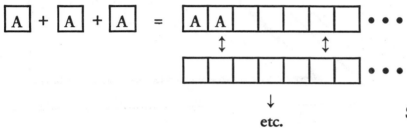

etc.

See Border Application Diagram, page 195.

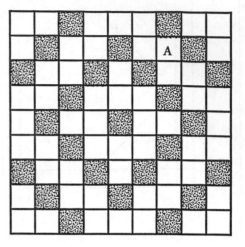

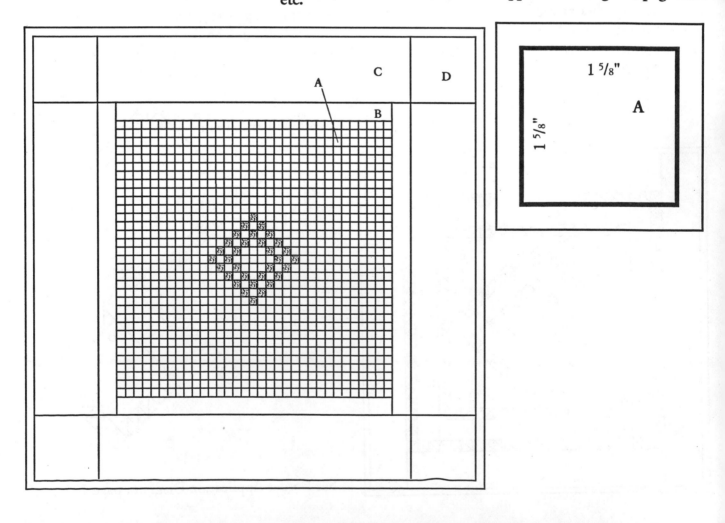

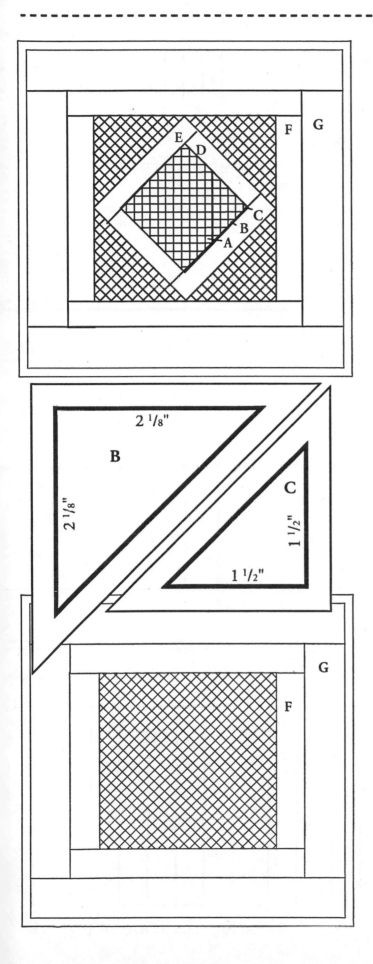

Variation 2 — Center Diamond

Measurements given <u>without</u> seam allowance

A — square template given
B — triangle template given
C — triangle template given
D — 24 inches x 6 inches
E — 36 ¼ inches x 6 inches
F — width of inner border 6 inches
G — width of outer border 16 inches

Assembly instructions:

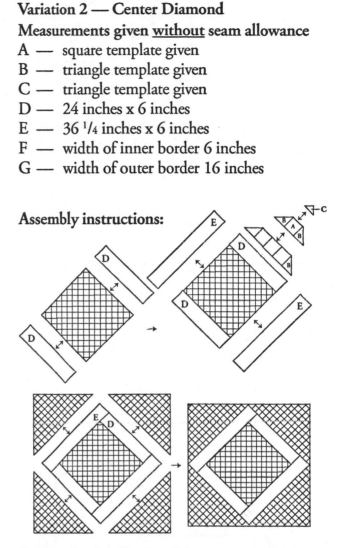

See Border Application Diagram, page 195.

Variation 3

Use templates A, B, and C and other indicated measurements from Variation 2.

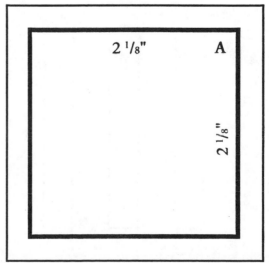

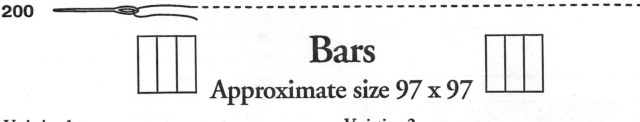

Bars
Approximate size 97 x 97

Variation 1

Measurements given **without** seam allowance
A — 8 ¹/₄ inches x 57 ³/₄ inches
B — 4 ³/₄ inches x 57 ³/₄ inches
C — 4 ³/₄ inches square
D — 15 inches x 67 ¹/₄ inches
E — 15 inches square

Variation 2

Measurements given **without** seam allowance
A — 9 ¹/₂ inches x 66 ¹/₂ inches
B — 15 inches x 66 ¹/₂ inches
C — 15 inches square

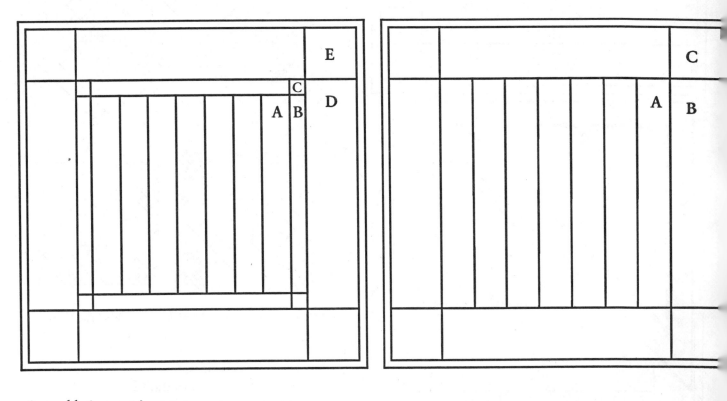

Assembly instructions:

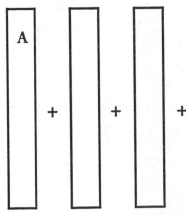
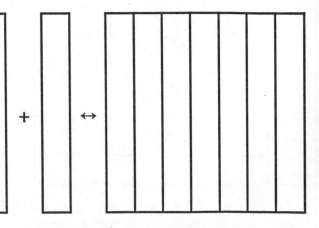

See Border Application Diagram, page 195.

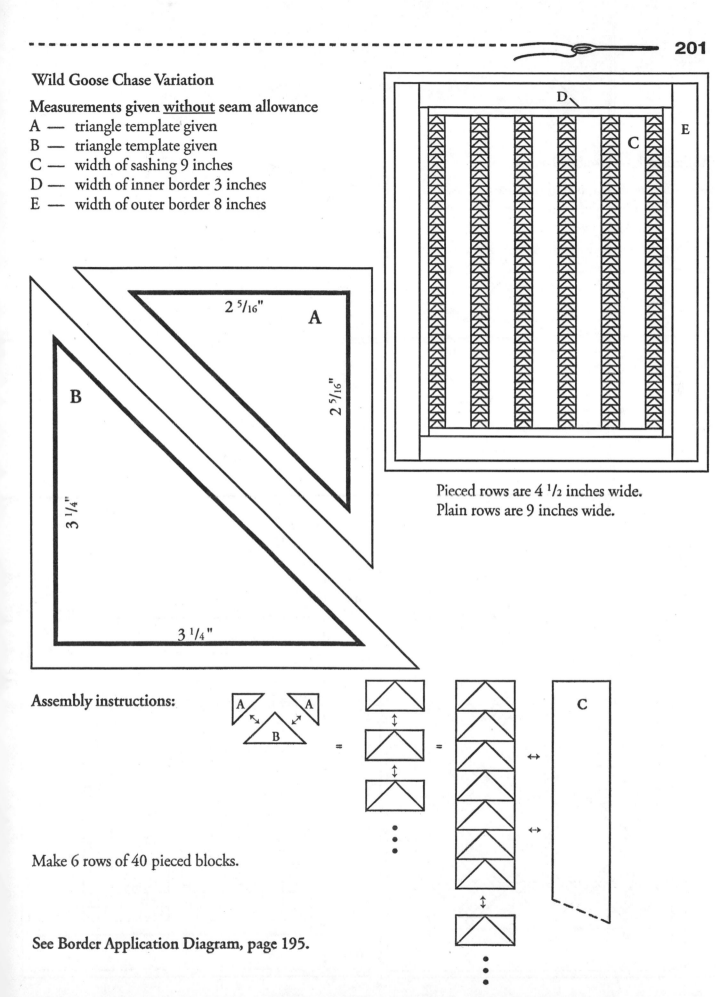

Wild Goose Chase Variation

Measurements given <u>without</u> seam allowance
A — triangle template given
B — triangle template given
C — width of sashing 9 inches
D — width of inner border 3 inches
E — width of outer border 8 inches

2 ⁵/₁₆"   A

2 ⁵/₁₆"

B

3 ¹/₄"

3 ¹/₄"

Pieced rows are 4 ¹/₂ inches wide.
Plain rows are 9 inches wide.

Assembly instructions:

A   A

B   =   =   C

Make 6 rows of 40 pieced blocks.

See Border Application Diagram, page 195.

Multiple Patch
Approximate size 96 x 118

Variation 1 — Double 9-Patch

Measurements given <u>without</u> seam allowance

A — template given
B — template given
C — cut 6 squares 15 $^3/_4$ inches x 15 $^3/_4$ inches
D — cut 10 triangles

E — cut 4 triangles

F — width of inner border 2 $^5/_8$ inches
G — width of outer border 12 inches

Make 12 pieced blocks 15 $^3/_4$ inches square.

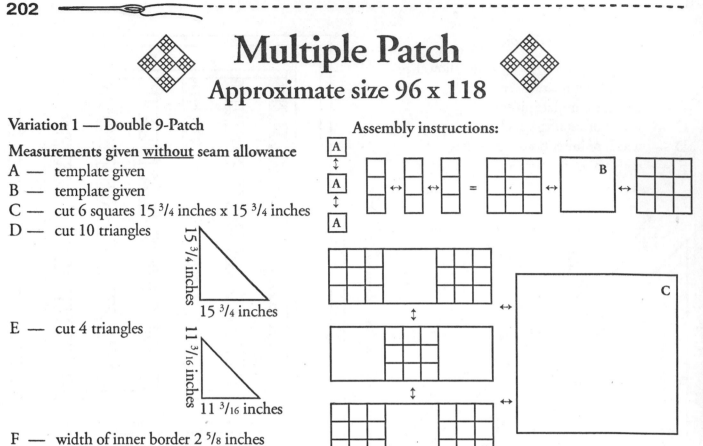

Assembly instructions:

See Diagram 6, page 193 (Total Quilt Assembly).
See Border Application Diagram, page 195.

Double 4-Patch
Approximate size 96 x 104

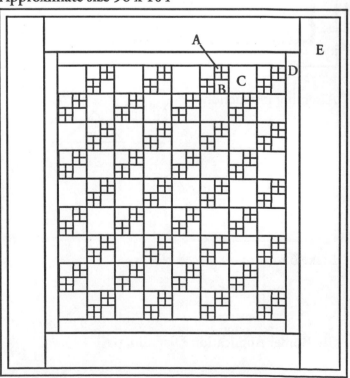

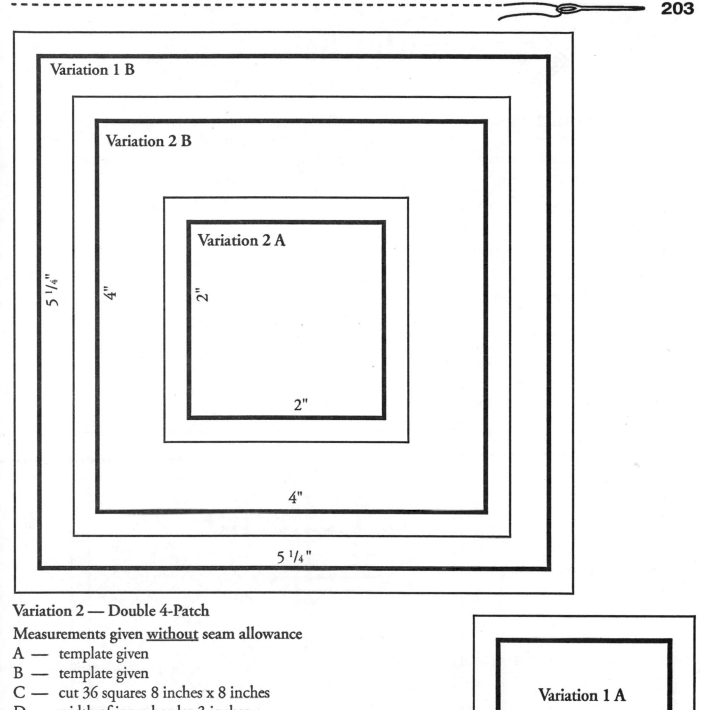

Variation 1 B

Variation 2 B

Variation 2 A

5 ¼"

4"

2"

2"

2"

4"

5 ¼"

Variation 2 — Double 4-Patch

Measurements given <u>without</u> seam allowance

A — template given
B — template given
C — cut 36 squares 8 inches x 8 inches
D — width of inner border 3 inches
E — width of outer border 13 inches

Make 20 pieced blocks 8 inches square.

Assembly instructions:

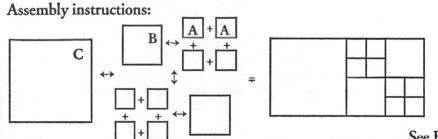

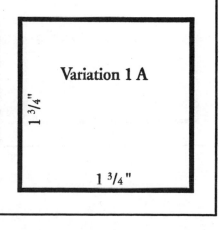

Variation 1 A

1 ¾"

1 ¾"

See Border Application Diagram, page 195.

Irish Chain
Approximate size 95 x 105

Measurements given <u>without</u> seam allowance

A — template given

B — cut 20 - 8 ¾-inch squares

C — cut 18 triangles

D — cut 4 triangles

E — width of inner border 3 ½ inches

F — width of outer border 12 inches

Make 30 pieced blocks 8 ¾ inches square. Plain blocks and triangles need template A and partial template A appliqued in the corners to complete the pattern.

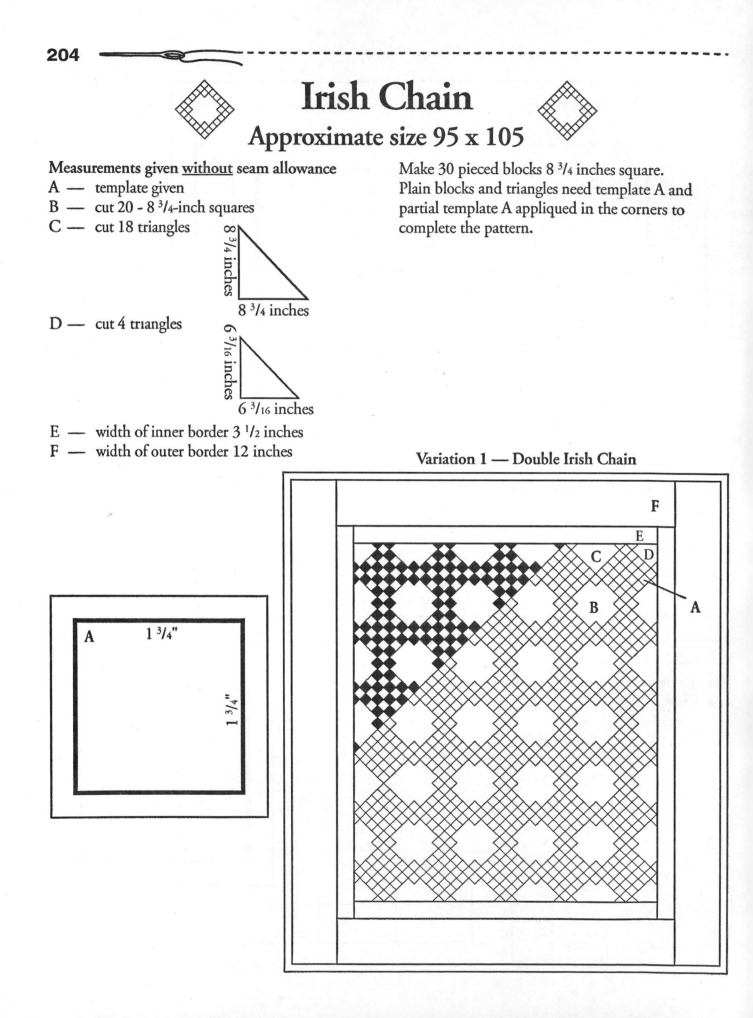

Variation 1 — Double Irish Chain

Assembly instructions:

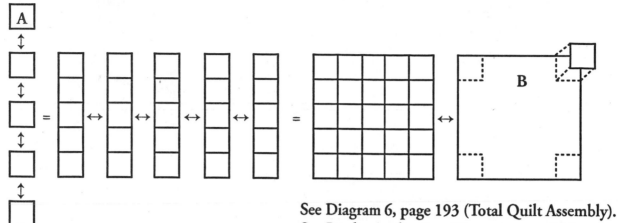

See Diagram 6, page 193 (Total Quilt Assembly).
See Border Application Diagram, page 195.

Variation 2 — Single Irish Chain
Proceed as in Variation 1 but eliminate appliqued
squares on plain alternate blocks.

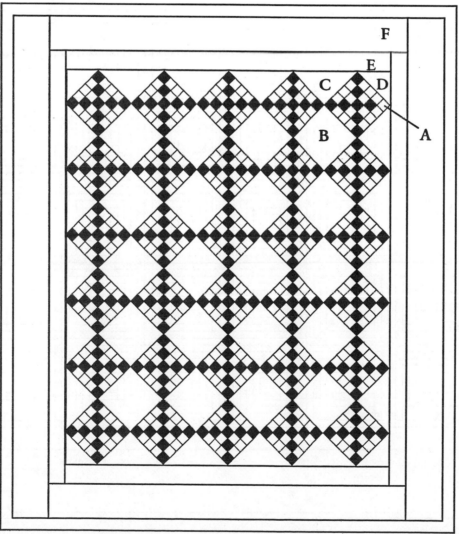

Log Cabin
Approximate size 96 x 108

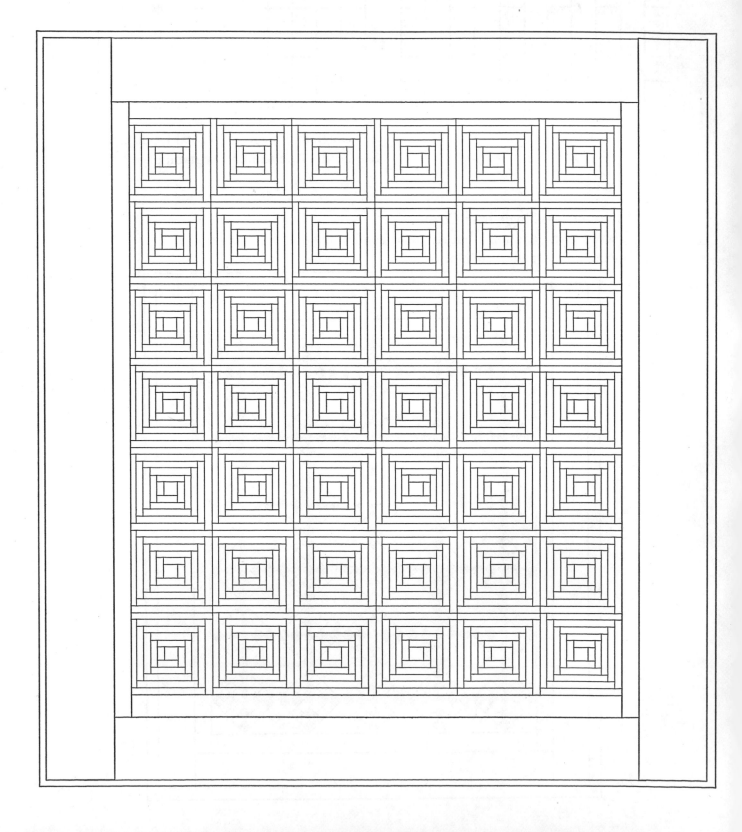

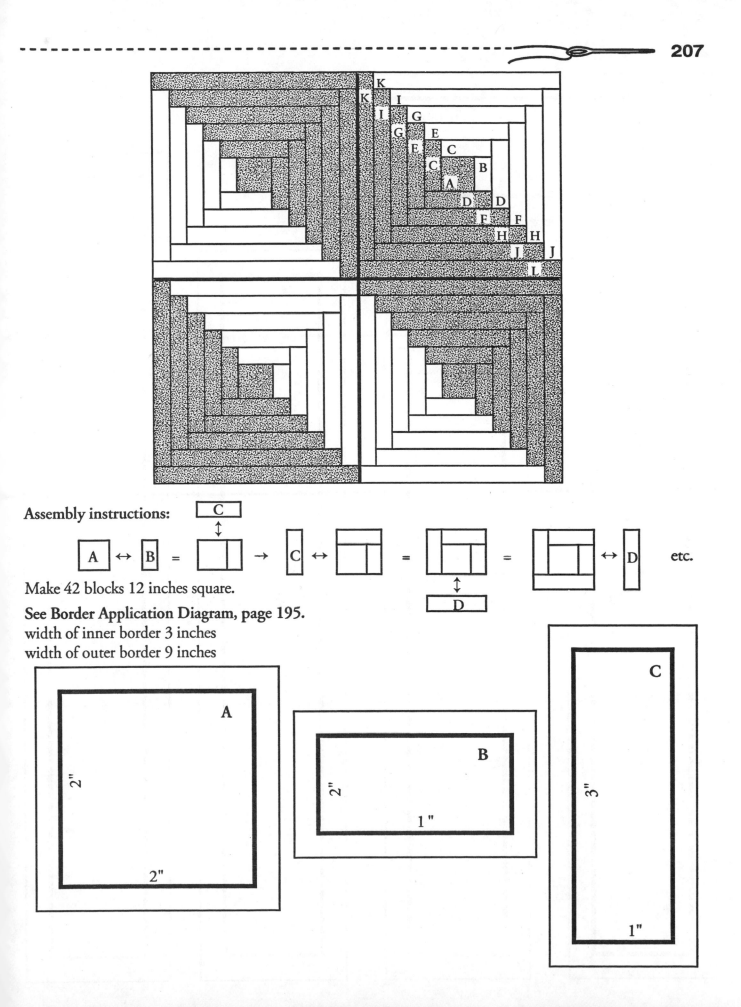

Assembly instructions:

A ↔ B = → C ↔ = = ↔ D etc.

Make 42 blocks 12 inches square.

See Border Application Diagram, page 195.
width of inner border 3 inches
width of outer border 9 inches

A
2"
2"

B
2"
1"

C
3"
1"

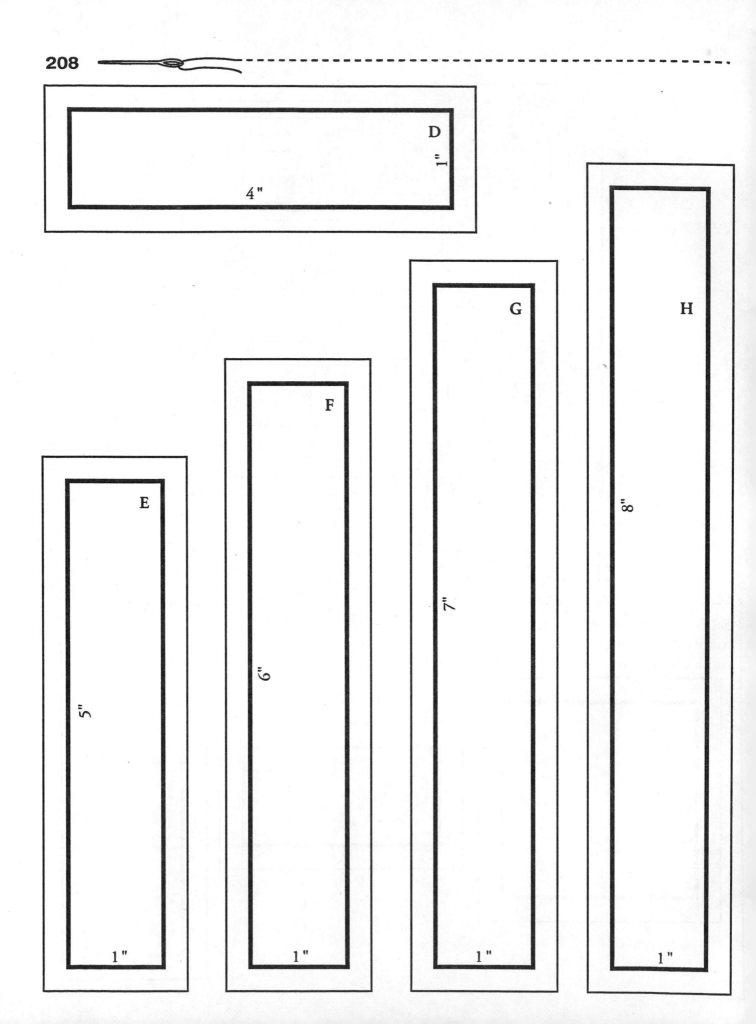

208

D

4"

1"

E

5"

1"

F

6"

1"

G

7"

1"

H

8"

1"

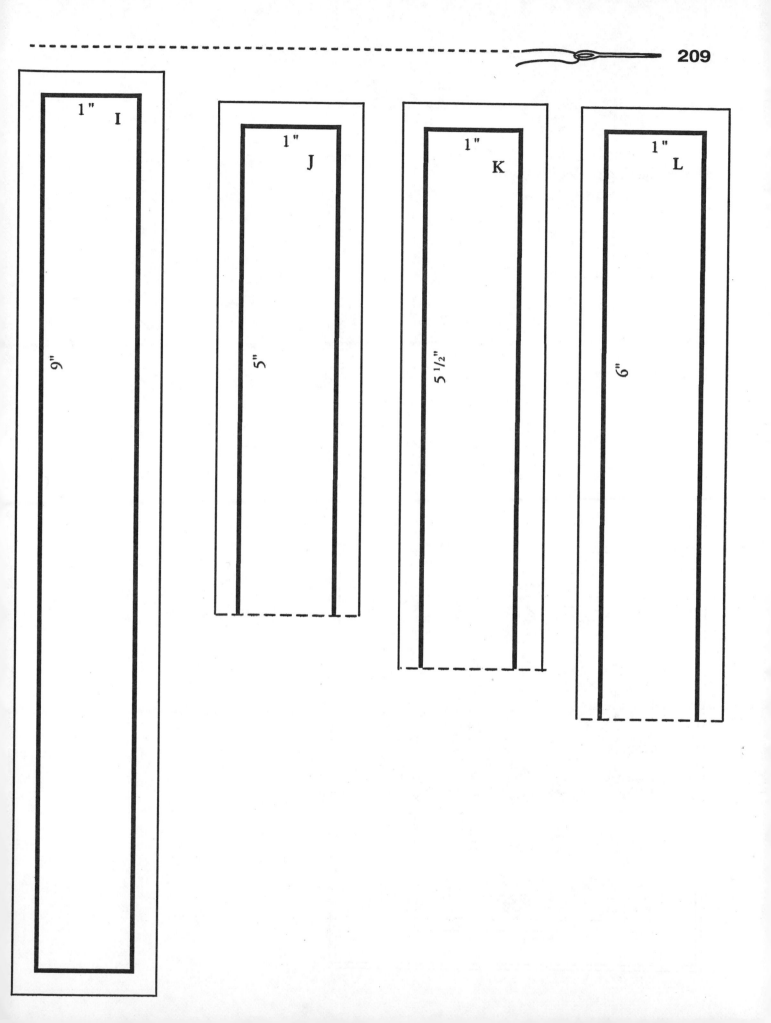

I
1"
9"

J
1"
5"

K
1"
5 1/2"

L
1"
6"

Double T
Approximate size 96 x 111

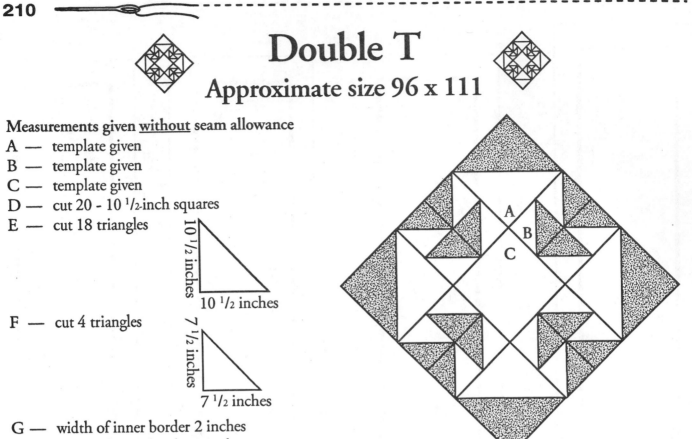

Measurements given <u>without</u> seam allowance

A — template given

B — template given

C — template given

D — cut 20 - 10 ½-inch squares

E — cut 18 triangles

F — cut 4 triangles

G — width of inner border 2 inches

H — width of outer border 9 inches

Make 30 pieced blocks 10 ½ inches square.

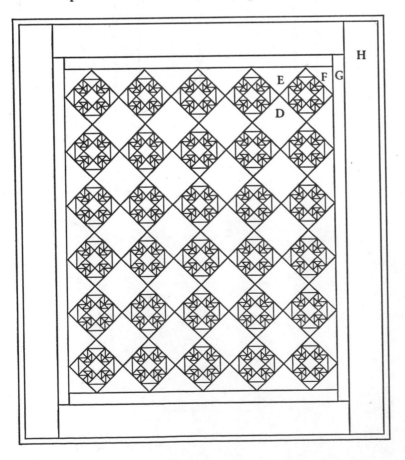

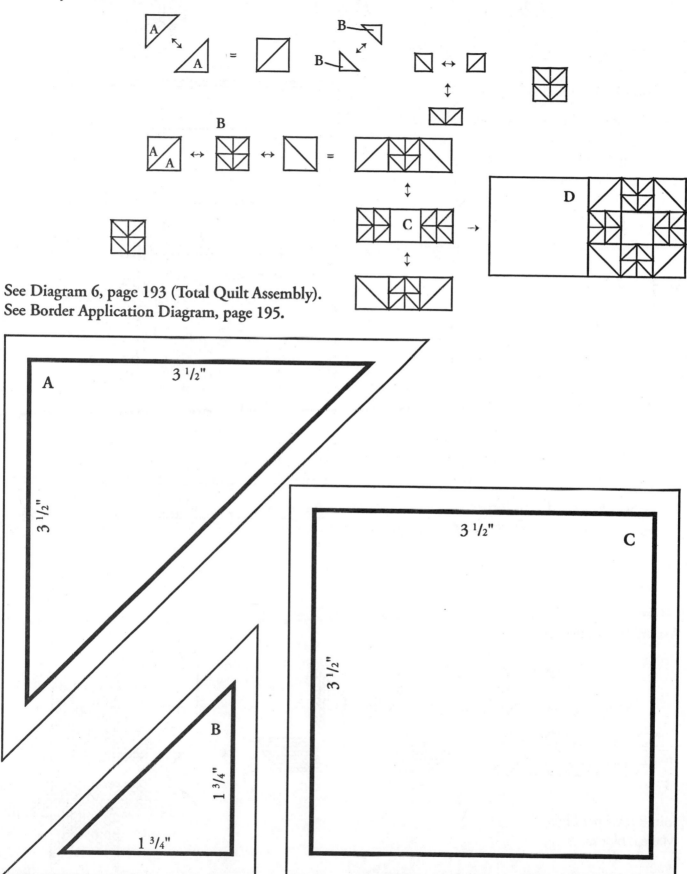

Assembly instructions:

See Diagram 6, page 193 (Total Quilt Assembly).
See Border Application Diagram, page 195.

Stars
Approximate size 94 x 105

Variation 1 — Lone Star

Measurements given <u>without</u> seam allowance

A — template given
B — cut 4 - 18-inch squares
C — cut 4 triangles

D — cut 9 triangles

E — cut 2 triangles

F — width of border 16 inches
G — cut 1 strip 11 ½ inches wide

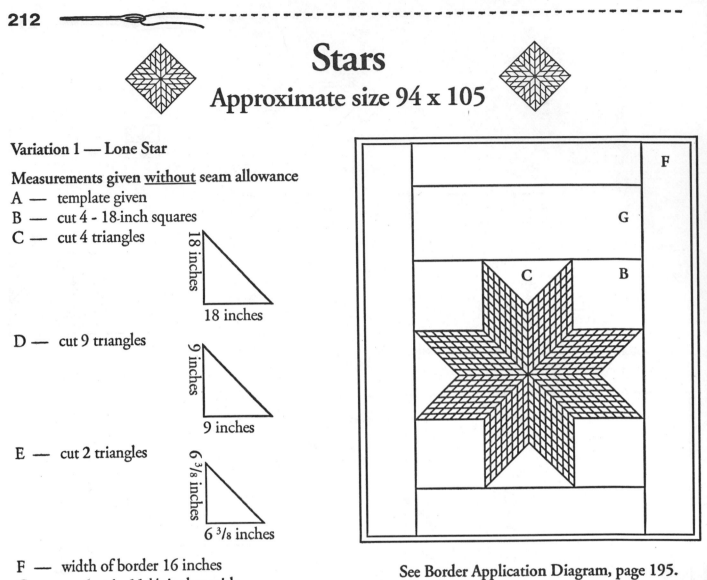

See Border Application Diagram, page 195.

Assembly instructions:

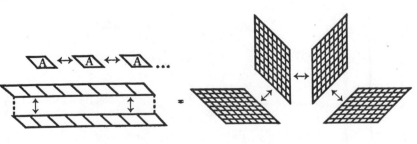

Join 8 rows per block.
Make 8 blocks.

Variation 2 — Broken Star

Measurements given <u>without</u> seam allowance

A — template given
B — cut 20 - 9-inch squares
C — cut 8 triangles

D — cut 1 strip 12 inches wide
E — width of border 16 inches

Assembly instructions:

Join 6 rows per block.
Make 32 blocks.

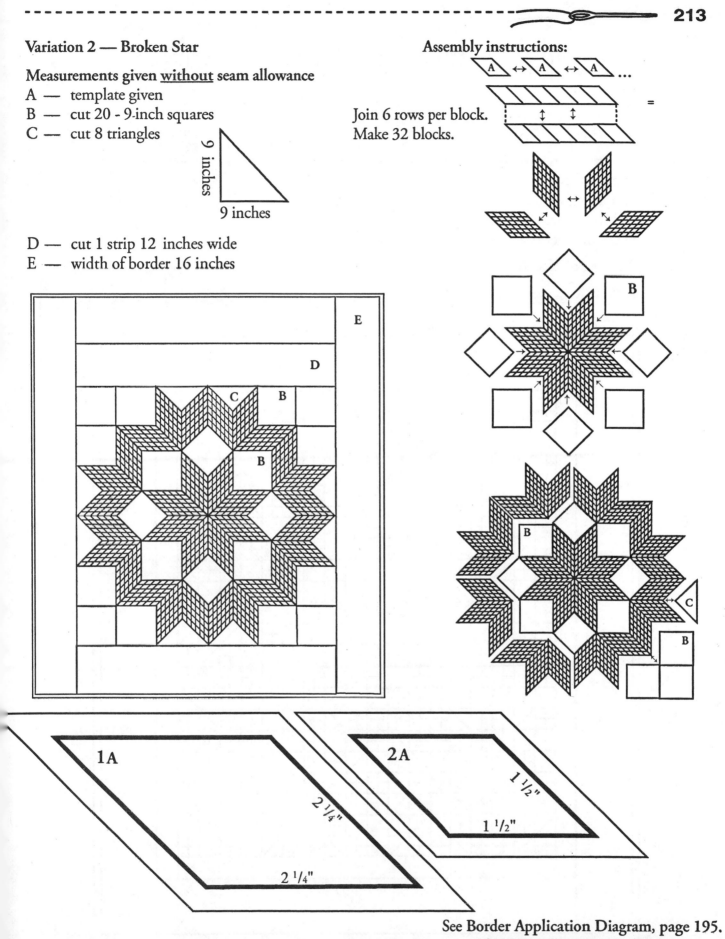

See Border Application Diagram, page 195.

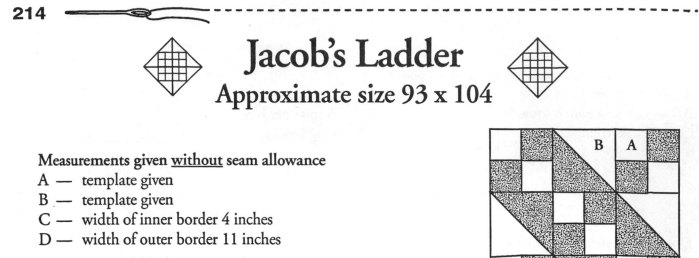

Jacob's Ladder
Approximate size 93 x 104

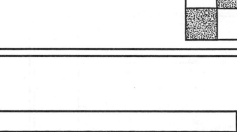

Measurements given <u>without</u> seam allowance

A — template given
B — template given
C — width of inner border 4 inches
D — width of outer border 11 inches

Make 42 pieced blocks 10 ½ inches square.

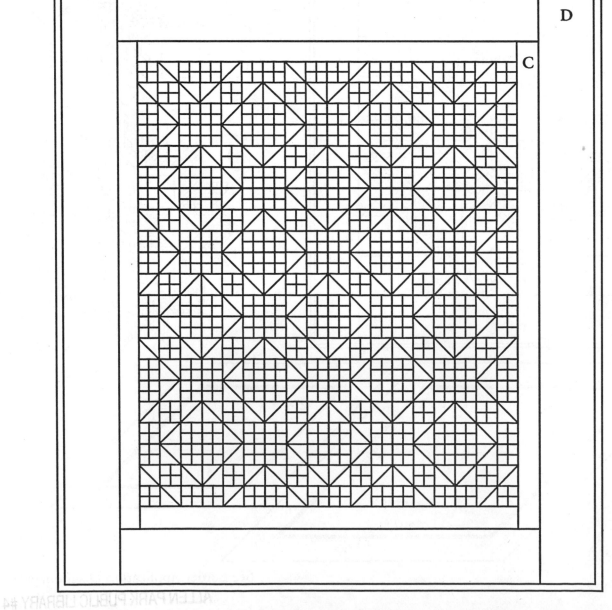

Assembly instructions:

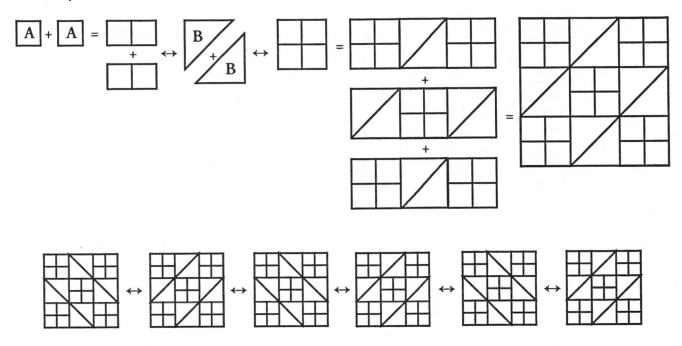

See Diagram 5, page 193 (Total Quilt Assembly).
See Border Application Diagram, page 195.

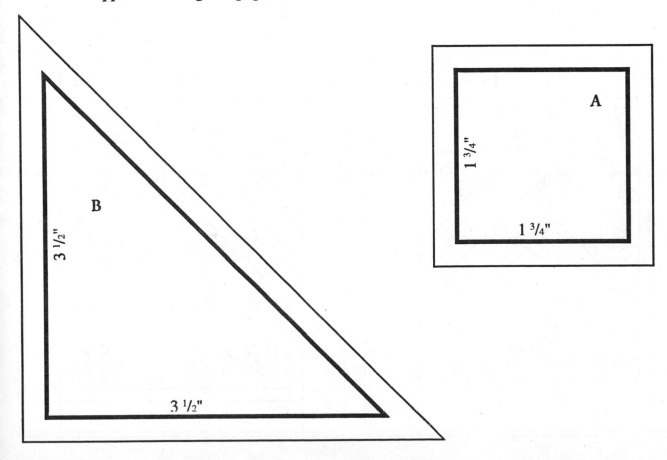

Baskets
Approximate size 90 x 105

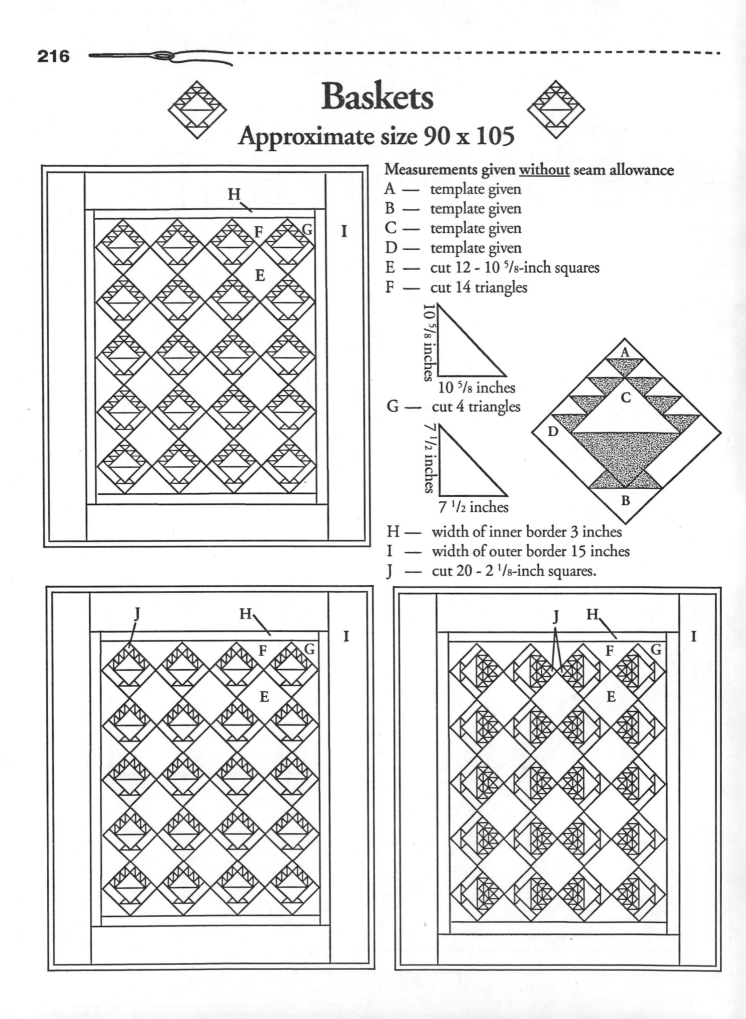

Measurements given <u>without</u> seam allowance

A — template given
B — template given
C — template given
D — template given
E — cut 12 - 10 $\frac{5}{8}$-inch squares
F — cut 14 triangles

10 $\frac{5}{8}$ inches / 10 $\frac{5}{8}$ inches

G — cut 4 triangles

7 $\frac{1}{2}$ inches / 7 $\frac{1}{2}$ inches

H — width of inner border 3 inches
I — width of outer border 15 inches
J — cut 20 - 2 $\frac{1}{8}$-inch squares.

Make 20 blocks 10 ⅝ inches square.

Assembly instructions:

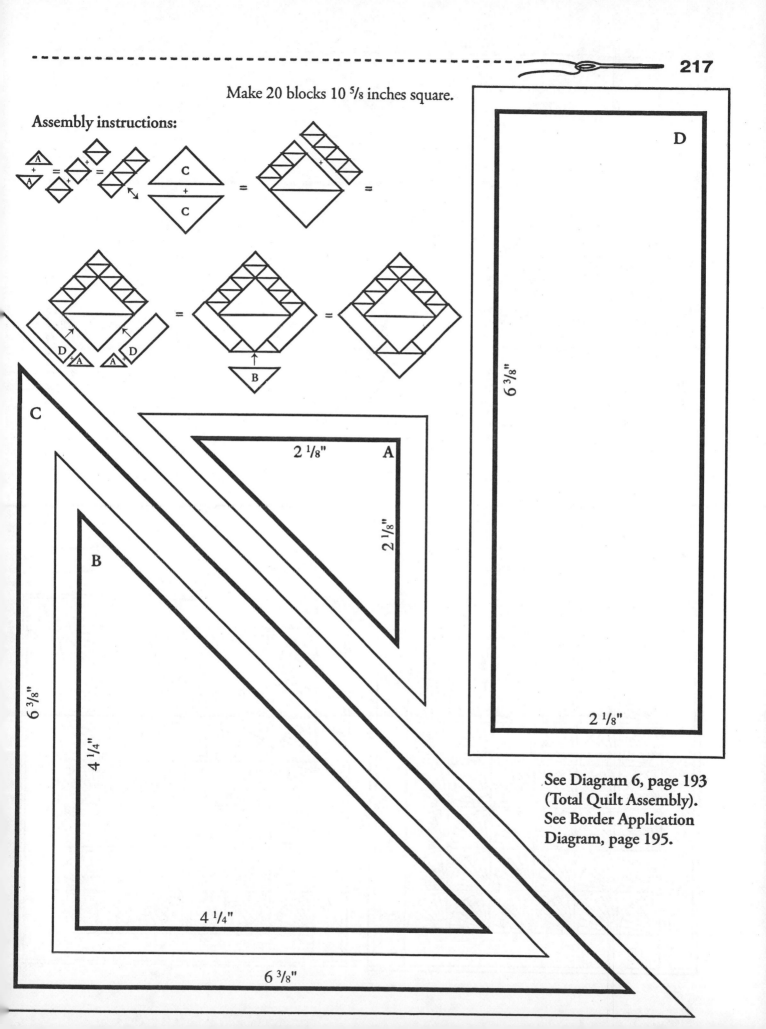

See Diagram 6, page 193
(Total Quilt Assembly).
See Border Application
Diagram, page 195.

Fan
Approximate size 96 x 107

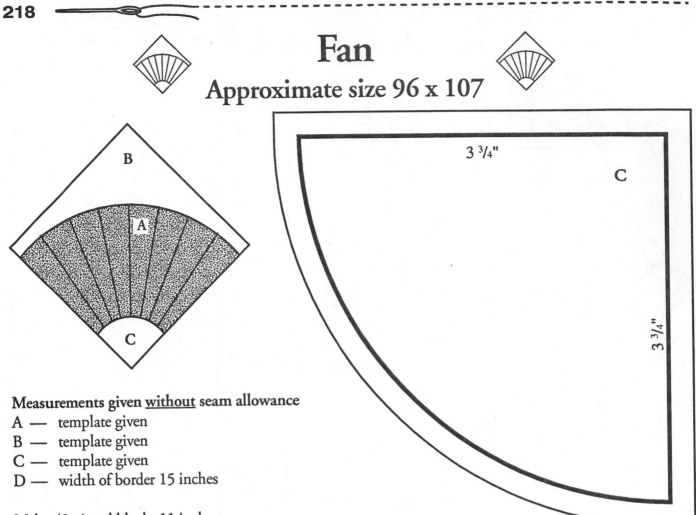

3 ¾"

3 ¾"

C

Measurements given <u>without</u> seam allowance

A — template given
B — template given
C — template given
D — width of border 15 inches

Make 42 pieced blocks 11 inches square.

D

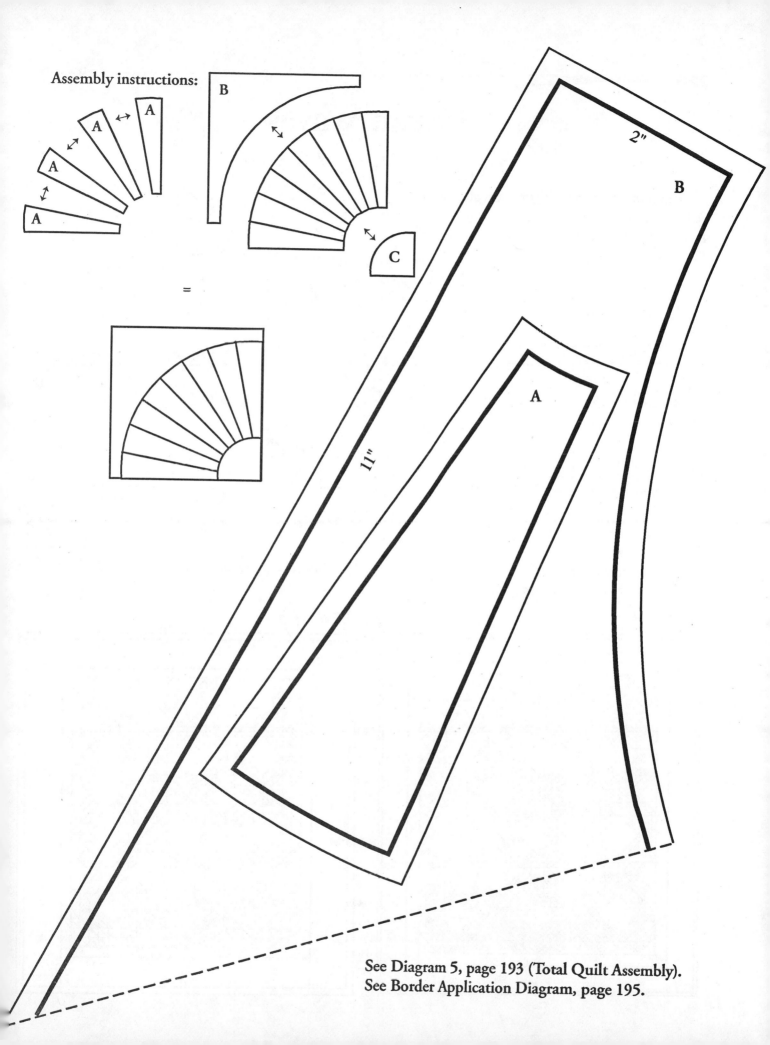

Assembly instructions:

B

A ↔ A
A ↔
A ↔
A

B ↔

C

=

2"

B

11"

A

See Diagram 5, page 193 (Total Quilt Assembly).
See Border Application Diagram, page 195.

Ocean Waves
Approximate size 95 x 107

Measurements given <u>without</u> seam allowance

A — template given

B — template given

C — cut 9 triangles

(triangle labeled 9 inches on vertical side, 9 inches on bottom)

D — cut 2 triangles

(triangle labeled 6 3/8 inches on vertical side, 6 3/8 inches on bottom)

E — width of inner border 3 inches

F — width of outer border 6 inches

Make 15 pieced blocks 18 inches square.

Make 11 half blocks

Make 2 quarter blocks

Darker line, below, indicates a single patch.

Assembly instructions:

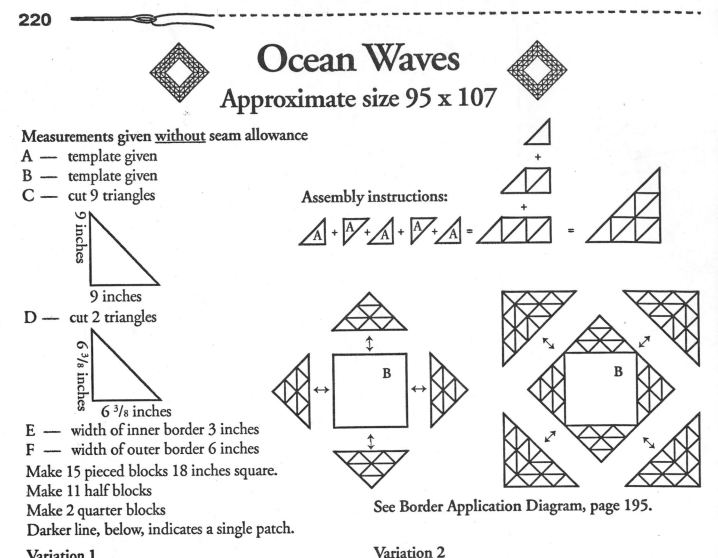

$$\boxed{A} + \boxed{A} + \boxed{A} + \boxed{A} + \boxed{A} = \cdots = \cdots$$

See Border Application Diagram, page 195.

Variation 1

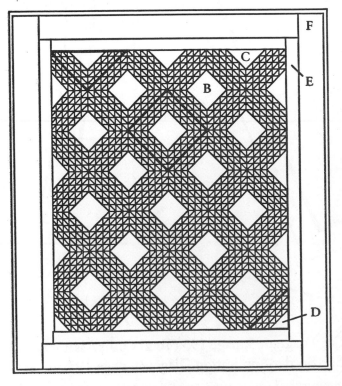

Variation 2

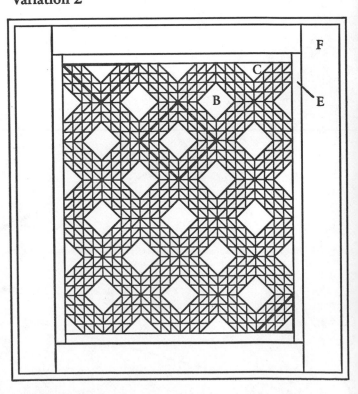

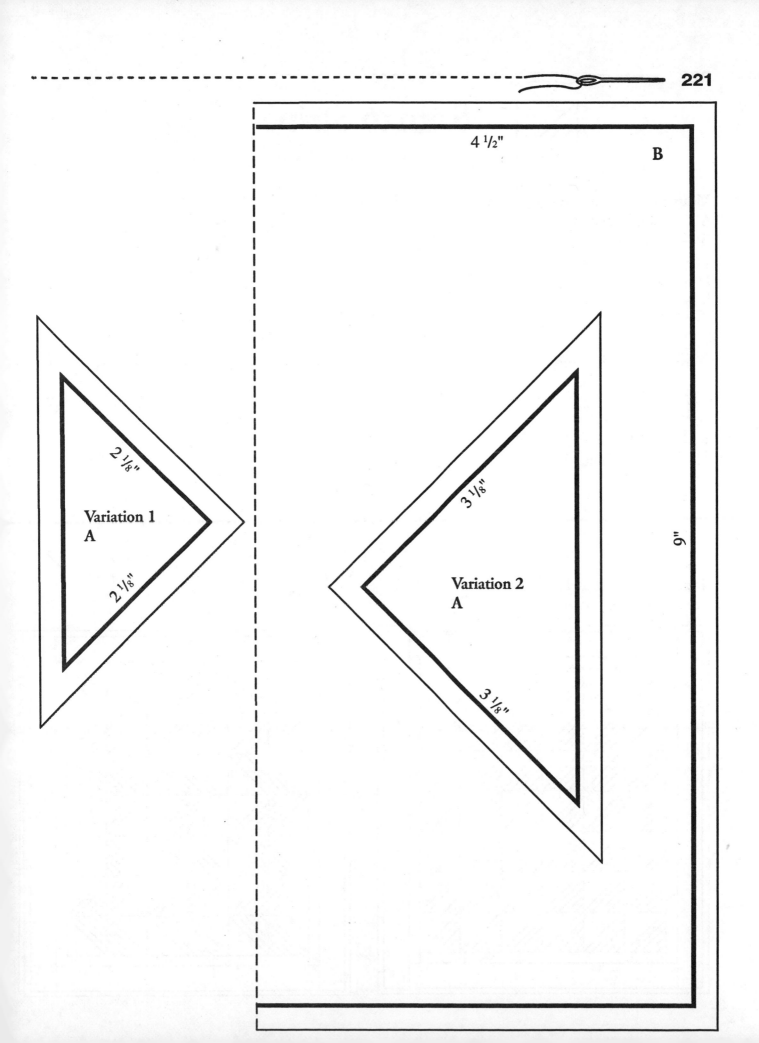

Variation 1
A

2 ⅛"

2 ⅛"

4 ½"

B

9"

Variation 2
A

3 ⅛"

3 ⅛"

Roman Stripe
Approximate size 96 x 106

Measurements given <u>without</u> seam allowance

A — template given
B — template given
C — template given
D — template given
E — template given
F — cut 42 triangles

10 inches

10 inches

G — width of inner border 3 inches
H — width of outer border 15 inches

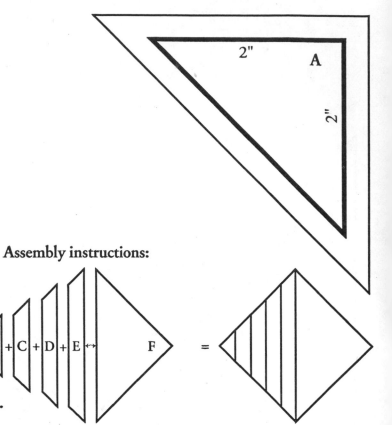

2"

A

2"

Assembly instructions:

A + B + C + D + E ↔ F =

See Diagram 5, page 193 (Total Quilt Assembly).
See Border Application Diagram, page 195.

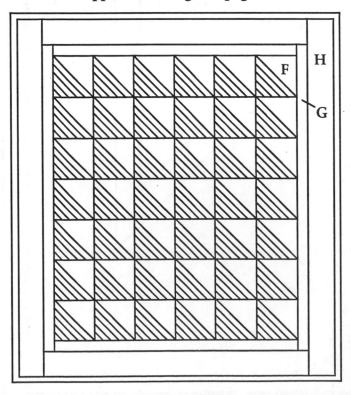

F

H

G

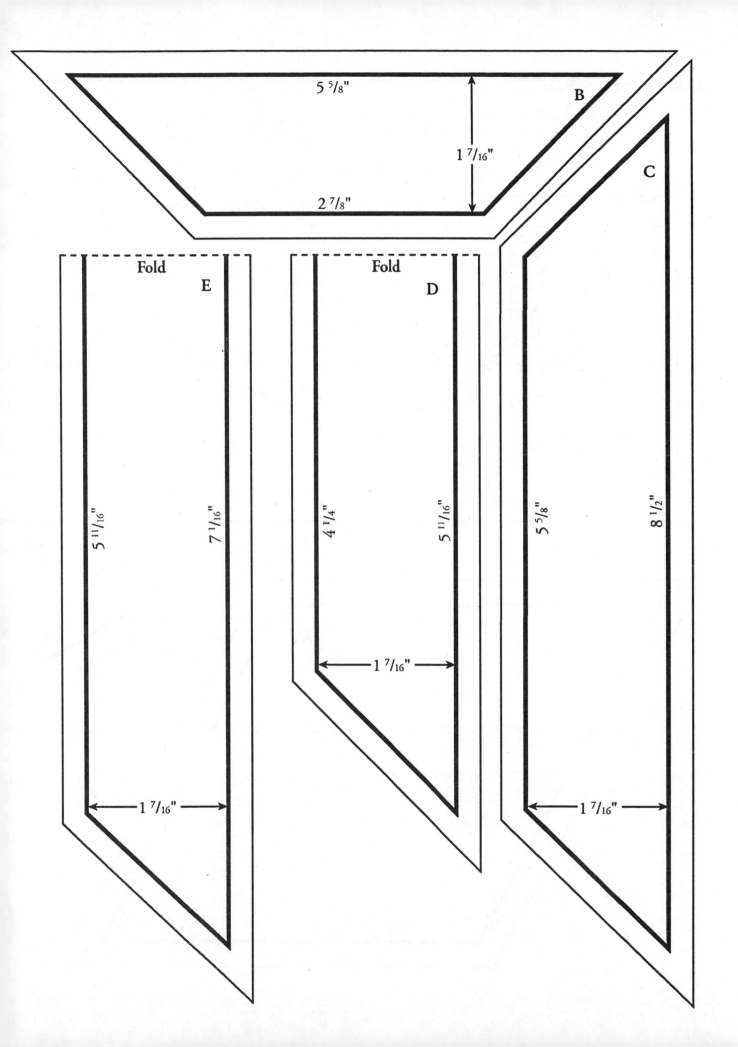

Tumbling Blocks
Approximate size 93 x 109

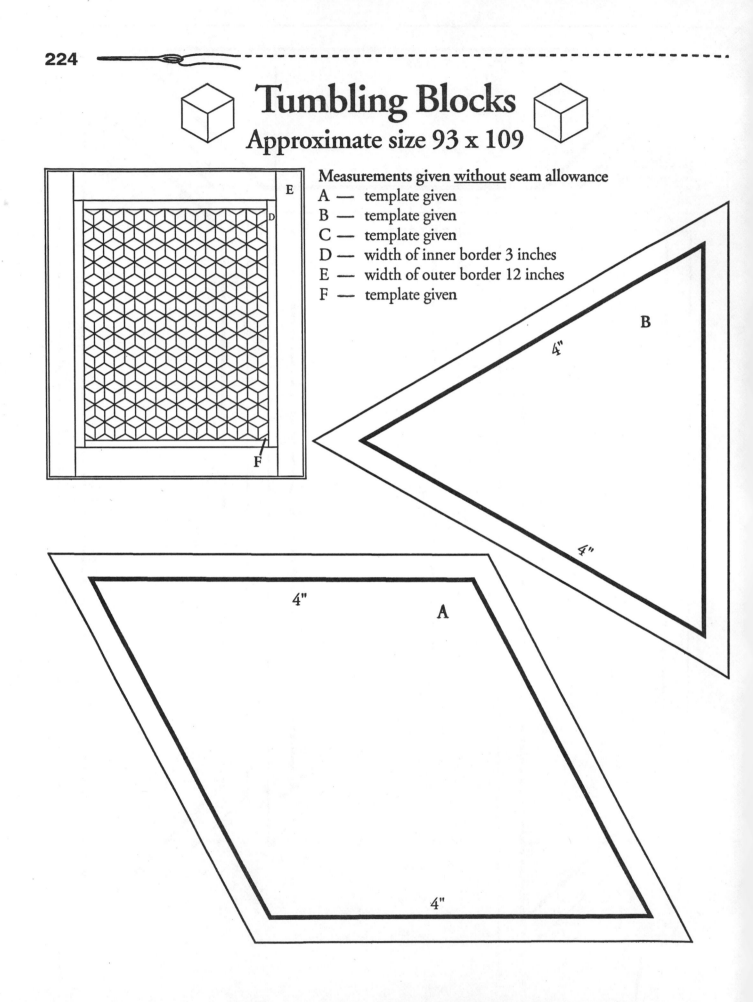

Measurements given <u>without</u> seam allowance
A — template given
B — template given
C — template given
D — width of inner border 3 inches
E — width of outer border 12 inches
F — template given

Assembly instructions:

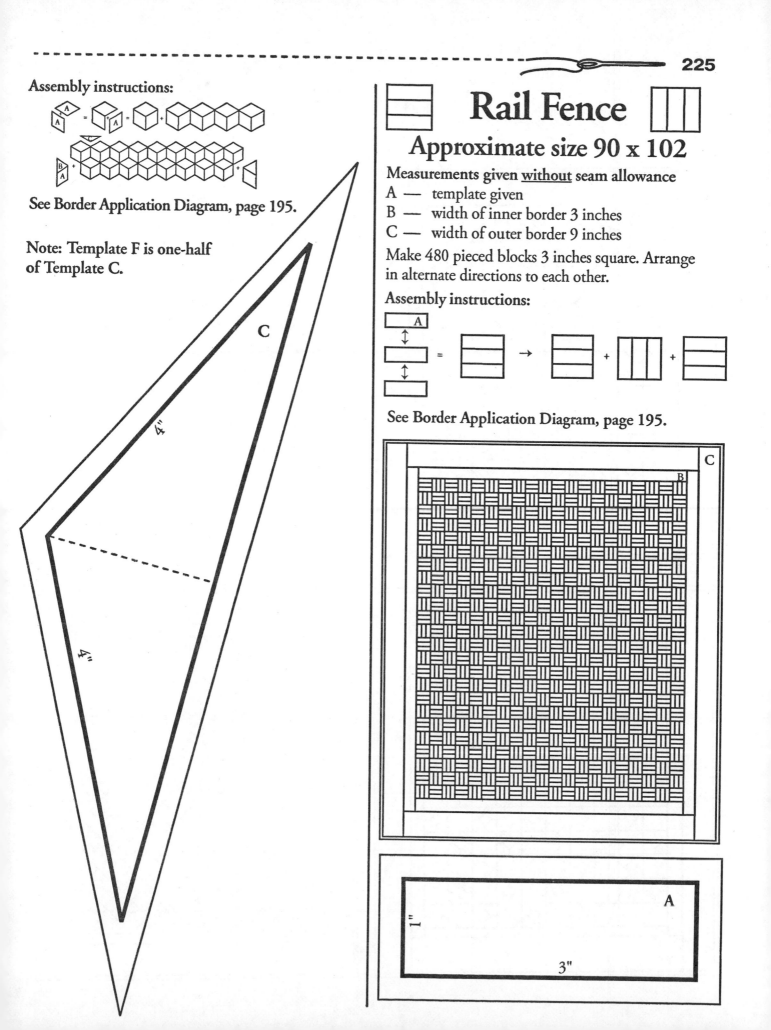

See Border Application Diagram, page 195.

Note: Template F is one-half of Template C.

C

4"

4"

Rail Fence
Approximate size 90 x 102

Measurements given <u>without</u> seam allowance

A — template given
B — width of inner border 3 inches
C — width of outer border 9 inches

Make 480 pieced blocks 3 inches square. Arrange in alternate directions to each other.

Assembly instructions:

A

See Border Application Diagram, page 195.

C

B

A

1"

3"

Bow Tie
Approximate size 95 x 107

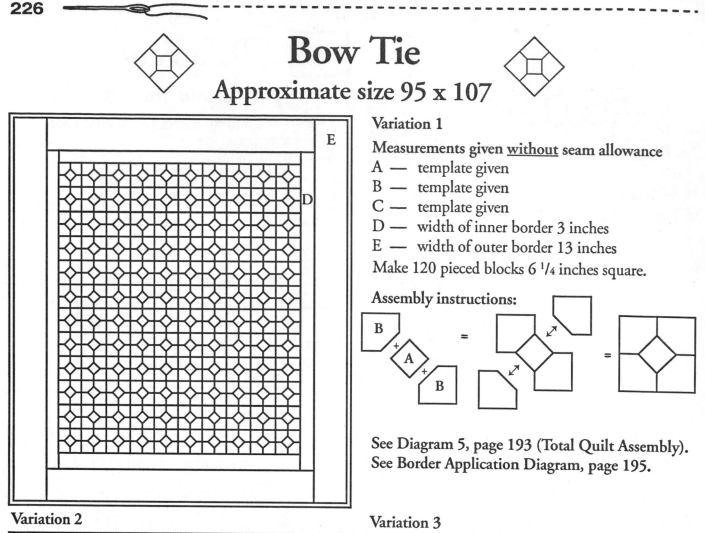

Variation 1

Measurements given <u>without</u> seam allowance

A — template given
B — template given
C — template given
D — width of inner border 3 inches
E — width of outer border 13 inches

Make 120 pieced blocks 6 $\frac{1}{4}$ inches square.

Assembly instructions:

See Diagram 5, page 193 (Total Quilt Assembly).
See Border Application Diagram, page 195.

Variation 2

Variation 3

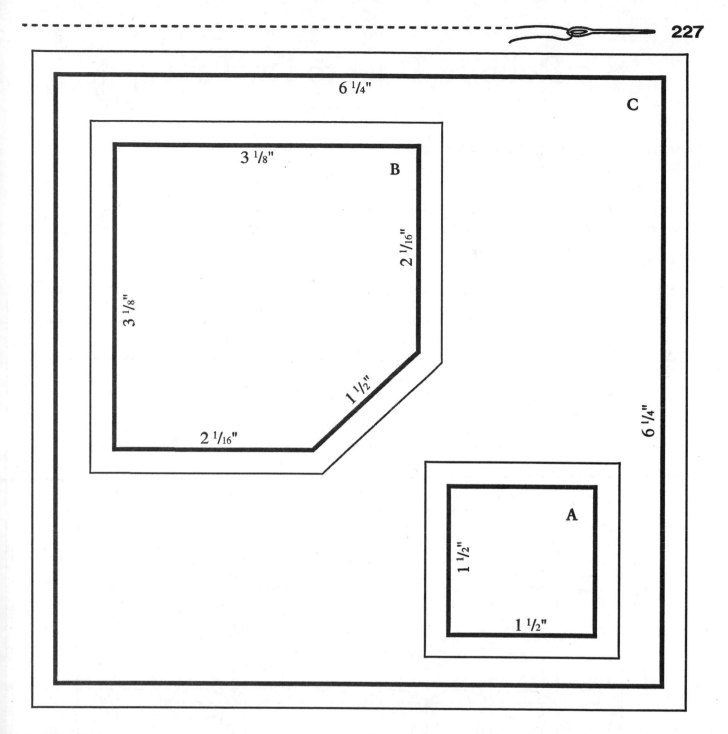

Variation 3

Measurements given <u>without</u> seam allowance

A — template given
B — template given
C — cut 48 squares, template given
D — cut 28 triangles

E — cut 4 triangles

F — width of inner border 3 inches
G — width of outer border 13 inches

Make 63 pieced blocks 6 ¼ inches square.

See Diagram 6, page 193 (Total Quilt Assembly).
See Border Application Diagram, page 195.

Robbing Peter to Pay Paul
Approximate size 96 x 106

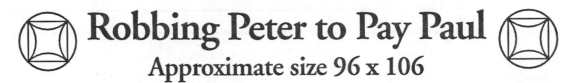

Measurements given <u>without</u> seam allowance

A — template given
B — template given
C — width of inner border 3 inches
D — width of outer border 10 inches

Make 56 pieced blocks 10 inches square.

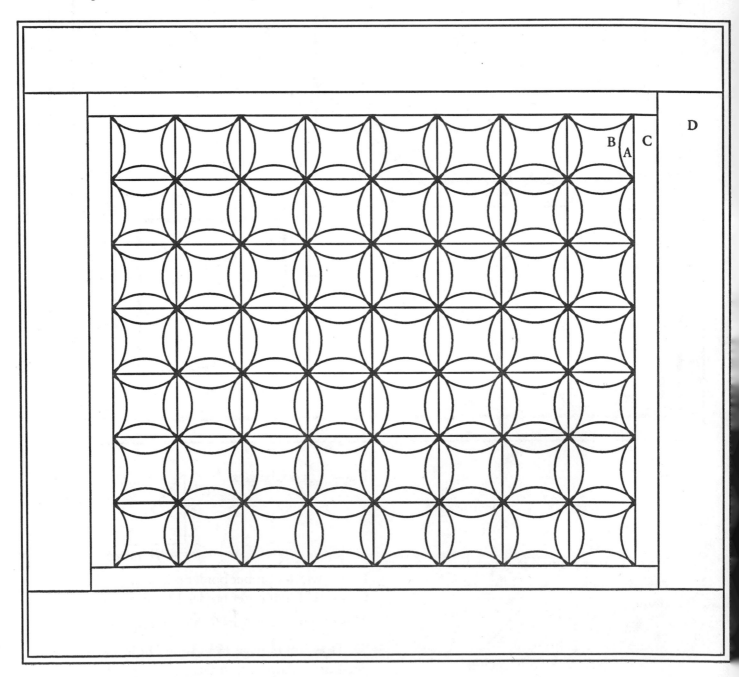

Assembly instructions:

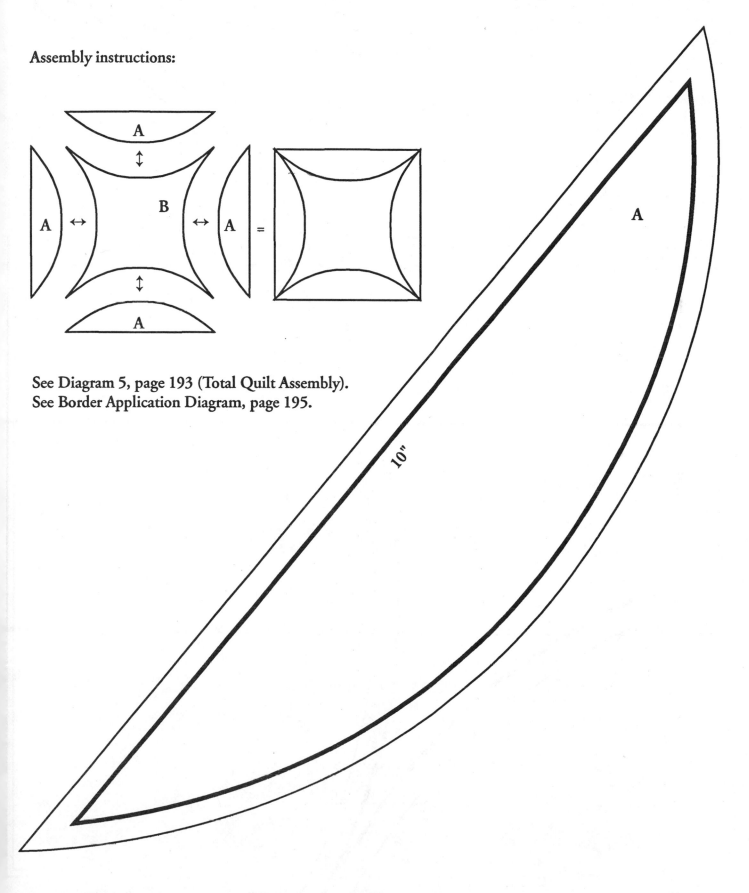

See Diagram 5, page 193 (Total Quilt Assembly).
See Border Application Diagram, page 195.

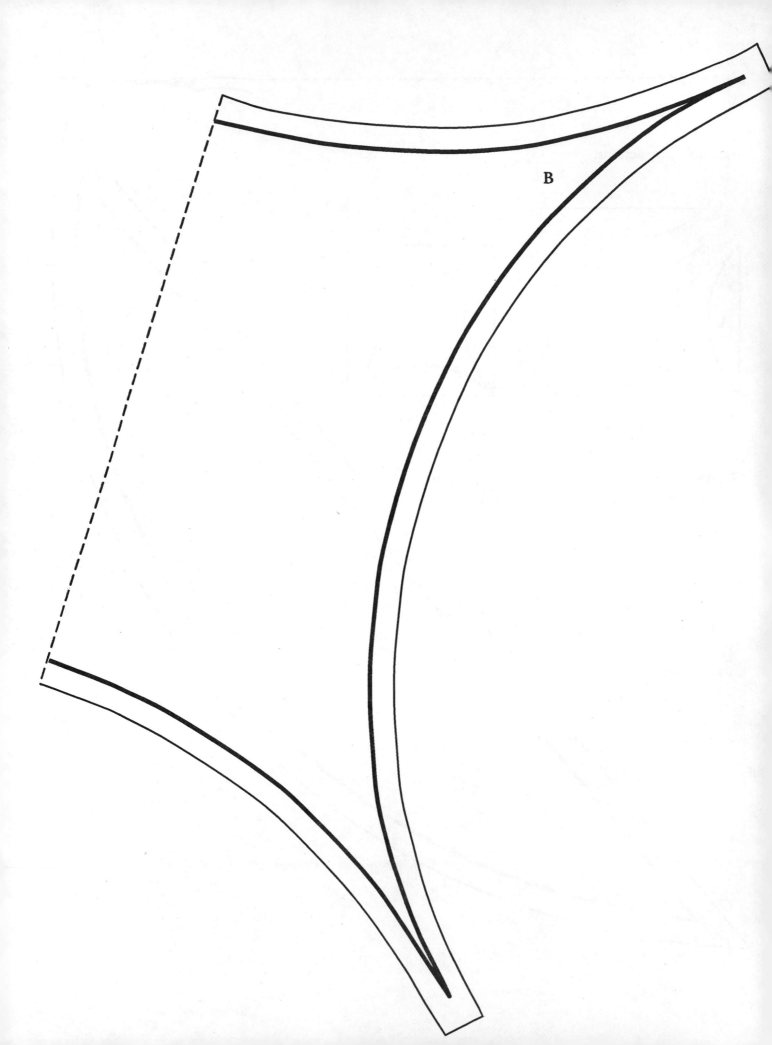

B

Shoo-fly
Approximate size 90 x 105

Measurements given **without** seam allowance

A — template given
B — template given
C — cut 12 - 10 ½ inch squares
D — cut 14 triangles

E — cut 4 triangles

F — width of inner border 3 inches
G — width of outer border 12 inches

Make 20 pieced blocks 10 ½ inches square.

See Diagram 6, page 193 (Total Quilt Assembly).
See Border Application Diagram, page 195.

Assembly instructions:

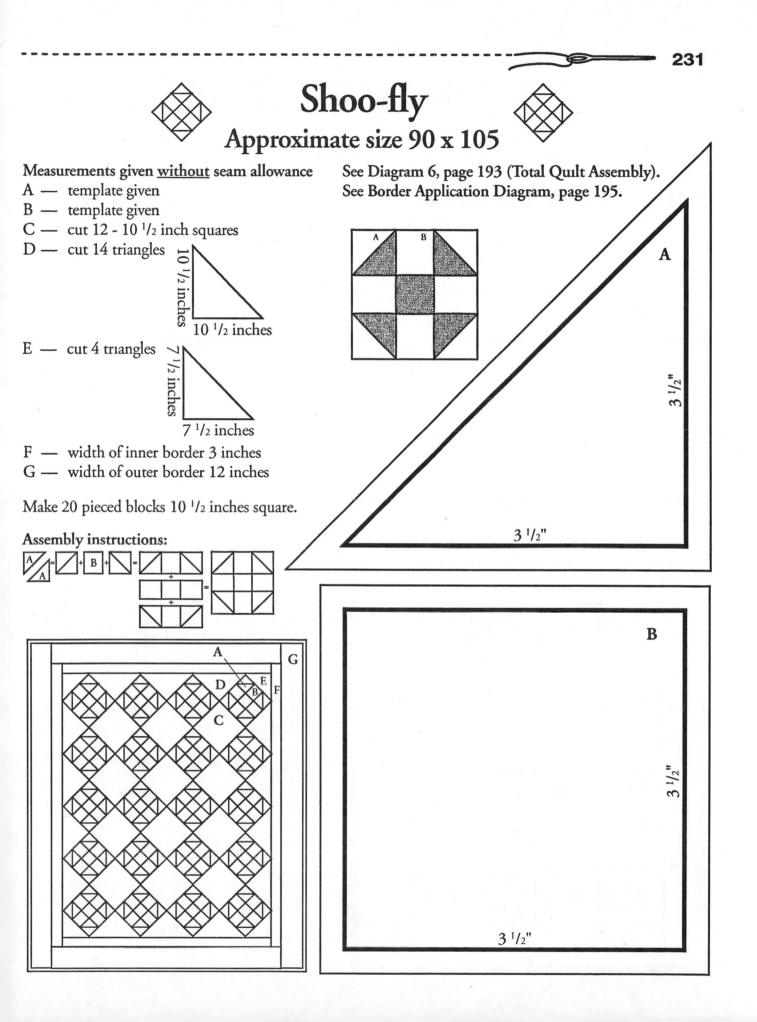

10 ½ inches
10 ½ inches

7 ½ inches
7 ½ inches

A
3 ½"
3 ½"

B
3 ½"
3 ½"

G
A
D
E
F
B
C

Monkey Wrench
Approximate size 89 x 104

Variation 1

Measurements given <u>without</u> seam allowance

A — template given
B — template given
C — width of sashing 4 ¹/₂ inches
D — width of border 12 inches

Make 20 pieced blocks 10 ⁵/₈ inches square.

Assembly instructions:

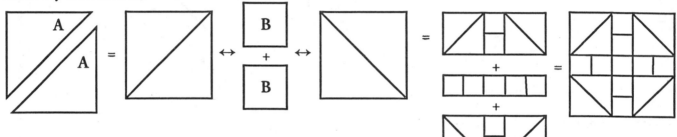

See Diagram 5, page 193 (Total Quilt Assembly).
See Border Application Diagram, page 195.

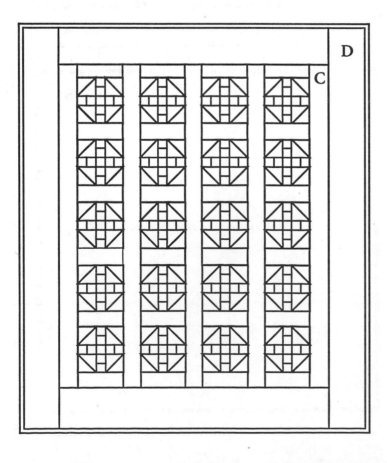

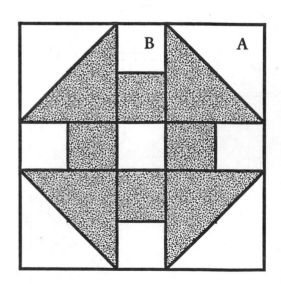

Variation 2

Measurements given without seam allowance

A — template given
B — template given
C — cut 12 - 10 ⅝-inch squares
D — cut 14 triangles

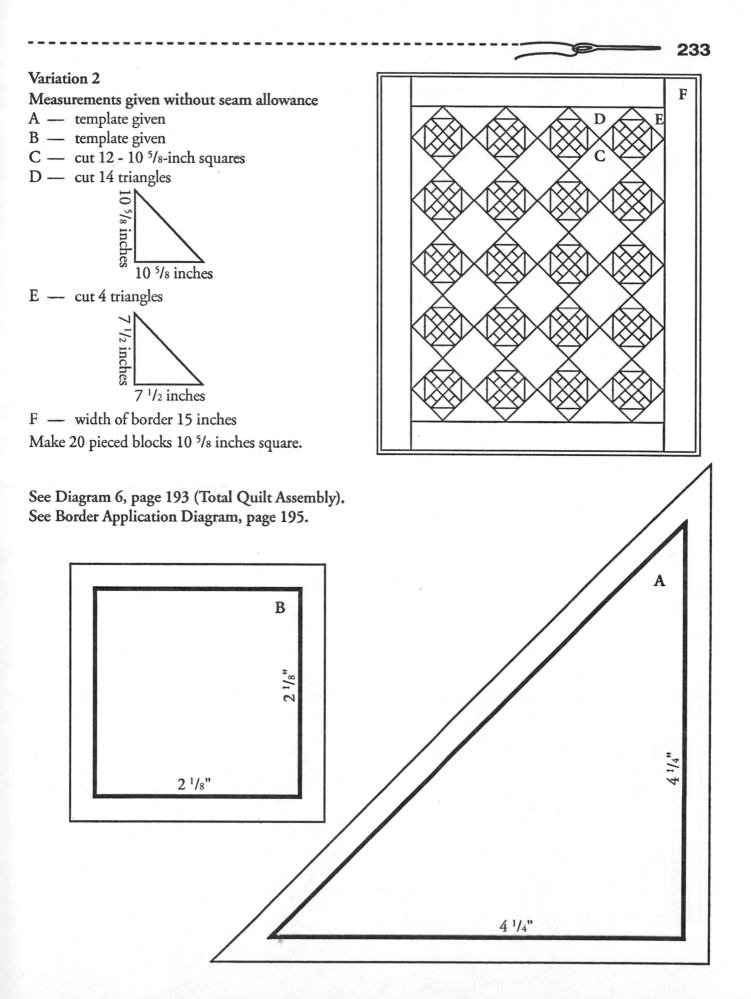

10 ⅝ inches
10 ⅝ inches

E — cut 4 triangles

7 ½ inches
7 ½ inches

F — width of border 15 inches

Make 20 pieced blocks 10 ⅝ inches square.

See Diagram 6, page 193 (Total Quilt Assembly).
See Border Application Diagram, page 195.

F

D   E

C

B

2 ⅛"

2 ⅛"

A

4 ¼"

4 ¼"

Carolina Lily
Approximate size 88 x 103

Measurements given <u>without</u> seam allowance

A — template given
B — template given
C — template given
D — template given
E — template given
F — template given
G — template given
H — template given
I — template given
J } Use narrow bias strips ³/₄ inches x 4 ¹/₂ inches and appliqué
K } stems to template F before piecing.
L — cut 12 - 10 ¹/₄-inch squares

M — cut 14 triangles

10 ¹/₄ inches
10 ¹/₄ inches

N — cut 4 triangles

7 ¹/₄ inches
7 ¹/₄ inches

O — width of inner border 3 inches
P — width of outer border 12 inches

Make 20 pieced blocks 10 ¹/₄ inches square.

Assembly instructions:

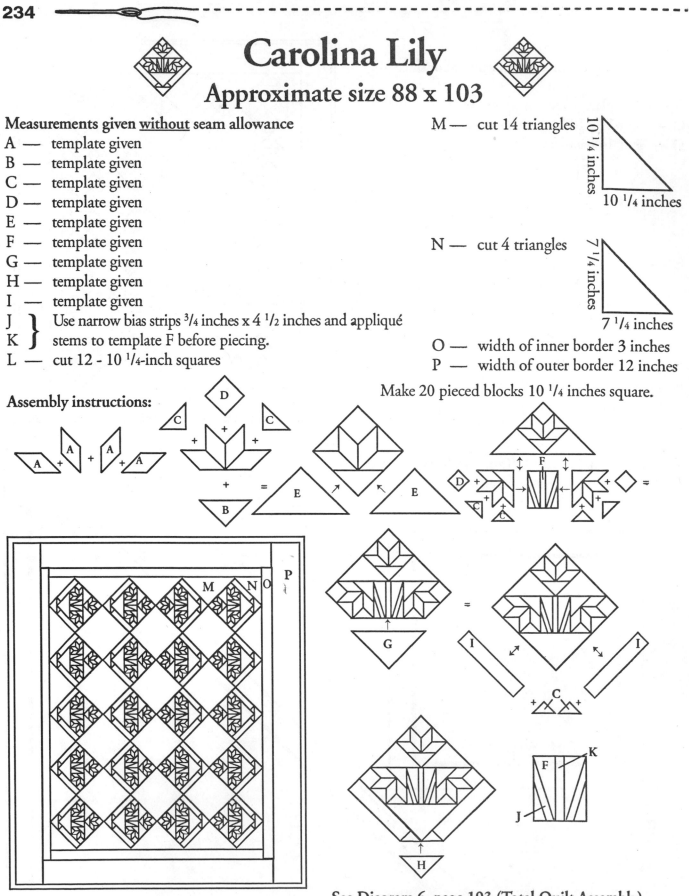

See Diagram 6, page 193 (Total Quilt Assembly).
See Border Application Diagram, page 195.

I

7 1/4"

1 1/2"

F

3"

3 5/8"

D

C

A

B

E

J

K

F

G

H

I

G

5 1/8"

B

2 1/8"

2 1/8"

5 1/8"

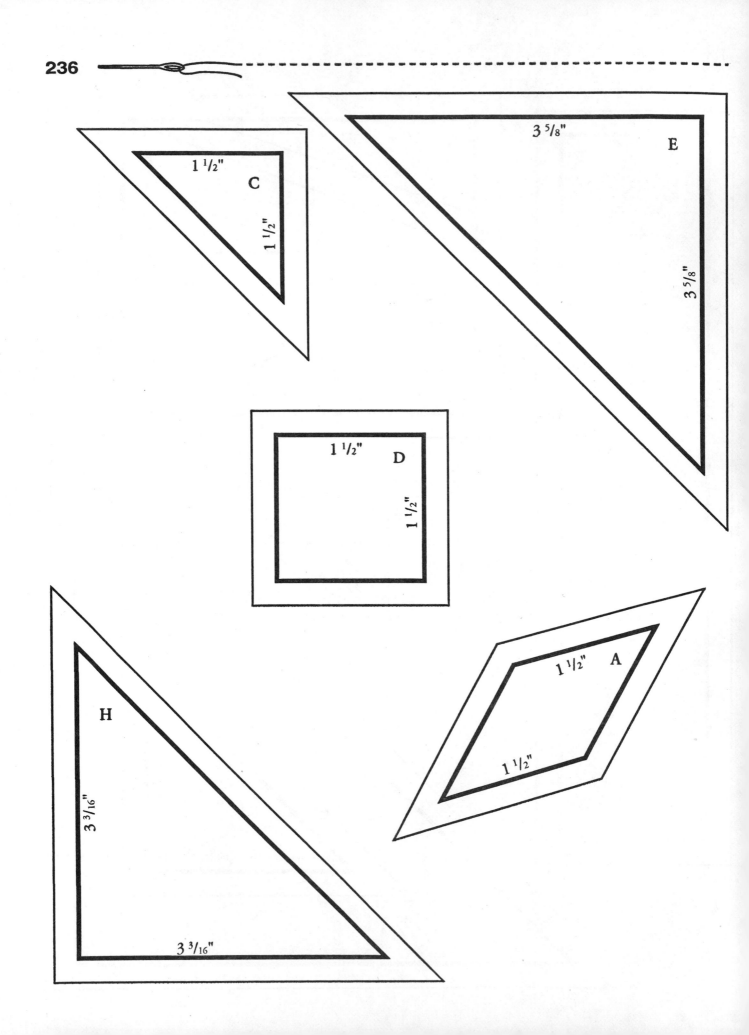

Crown of Thorns
Approximate size 90 x 105

Measurements given <u>without</u> seam allowance

A — template given
B — template given
C — cut 12 - 10 ½-inch squares
D — cut 14 triangles

E — cut 4 triangles

7 ½ inches / 7 ½ inches

F — width of inner border 3 inches
G — width of outer border 12 inches

Make 20 pieced blocks 10 ⅝ inches square.

10 ⅝ inches / 10 ⅝ inches

Assembly instructions:

A / A = □ + □ + B + ◻ + ◻ = ▨▨▨

A B

+ + + + =

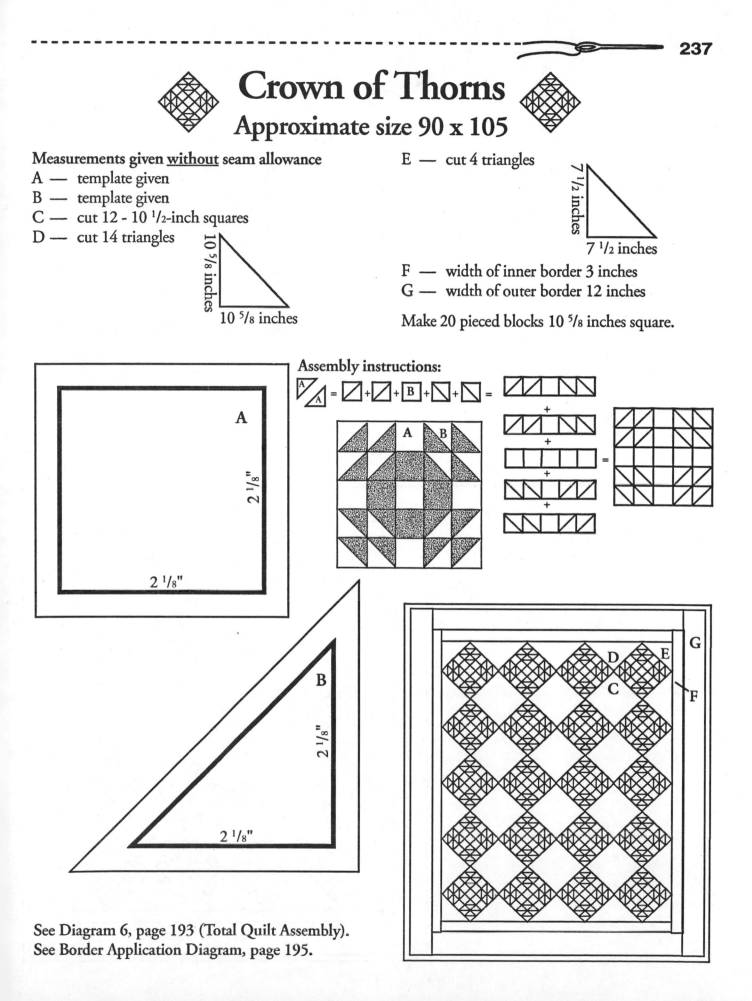

2 ⅛"
2 ⅛"
A

2 ⅛"
2 ⅛"
B

D E G
C F

See Diagram 6, page 193 (Total Quilt Assembly).
See Border Application Diagram, page 195.

Bear Paw
Approximate size 90 x 104

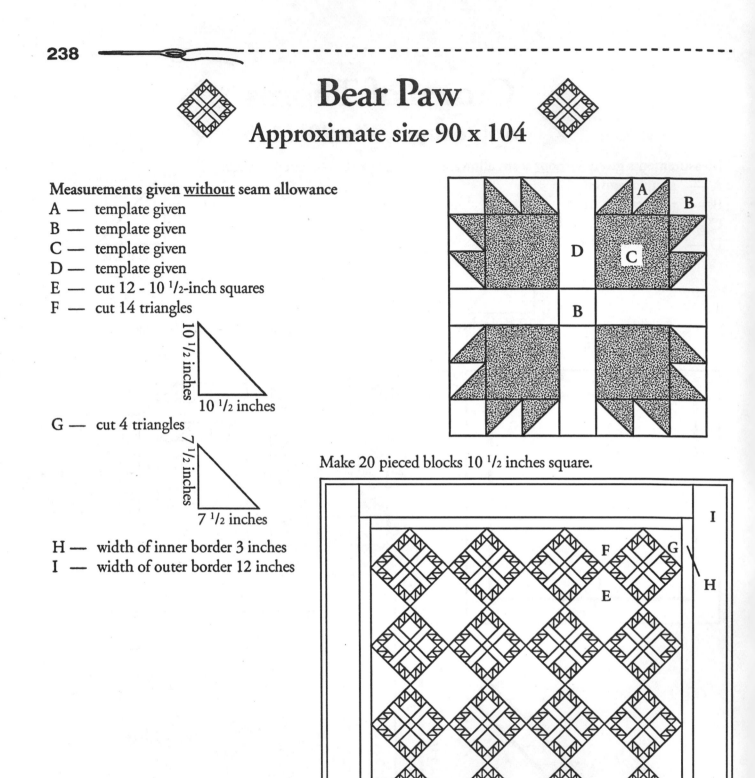

Measurements given <u>without</u> seam allowance

A — template given
B — template given
C — template given
D — template given
E — cut 12 - 10 ½-inch squares
F — cut 14 triangles

10 ½ inches / 10 ½ inches

G — cut 4 triangles

7 ½ inches / 7 ½ inches

H — width of inner border 3 inches
I — width of outer border 12 inches

Make 20 pieced blocks 10 ½ inches square.

Assembly instructions:

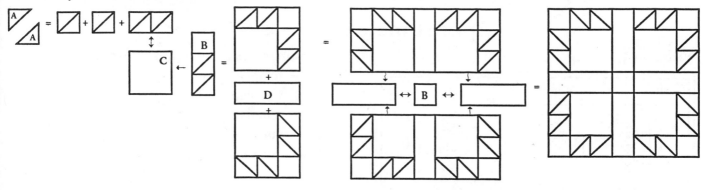

See Diagram 6, page 193 (Total Quilt Assembly).
See Border Application Diagram, page 195.

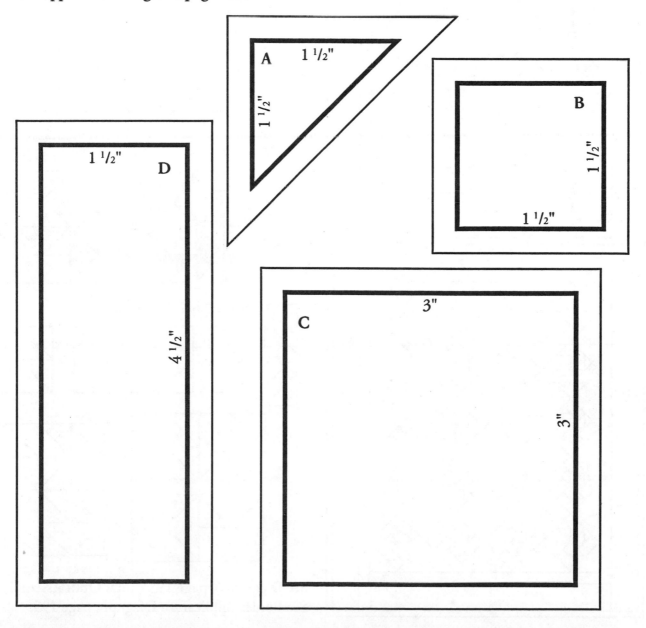

Pinwheel
Approximate size 90 x 104

Variation 1

Variation 2

Measurements given <u>without</u> seam allowance

A — template given
B — template given
C — template given
D — cut 12 - 10 ½-inch squares
E — cut 14 triangles

10 ½ inches / 10 ½ inches

F — cut 4 triangles

7 ½ inches / 7 ½ inches

G — width of inner border 3 inches
H — width of outer border 12 inches
Make 20 pieced blocks 10 ½ inches square.

Variation 1   Variation 2

Assembly instructions:

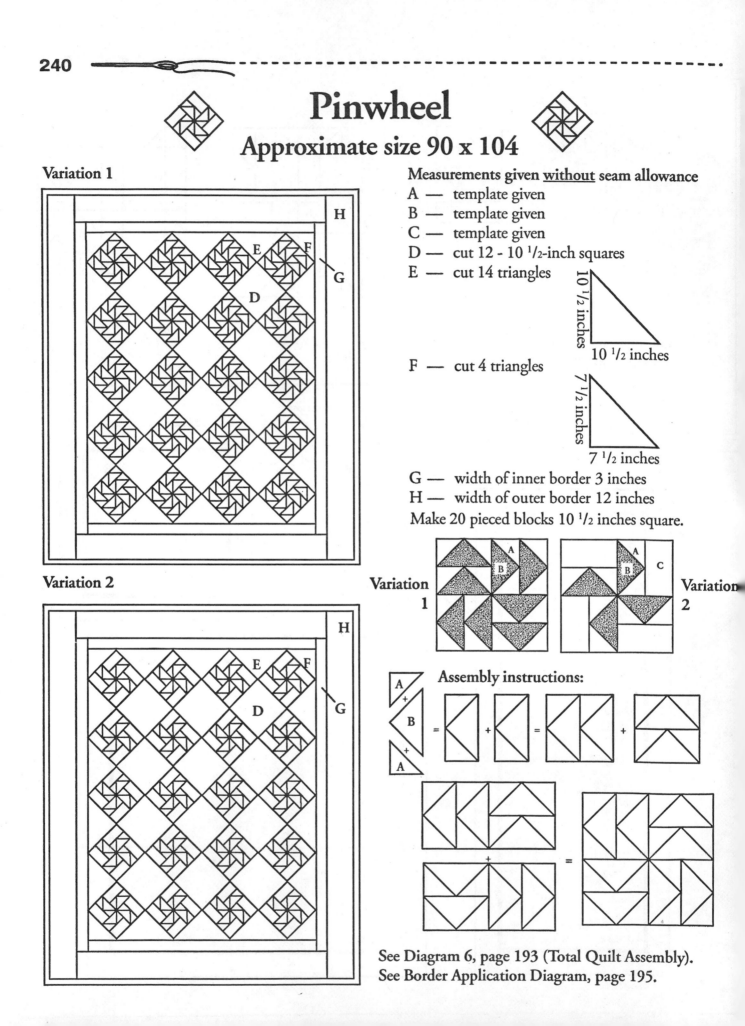

See Diagram 6, page 193 (Total Quilt Assembly).
See Border Application Diagram, page 195.

Variation 3   B — template given
                  D — template given

Use same measurements and procedures as in Variation 1
Assembly instructions:

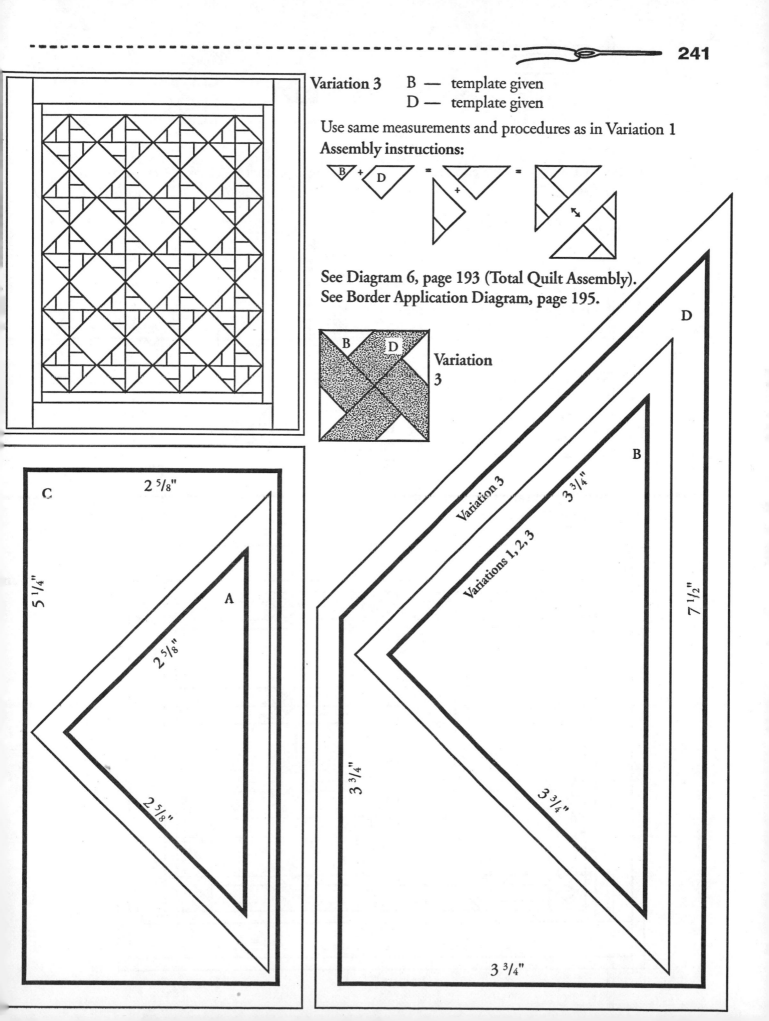

See Diagram 6, page 193 (Total Quilt Assembly).
See Border Application Diagram, page 195.

Variation
3

C

2 5/8"

5 1/4"

A

2 5/8"

2 5/8"

Variation 3

Variations 1, 2, 3   3 3/4"

D

B

7 1/2"

3 3/4"

3 3/4"

3 3/4"

Garden Maze
Approximate size 86 x 103

Measurements given <u>without</u> seam allowance

A — template given
B — template given
C — template given
D — template given
E — template given
F — cut 12 - 10-inch squares
G — width of inner border 3 inches
H — width of outer border 12 inches

Assembly instructions:

Make 20 corner blocks 6 1/2 inches square.
Make 31 pieced strips 6 1/2 inches x 10 inches.

See Diagram 5, page 193 (Total Quilt Assembly).
See Border Application Diagram, page 195.

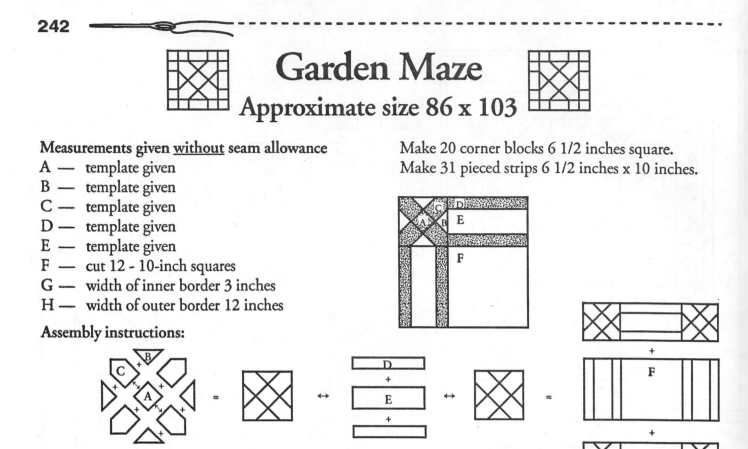

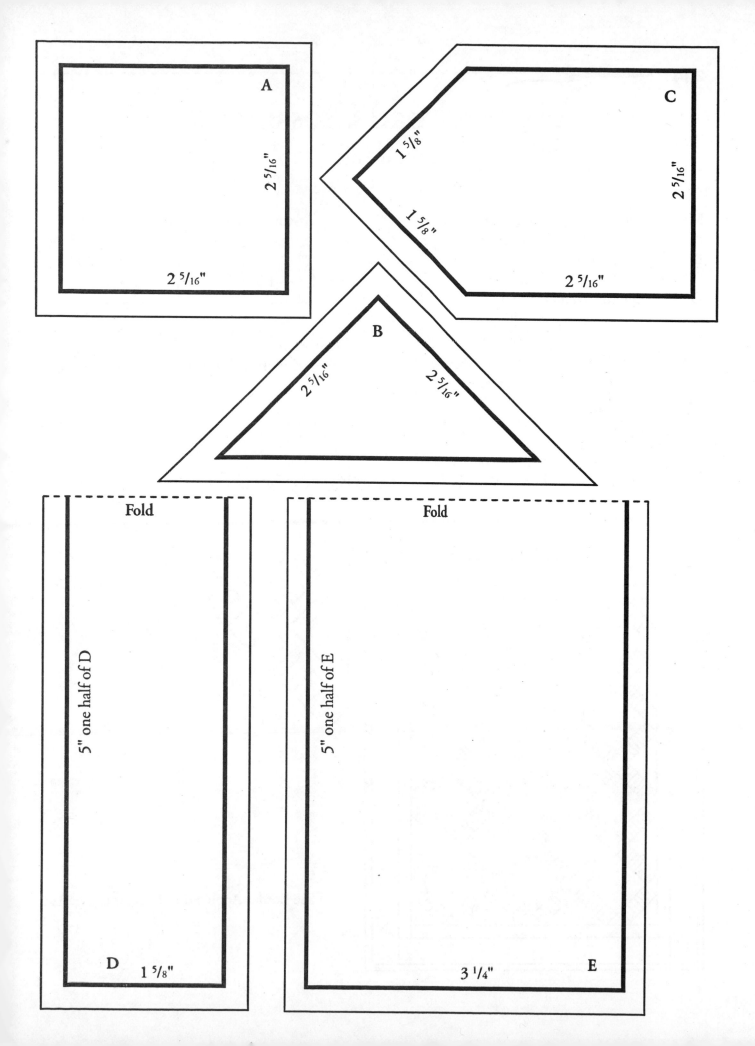

A

2 5/16"

2 5/16"

C

1 5/8"

1 5/8"

2 5/16"

2 5/16"

B

2 5/16"

2 5/16"

Fold

Fold

5" one half of D

5" one half of E

D   1 5/8"

3 1/4"   E

Railroad Crossing
Approximate size 93 x 114

Measurements given <u>without</u> seam allowance
A — template given
B — template given
C — cut 18 - 10 $\frac{1}{8}$-inch squares
D — cut 10 triangles

10 $\frac{1}{8}$ inches
10 $\frac{1}{8}$ inches

E — template given
F — template given
G — width of inner border 3 inches
H — width of outer border 12 inches

Assembly instructions:

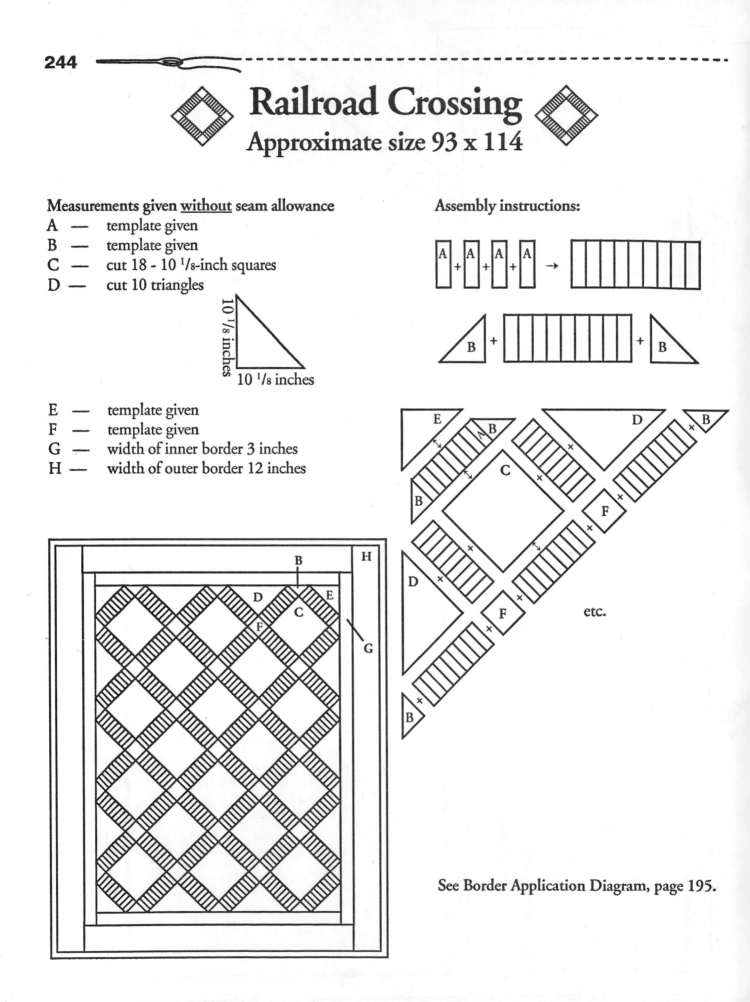

etc.

See Border Application Diagram, page 195.

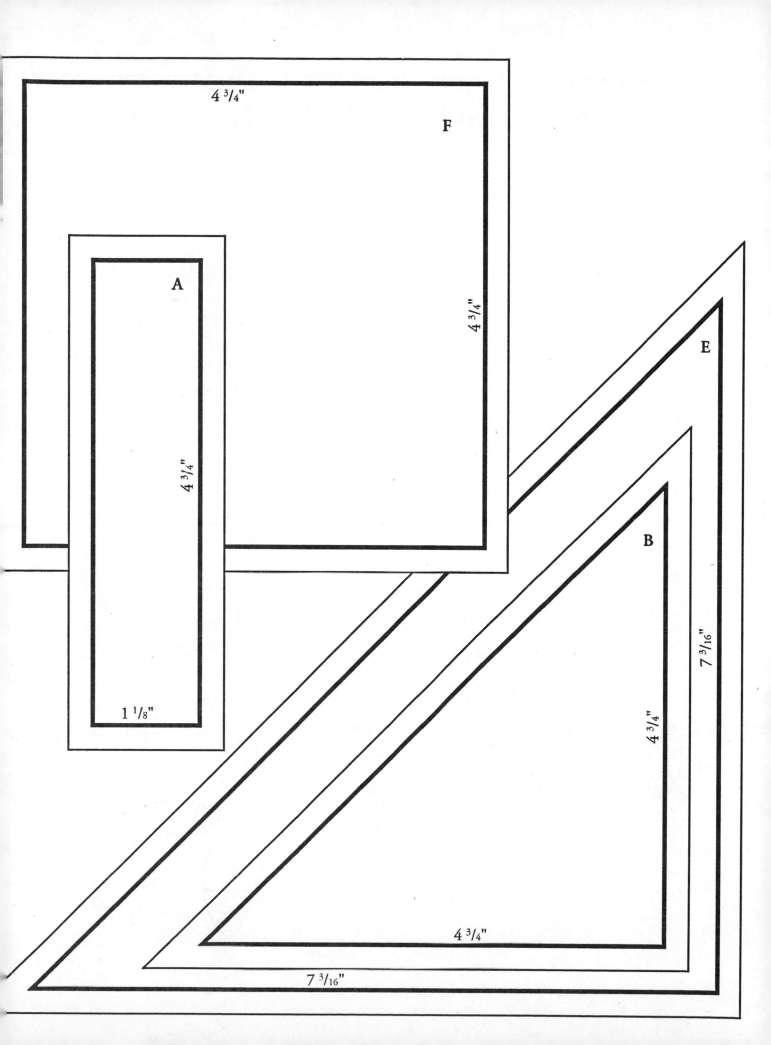

Double Wedding Ring
Approximate size 91 x 105

A — template given
B — template given
C — template given
D — template given
E — template given
F — template given

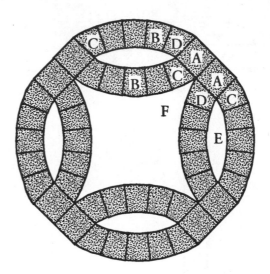

Make 97 pieced oval blocks.
Cut 42 full-size Template F.
Assemble as in diagram below.

Assembly instructions:

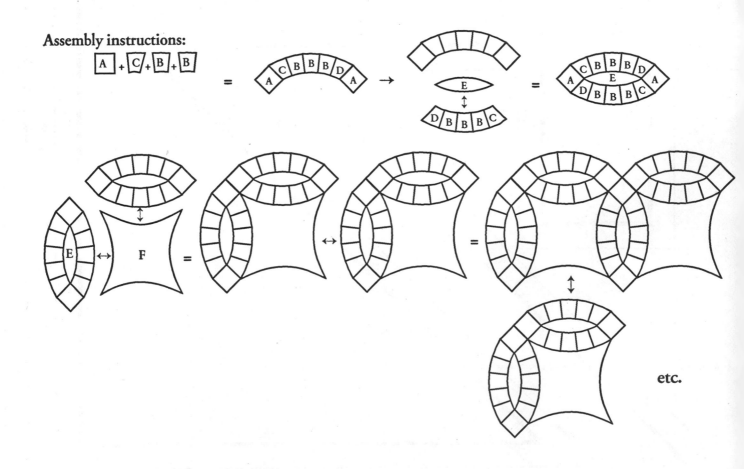

etc.

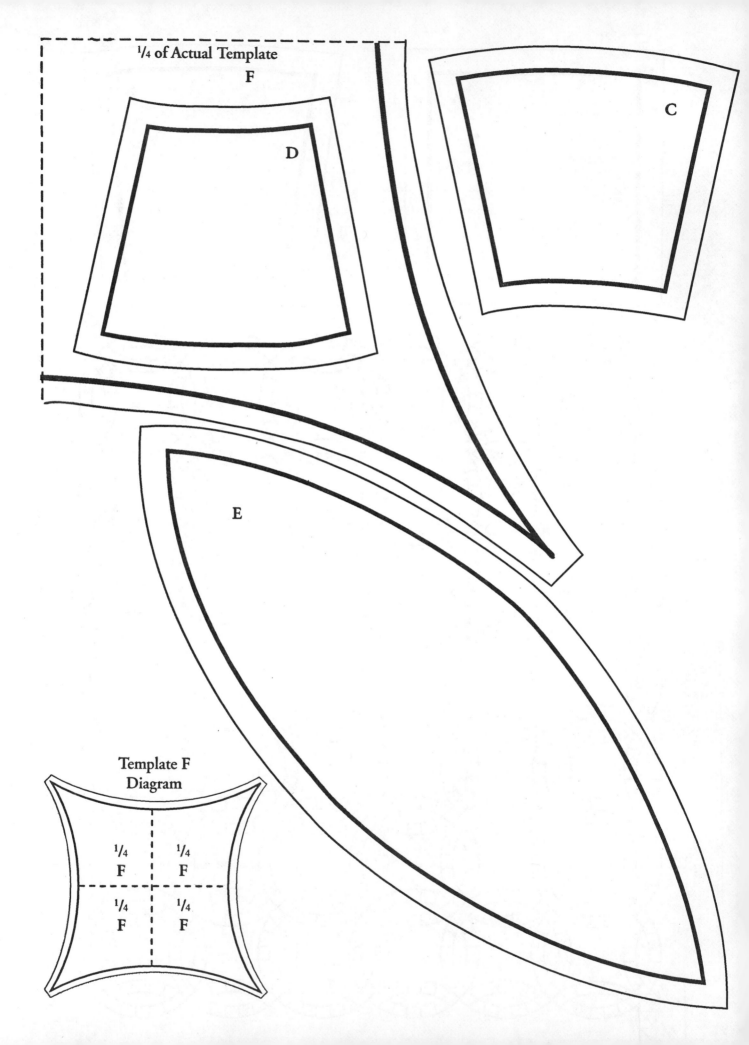

¹/₄ of Actual Template

F

D

C

E

Template F
Diagram

¹/₄
F

¹/₄
F

¹/₄
F

¹/₄
F

Diagonal Triangles
Approximate size 90 x 96

Measurements given <u>without</u> seam allowance
A — template given
B — width of inner border 3 inches
C — width of outer border 12 inches
Make 22 rows of 20 pieced blocks 3 inches square.

Assembly instructions:

See Border Application Diagram, page 195.

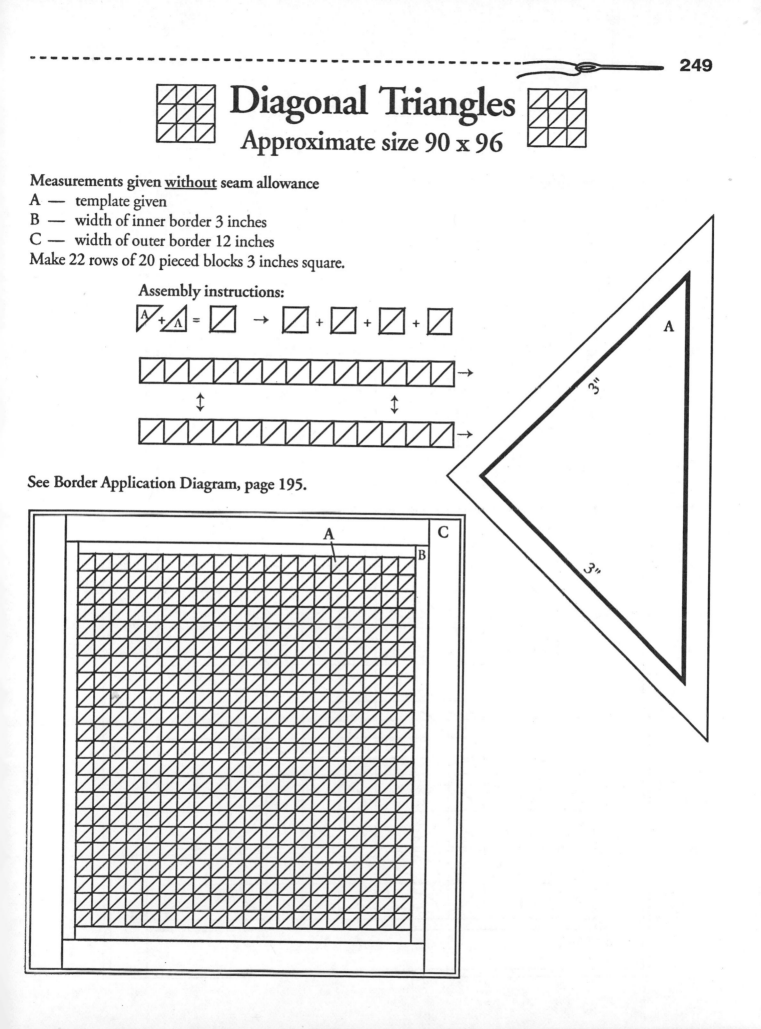

Drunkard's Path
Approximate size 102 x 128

Measurements given <u>without</u> seam allowance

A — template given
B — template given
C — width of inner border 3 inches
D — width of outer border 9 inches

Make 192 pieced blocks 6 ½ inches square.
Alternate placement of blocks to match diagram.

Assembly instructions:

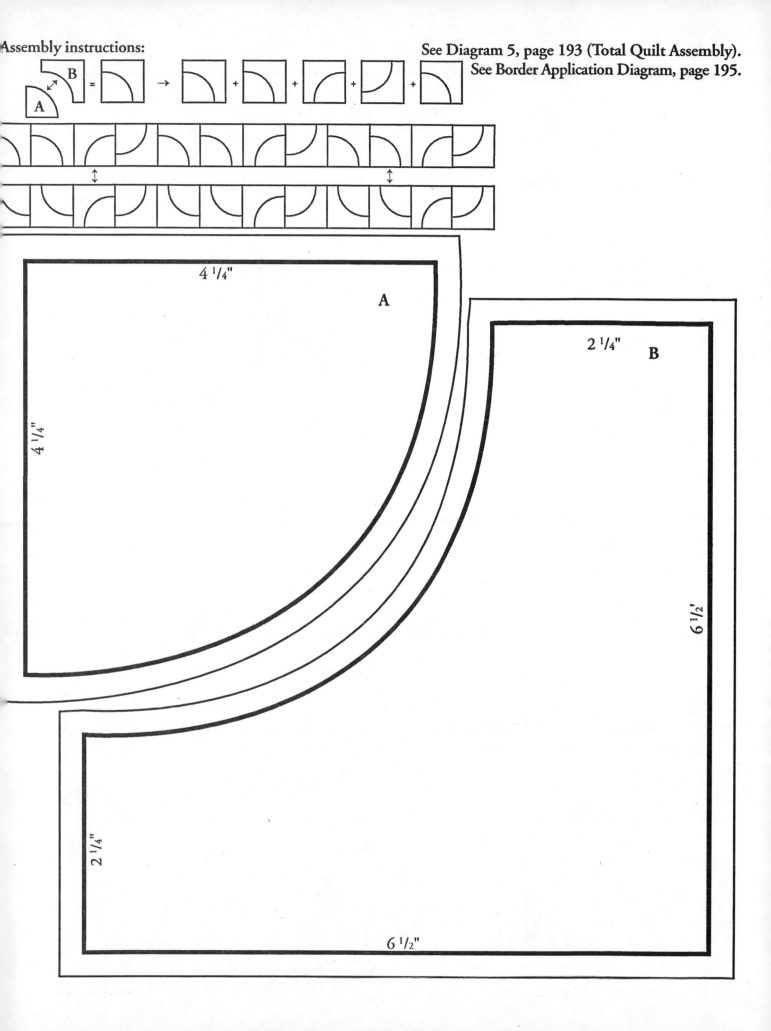

See Diagram 5, page 193 (Total Quilt Assembly).
See Border Application Diagram, page 195.

A

4 1/4"

4 1/4"

B

2 1/4"

6 1/2'

2 1/4"

6 1/2"

Tree of Life
Approximate size 94 x 114

Measurements given <u>without</u> seam allowance

Make 12 pieced blocks 15 ³/₄ inches square.

A — template given
B — template given
C — template given
D — template given
E — template given
F — template given
G — cut 6 - 15 ³/₄-inch squares
H — cut 10 triangles

15 ³/₄ inches
15 ³/₄ inches

I — cut 4 triangles

11 ¹/₈ inches
11 ¹/₈ inches

J — width of inner border 3 inches
K — width of outer border 12 inches

Assembly instructions:

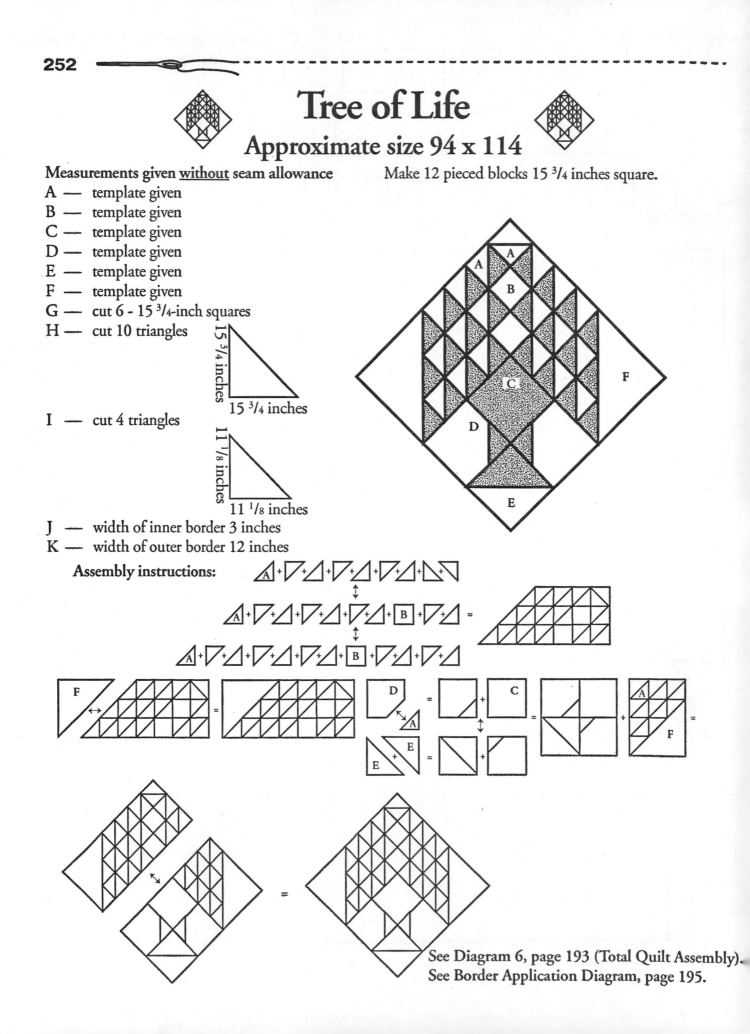

See Diagram 6, page 193 (Total Quilt Assembly).
See Border Application Diagram, page 195.

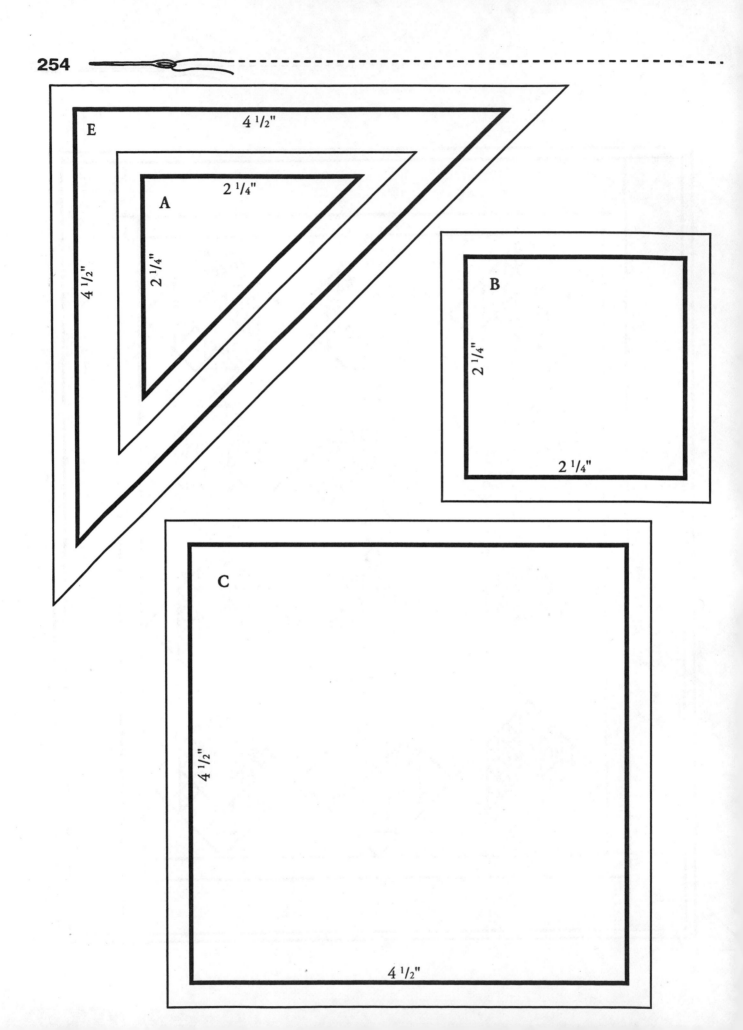

E

4 ½"

A

2 ¼"

2 ¼"

4 ½"

B

2 ¼"

2 ¼"

C

4 ½"

4 ½"

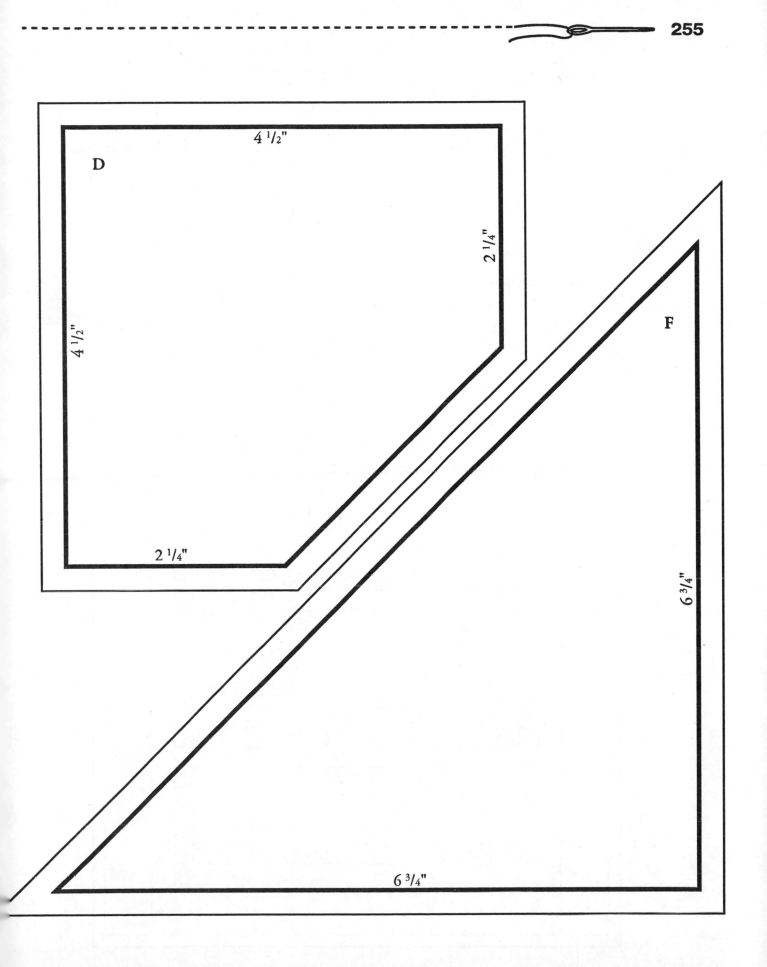

Bachelor's Puzzle
Approximate size 96 x 110

Measurements given <u>without</u> seam allowance

A — template given
B — template given
C — template given
D — width of inner border 3 inches
E — width of outer border 12 inches

Make 120 pieced Four-Patch blocks 3 ¹/₂ inches square.
Make 218 pieced triangle blocks 3 ¹/₂ inches square.

Pieced blocks must be alternated as in diagram to create the proper pattern.

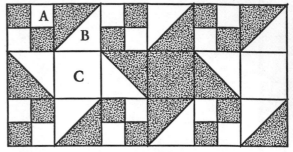

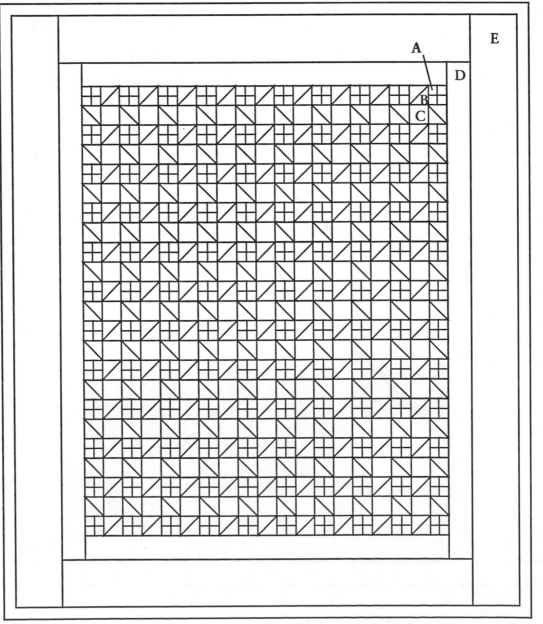

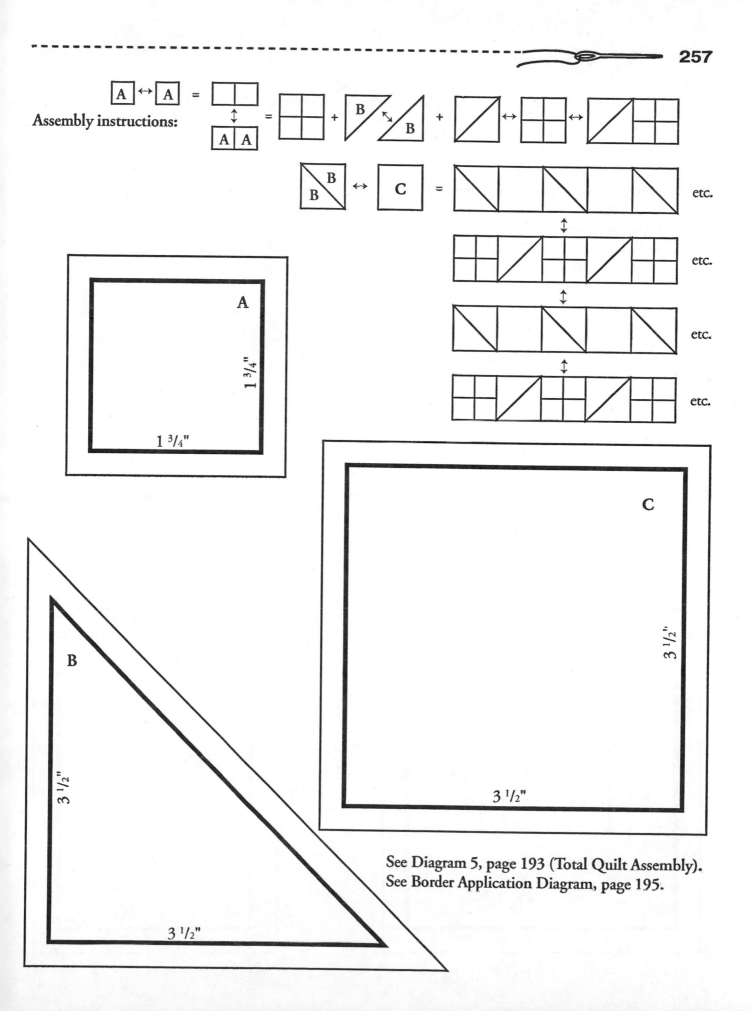

See Diagram 5, page 193 (Total Quilt Assembly).
See Border Application Diagram, page 195.

Rolling Stone
Approximate size 91 x 106

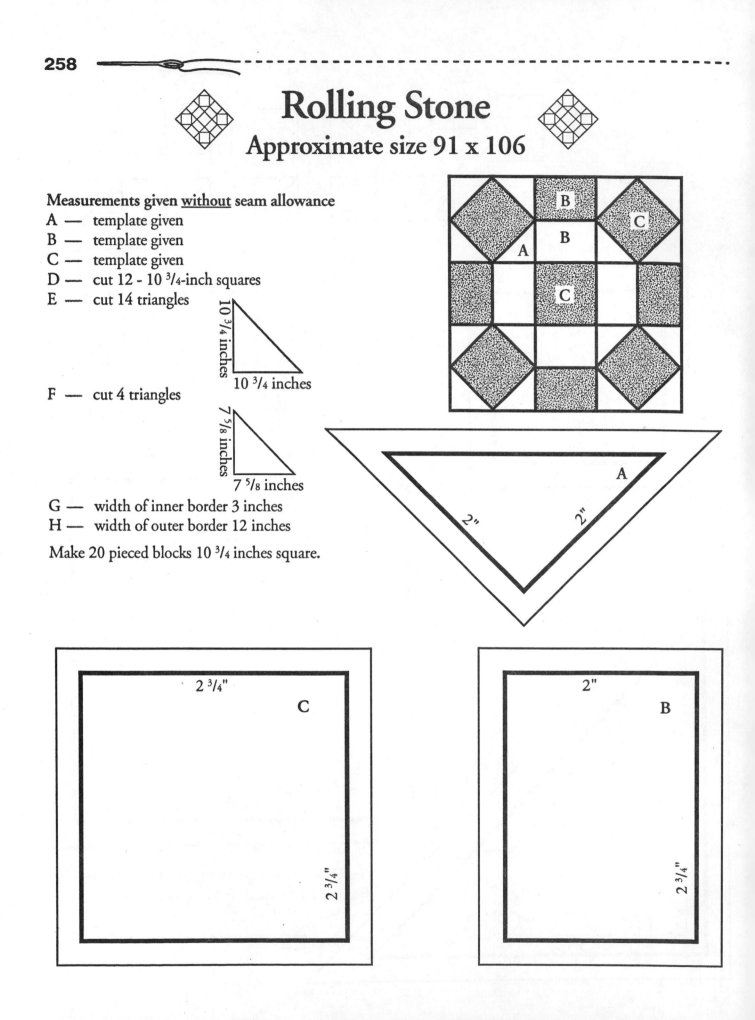

Measurements given <u>without</u> seam allowance

A — template given
B — template given
C — template given
D — cut 12 - 10 ³/₄-inch squares
E — cut 14 triangles

10 ³/₄ inches / 10 ³/₄ inches

F — cut 4 triangles

7 ⁵/₈ inches / 7 ⁵/₈ inches

G — width of inner border 3 inches
H — width of outer border 12 inches

Make 20 pieced blocks 10 ³/₄ inches square.

A — 2" — 2"

C — 2 ³/₄" — 2 ³/₄"

B — 2" — 2 ³/₄"

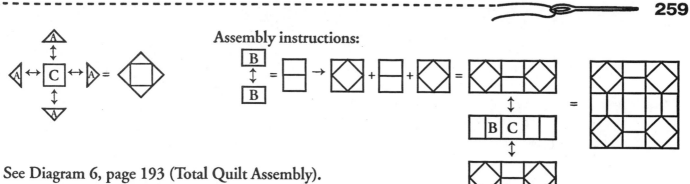

Assembly instructions:

See Diagram 6, page 193 (Total Quilt Assembly).
See Border Application Diagram, page 195.

Amish Quilt Patterns Small Version

Center Diamond
Approximate size 48 x 48

Variation 1

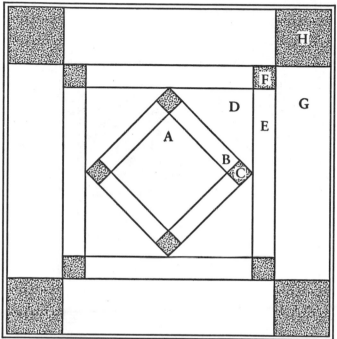

Variation 2

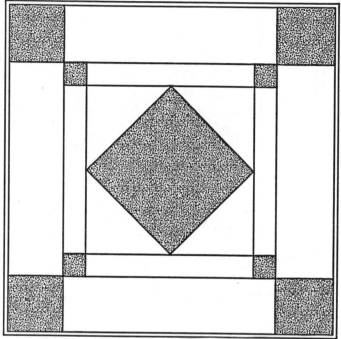

Measurements given <u>without</u> seam allowance

A — 13 ³/₄ inches square

B — 13 ³/₄ inches x 3 inches

C — 3 inches square

D —

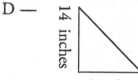

14 inches / 14 inches

E — 3 inches x 28 inches

F — 3 inches square

G — width of outer border 8 inches

H — 8 inches square

Variation 2: All measurements are the same except for Center Diamond which measures 19 ³/₄ inches square (add seam allowance).

Assembly instructions:

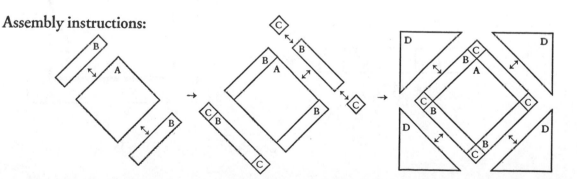

Sunshine and Shadow
Approximate size 48 x 48

Variation 1

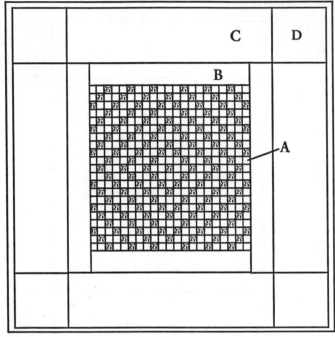

Variation 2 — Center Diamond

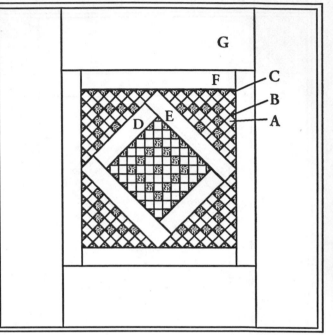

Measurements given <u>without</u> seam allowance

A — template given
B — width of inner border 3 inches
C — width of outer border 8 inches
D — 8 inches square

Measurements given <u>without</u> seam allowance

A — template given
B — template given
C — template given
D — 2 ³/₄ inches x 10 ⁵/₈ inches
E — 2 ³/₄ inches x 16 ¹/₄ inches
F — width of inner border 2 ³/₄ inches
G — width of outer border 8 inches

Assembly instructions:

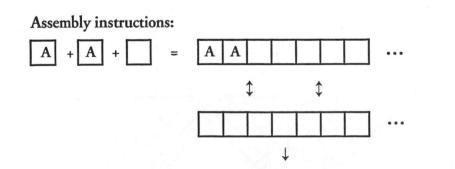

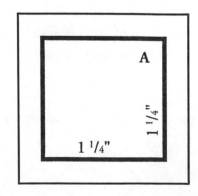

See Border Application Diagram, page 195.

Variation 3

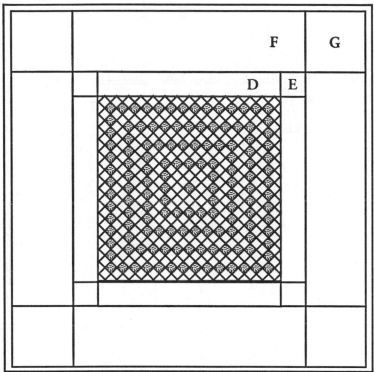

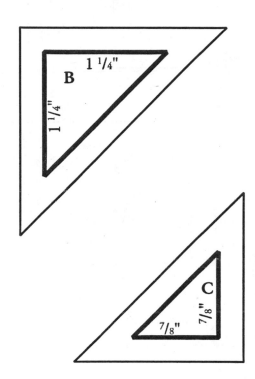

Measurements given <u>without</u> seam allowance

A — template given
B — template given
C — template given
D — width of inner border 3 inches
E — 3 inches square
F — width of outer border 8 inches
G — 8 inches square

Assembly instructions Variation 2:

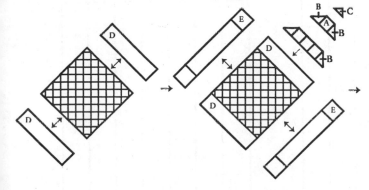

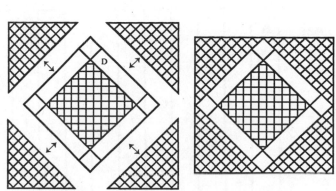

See Border Application Diagram, page 195.

Bars
Approximate size 48 x 48

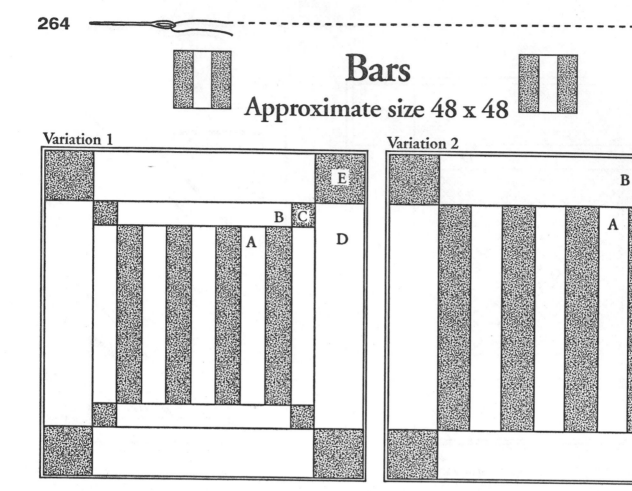

Variation 1

Variation 2

Measurements given <u>without</u> seam allowance

A — 3 $^3/_4$ inches x 26 $^1/_4$ inches
B — 3 inches x 26 $^1/_4$ inches
C — 3 inches square
D — 8 inches x 32 $^1/_4$ inches
E — 8 inches square

Measurements given <u>without</u> seam allowance

A — 4 $^1/_2$ inches x 31 $^1/_2$ inches
B — 8 inches x 31 $^1/_2$ inches
C — 8 inches square

Assembly instructions:

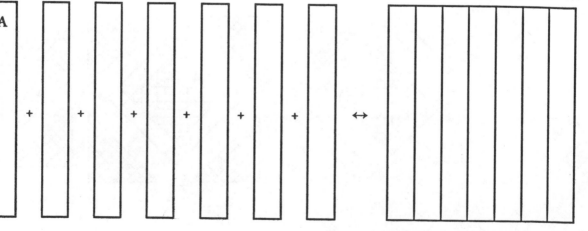

See Border Application Diagram, page 195.

Wild Goose Chase Variation — Approximate size 44 x 58

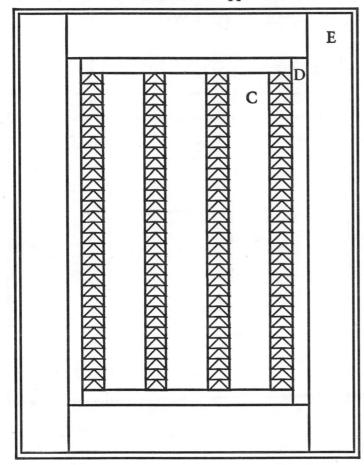

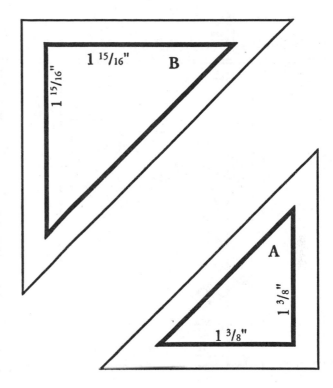

Measurements given <u>without</u> seam allowance

A — template given
B — template given
C — width of sashing 5 ¹/₂ inches
D — width of inner border 2 inches
E — width of outer border 6 inches

Size of pieced rectangle block 2 ³/₄ inches x 1 ³/₈ inches.
Make 4 rows of 30 blocks each.

Assembly instructions:

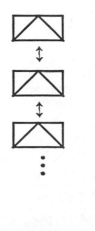

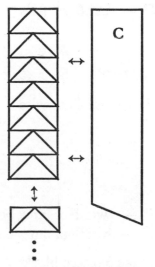

See Border Application Diagram, page 195.

Multiple Patch
Approximate size 48 x 60

Variation 1 — Double 9-Patch

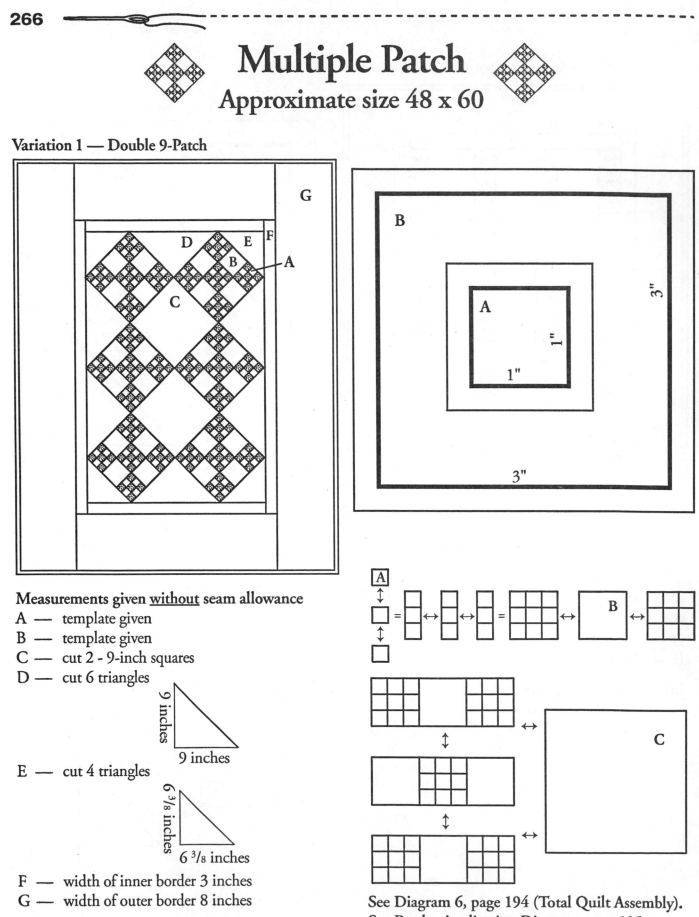

Measurements given <u>without</u> seam allowance

A — template given
B — template given
C — cut 2 - 9-inch squares
D — cut 6 triangles

9 inches / 9 inches

E — cut 4 triangles

6 3/8 inches / 6 3/8 inches

F — width of inner border 3 inches
G — width of outer border 8 inches

Make 6 pieced blocks 9 inches square.

See Diagram 6, page 194 (Total Quilt Assembly).
See Border Application Diagram, page 195.

Variation 2 — Double 4-Patch

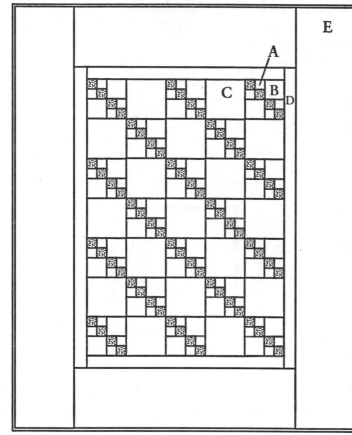

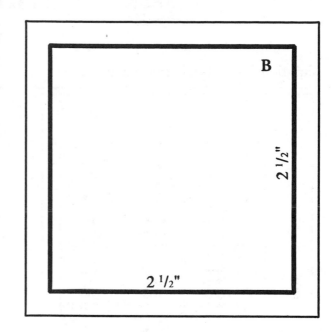

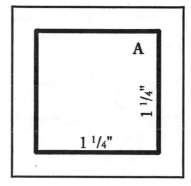

Measurements given <u>without</u> seam allowance

A — template given
B — template given
C — cut 17 - 5-inch squares
D — width of inner border 2 inches
E — width of outer border 8 inches

Make 18 pieced blocks 5 inches square.

Assembly instructions:

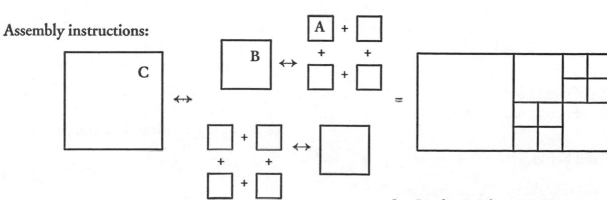

See Border Application Diagram, page 195.

Irish Chain
Approximate size 47 x 55

Variation 1 — Double Irish Chain

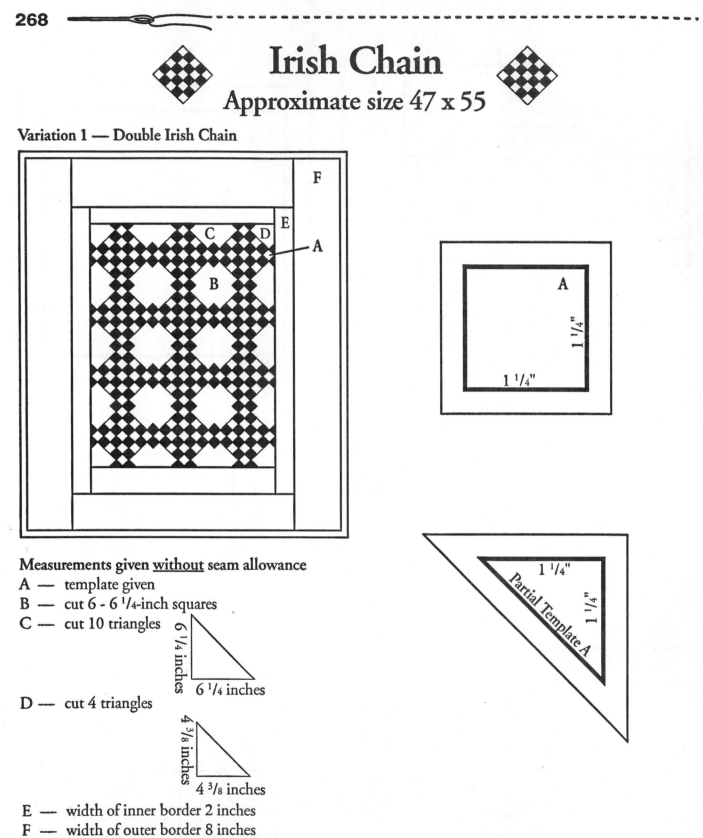

Measurements given <u>without</u> seam allowance

A — template given

B — cut 6 - 6 ¼-inch squares

C — cut 10 triangles

D — cut 4 triangles

E — width of inner border 2 inches

F — width of outer border 8 inches

See Border Application Diagram, page 195.

Make 12 pieced blocks 6 ¼ inches square.

Plain blocks and triangles need Template A and Partial Template A appliquéd in the corners to complete the pattern.

Variation 2 — Single Irish Chain

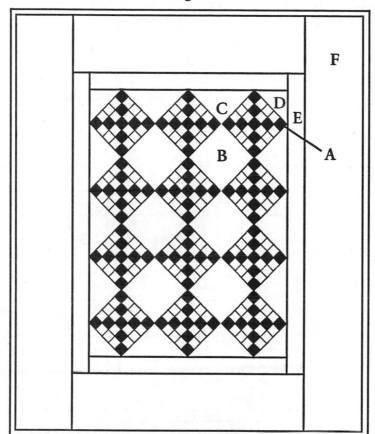

Proceed as in Variation 1 but eliminate
appliquéd squares on plain alternate blocks.

See Diagram 6, page 194 (Total Quilt Assembly).
See Border Application Diagram, page 195.

Assembly instructions:

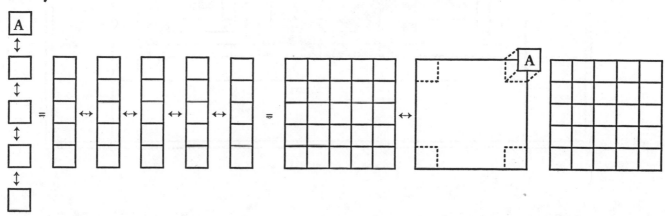

Log Cabin
Approximate size 45 x 53

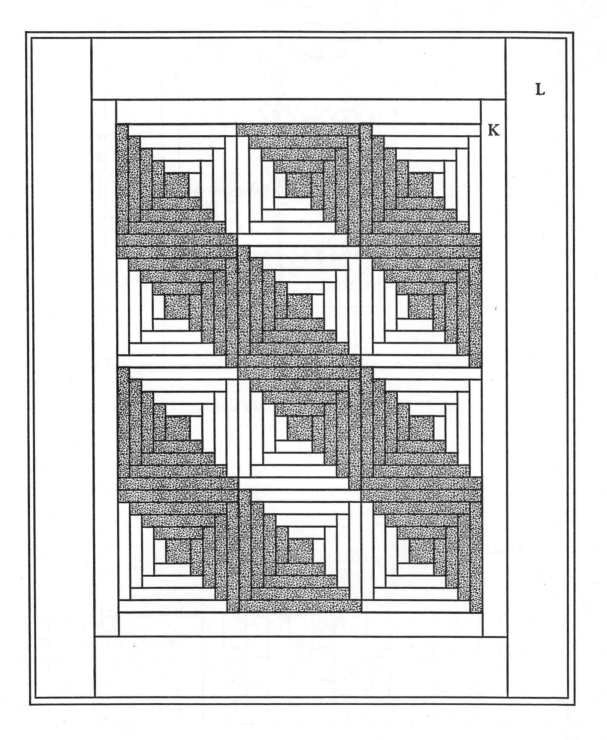

K — width of inner border 2 inches
L — width of outer border 8 inches

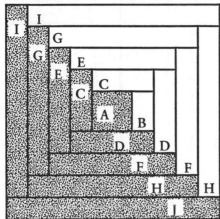

Make 12 pieced blocks 8 ¼ inches square.

Assembly instructions: Beginning with A and B, add fabric strips in order to complete Log Cabin block.

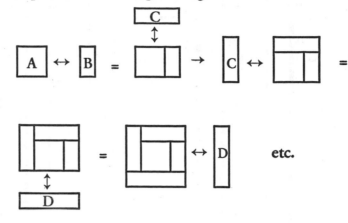

See **Border Application Diagram, page 195.**

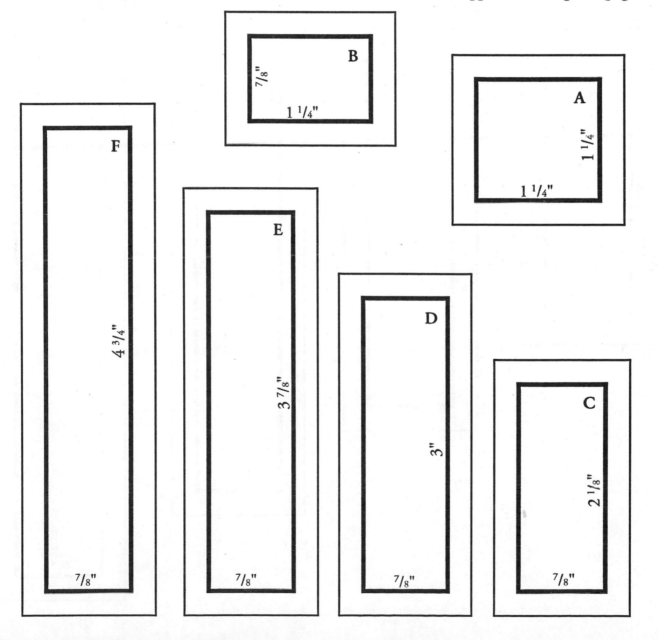

B   ⁷/₈"   1 ¼"

A   1 ¼"   1 ¼"

F   4 ³/₄"   ⁷/₈"

E   3 ⁷/₈"   ⁷/₈"

D   3"   ⁷/₈"

C   2 ¹/₈"   ⁷/₈"

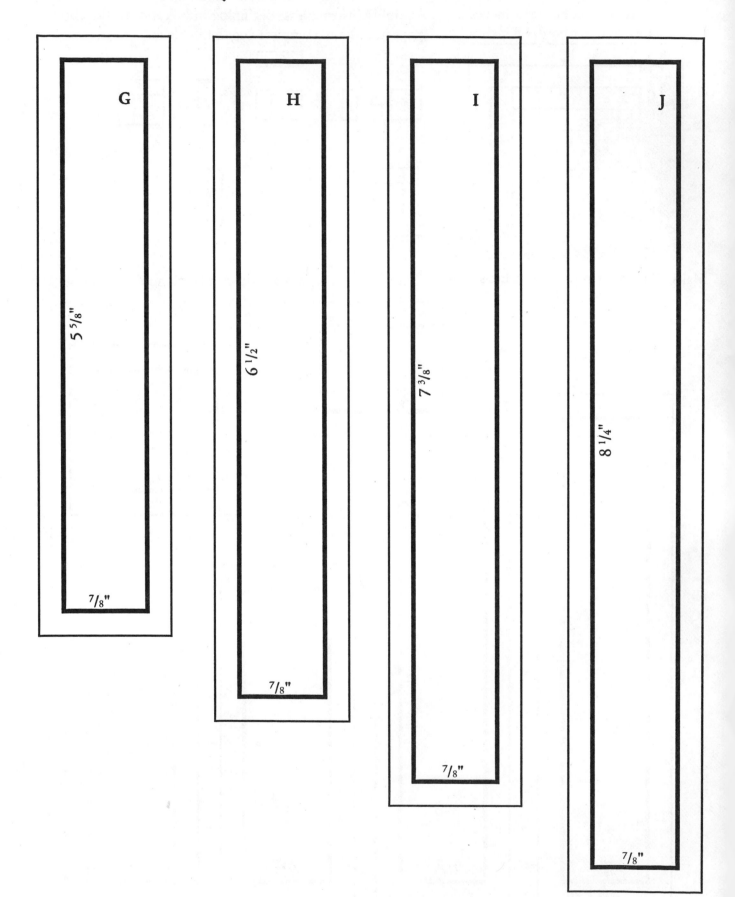

G

5 5/8"

7/8"

H

6 1/2"

7/8"

I

7 3/8"

7/8"

J

8 1/4"

7/8"

Rail Fence
Approximate size 47 x 56

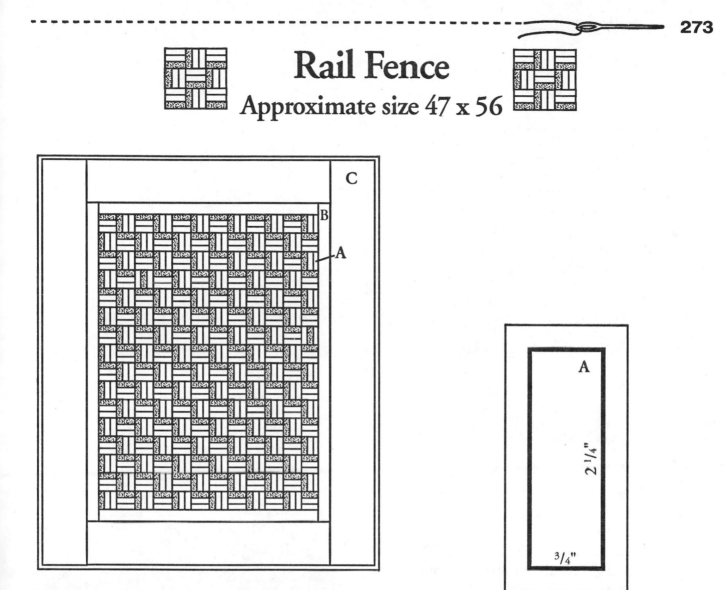

Measurements given <u>without</u> seam allowance

A — template given
B — width of inner border 2 inches
G — width of outer border 8 inches

Make 192 pieced blocks 2 ¼ inches square.
Arrange in alternate directions to each other.

See Diagram 6, page 194 (Total Quilt Assembly).
See Border Application Diagram, page 195.

Assembly instructions:

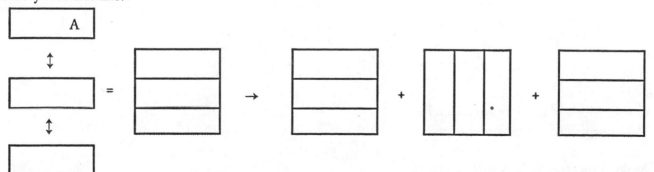

Double T
Approximate size 46 x 58

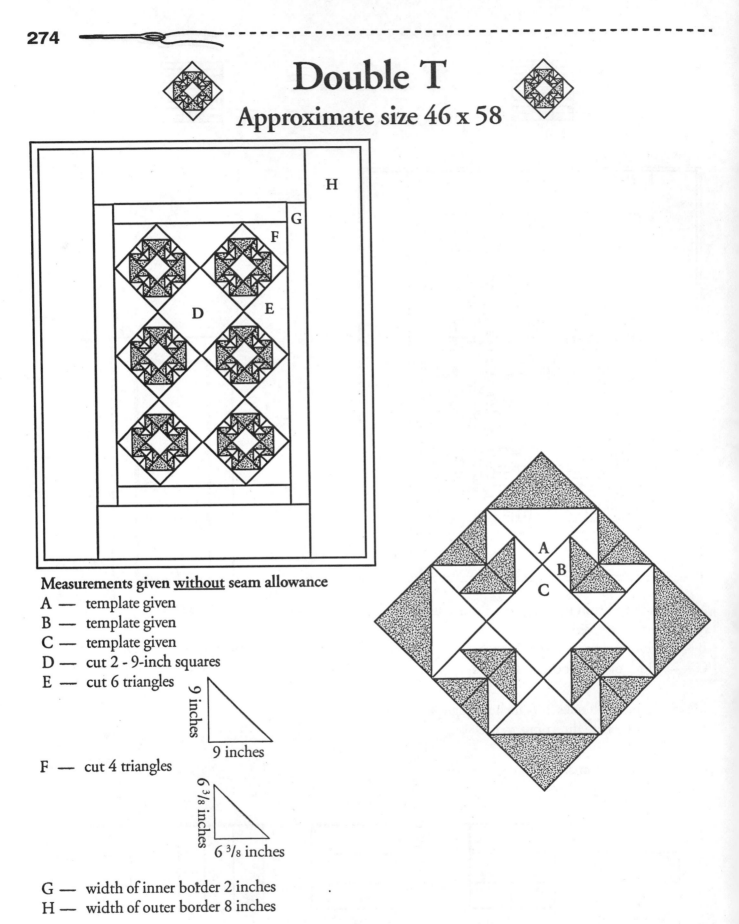

Measurements given <u>without</u> seam allowance

A — template given
B — template given
C — template given
D — cut 2 - 9-inch squares
E — cut 6 triangles

9 inches / 9 inches

F — cut 4 triangles

6 3/8 inches / 6 3/8 inches

G — width of inner border 2 inches
H — width of outer border 8 inches

Make 6 pieced blocks 9 inches square.

Assembly instructions:

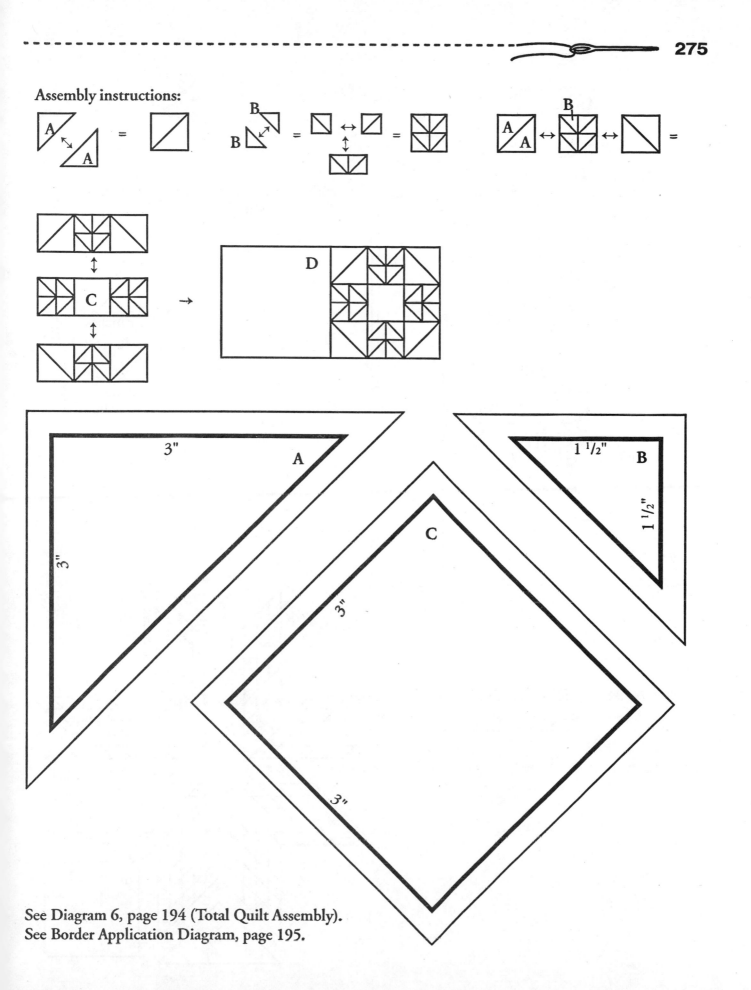

See Diagram 6, page 194 (Total Quilt Assembly).
See Border Application Diagram, page 195.

Stars
Approximate size 48 x 57

Variation 1 — Lone Star

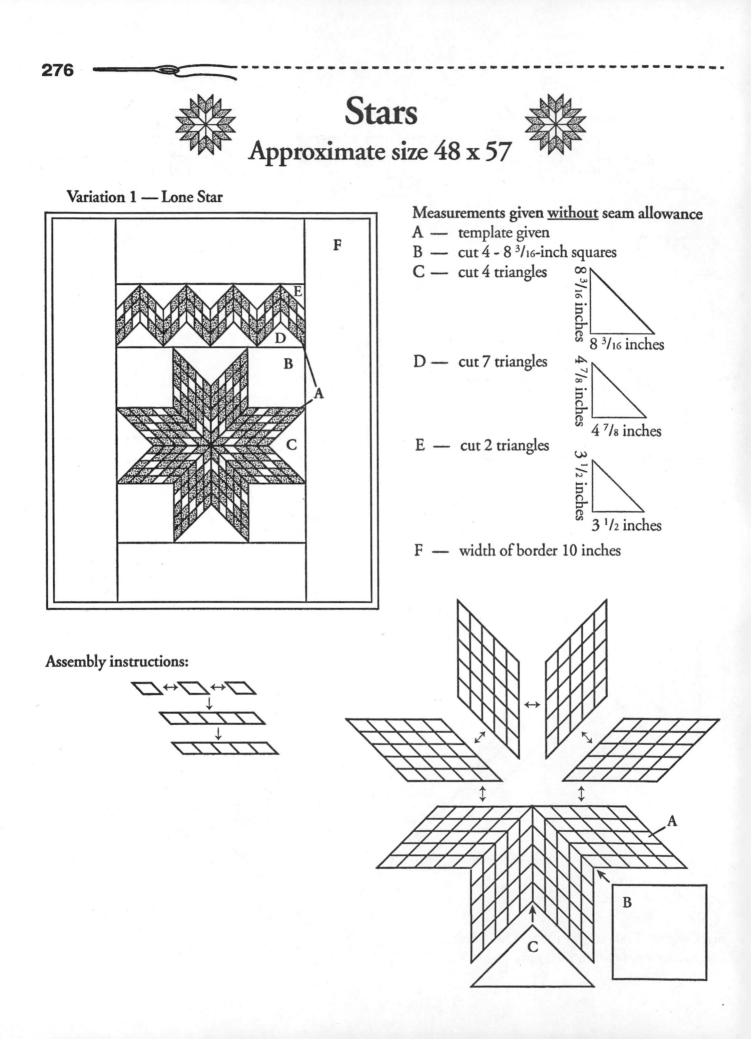

Measurements given <u>without</u> seam allowance
A — template given
B — cut 4 - 8 3/16-inch squares
C — cut 4 triangles

8 3/16 inches
8 3/16 inches

D — cut 7 triangles

4 7/8 inches
4 7/8 inches

E — cut 2 triangles

3 1/2 inches
3 1/2 inches

F — width of border 10 inches

Assembly instructions:

F

E

D

B

A

C

A

B

C

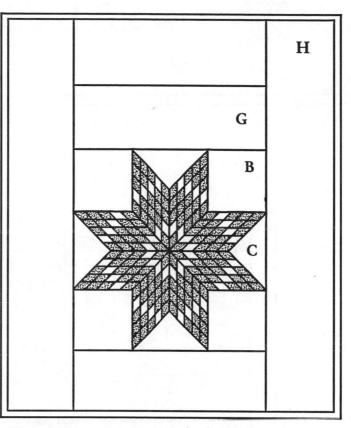

Variation 2 — Lone star with plain pillow throw same as Variation 1 except eliminate D and E and replace with G — 8 ½ inches x width of pieced star

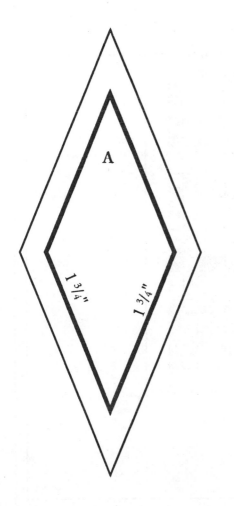

See Border Application Diagram, page 195.

Jacob's Ladder
Approximate size 44 x 56

D

C

Measurements given <u>without</u> seam allowance
A — template given
B — template given
C — width of inner border 2 inches
D — width of outer border 8 inches

Make 24 pieced blocks 6 inches square.

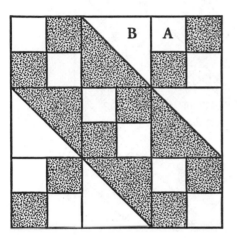

See Diagram 5, page 194 (Total Quilt Assembly).
See Border Application Diagram, page 195.

Assembly instructions:

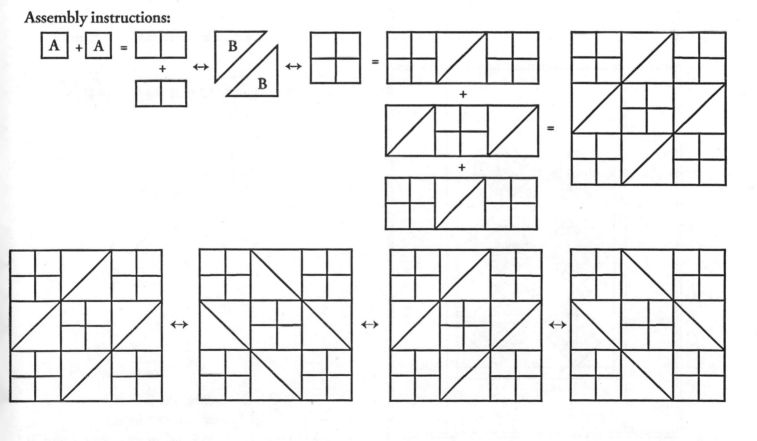

Baskets
Approximate size 45 x 57

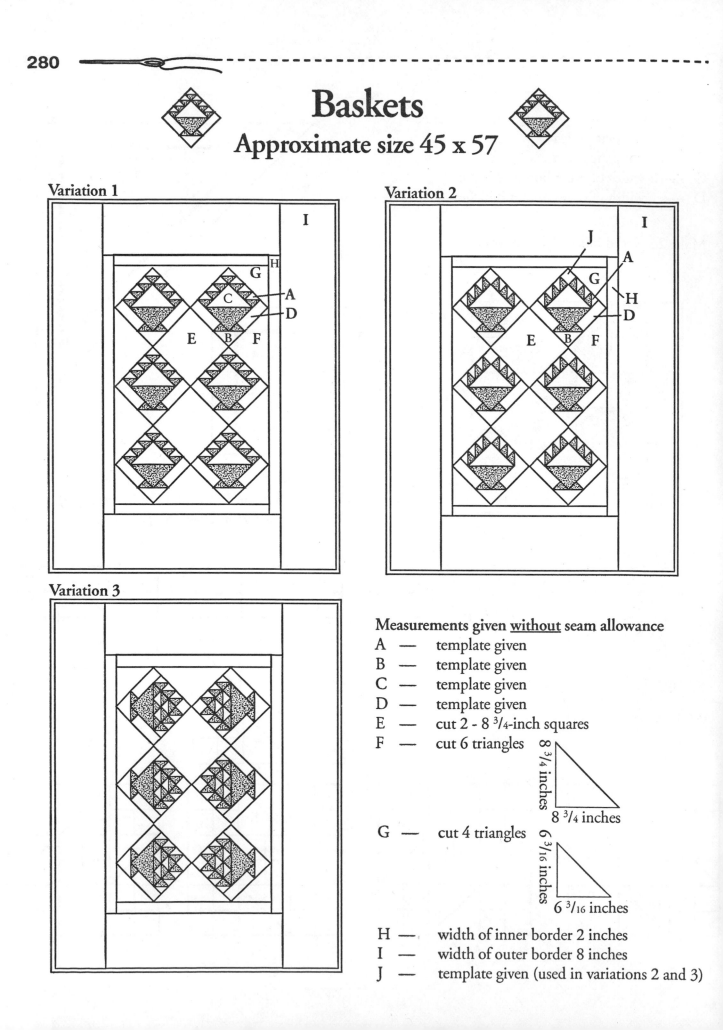

Variation 1

Variation 2

Variation 3

Measurements given <u>without</u> seam allowance

A — template given
B — template given
C — template given
D — template given
E — cut 2 - 8 ¾-inch squares
F — cut 6 triangles

G — cut 4 triangles

H — width of inner border 2 inches
I — width of outer border 8 inches
J — template given (used in variations 2 and 3)

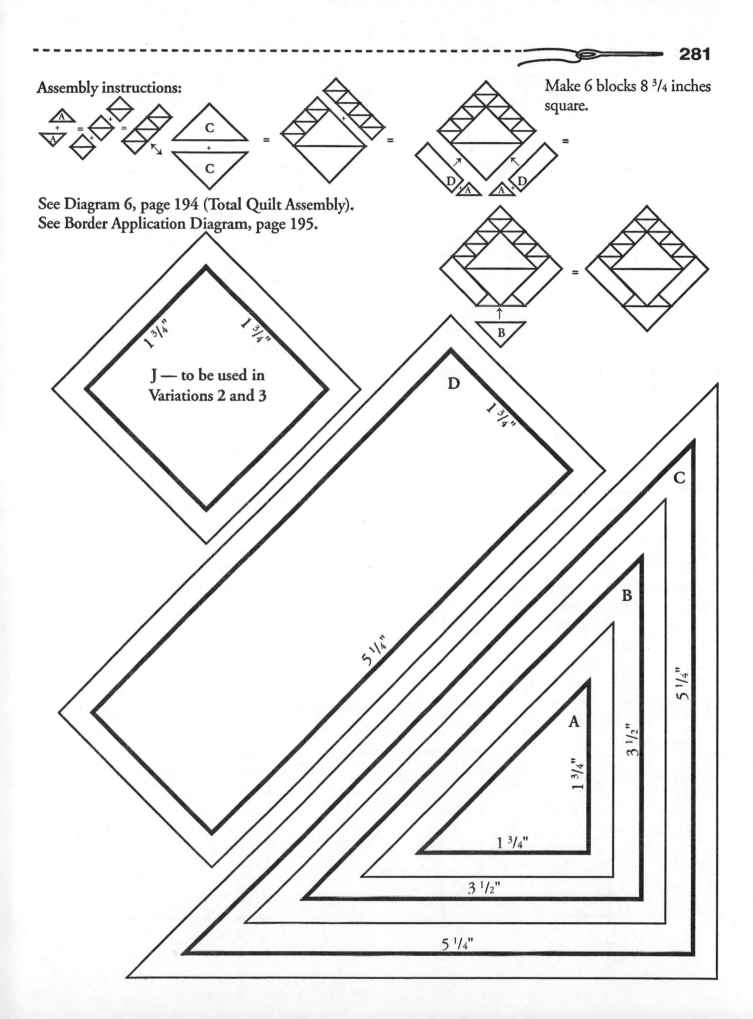

Assembly instructions:

Make 6 blocks 8 ¾ inches square.

See Diagram 6, page 194 (Total Quilt Assembly).
See Border Application Diagram, page 195.

J — to be used in Variations 2 and 3

1 ¾"   1 ¾"

D   1 ¾"

C   5 ¼"

B   3 ½"

A   1 ¾"

1 ¾"

3 ½"

5 ¼"

5 ¼"

Fan

Approximate size 47 x 56

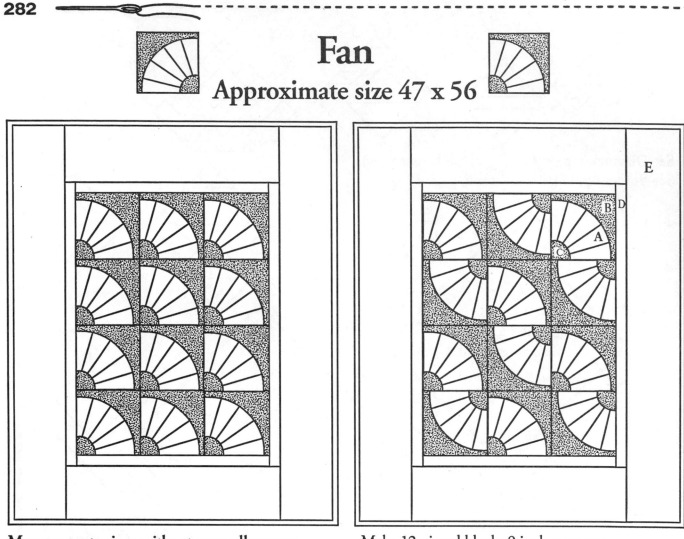

Measurements given <u>without</u> seam allowance

A — template given
B — template given
C — template given
D — width of inner border 2 inches
E — width of outer border 8 inches

Make 12 pieced blocks 9 inches square.

See Diagram 6, page 194 (Total Quilt Assembly).
See Border Application Diagram, page 195.

Assembly instructions:

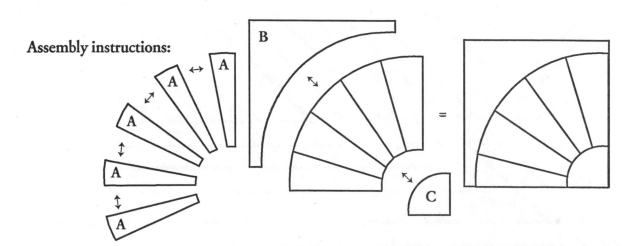

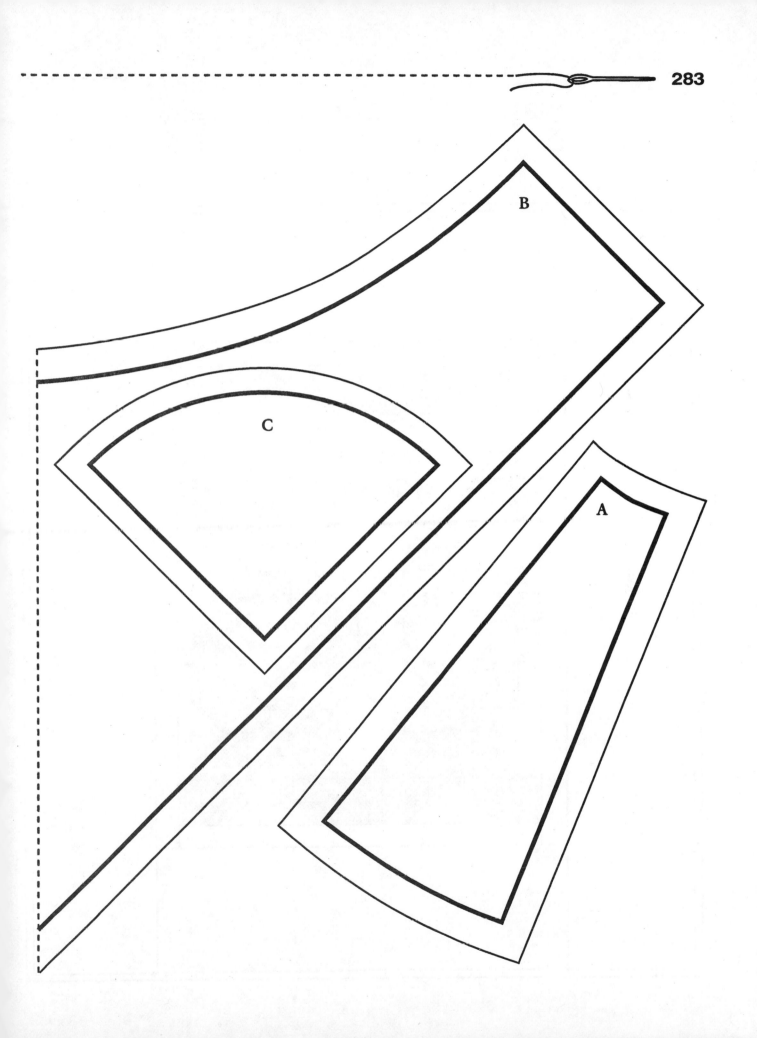

Ocean Waves
Approximate size 48 x 55

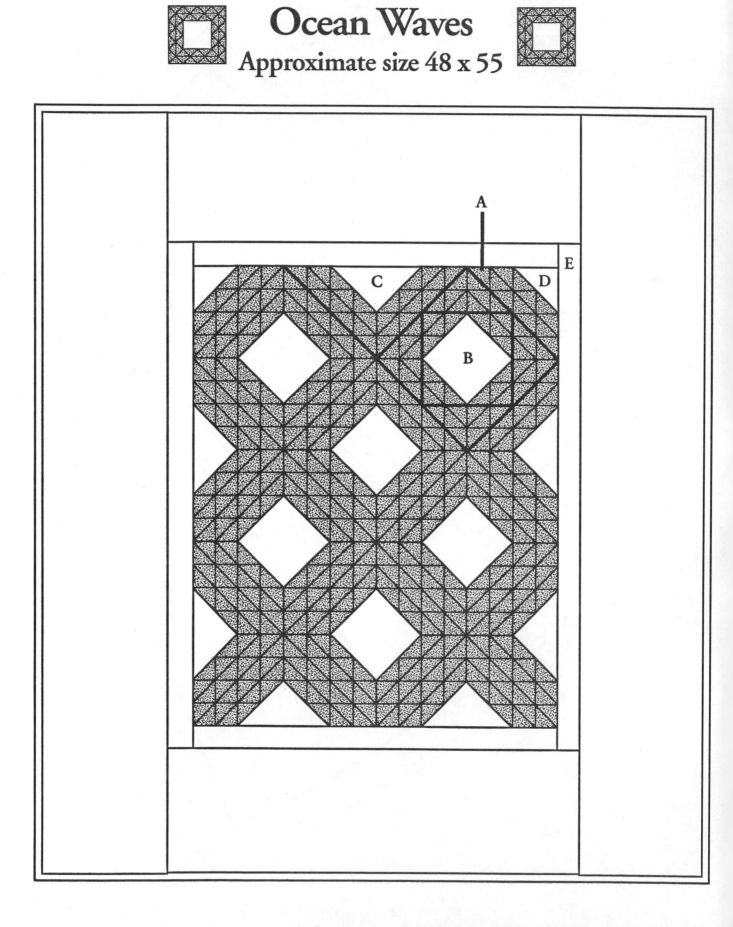

Measurements given <u>without</u> seam allowance

A — template given
B — template given
C — cut 7 triangles

5 inches
5 inches

D — cut 2 triangles

3 ½ inches
3 ½ inches

E — width of inner border 2 inches
F — width of outer border 8 inches

Make 15 pieced blocks

B

Make 11 half blocks

C

Make 2 quarter blocks

D

Assembly instructions:

See Border Application Diagram, page 195.

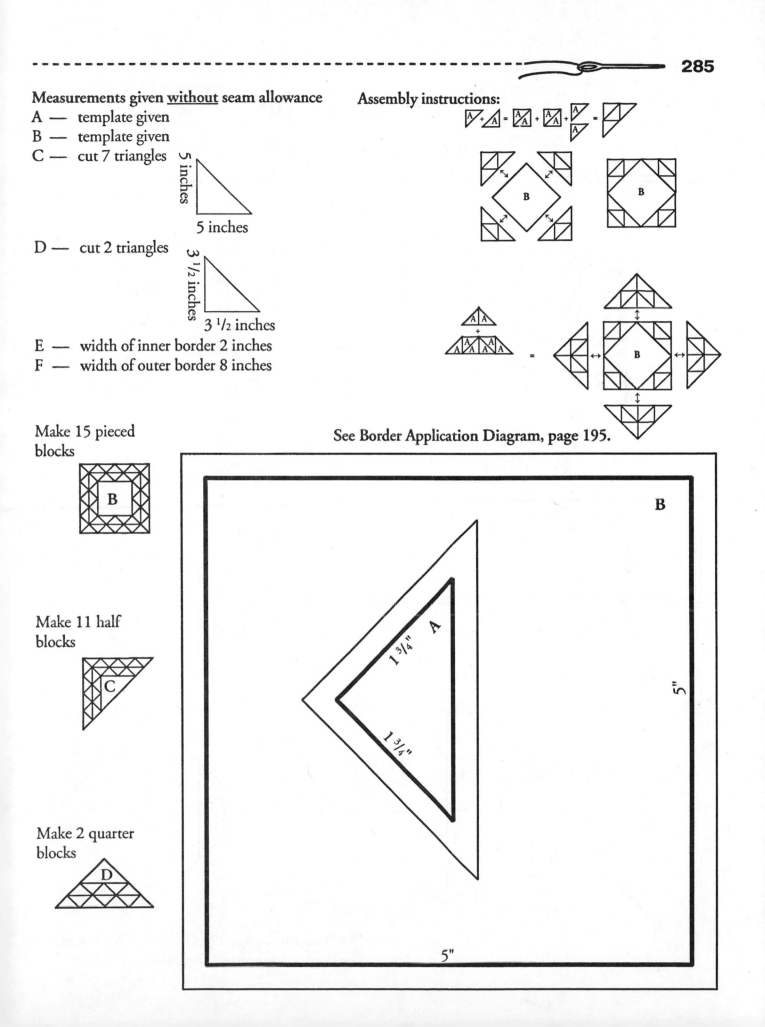

B

A

1 ¾"

1 ¾"

5"

5"

Roman Stripe
Approximate size 48 x 55

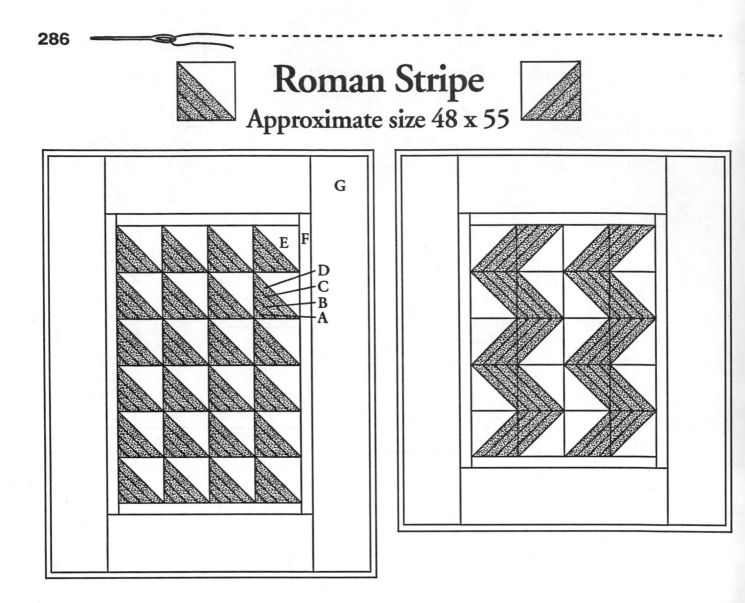

G

E F

D
C
B
A

Assembly instructions:

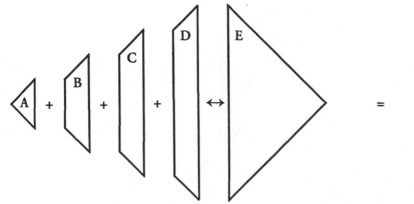

A + B + C + D ↔ E =

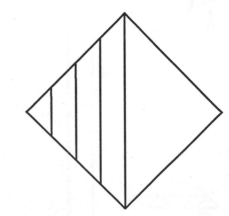

See Diagram 5, page 194 (Total Quality Assembly).
See Border Application Diagram, page 195.

Measurements given without seam allowance

A — template given
B — template given
C — template given
D — template given
E — cut 24 triangles

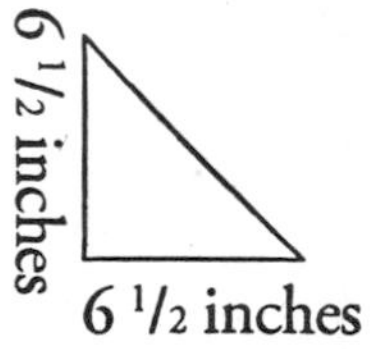

6 ½ inches / 6 ½ inches

F — width of inner border 3 inches
G — width of outer border 8 inches

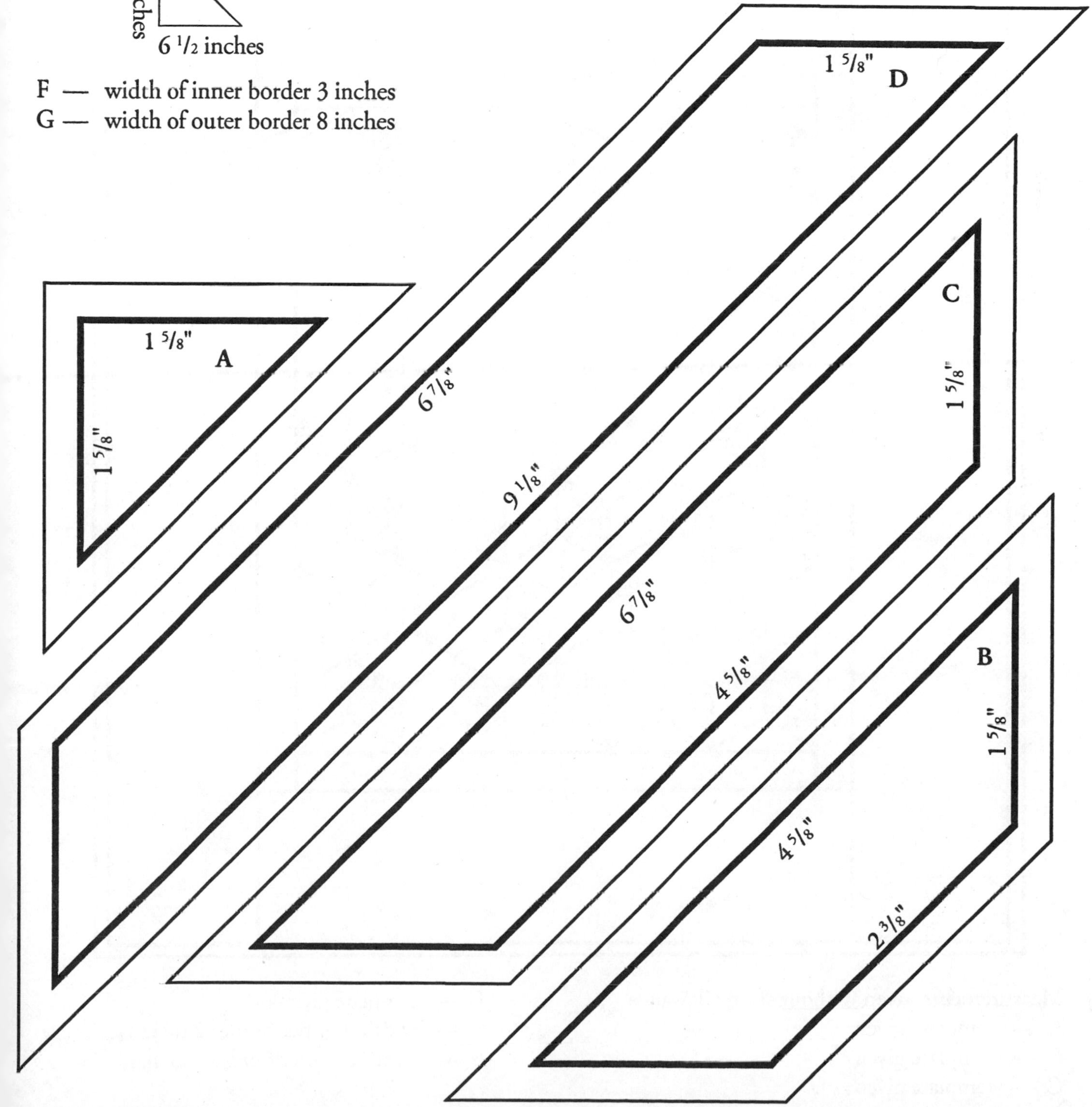

1 ⁵/₈" D

1 ⁵/₈" A

1 ⁵/₈"

C

1 ⁵/₈"

6 ⁷/₈"

9 ⅛"

6 ⁷/₈"

4 ⁵/₈"

B

1 ⁵/₈"

4 ⁵/₈"

2 ³/₈"

Tumbling Blocks
Approximate size 48 x 54

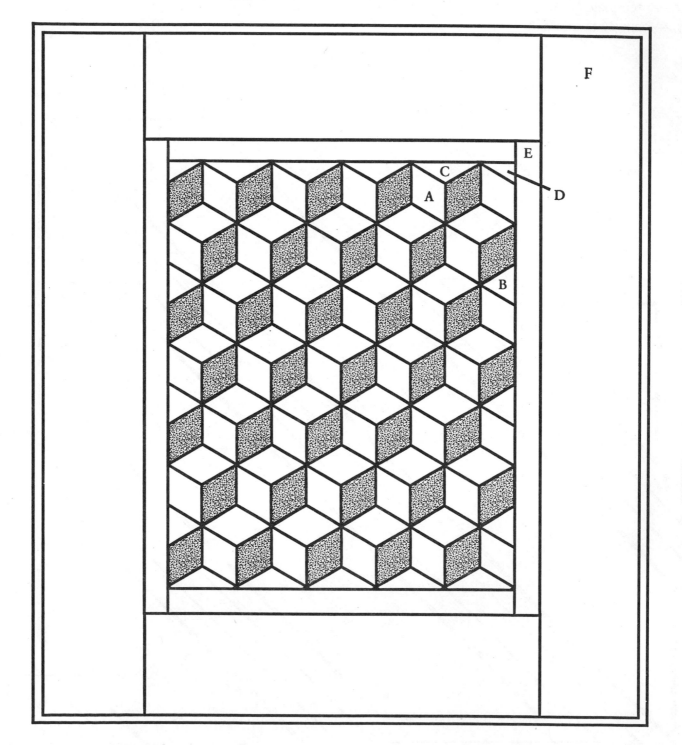

Measurements given <u>without</u> seam allowance

A — template given

B — template given

C — template given

D — template given

E — width of inner border 2 inches

F — width of outer border 8 inches

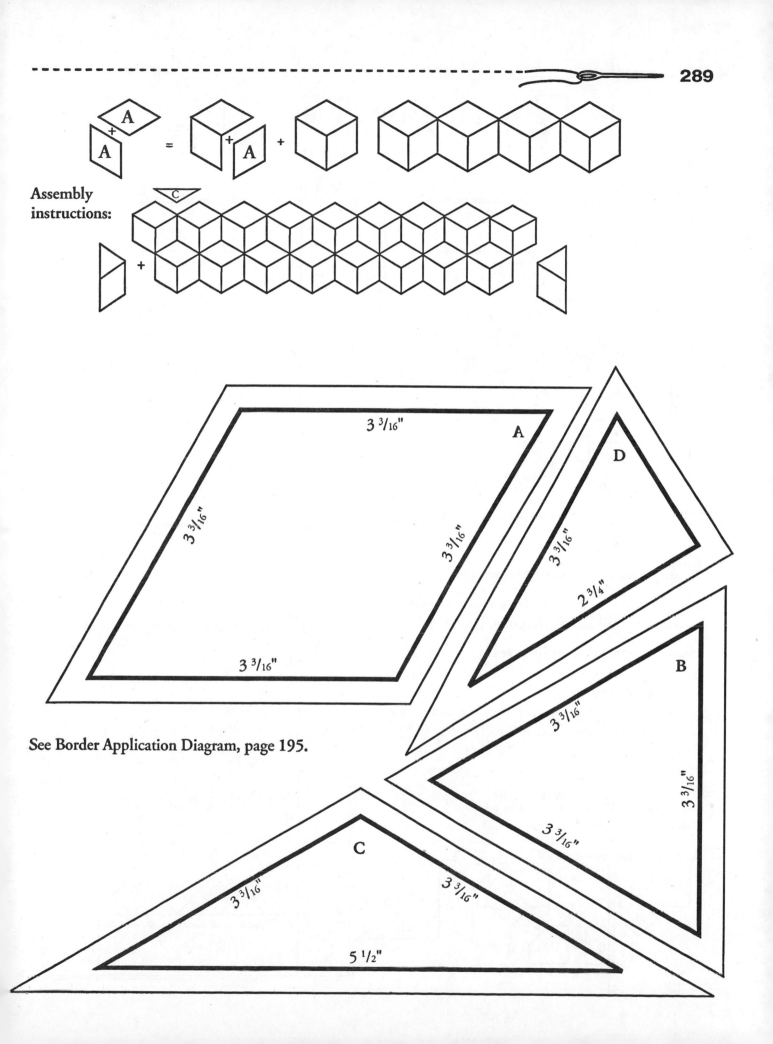

Assembly instructions:

See Border Application Diagram, page 195.

A

3 3/16"

3 3/16"

3 3/16"

3 3/16"

D

3 3/16"

2 3/4"

B

3 3/16"

3 3/16"

3 3/16"

C

3 3/16"

3 3/16"

5 1/2"

Bow Tie
Approximate size 45 x 55

Variation 1

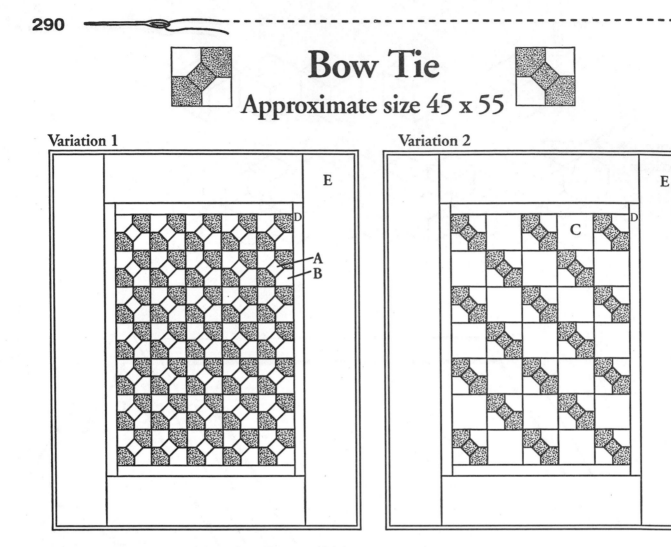

E

D

A
B

Variation 2

E

D

C

See Diagram 5, page 194 (Total Quilt Assembly).
See Border Application Diagram, page 195.

Measurements given <u>without</u> seam allowance
A — template given
B — template given
C — template given (used only for Variations 2 and 3)
D — width of inner border 2 inches
E — width of outer border 8 inches

Make 35 pieced blocks 5 inches square.
Variation 2, make 18 pieced blocks.

Assembly instructions:

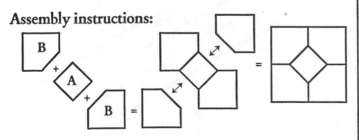

Variation 3

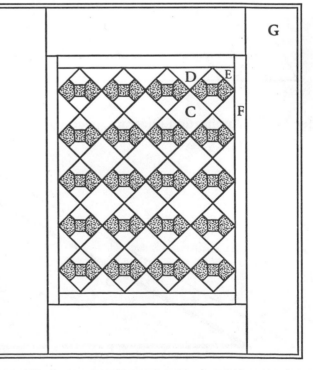

G

D   E

C   F

Variation 3

Measurements given <u>without</u> seam allowance

A — template given
B — template given
C — 12 squares template given
D — cut 14 triangles

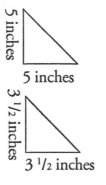

E — cut 4 triangles

E — width of inner border 2 inches
F — width of outer border 8 inches

Make 20 pieced blocks 5 inches square.

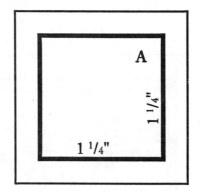

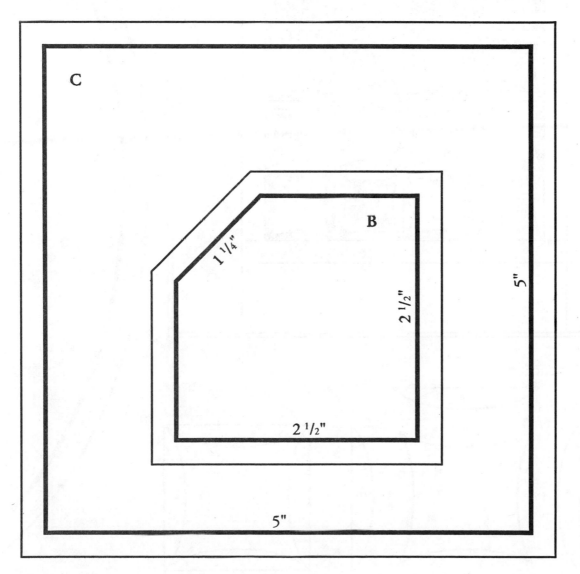

Robbing Peter to Pay Paul
Approximate size 49 x 56

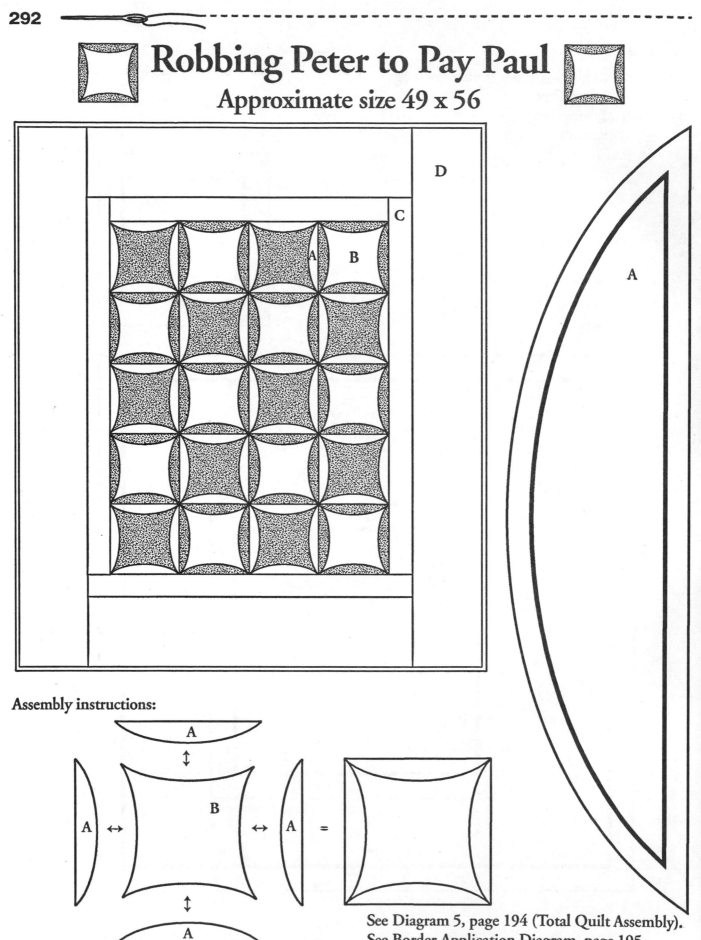

Assembly instructions:

See Diagram 5, page 194 (Total Quilt Assembly).
See Border Application Diagram, page 195.

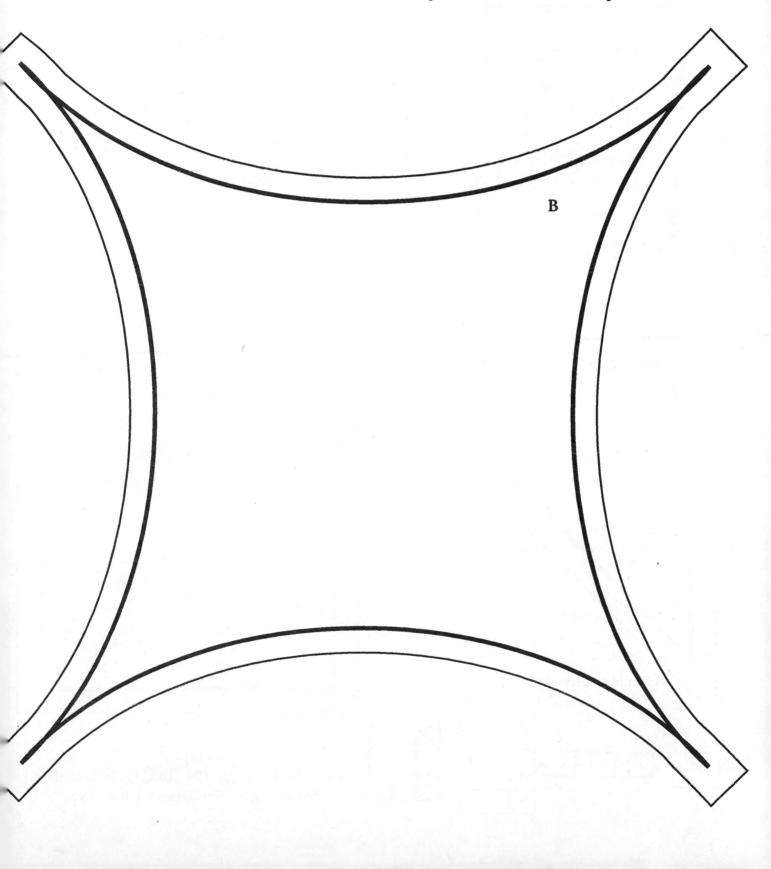

Measurements given <u>without</u> seam allowance
A — template given
B — template given

C — width of inner border 2 inches
D — width of outer border 8 inches
Make 20 pieced blocks 7 1/8 inches square.

B

Shoo-Fly
Approximate size 46 x 58

Measurements given <u>without</u> seam allowance
A — template given
B — template given
C — cut 2 - 9-inch squares
D — cut 6 triangles

9 inches / 9 inches

E — cut 4 triangles

6 3/8 inches / 6 3/8 inches

F — width of inner border 2 inches
G — width of outer border 8 inches

Make 6 pieced blocks 9 inches square.

3"

3"   A

3"

B

3"

3"

Assembly instructions:

See Diagram 6, page 194 (Total Quilt Assembly).
See Border Application Diagram, page 195.

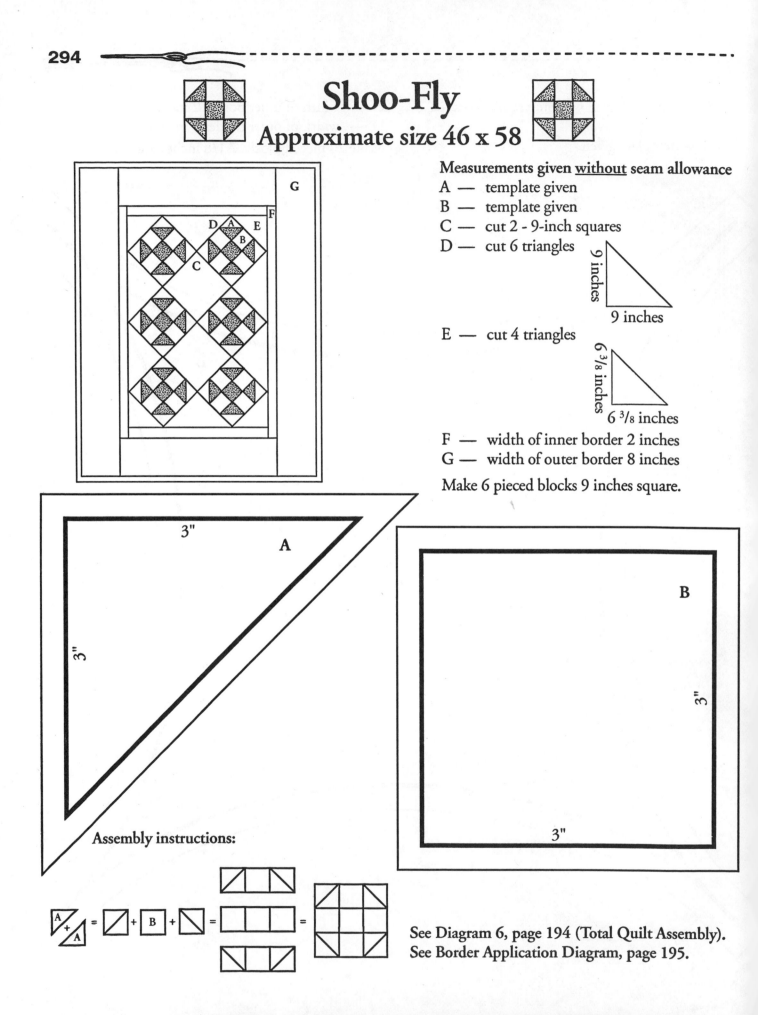

Crown of Thorns
Approximate size 45 x 57

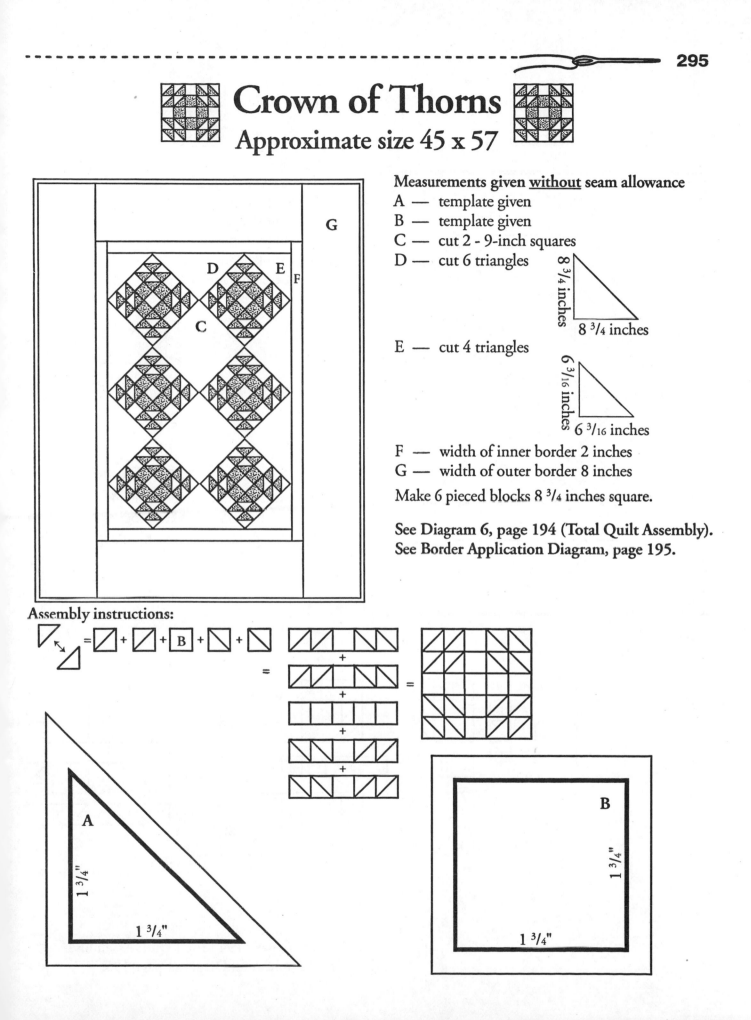

Measurements given **without** seam allowance

A — template given
B — template given
C — cut 2 - 9-inch squares
D — cut 6 triangles

8 ³/₄ inches / 8 ³/₄ inches

E — cut 4 triangles

6 ³/₁₆ inches / 6 ³/₁₆ inches

F — width of inner border 2 inches
G — width of outer border 8 inches

Make 6 pieced blocks 8 ³/₄ inches square.

See Diagram 6, page 194 (Total Quilt Assembly).
See Border Application Diagram, page 195.

Assembly instructions:

A
1 ³/₄"
1 ³/₄"

B
1 ³/₄"
1 ³/₄"

Bear Paw
Approximate size 45 x 57

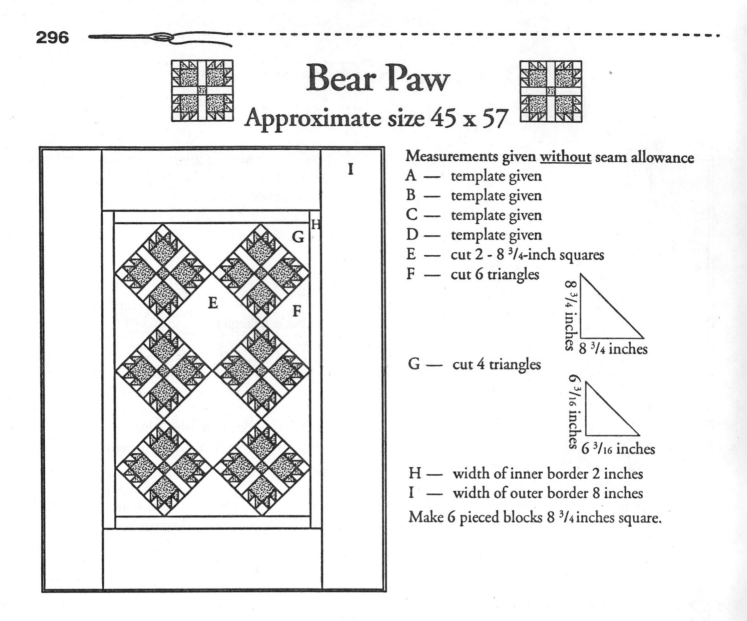

Measurements given <u>without</u> seam allowance

A — template given
B — template given
C — template given
D — template given
E — cut 2 - 8 ³/₄-inch squares
F — cut 6 triangles

8 ³/₄ inches
8 ³/₄ inches

G — cut 4 triangles

6 ³/₁₆ inches
6 ³/₁₆ inches

H — width of inner border 2 inches
I — width of outer border 8 inches

Make 6 pieced blocks 8 ³/₄ inches square.

Assembly instructions:

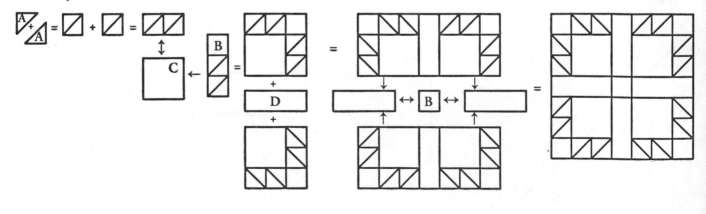

See Diagram 6, page 194 (Total Quilt Assembly).
See Border Application Diagram, page 195.

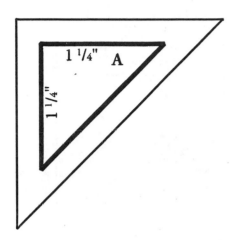

1 1/4" A

1 1/4"

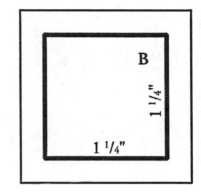

B

1 1/4"

1 1/4"

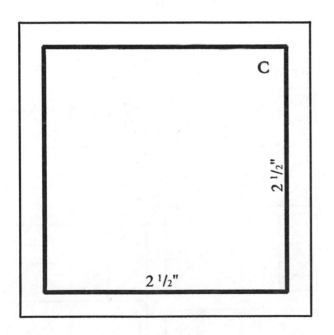

C

2 1/2"

2 1/2"

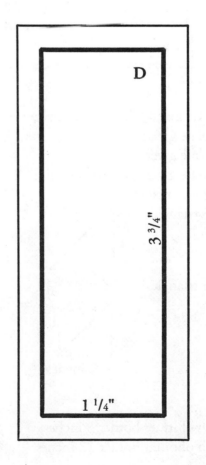

D

3 3/4"

1 1/4"

Pinwheel
Approximate size 46 x 58

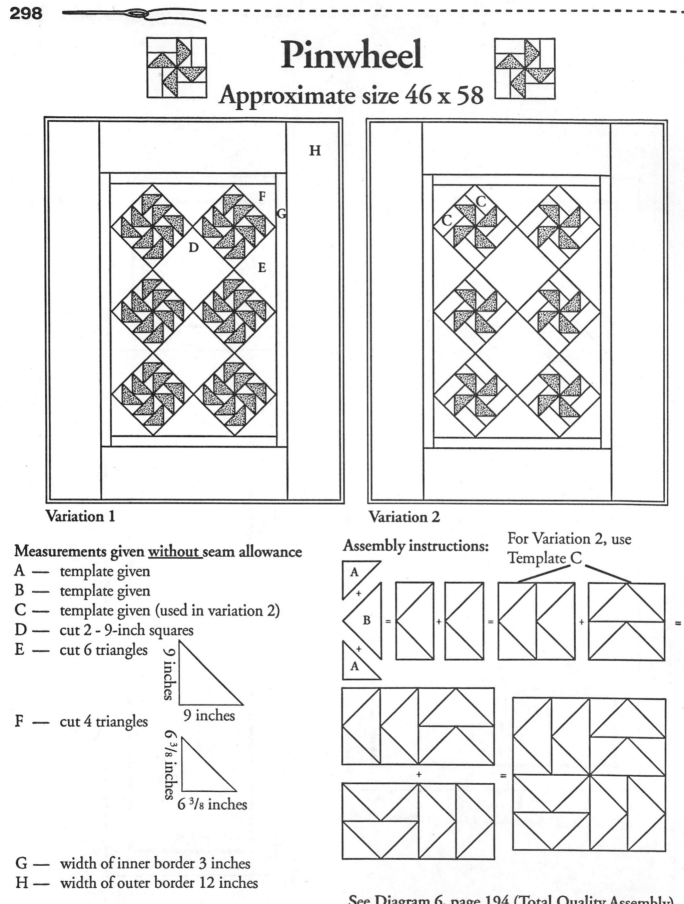

Variation 1

Variation 2

Measurements given <u>without</u> seam allowance

A — template given

B — template given

C — template given (used in variation 2)

D — cut 2 - 9-inch squares

E — cut 6 triangles

F — cut 4 triangles

9 inches / 9 inches

6 ³/₈ inches / 6 ³/₈ inches

G — width of inner border 3 inches

H — width of outer border 12 inches

Make 6 pieced blocks 9 inches square.

Assembly instructions:

For Variation 2, use Template C

See Diagram 6, page 194 (Total Quality Assembly).
See Border Application Diagram, page 195.

Variation 3

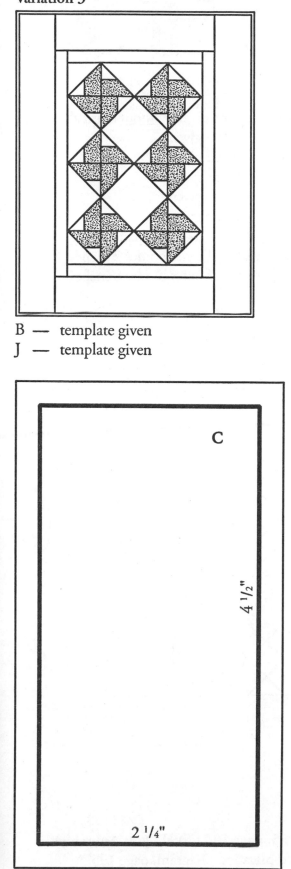

B — template given
J — template given

Use same measurements and procedures as in Variation 1.

Assembly instructions:

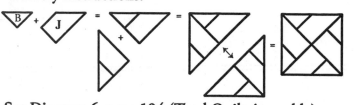

See Diagram 6, page 194 (Total Quilt Assembly).
See Border Application Diagram, page 195.

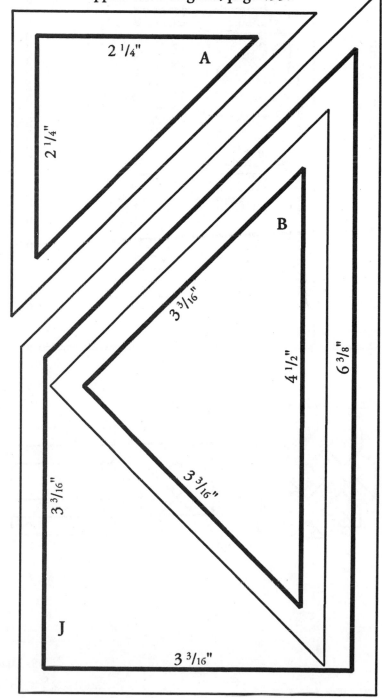

A — 2 1/4" × 2 1/4"

B — 3 3/16" / 4 1/2" / 6 3/8"

J — 3 3/16" × 3 3/16" × 3 3/16"

C — 4 1/2" × 2 1/4"

Garden Maze
Approximate size 48 x 60

Measurements given <u>without</u> seam allowance

A — template given
B — template given
C — template given
D — template given
E — template given
F — cut 6 - 7 $\frac{1}{4}$-inch squares
G — width of inner border 2 inches
H — width of outer border 8 inches

Make 12 small pieced corner blocks
4 $\frac{1}{2}$ inches square.

Make 17 small pieced strips 4 $\frac{1}{2}$ inches
x 7 $\frac{1}{4}$ inches.

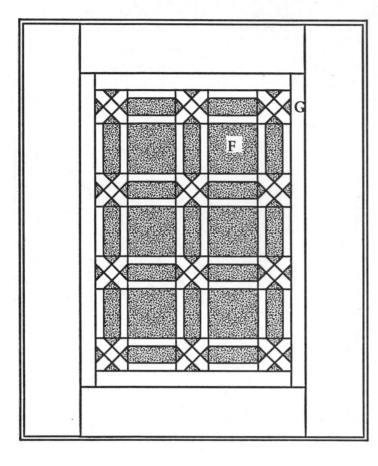

Assembly instructions:

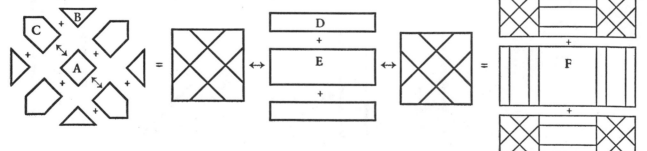

See Diagram 5, page 194 (Total Quilt Assembly).
See Border Application Diagram, page 195.

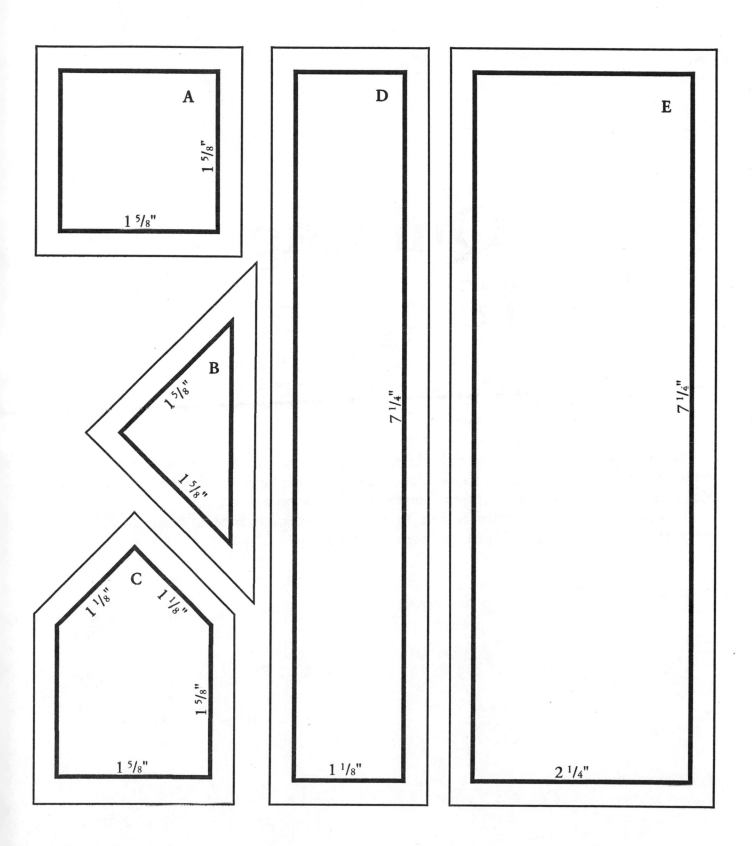

Quilting Templates Large Version

The following are several traditional quilting templates given in full size. Many of the templates extend over several pages. Copy these pages on a copier or trace, using tracing paper. Match corresponding letters along dotted lines and tape pages together to form the complete template.

One quarter of the Circular Feather is given. To make a complete circle, trace the section given, make a one-quarter turn and trace again. Repeat until circle is complete.

To create finished template, match corresponding letters
along dotted lines and tape.

Completed pattern motif will look like this:

Circular Feather — i.

Trim along dotted lines.

Trim along dotted lines.

A→

A→

A→

Circular Feather — ii.

A

A

B

Trim along dotted lines.

Circular Feather — iii.

Pumpkin Seed

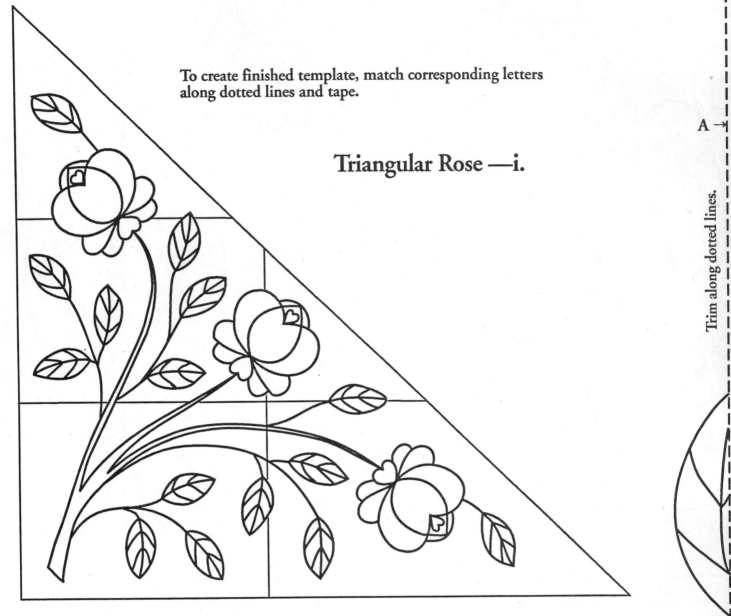

To create finished template, match corresponding letters along dotted lines and tape.

Triangular Rose —i.

A →

Trim along dotted lines.

Completed pattern motif will look like this:

A →

D

D

Triangular Rose —ii.

←A

←A

B

B

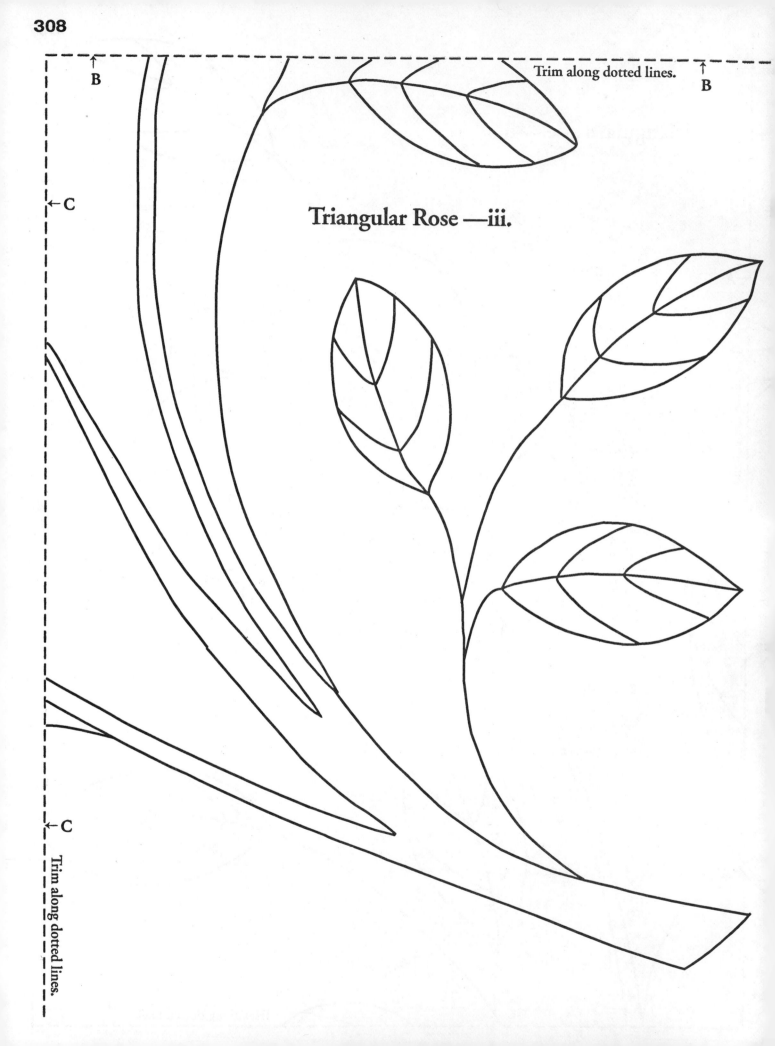

B

Trim along dotted lines.

B

C

Triangular Rose —iii.

C

Trim along dotted lines.

Trim along dotted lines.

D

D

Triangular Rose —iv.

E

C →

Trim along dotted lines.

C →

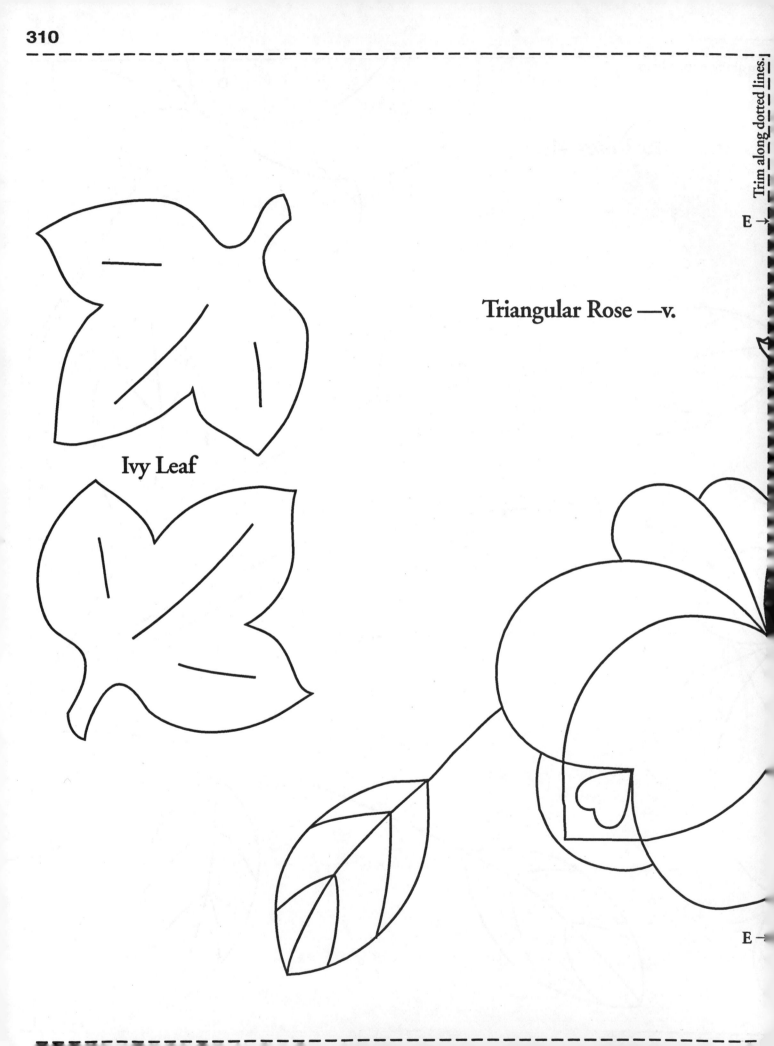

Ivy Leaf

Triangular Rose —v.

Trim along dotted lines.

E →

E →

Feather Border — i.

Completed pattern motif will look like this:

To create finished template, match corresponding letters along dotted lines and tape.

A

B

Feather Border — ii.

C

C

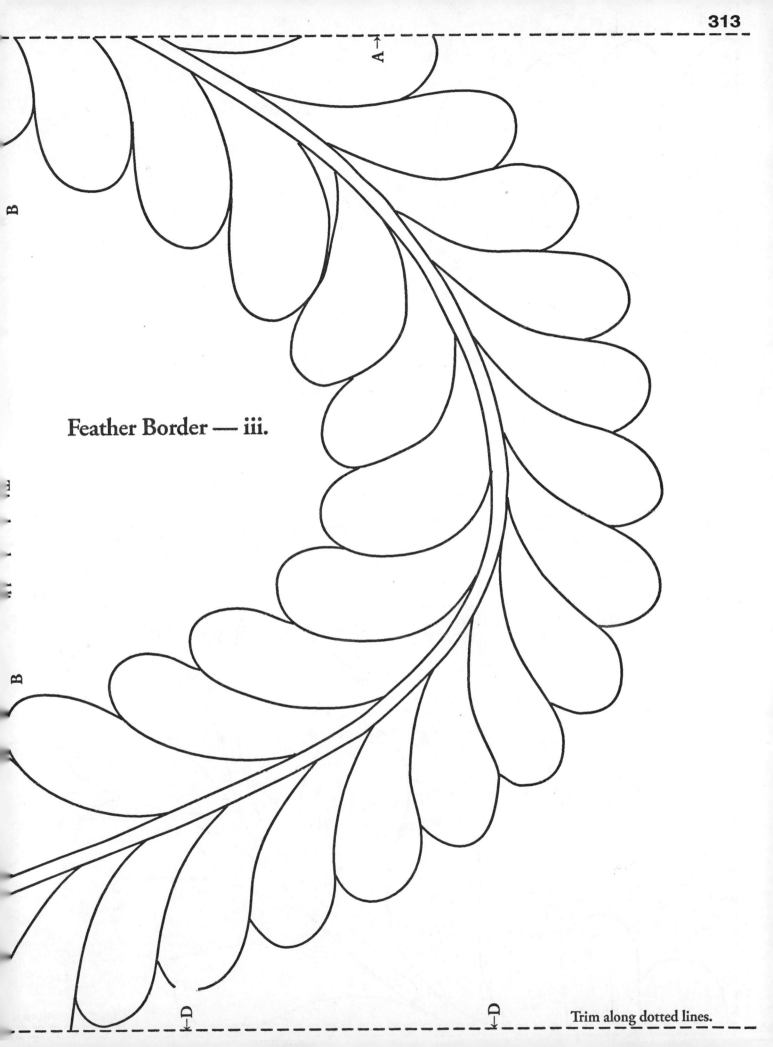

Feather Border — iii.

Feather Border — iv.

Trim along dotted li

Feather Border — v.

Trim along dotted lines.

E

E

D

D

Grapes with Leaves

Fiddlehead Fern — i.

To create finished template, match corresponding letters
along dotted lines and tape.

Completed pattern motif will look like this:

Trim along dotted lines.

A →

D

Trim along dotted lines.

D

Fiddlehead Fern — ii.

← A

Trim along dotted lines.

← A

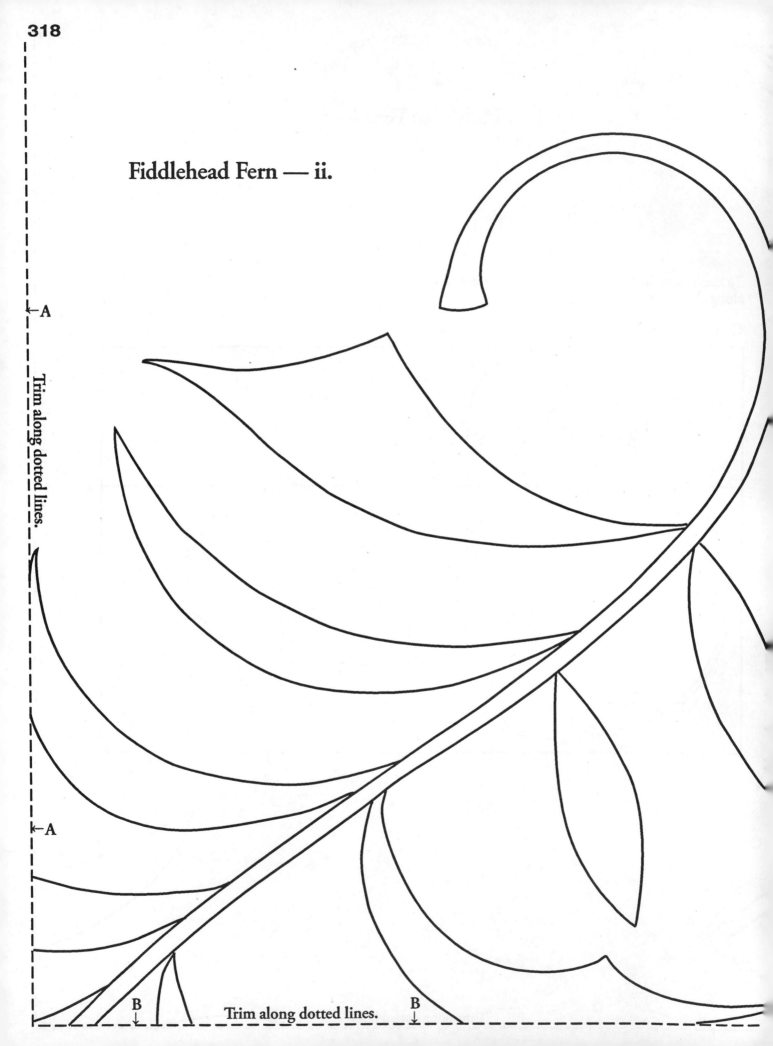

B

Trim along dotted lines.

B

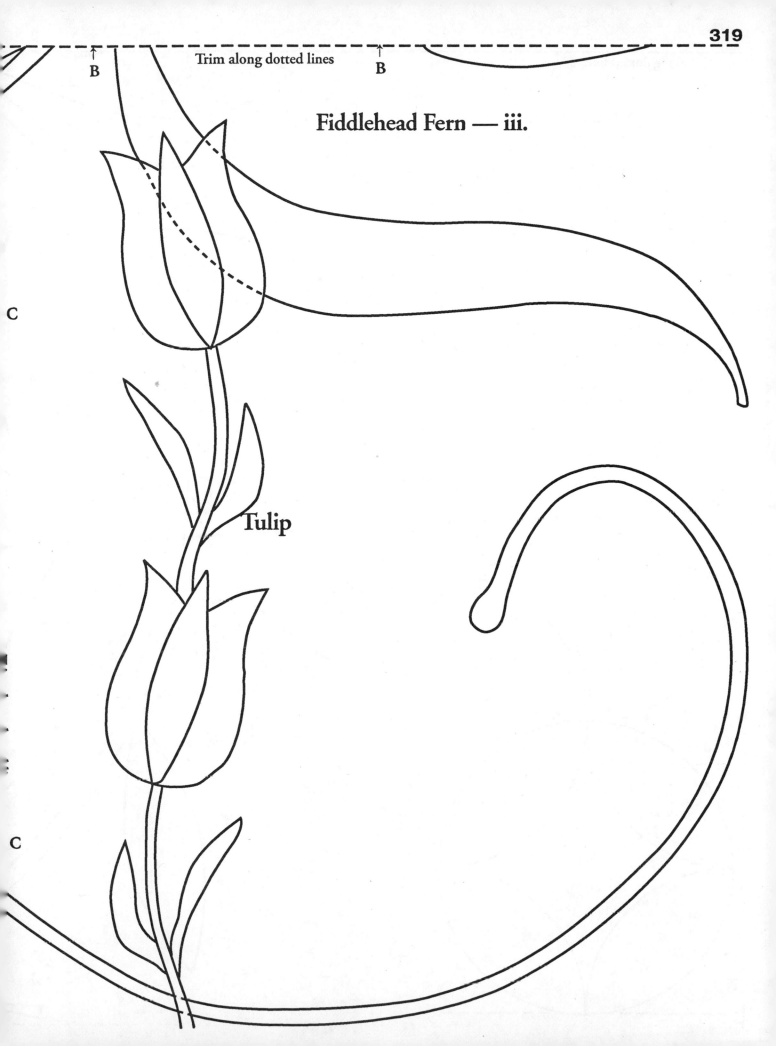

Fiddlehead Fern — iii.

C

Tulip

C

Cut along dotted line.   ↑
                          D

Pumpkin Seed

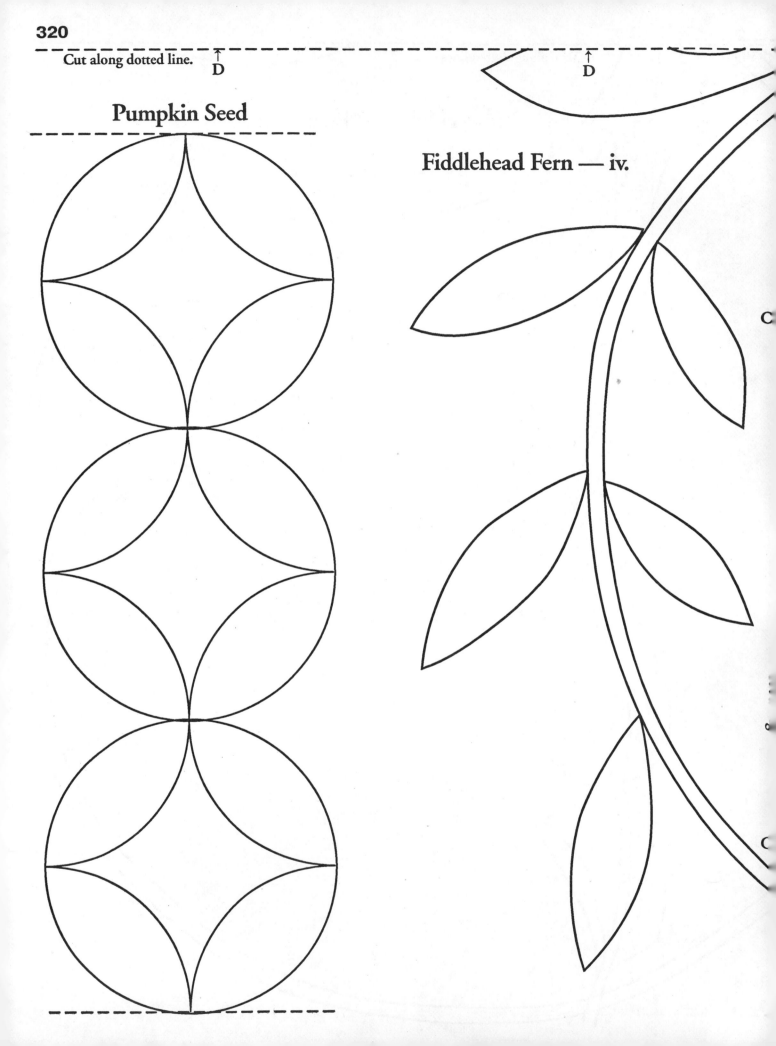

↑
D

Fiddlehead Fern — iv.

C

C

Trim along dotted lines.

Cable — i.

A →

A →

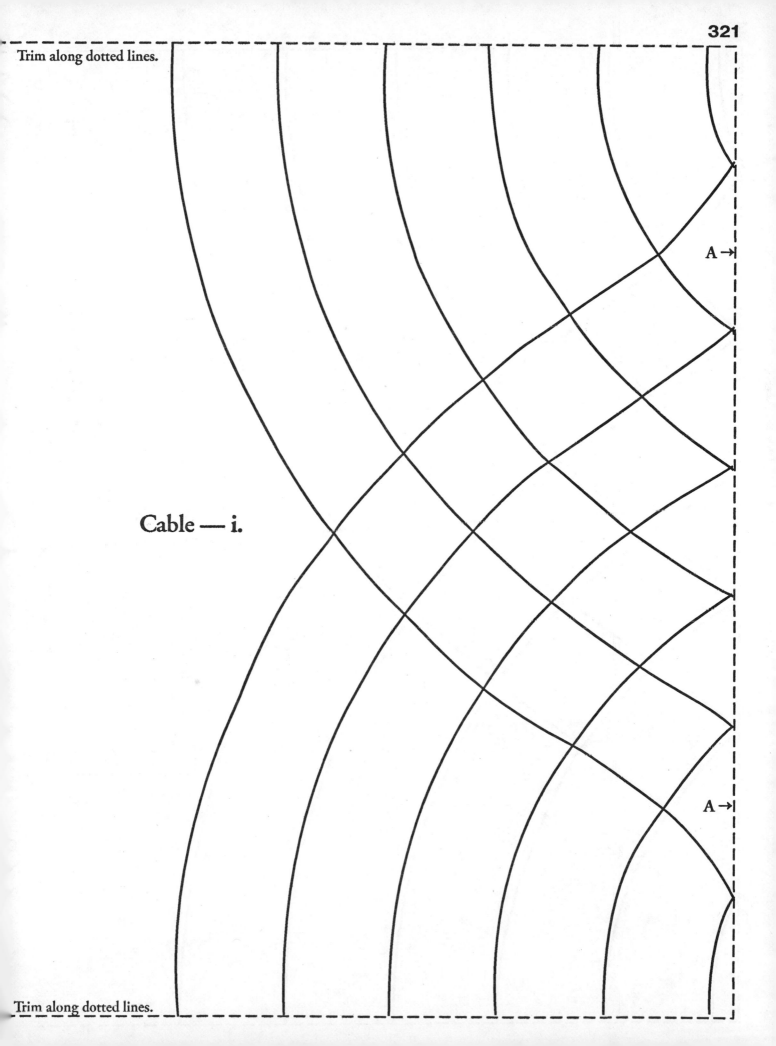

Cable — ii.

←A

←A

Trim along dotted lines.

Cable — iii.

324

Floral Border Design

Dogwood

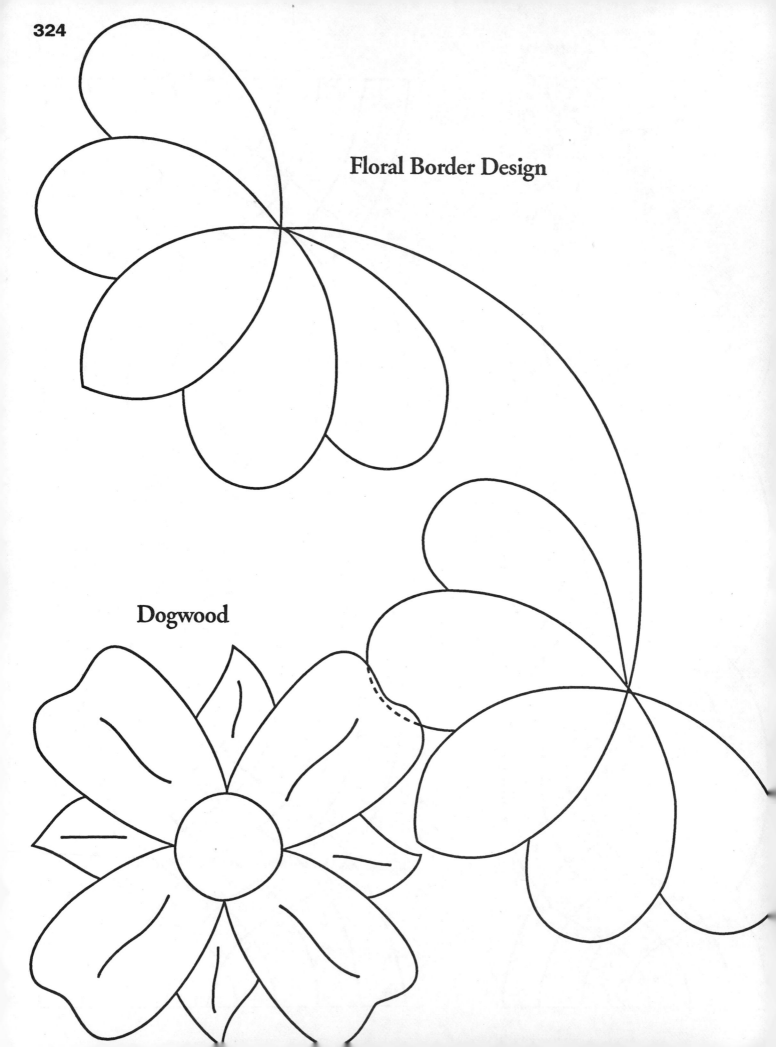

Quilting Templates
Small Version

Circular Feather

Trim along dotted line.

Completed pattern
motif will look like this:

Trim along dotted line.

Triangular Rose — i.

Completed pattern motif will look like this:

To complete finished template, match corresponding letters along dotted lines and tape.

M

Trim along dotted line.

M

Triangular Rose —ii.

Trim along dotted line.

M · M

Floral Corner A

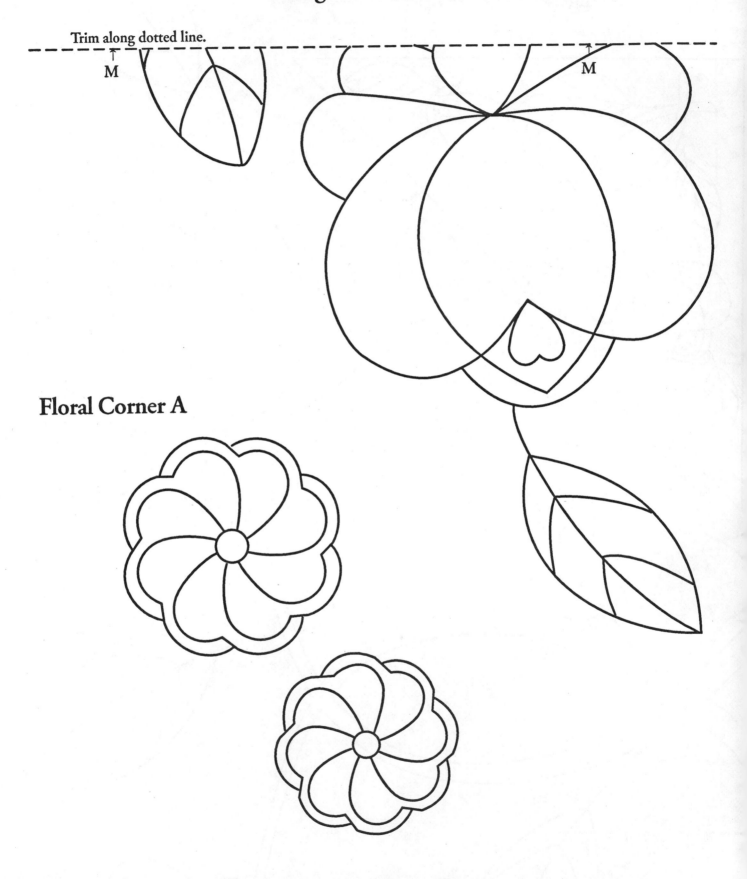

Feather Border — i.

Completed pattern motif will look like this:

To create finished template, match corresponding
letters along dotted lines and tape.

D

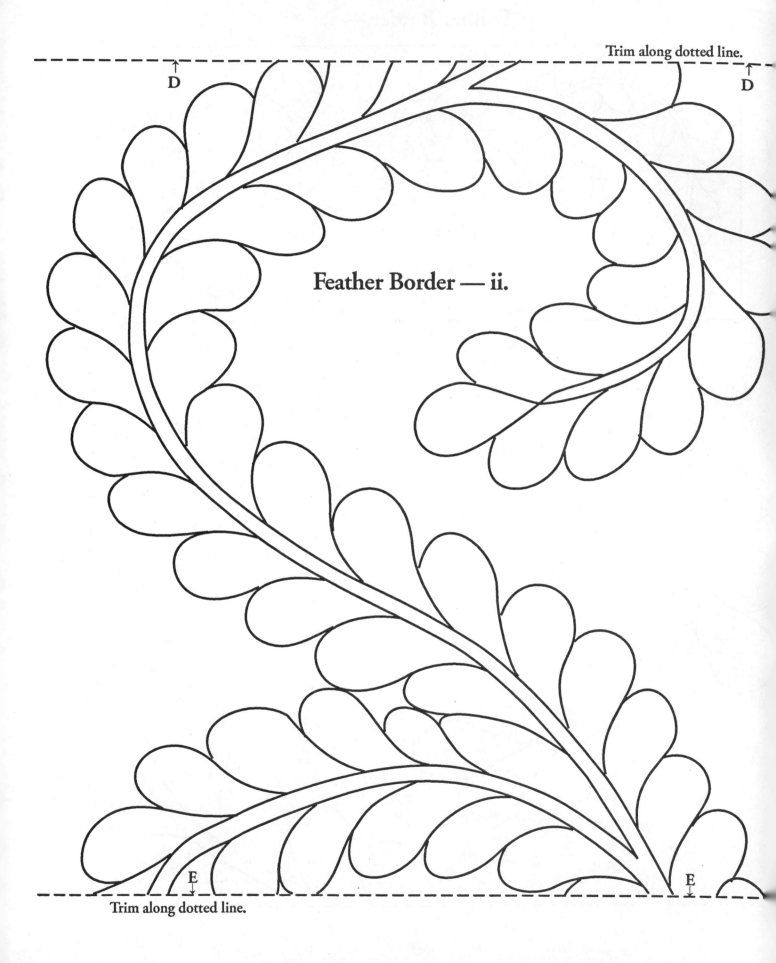

Trim along dotted line.

D

D

Feather Border — ii.

E

E

Trim along dotted line.

Trim along dotted line.

E

Feather Border — iii.

E

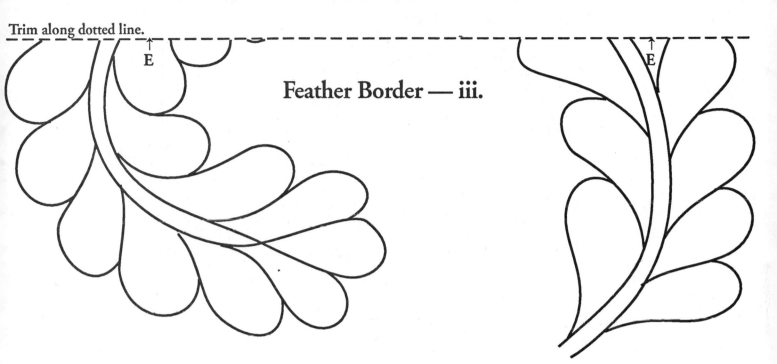

Ivy Leaf

Floral Corner B

Completed pattern motif will look like this:

To create finished template, match corresponding
letters along dotted lines and tape.

Fiddlehead Fern — i.

Trim along dotted line.

F

F

Fiddlehead Fern — ii.

Trim along dotted line.

F   F

Floral Corner C

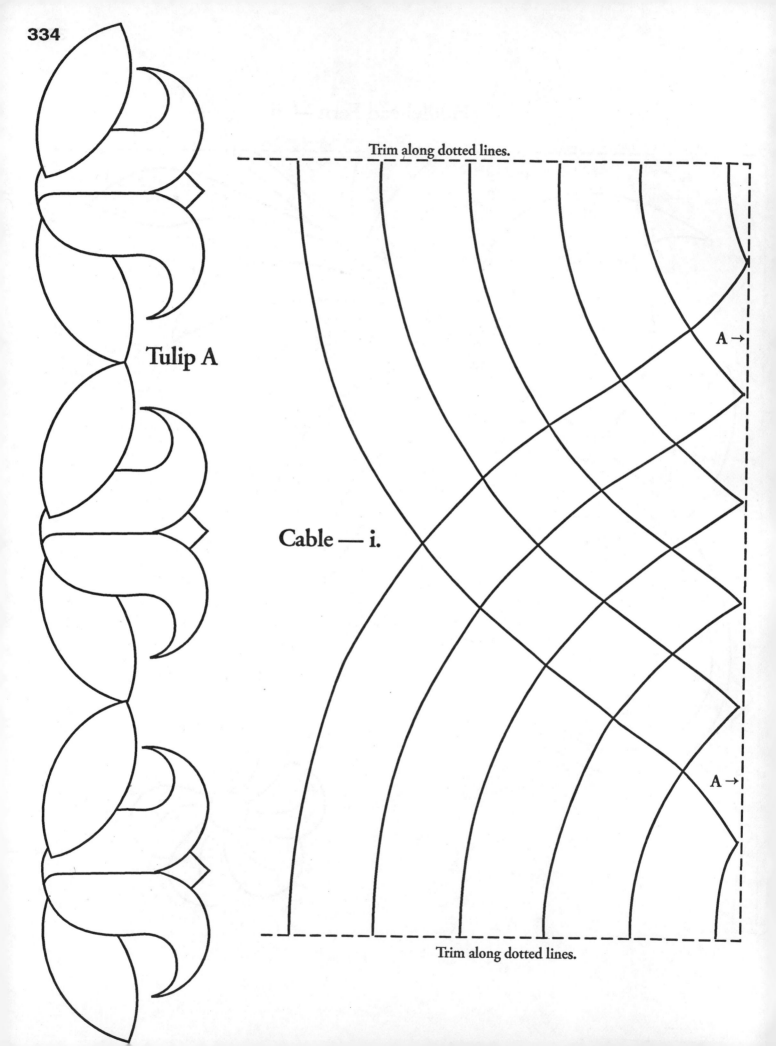

Tulip A

Cable — i.

Trim along dotted lines.

A →

A →

Trim along dotted lines.

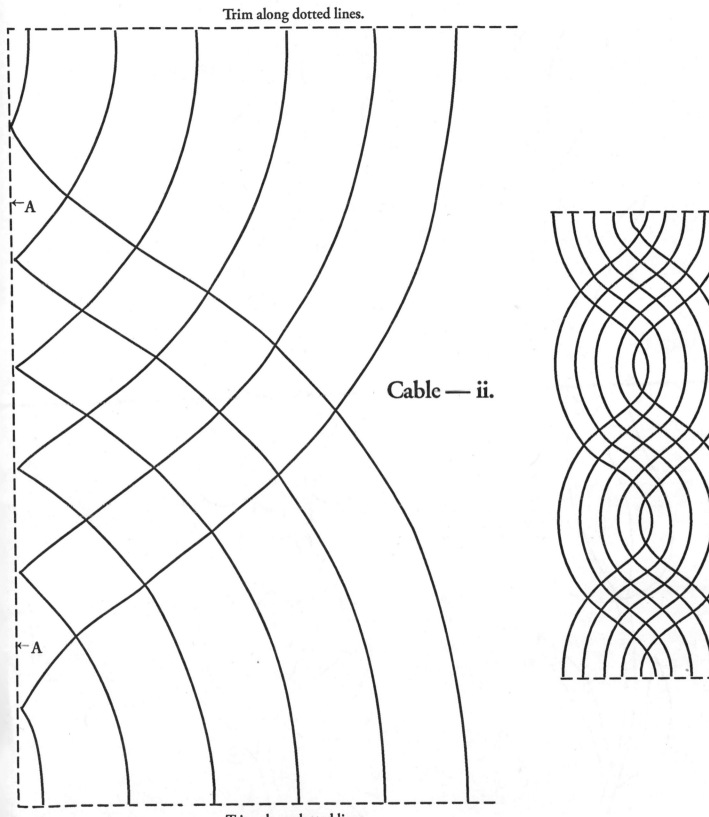

Trim along dotted lines.

← A

← A

Cable — ii.

Trim along dotted lines.

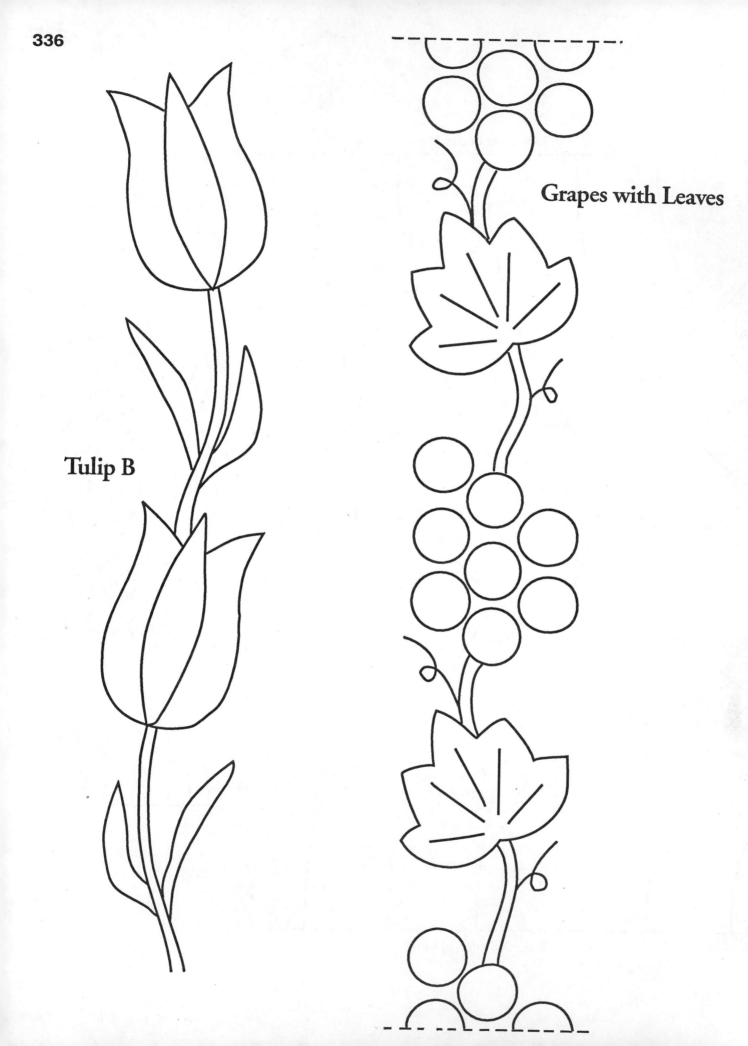

Tulip B

Grapes with Leaves

Pumpkin Seed

Floral Border Design

Dogwood

338

Fan A

Basket with Tulip — i.

K →

K →

Basket with Tulip — ii.

←K

←K

Trim along dotted line.

Leaves

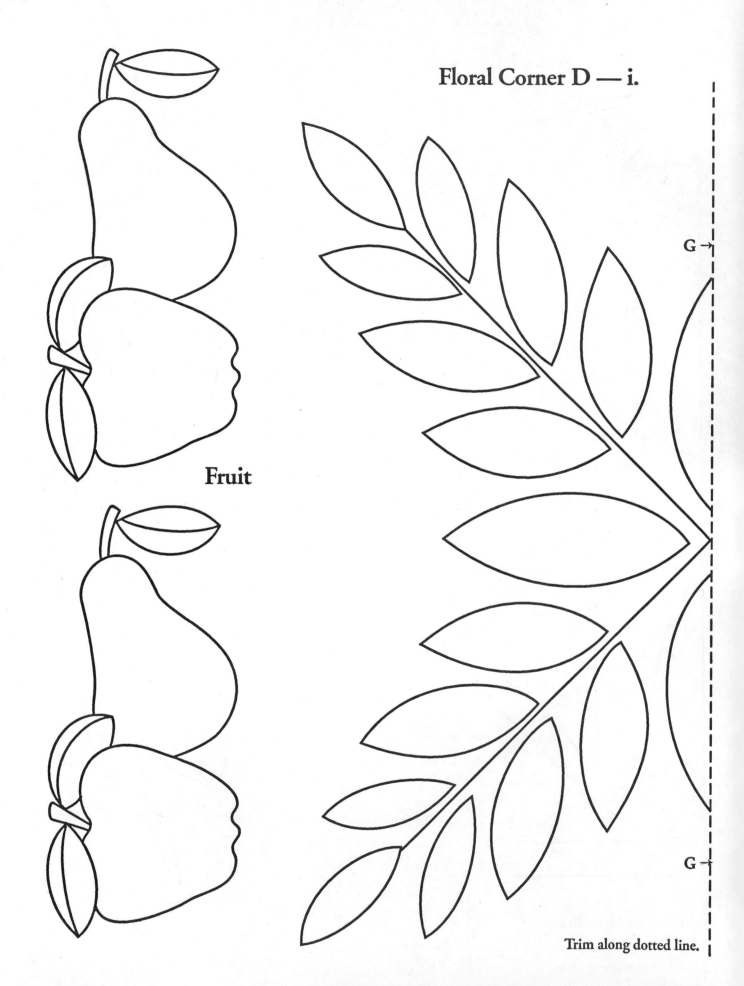

Floral Corner D — i.

Fruit

G →

G →

Trim along dotted line.

Floral Corner D — ii.

← G

← G

Trim along dotted line.

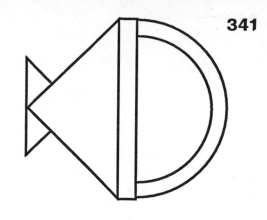

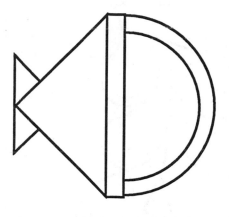

Baskets

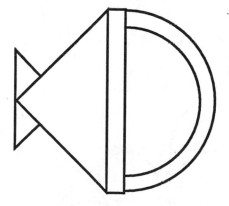

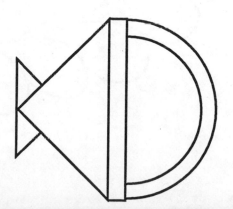

Feather Heart with Cross-Hatching

Fan B

Diamond

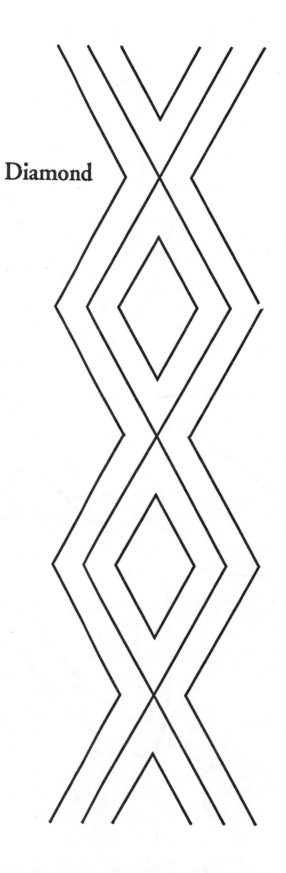

Floral Corner E

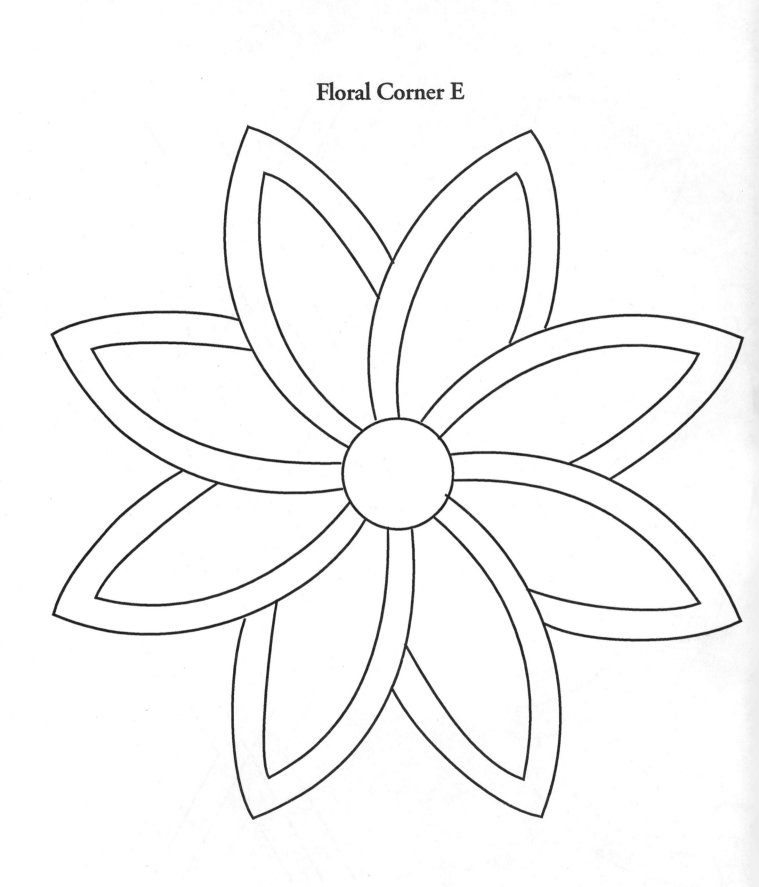

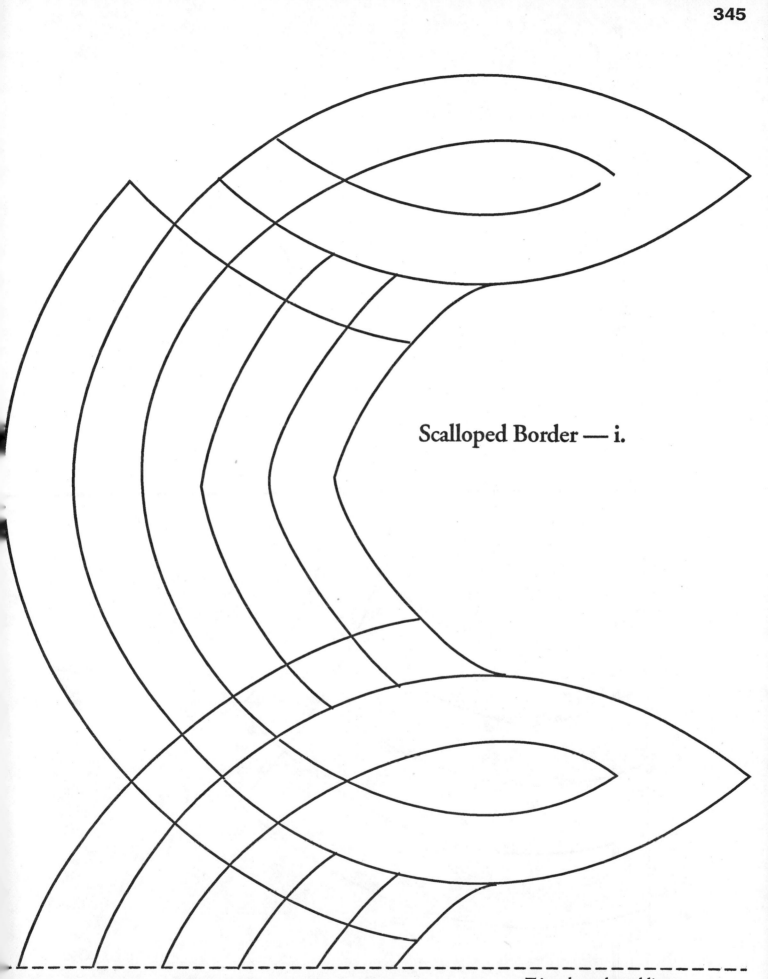

Scalloped Border — i.

Trim along dotted line.

Scalloped Border — ii.

Trim along dotted line.

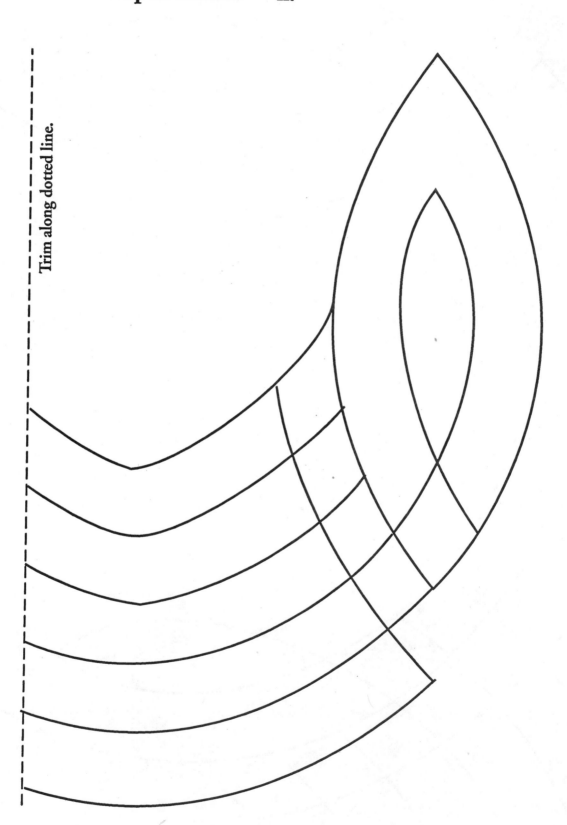

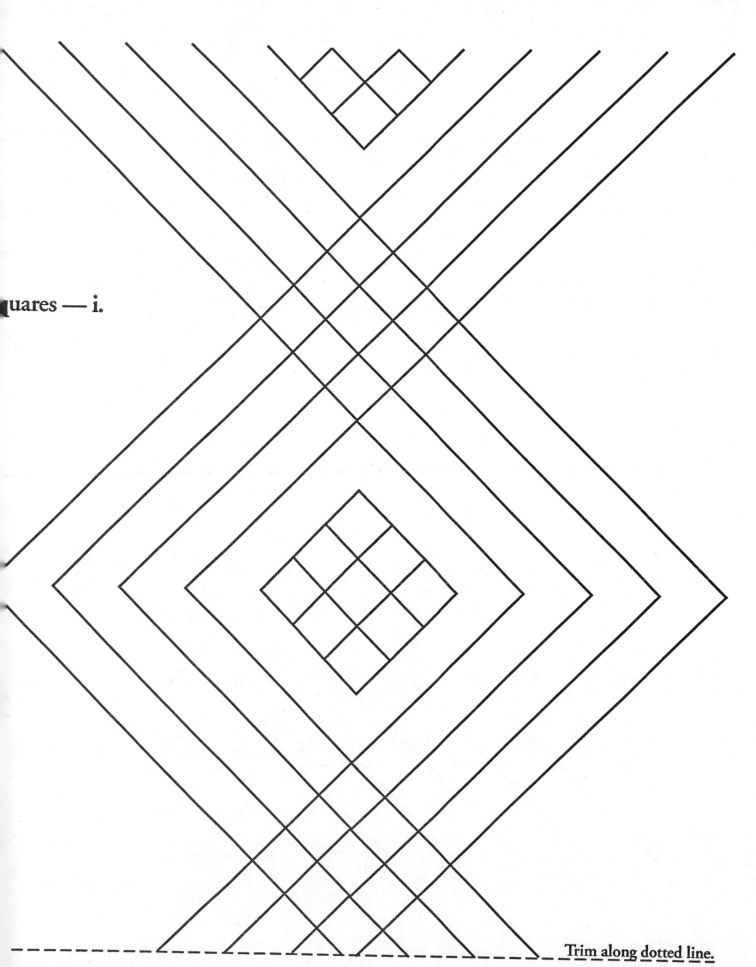

quares — i.

Trim along dotted line.

Squares — ii.

Trim along dotted line.

Hearts

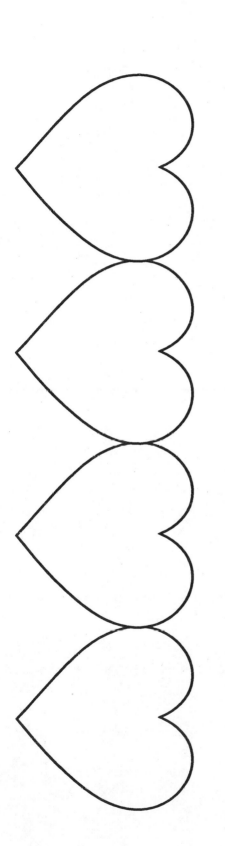

Index